Art Appreciation

Art Appreciation

EDITED BY ASSOCIATE PROFESSOR EMERITUS BRUCE SCHWABACH

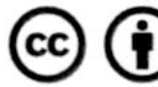

Published by SUNY OER Services

State University of New York Office of Library and Information Services
10 N Pearl St
Albany, NY 12207

The online version of this textbook can be found on Lumen Learning at https://courses.lumenlearning.com/masteryart1-91/

Cover image by "Google Street View — Sao Paulo graffiti" by Kevin Dooley from https://flic.kr/p/eZuSv2 licensed under a Creative Commons Attribution License.

ISBN: 978-1-64176-082-9

Contents

Chapter 5: Fine Art Media and Technique

Chapter 6: Research, Communicate, and Evaluate Arts Information

Introduction

Welcome

This course is taught using a mastery approach. It was designed to give you the best opportunity for success. Your instructor will guide you through the process, but below are some important things to keep in mind as you begin.

Course Structure

- Each course is built around **Competencies**, which are important skills or knowledge that can be used in the real world
- Each Competency has enabling **Learning Outcomes** that teach you what you need to know to master the Competency
- Each Learning Outcome is supported by **Open Educational Resources**, which are a range of materials that will help you build your skills and knowledge of the learning outcomes.

Demonstrating Mastery

- There is a graded **Quiz** for each Competency

  ◦ You must attain 80 percent on the quiz to demonstrate mastery
  ◦ You can retake the quiz as many times as you need to get to 80 percent
  ◦ If you are struggling to pass a quiz after three attempts, your instructor will provide you with support and guidance to help you be successful on your next attempt

- There are also graded **Performance Assessments** for groups of Competencies

  ◦ You must attain 80 percent on the Performance Assessment to demonstrate mastery
  ◦ You can resubmit the Performance Assessment as many times as you need to get to 80 percent
  ◦ If you do not achieve 80 percent on a Performance Assessment, your instructor will provide you with support and guidance to help you be successful on your next attempt

How to Approach this Content

Start by reflecting on the learning outcomes for each section. Do the concepts seem familiar? Plan to spend most of your time on concepts that are new or complicated. Always review page headings, and pay special attention to introductory and concluding sections. When you have finished a section, review what you have learned. The more you stop and ask yourself whether you understand, the better prepared you will be to demonstrate mastery in an assessment. Take notes on your reflections and reach out to your instructor if you need help with difficult or confusing concepts.

About this Book

Your Art Appreciation textbook is a compilation of articles written by instructors for universities around the country. The entire compilation is provided free of charge online through a Creative Commons license. You can access or even copy all the material here, for your own reference, even after the semester ends.

Different Versions

An electronic version is made available via your course in Blackboard, through the College Library, and at https://courses.lumenlearning.com/masteryart1-91/. You may also purchase a physical copy at the College Bookstore. The electronic version has access to multimedia content including video, slideshows, and interactive activities. The print version will have all the same reading material, but not include the multimedia content.

About the Author

There are many different authors; look to the "Licenses and Attributions" section at the end of each chapter to identify contributors. This compilation was edited by Bruce Schwabach at Herkimer County Community College.

Bruce Schwabach taught studio art, and art history for over 35 years at Herkimer College of SUNY. He also is an early advocate of the SUNY Learning Network, promoting online learning.

With an BFA from SUNY New Paltz, and an MFA from Pennsylvania State University, he is a nationally recognized painter, and photographer.

Recently his photograph, "Ponderosa Pines in Yosemite National Park", was on view at The National Botanical Gardens in Washington, DC.

Currently, Schwabach is one of the SUNY OER panelists promoting open-sourced learning on SUNY campuses.

CHAPTER 1: ELEMENTS AND PRINCIPLES OF DESIGN

Why It Matters

Identify, define, and discuss the visual elements and principles of design and their use in art and visual communication (course level learning objective)

Introduction

Whether an artist creates two-dimensional or three-dimensional art, works in a traditional medium like painting, or makes art using the latest technology, all artists use the same basic visual building blocks of form (elements) and strategies of visual organization (principles) to achieve visual unity.

In this section you will learn about the differences between form and content and be introduced to the basic elements and principles of design. You'll also learn about types of representation in art. All of these concepts are integral to formalism, which is a method of studying artwork by analyzing and describing it in purely in terms of visual effects.

Check out this video for a quick introduction to formalism:

- https://youtu.be/72cGGeVwd2g

Take a look at Picasso's painting, *Guernica*, completed in 1937. At first glance it's an incredibly busy and complex arrangement of forms. How can formalism be used to provide compositional understanding of this work? How can it be used to analyze and describe the arrangement of forms and how they contribute to a viewer's experience and interpretation of the painting? Read on, and you'll find out.

LEARNING OUTCOMES

- Identify and describe the difference between form and content as used in art
- Identify and define the five elements of design
- Identify and distinguish how the principles of design are used to visually organize the elements of design
- Distinguish between representational (realistic), abstract, and nonrepresentational (or non-objective) imagery

---

How to Study for the Performance Assessment (PA)

The PA for this module is a short paper where you will choose an artwork from the list to analyze through formalism. Again, read the PA before you begin the module content. As you read through the content, take notes on how all the elements of form are defined, as well as the principles of design. Understanding these key terms will help you consider your artwork in relation to how the artist used the elements and principles. Finally, from the artwork list, choose an artwork that you will enjoy describing and analyzing.

OK, let's get started!

Form and Content

Identify and describe the difference between form and content as used in art

LEARNING ACTIVITIES

The learning activities for this section include:

- Reading: Formalism and Content
- Video: Introducing Formal Analysis: Landscape

Take time to review and reflect on each of these activities in order to improve your performance on the assessment for this section.

Reading: Formalism and Content

This is an overview of some important terms related to writing about and discussing art. The term *formalism* comes from critical art theory, which resembles "aesthetics discussion." *Content* is one aspect of the artwork. This will also touch on point of view (POV), which is an important factor as we look at and discuss artworks.

Viewing Art

Personal Level

When we are looking at art, when we find or "run into" an artwork or exhibition, we typically have an initial response or impression. This response to what we see (or hear, etc.) is formed by a lifetime of knowledge and experience and the culture and time in which we live. The expression "Beauty lies in the eye of the beholder" gets at the subjective and personal nature of perception—and of the "first impression," in particular. There's nothing wrong with one's first impression or response—it is, after all, a personal response. It's *your* point of view.

Formal Analysis

Formal analysis is a close and analytical way of looking at and discussing a work of art. It includes describing the work in terms of various design elements, such as color, shape, texture, line, lighting, mass, and space, as well as a discussion of how those elements have been used (the design principles). Formal analysis moves *beyond* description of the artwork and its content by linking the elements of the work to the effects that they have on the viewer. This is discussion of the artwork from the point of view of "here is the artwork, and this is what I see and can make sense of . . ." Formal analysis uses art terminology to consider the effects of an artwork the viewer (you), and it's a process that enables us to think about and consider the overall meaning of the artwork.

NOTE: Formal analysis does not use or require research and is based on your POV. The more informed you are, the deeper your analysis will go—but that depth depends on experience and knowledge, not on research.

Content

Content is simply the the subject matter of an artwork. It's the images you see—like the trees in a painting of a forest, or the town, the sky, and the moon in Van Gogh's *Starry Night*. Content can play a role in formal analysis, but the content aspect is less important than the "artwork" aspect.

Video: Introducing Formal Analysis: Landscape

- https://youtu.be/AlbTrG-SIDE

Elements of Design

Identify and define the five elements of design

LEARNING ACTIVITIES

The learning activities for this section include:

- Reading: Artistic Elements
- Videos: Elements of Art

Take time to review and reflect on each of these activities in order to improve your performance on the assessment for this section.

Reading: Artistic Elements

The Point

A **point** is the visual element upon which all others are based. It can be defined as a singularity in space or, in geometric terms, the area where two coordinates meet. When an artist marks a simple point on a surface, (also referred to as the **ground**), they immediately create a **figure-ground relationship**. That is, they divide the work between its surface and anything added to it. Our eyes differentiate between the two, and their arrangement has everything to do with how we see a final composition. The point itself can be used as a way to create forms. For example, *Pointillism* is a style of painting made famous by the French artist Georges Seurat in the late nineteenth century. He and others in the Pointillist group created paintings by juxtaposing points—or dots—of color that optically mixed to form lines, shapes and forms within a composition. Look at a detail from Seurat's *La Parade de Cirque* to see how this works. His large canvas *Sunday Afternoon on the Grande Jatte* is a testament to the pointillist style and aesthetic. Its creation was a painstaking process but one that generated new ways of thinking about color and form.

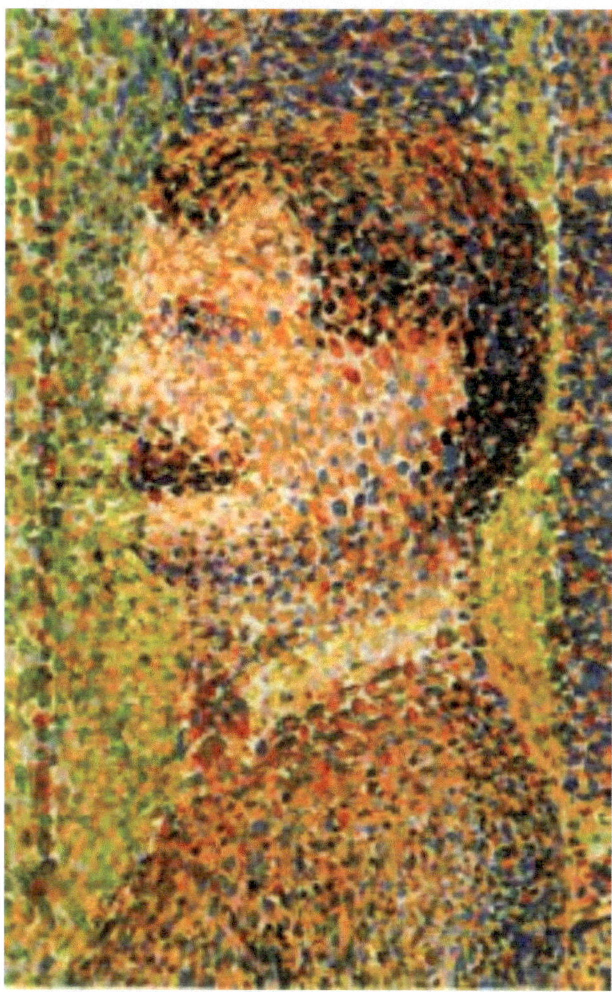

Georges Seurat, La Parade de Cirque, detail, 1887-89. The Metropolitan Museum of Art, New York. CC BY-SA

Definitions and Qualities of Line

Essentially, when you put two or more points together you create a line. A line can be lyrically defined as a point in motion. There are many different types of lines, all characterized by their length being greater than their width. Lines can be static or dynamic depending on how the artist chooses to use them. They help determine the motion, direction and energy in a work of art. We see line all around us in our daily lives; telephone wires, tree branches, jet contrails and winding roads are just a few examples. Look at the photograph below to see how line is part of natural and constructed environments.

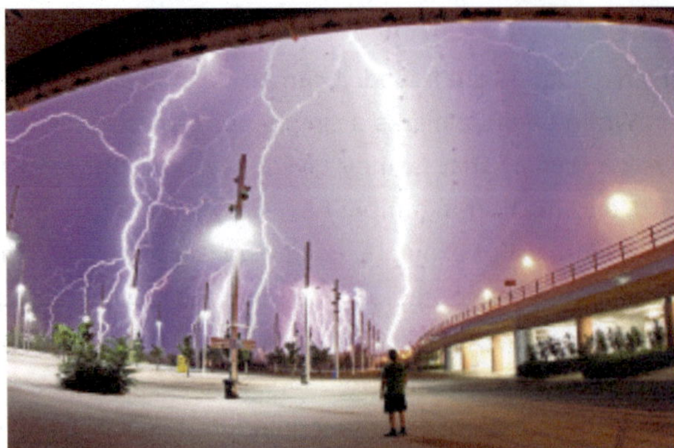

Photo by NASA. CC BY-NC

In this image of a lightning storm we can see many different lines. Certainly the jagged, meandering lines of the lightning itself dominate the image, followed by the straight lines of the light standards, the pillars holding up the overpass on the right and the guard rails attached to its side. There are more subtle lines too, like the gently arced line at the top of the image and the shadows cast by the poles and the standing figure in the middle. Lines are even implied by falling water droplets in the foreground.

The Nazca lines in the arid coastal plains of Peru date to nearly 500 BCE were scratched into the rocky soil, depicting animals on an incredible scale, so large that they are best viewed from the air. Let's look at how the different kinds of line are made.

Diego Velazquez's *Las Meninas* from 1656, ostensibly a portrait of the Infanta Margarita, the daughter of King Philip IV and Queen Mariana of Spain, offers a sumptuous amount of artistic genius; its shear size (almost ten feet square), painterly style of naturalism, lighting effects, and the enigmatic figures placed throughout the canvas–including the artist himself –is one of the great paintings in western art history. Let's examine it (below) to uncover how Velazquez uses basic elements and principles of art to achieve such a masterpiece.

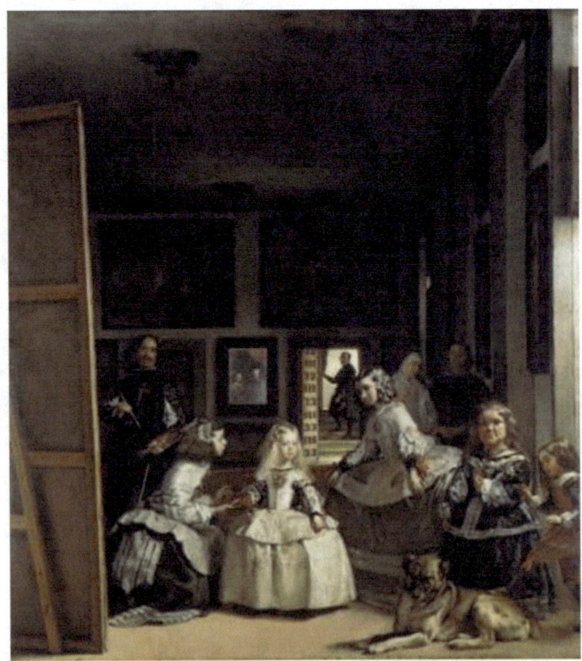

Diego Velazquez, Las Meninas, 1656, oil on canvas, 125.2" x 108.7". Prado, Madrid. CC BY-SA

Actual lines are those that are physically present. The edge of the wooden stretcher bar at the left of *Las Meninas* is an actual line, as are the picture frames in the background and the linear decorative elements on some of the figures' dresses. How many other actual lines can you find in the painting?

Implied lines are those created by visually connecting two or more areas together. The space between the Infanta Margarita—the blonde central figure in the composition—and the *meninas*, or maids of honor, to the left and right of her, are implied lines. Both set up a diagonal relationship that implies movement. By visually connecting the space between the heads of all the figures in the painting we have a sense of jagged motion that keeps the lower part of the composition in motion, balanced against the darker, more static upper areas of the painting. Implied lines can also be created when two areas of different colors or tones come together. Can you identify more implied lines in the painting? Where? Implied lines are found in three-dimensional artworks, too. The sculpture of the *Laocoon* below, a figure from Greek and Roman mythology, is, along with his sons, being strangled by sea snakes sent by the goddess Athena as wrath against his warnings to the Trojans not to accept the Trojan horse. The sculpture sets implied lines in motion as the figures writhe in agony against the snakes.

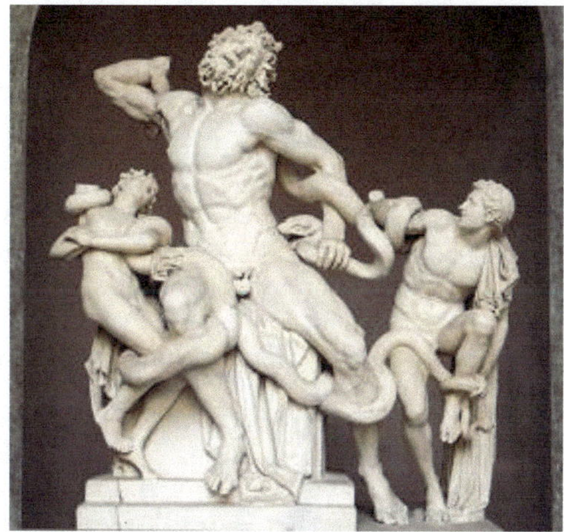

Laocoon Group, Roman copy of Greek original, Vatican Museum, Rome. Photo by Marie-Lan Nguyen. CC BY-SA

Straight or classic lines provide structure to a composition. They can be oriented to the horizontal, vertical, or diagonal axis of a surface. Straight lines are by nature visually stable, while still giving direction to a composition. In *Las Meninas*, you can see them in the canvas supports on the left, the wall supports and doorways on the right, and in the background in matrices on the wall spaces between the framed pictures. Moreover, the small horizontal lines created in the stair edges in the background help anchor the entire visual design of the painting.

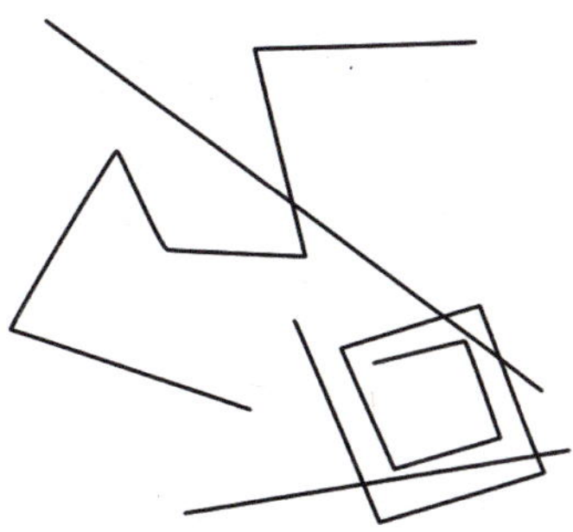

Straight lines, 11 July 2012, Creator: Oliver Harrison. CC BY

Expressive lines are curved, adding an organic, more dynamic character to a work of art. Expressive lines are often rounded and follow undetermined paths. In *Las Meninas* you can see them in the aprons on the girls' dresses and in the dog's folded hind leg and coat pattern. Look again at the *Laocoon* to see expressive lines in the figures' flailing limbs and the sinuous form of the snakes. Indeed, the sculpture seems to be made up of nothing but expressive lines, shapes and forms.

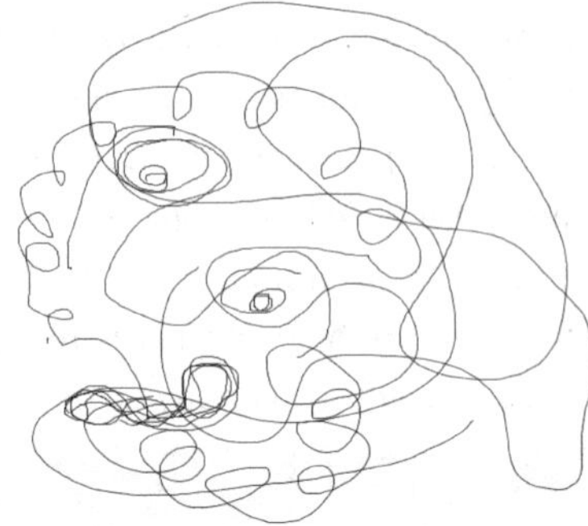

Organic lines, 11 July 2012, Creator: Oliver Harrison. CC BY

There are other kinds of line that encompass the characteristics of those above yet, taken together, help create additional artistic elements and richer, more varied compositions. Refer to the images and examples below to become familiar with these types of line.

Outline, or contour line is the simplest of these. They create a path around the edge of a shape. In fact, outlines define shapes.

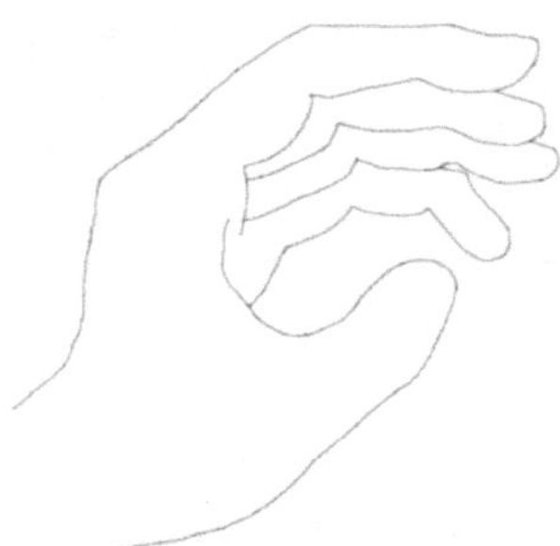

Outline, 11 July 2012, Creator: Oliver Harrison. CC BY

Cross contour lines follow paths across a shape to delineate differences in surface features. They give flat shapes a sense of form (the illusion of three dimensions), and can also be used to create shading.

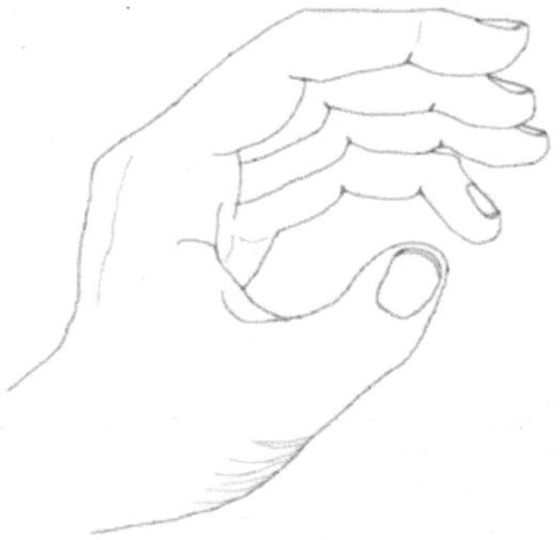

Cross Contour, 11 July 2012, Creator: Oliver Harrison. CC BY

Hatch lines are repeated at short intervals in generally one direction. They give shading and visual texture to the surface of an object.

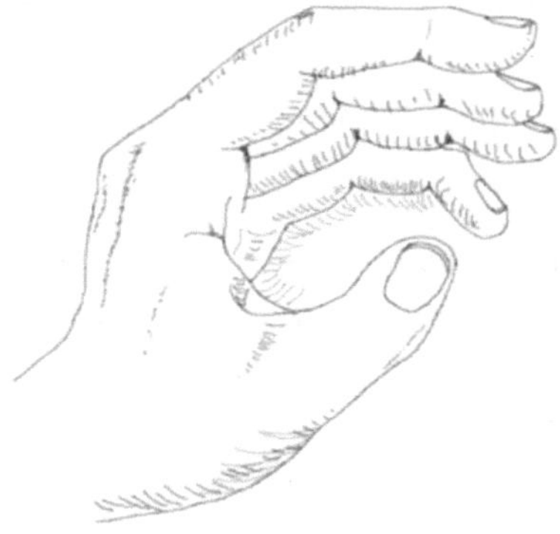

Hatch, 11 July 2012, Creator: Oliver Harrison. CC BY

Crosshatch lines provide additional tone and texture. They can be oriented in any direction. Multiple layers of crosshatch lines can give rich and varied shading to objects by manipulating the pressure of the drawing tool to create a large range of values.

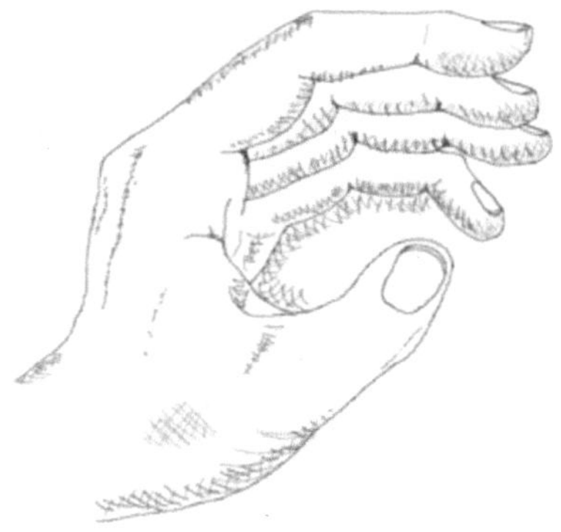

Crosshatch, 11 July 2012, Creator: Oliver Harrison. CC BY

Line quality is that sense of character embedded in the way a line presents itself. Certain lines have qualities that distinguish them from others. Hard-edged, jagged lines have a staccato visual movement while organic, flowing lines create a more comfortable feeling. Meandering lines can be either geometric or expressive, and you can see in the examples how their indeterminate paths animate a surface to different degrees.

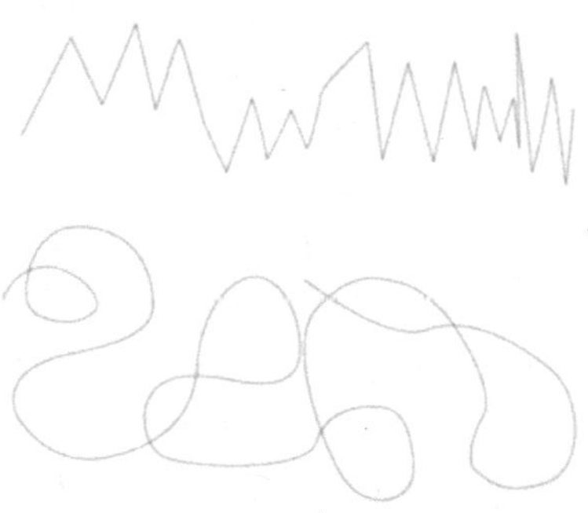

A Line, 11 July 2012, Creator: Oliver Harrison. CC BY

Although line as a visual element generally plays a supporting role in visual art, there are wonderful examples in which line carries a strong cultural significance as the primary subject matter.

Calligraphic lines use quickness and gesture, more akin to paint strokes, to imbue an artwork with a fluid, lyrical character. To see this unique line quality, view the work of Chinese poet and artist Dong Qichang's Du Fu's Poem, dating from the Ming dynasty (1555-1637). A more geometric example from the Koran, created in the Arabic calligraphic style, dates from the 9th century.

Both these examples show how artists use line as both a form of writing and a visual art form. American artist Mark Tobey (1890–1976) was influenced by Oriental calligraphy, adapting its form to the act of pure painting within a modern abstract style described as white writing.

Shapes: Positive, Negative and Planar Issues

A shape is defined as an enclosed area in two dimensions. By definition shapes are always implied and flat in nature. They can be created in many ways, the simplest by enclosing an area with an outline. They can also be made by surrounding an area with other shapes or the placement of different textures next to each other—for instance, the shape of an island surrounded by water. Because they are more complex than lines, shapes do much of the heavy lifting in arranging compositions. The abstract examples below give us an idea of how shapes are made.

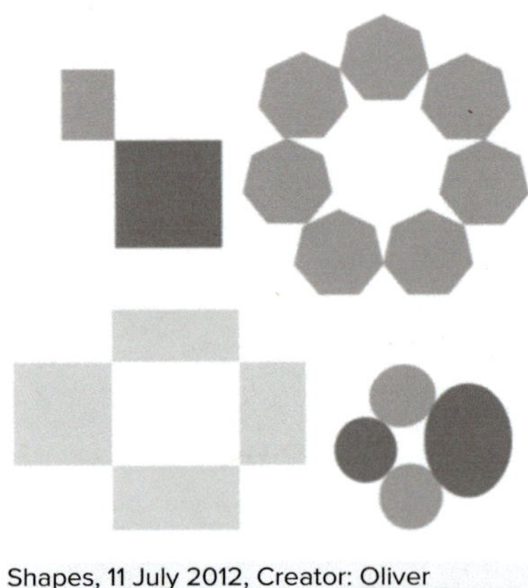

Shapes, 11 July 2012, Creator: Oliver Harrison. CC BY

Referring back to Velazquez's *Las Meninas*, it is fundamentally an arrangement of shapes; organic and hard-edged, light, dark and mid-toned, that solidifies the composition within the larger shape of the canvas. Looking at it this way, we can view any work of art, whether two or three-dimensional, realistic, abstract or non-objective, in terms of shapes alone.

Positive / Negative Shapes and Figure / Ground Relationships

Shapes animate figure-ground relationships. We visually determine **positive** shapes (the figure) and **negative** shapes (the ground). One way to understand this is to open your hand and spread your fingers apart. Your hand is the positive shape, and the space around it becomes the negative shape. You can also see this in the example above. The shape formed by the black outline becomes positive because it's enclosed. The area around it is negative. The same visual arrangement goes with the gray circle and the purple square. But identifying positive and negative shapes can get tricky in a more complex composition. For instance, the four blue rectangles on the left have edges that touch each other, thus creating a solid white shape in the center. The four green rectangles on the right don't actually connect yet still give us an implied shape in the center. Which would you say is the positive shape? What about the red circles surrounding the gray star shape? Remember that a positive shape is one that is distinguished from the background. In *Las Meninas* the figures become the positive shapes because they are lit dramatically and hold our attention against the dark background. What about the dark figure standing in the doorway? Here the dark shape becomes the positive one, surrounded by a white background. Our eyes always return to this figure as an anchor to the painting's entire composition. In three dimensions, positive shapes are those that make up the actual work. The negative shapes are the empty spaces around, and sometimes permeating through the work itself. The *Laocoon* is a good example of this. A modern work that uses shapes to a dramatic effect is Alberto Giacometti's *Reclining Woman Who Dreams* from 1929. In an abstract style the artist weaves positive and negative shapes together, the result is a dreamy, floating sensation radiating from the sculpture.

Plane

A ***plane*** is defined as any surface area in space. In two-dimensional art, the picture plane is the flat surface an image is created upon; a piece of paper, stretched canvas, wood panel, etc. A shape's orientation within the picture plane creates a visually implied plane, inferring direction and depth in relation to the viewer. The graphic below shows three examples.

Shape Planes, 11 July 2012, Creator: Oliver Harrison. CC BY

Traditionally the picture plane has been likened to a window the viewer looks through to a scene beyond, the artist constructing a believable image showing implied depth and planar relationships. *Landscape with the Fall of Icarus*, painted by Pieter Breughel the Elder in 1558 (below), presents us with the tragic ending to the Greek myth involving Icarus, son of Daedalus, who, trying to escape from the island of Crete with wings of wax, flies too close to the sun and falls to earth. Breughel shows us an idyllic landscape with farmers tilling their fields, each terraced row a different plane of earth, and shepherds tending their flocks of sheep in the foreground. He depicts the livestock in positions that infer they are moving in different directions in relation to the "window" of the picture plane. We look further to see a gradual recession to the sea and a middle ground dominated by a ship under sail. The curves of the billowing sails imply two or three different planes. The background of the painting shows the illusion of deep space, the massive cliffs now small in relation to the foreground, and the distant ship near the center as smaller and lighter in tone. In the grandeur of the scene Icarus falls into the sea unnoticed just off shore to the lower right, only his legs still above water. The artist's use of planar description is related to the idea of space and how it's depicted in two dimensions. We will look at the element of space just ahead.

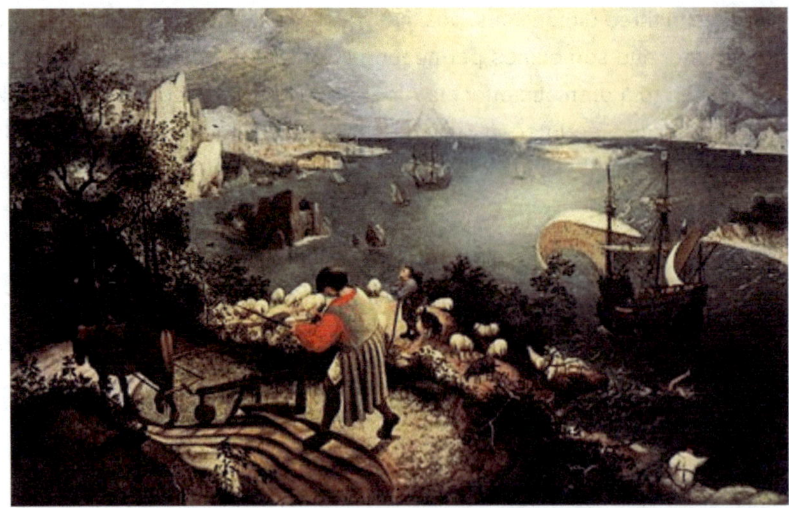

Landscape with the Fall of Icarus, Peter Breughel the Elder, 1558. Musee des Beaux-arts, Brussels. CC BY-SA

Space

Space is the empty area surrounding real or implied objects. Humans categorize space: there is outer space, that limitless void we enter beyond our sky; inner space, which resides in people's minds and imaginations, and personal space, the important but intangible area that surrounds each individual and which is violated if someone else gets too close. Pictorial space is flat, and the digital realm resides in cyberspace. Art responds to all of these kinds of space.

Clearly artists are as concerned with space in their works as they are with, say, color or form. There are many ways for the artist to present ideas of space. Remember that many cultures traditionally use pictorial space as a window to view realistic subject matter through, and through the subject matter they present ideas, narratives and symbolic content. The innovation of **linear perspective,** an implied geometric pictorial construct dating from fifteenth-century Europe, affords us the accurate illusion of three-dimensional space on a flat surface, and appears to recede into the distance through the use of a **horizon line** and **vanishing points**. See how perspective is set up in the schematic examples below:

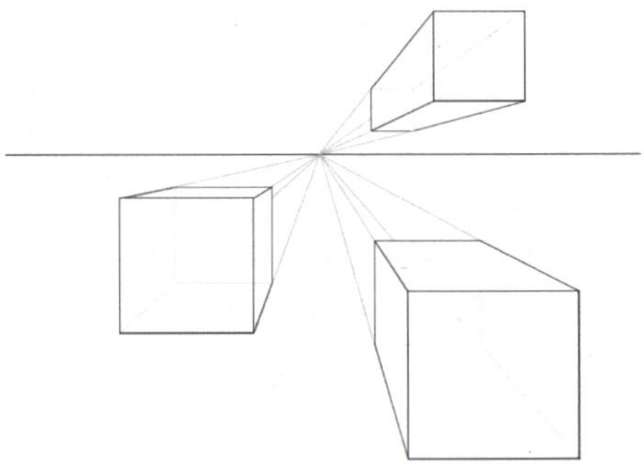

One Point Perspective, 11 July 2012, Creator: Oliver Harrison. CC BY

One-point perspective occurs when the receding lines appear to converge at a single point on the horizon and used when the flat front of an object is facing the viewer. Note: Perspective can be used to show the relative size and recession into space of any object, but is most effective with hard-edged three-dimensional objects such as buildings.

A classic Renaissance artwork using one point perspective is Leonardo da Vinci's *The Last Supper* from 1498. Da Vinci composes the work by locating the vanishing point directly behind the head of Christ, thus drawing the viewer's attention to the center. His arms mirror the receding wall lines, and, if we follow them as lines, would converge at the same vanishing point.

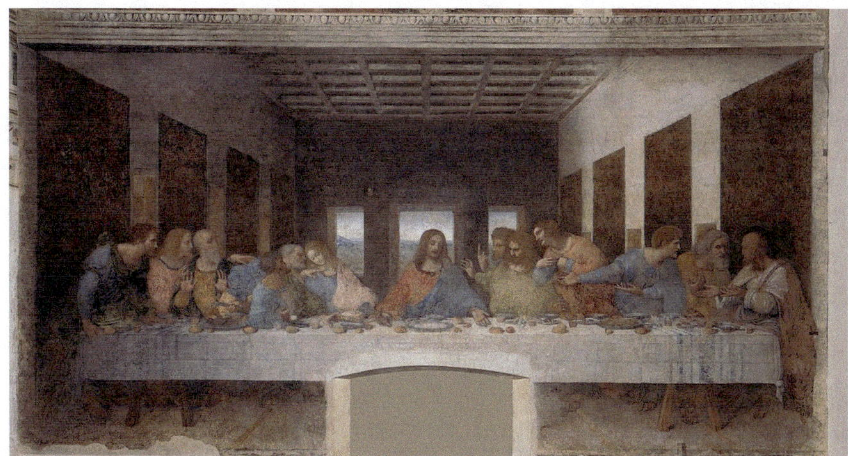

Leonardo da Vinci, The Last Supper, 1498. Fresco. Santa Maria della Grazie. Work is in the public domain.

Two-point perspective occurs when the vertical edge of a cube is facing the viewer, exposing two sides that recede into the distance, one to each vanishing point.

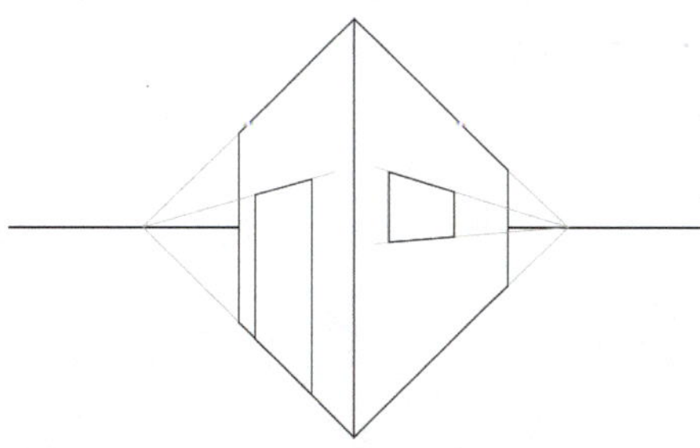

Two Point Perspective, 11 July 2012, Creator: Oliver Harrison. CC BY

View Gustave Caillebotte's Paris Street, Rainy Weather from 1877 to see how two-point perspective is used to give an accurate view to an urban scene. The artist's composition, however, is more complex than just his use of perspective. The figures are deliberately placed to direct the viewer's eye from the front right of the picture to the building's front edge on the left, which, like a ship's bow, acts as a cleaver to plunge both sides toward the horizon. In the midst of this visual recession a lamp post stands firmly in the middle to arrest our gaze from going right out the back of the painting. Caillebotte includes the little metal arm at the top right of the post to direct us again along a horizontal path, now keeping us from traveling off the top of the canvas. As relatively spare as the left side of the work is, the artist crams the right side with hard-edged and organic shapes and forms in a complex play of positive and negative space.

Three-point perspective is used when an artist wants to project a "bird's-eye view", that is, when the projection lines recede to two points on the horizon and a third either far above or below the horizon line. In this case the parallel lines that make up the sides of an object are not parallel to the edge of the ground the artist is working on (paper, canvas, etc).

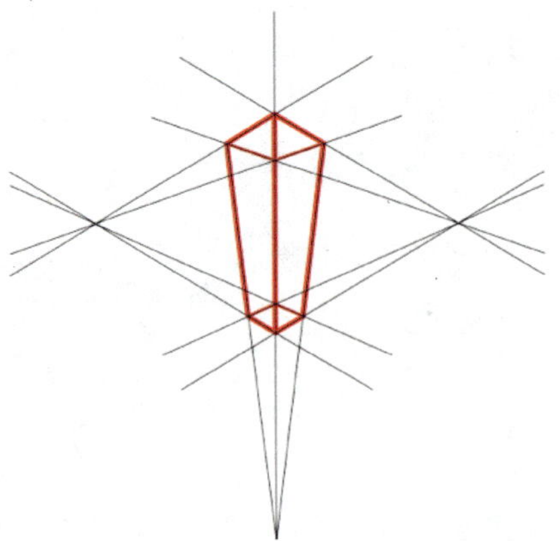

Three-point perspective (with vanishing points above and below the horizon line shown at the same time). Design by Shazz, CC BY

The perspective system is a cultural convention well suited to a traditional western European idea of the "truth," that is, an accurate, clear rendition of observed reality. Even after the invention of linear perspective, many cultures traditionally use a flatter pictorial space, relying on overlapped shapes or size differences in forms to indicate this same truth of observation. Examine the miniature painting of the *Third Court of the Topkapi Palace* from fourteenth-century Turkey to contrast its pictorial space with that of linear perspective. It's composed from a number of different vantage points (as opposed to vanishing points), all very flat to the picture plane. While the overall image is seen from above, the figures and trees appear as cutouts, seeming to float in mid air. Notice the towers on the far left and right are sideways to the picture plane. As "incorrect" as it looks, the painting gives a detailed description of the landscape and structures on the palace grounds.

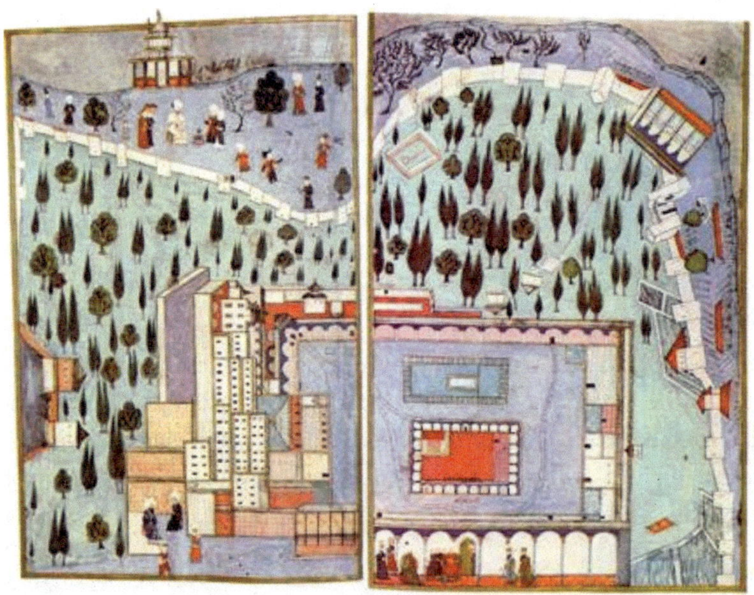

Third Court of the Topkapi Palace, from the Hunername, 1548. Ottoman miniature painting, Topkapi Museum, Istanbul. CC BY-SA

After nearly five hundred years using linear perspective, western ideas about how space is depicted accurately in two dimensions went through a revolution at the beginning of the 20th century. A young Spanish artist, Pablo Picasso, moved to Paris, then western culture's capital of art, and largely reinvented pictorial space with the invention of Cubism, ushered in dramatically by his painting Les Demoiselles d'Avignon in 1907. He was influenced in part by the chiseled forms, angular surfaces and disproportion of African sculpture (refer back to the *Male Figure* from Cameroon) and mask-like faces of early Iberian artworks. For more information about this important painting, listen to the following question and answer.

- https://youtu.be/pngGDycLQuE

Picasso, his friend Georges Braque and a handful of other artists struggled to develop a new space that relied on, ironically, the flatness of the picture plane to carry and animate traditional subject matter including figures, still life and landscape. Cubist pictures, and eventually sculptures, became amalgams of different points of view, light sources and planar constructs. It was as if they were presenting their subject matter in many ways at once, all the while shifting foreground, middle ground and background so the viewer is not sure where one starts and the other ends. In an interview, the artist explained cubism this way: "The problem is now to pass, to go around the object, and give a plastic expression to the result. All of this is my struggle to break with the two-dimensional aspect*"(from Alexander Liberman, *An Artist in His Studio, 1960, page 113*). Public and critical reaction to cubism was understandably negative, but the artists' experiments with spatial relationships reverberated with others and became – along with new ways of using color – a driving force in the development of a modern art movement that based itself on the flatness of the picture plane. Instead of a window to look into, the flat surface becomes a ground on which to construct formal arrangements of shapes, colors and compositions. For another perspective on this idea, refer back to module one's discussion of 'abstraction'.

You can see the radical changes cubism made in George Braque's landscape *La Roche Guyon* from 1909. The trees, houses, castle and surrounding rocks comprise almost a single complex form, stair-stepping up the canvas to mimic the distant hill at the top, all of it struggling upwards and leaning to the right within a shallow pictorial space.

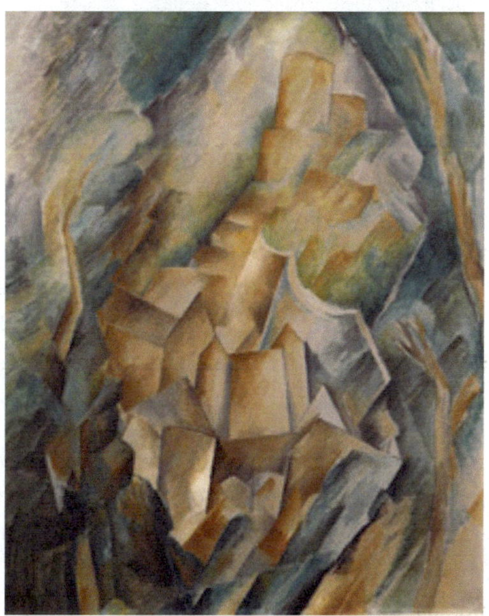

George Braque, Castle at La Roche Guyon, 1909. Oil on canvas. Stedelijk van Abbe Museum, Eindhoven, Netherlands. Licensed through GNU and Creative Commons

As the cubist style developed, its forms became even flatter. Juan Gris's *The Sunblind* from 1914 splays the still life it represents across the canvas. Collage elements like newspaper reinforce pictorial flatness.

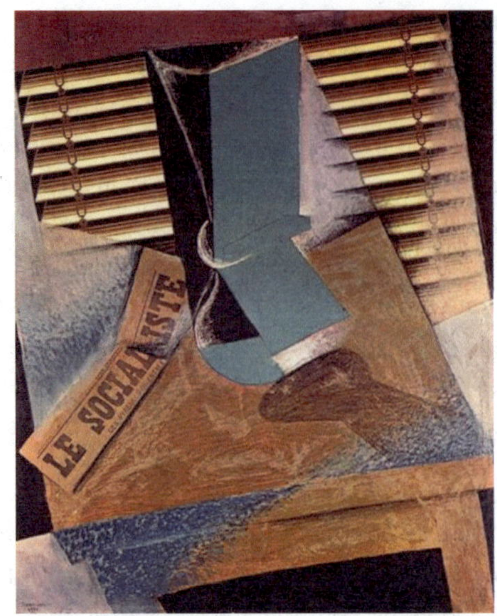

Juan Gris, The Sunblind, 1914. Gouache, collage, chalk, and charcoal on canvas. Tate Gallery, London. Image licensed under GNU Free Documentation License

It's not so difficult to understand the importance of this new idea of space when placed in the context of comparable advances in science surrounding the turn of the nineteenth century. The Wright Brothers took to the air with powered flight in 1903, the same year Marie Curie won the first of two Nobel prizes for her pioneering work in radiation. Sigmund Freud's new ideas on the inner spaces of the mind and its effect on behavior were published in 1902, and Albert Einstein's calculations on relativity, the idea that space and time are intertwined, first appeared in 1905. Each of these discoveries added to human understanding and realligned the way we look at ourselves and our world. Indeed, Picasso, speaking of his struggle to define cubism, said "Even Einstein did not know it either! The condition of discovery is outside ourselves; but the terrifying thing is that despite all this, we can only find what we know" (from *Picasso on Art, A Selection of Views* by Dore Ashton, (Souchere, 1960, page 15).

Three-dimensional space doesn't undergo this fundemental transformation. It remains a visual tug between positive and negative spaces. Sculptors influenced by cubism do, however, develop new forms to fill this space; abstract and non-objective works that chanllenge us to see them on their own terms. Constantin Brancusi, a Romanian sculptor living in Paris, became a leading artist to champion the new forms of modern art. His sculpture Bird in Space is an elegant example of how abstraction and formal arrangement combine to symbolize the new movement. The photograph of Brancusi's studio below gives further evidence of sculpture's debt to cubism and the struggle "to go around the object, to give it plastic expression."

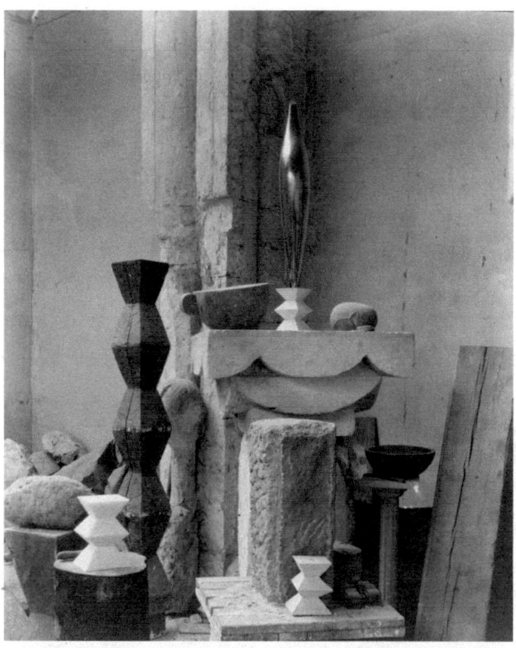

Edward Steichen, Brancusi's studio, 1920. Metropolitan Museum, New York. This photograph is in the public domain.

Now that we've established line, shape, and spatial relationships, we can turn our attention to surface qualities and their importance in works of art. Value (or tone), color and texture are the elements used to do this.

Value is the relative lightness or darkness of a shape in relation to another. The value scale, bounded on one end by pure white and on the other by black, and in between a series of progressively darker shades of grey, gives an artist the tools to make these transformations. The value scale below shows the standard variations in tones. Values near the lighter end of the spectrum are termed high-keyed, those on the darker end are low-keyed.

Value Scale, 11 July 2012, Creator: Oliver Harrison, CC BY

In two dimensions, the use of value gives a shape the illusion of mass and lends an entire composition a sense of light and shadow. The two examples below show the effect value has on changing a shape to a form.

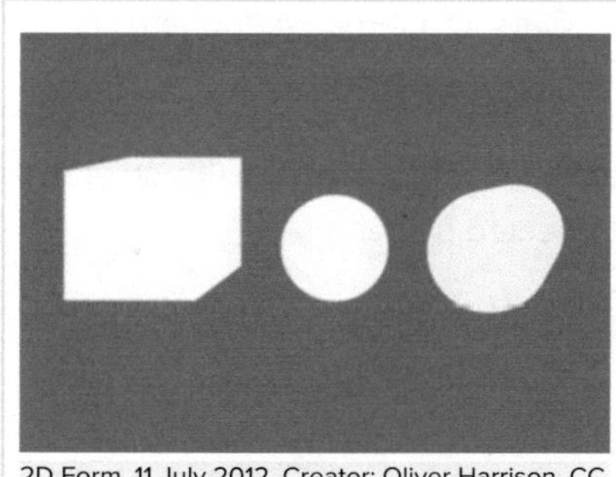

2D Form, 11 July 2012, Creator: Oliver Harrison, CC BY

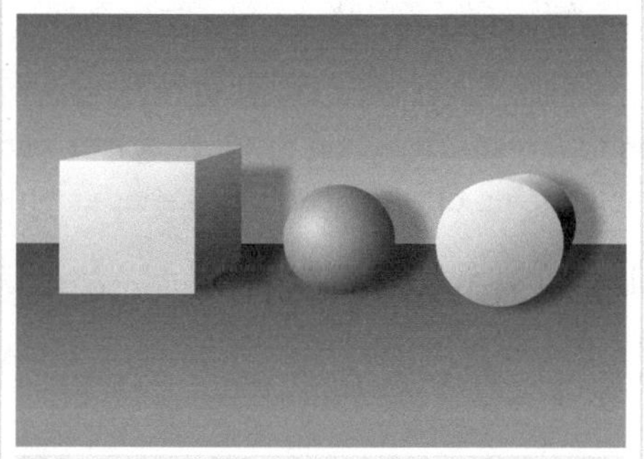

3D Form, 11 July 2012, Creator: Oliver Harrison, CC BY

This same technique brings to life what begins as a simple line drawing of a young man's head in Michelangelo's Head of a Youth and a Right Hand from 1508. Shading is created with line (refer to our discussion of *line* earlier in this module) or tones created with a pencil. Artists vary the tones by the amount of resistance they use between the pencil and the paper they're drawing on. A drawing pencil's leads vary in hardness, each one giving a different tone than another. Washes of ink or color create values determined by the amount of water the medium is dissolved into.

The use of **high contrast,** placing lighter areas of value against much darker ones, creates a dramatic effect, while **low contrast** gives more subtle results. These differences in effect are evident in 'Guiditta and Oloferne' by the Italian painter Caravaggio, and Robert Adams' photograph Untitled, Denver from 1970-74. Caravaggio uses a high contrast palette to an already dramatic scene to increase the visual tension for the viewer, while Adams deliberately makes use of low contrast to underscore the drabness of the landscape surrounding the figure on the bicycle.

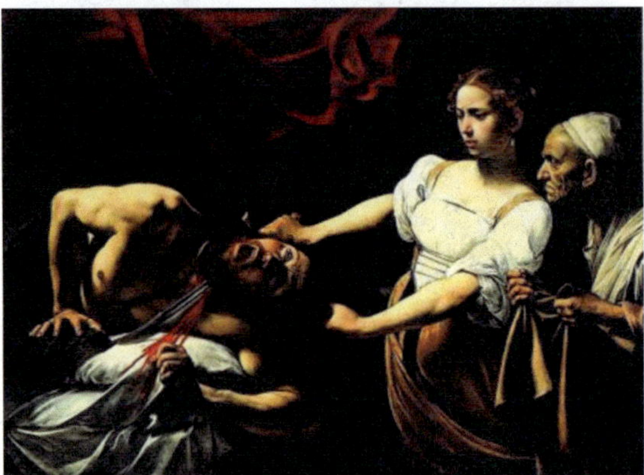

Caravaggio, Guiditta Decapitates Oloferne, 1598, oil on canvas. National Gallery of Italian Art, Rome. This work is in the public domain

Color

Color is the most complex artistic element because of the combinations and variations inherent in its use. Humans respond to color combinations differently, and artists study and use color in part to give desired direction to their work.

Color is fundamental to many forms of art. Its relevance, use and function in a given work depend on the medium of that work. While some concepts dealing with color are broadly applicable across media, others are not.

The full **spectrum** of colors is contained in white light. Humans perceive colors from the light reflected off objects. A red object, for example, looks red because it reflects the red part of the spectrum. It would be a different color under a different light. Color theory first appeared in the 17th century when English mathematician and scientist Sir Isaac Newton discovered that white light could be divided into a spectrum by passing it through a prism.

The study of color in art and design often starts with *color theory*. Color theory splits up colors into three categories: primary, secondary, and tertiary.

The basic tool used is a color wheel, developed by Isaac Newton in 1666. A more complex model known as the color tree, created by Albert Munsell, shows the spectrum made up of sets of tints and shades on connected planes.

There are a number of approaches to organizing colors into meaningful relationships. Most systems differ in structure only.

Traditional Model

Traditional color theory is a qualitative attempt to organize colors and their relationships. It is based on Newton's color wheel, and continues to be the most common system used by artists.

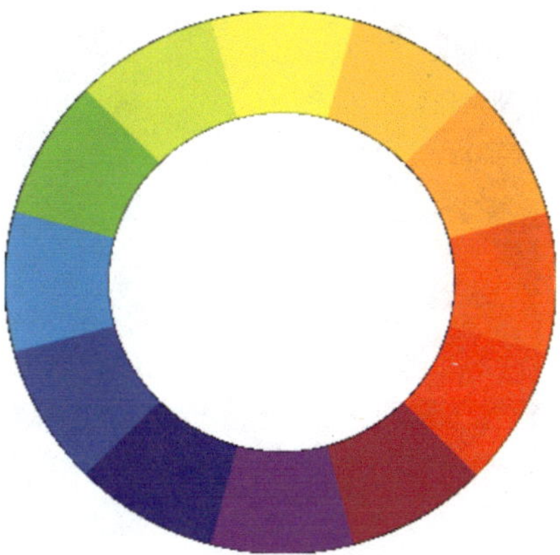

Blue Yellow Red Color Wheel. Released under
the GNU Free Documentation License

Traditional color theory uses the same principles as subtractive color mixing (see below) but prefers different primary colors.

- The ***primary*** colors are red, blue, and yellow. You find them equidistant from each other on the color wheel. These are the "elemental" colors; not produced by mixing any other colors, and all other colors are derived from some combination of these three.
- The ***secondary*** colors are orange (mix of red and yellow), green (mix of blue and yellow), and violet (mix of blue and red).
- The***tertiary*** colors are obtained by mixing one primary color and one secondary color. Depending on amount of color used, different hues can be obtained such as red-orange or yellow-green. Neutral colors (browns and grays) can be mixed using the three primary colors together.
- White and black lie outside of these categories. They are used to lighten or darken a color. A lighter color (made by adding white to it) is called a ***tint***, while a darker color (made by adding black) is called a ***shade***.

Color Mixing

A more quantifiable approach to color theory is to think about color as the result of light reflecting off a surface. Understood in this way, color can be represented as a ratio of amounts of primary color mixed together.

Additive color theory is used when different colored lights are being ***projected*** on top of each other. Projected media produce color by projecting light onto a reflective surface. Where subtractive mixing creates the impression of color by selectively absorbing part of the spectrum, additive mixing produces color by selective projection of part of the spectrum. Common applications of additive color theory are theater lighting and television screens. RGB color is based on additive color theory.

- The primary colors are red, blue, and green.
- The secondary colors are yellow (mix of red and green), cyan (mix of blue and green), and magenta (mix of blue and red).
- The tertiary colors are obtained by mixing the above colors at different intensities.

White is created by the confluence of the three primary colors, while black represents the absence of all color. The lightness or darkness of a color is determined by the intensity/density of its various parts. For instance: a middle-toned gray could be produced by projecting a red, a blue and a green light at the same point with 50% intensity.

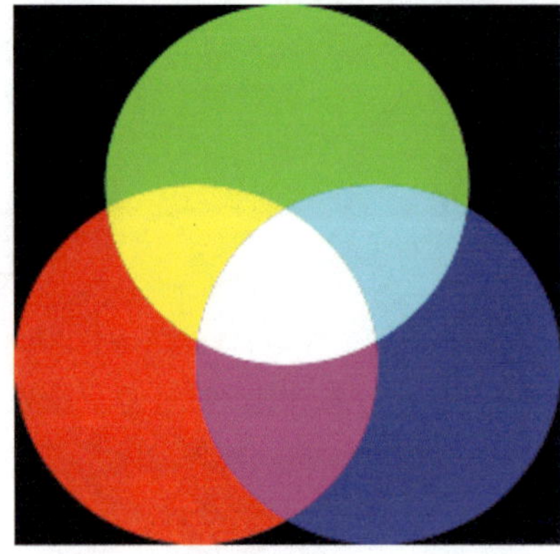

Additive Color Representation. This image is in the public domain.

The primaries are red, green and blue. White is the confluence of all the primary colors; black is the absence of color.

Subtractive color theory ("process color") is used when a single light source is being **_reflected_** by different colors laid one on top of the other. Color is produced when parts of the external light source's spectrum are absorbed by the material and not reflected back to the viewer's eye. For example, a painter brushes blue paint onto a canvas. The chemical composition of the paint allows all of the colors in the spectrum to be absorbed except blue, which is reflected from the paint's surface. Subtractive color works as the reverse of additive color theory. Common applications of subtractive color theory are used in the visual arts, color printing and processing photographic positives and negatives. The primary colors are red, yellow, and blue.

- The secondary colors are orange, green and violet.
- The tertiary colors are created by mixing a primary with a secondary color.
- Black is mixed using the three primary colors, while white represents the absence of all colors. Note: because of impurities in subtractive color, a true black is impossible to create through the mixture of primaries. Because of this the result is closer to brown. Similar to additive color theory, lightness and darkness of a color is determined by its intensity and density.

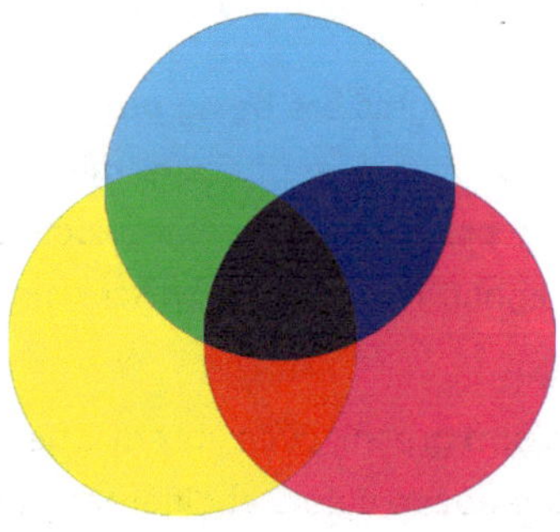

Subtractive Color Mixing. Released under the GNU Free Documentation License

The primaries are blue, yellow and red.

Color Attributes

There are many attributes to color. Each one has an effect on how we perceive it.

- **Hue** refers to color itself, but also to the variations of a color.
- **Value** (as discussed previously)refers to the relative lightness or darkness of one color next to another. The value of a color can make a difference in how it is perceived. A color on a dark background will appear lighter, while that same color on a light background will appear darker.

- **Tone** refers to the gradation or subtle changes made to a color when it's mixed with a gray created by adding two complements (see *Complementary Color* below). You can see various color tones by looking at the color tree mentioned in the paragraph above.
- **Saturation** refers to the purity and intensity of a color. The primaries are the most intense and pure, but diminish as they are mixed to form other colors. The creation of tints and shades also diminish a color's saturation. Two colors work strongest together when they share the same intensity. This is called equiluminance.

Color Interactions

Beyond creating a mixing hierarchy, color theory also provides tools for understanding how colors work together.

Monochrome

The simplest color interaction is monochrome. This is the use of variations of a single hue. The advantage of using a monochromatic color scheme is that you get a high level of unity throughout the artwork because all the tones relate to one another. See this in Mark Tansey's Derrida Queries de Man from 1990.

Analogous Color

Analogous colors are similar to one another. As their name implies, analogous colors can be found *next* to one another on any 12-part color wheel:

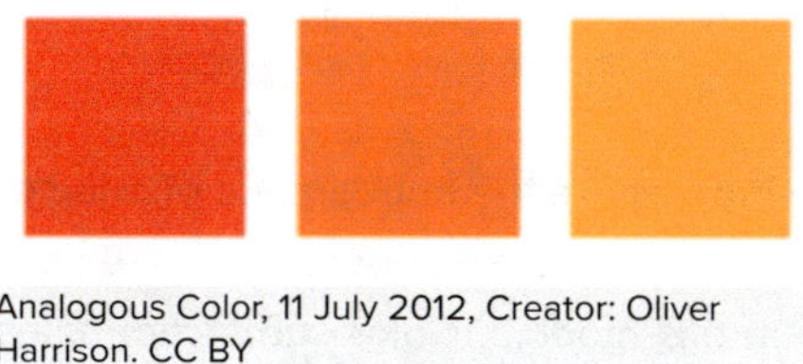

Analogous Color, 11 July 2012, Creator: Oliver Harrison. CC BY

You can see the effect of analogous colors in Paul Cezanne's oil painting Auvers Panoromic View

Color Temperature

Colors are perceived to have *temperatures* associated with them. The color wheel is divided into *warm* and *cool* colors. Warm colors range from yellow to red, while cool colors range from yellow-green to violet. You can achieve complex results using just a few colors when you pair them in warm and cool sets.

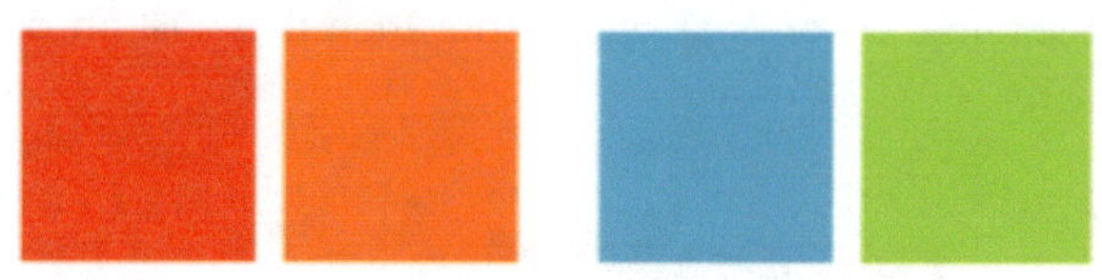

Warm cool color, 11 July 2012, Creator: Oliver Harrison. CC BY

Complementary Colors

Complementary colors are found directly *opposite* one another on a color wheel. Here are some examples:

- purple and yellow
- green and red
- orange and blue

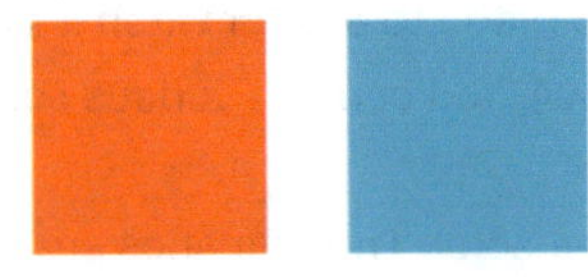

Complementary Color, 11 July 2012,
Creator: Oliver Harrison. CC BY

Blue and orange are complements. When placed near each other, complements create a visual tension. This color scheme is desirable when a dramatic effect is needed using only two colors. The painting Untitled by Keith Haring is an example. You can click the painting to create a larger image.

A **split complementary** color scheme uses one color plus the two colors on each side of the first color's complement on the color wheel. Like the use of complements, a split complement creates visual tension but includes the variety of a third color.

Split Complementary Color, 11 July
2012, Creator: Oliver Harrison. CC BY

Color Subtraction refers to a visual phenomenon where the appearance of one color will lessen its presence in a nearby color. For instance, orange (red + yellow) on a red background will appear more like yellow. Don't confuse color subtraction with the *subtractive color system* mentioned earlier in this module. Color subtraction uses specific hues within a color scheme for a certain visual effect.

Simultaneous Contrast

Neutrals on a colored background will appear tinted toward that color's complement, because the eye attempts to create a balance. (Grey on a red background will appear more greenish, for example.) In other words, the color will shift *away* from the surrounding color. Also, non-dominant colors will appear tinted towards the complement of the dominant color.

Color interaction affect values, as well. Colors appear darker on or near lighter colors, and lighter on or near darker colors. Complementary colors will look more intense on or near each other than they will on or near grays (refer back to the Keith Haring example above to see this effect).

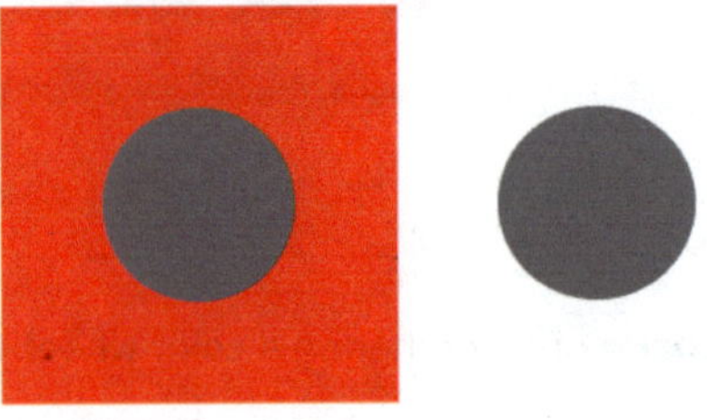

Simultaneous Contrast, 11 July 2012, Creator: Oliver Harrison. CC BY

Videos: Elements of Art

- https://youtu.be/BDePyEFT1gQ?list=PLiOil1qP-cMURN_8baOr3QWfySmljqKlj

Principles of Design

Identify and distinguish how the principles of design are used to visually organize the elements of design

LEARNING ACTIVITIES

The learning activities for this section include:

- Reading: Artistic Principles

Take time to review and reflect on each of these activities in order to improve your performance on the assessment for this section.

Reading: Artistic Principles

Art As Visual Input

Visual art manifests itself through media, ideas, themes and sheer creative imagination. Yet all of these rely on basic structural principles that, like the elements we've been studying, combine to give voice to artistic expression. Incorporating the principles into your artistic vocabulary not only allows you to objectively describe artworks you may not understand, but contributes in the search for their meaning.

The first way to think about a principle is that it is something that can be repeatedly and dependably done with elements to produce some sort of visual effect in a composition.

The principles are based on sensory responses to visual input: elements APPEAR to have visual weight, movement, etc. The principles help govern what might occur when particular elements are arranged in a particular way. Using a chemistry analogy, the principles are the ways the elements "stick together" to make a "chemical" (in our case, an image). Principles can be confusing. There are at least two very different but correct ways of thinking about principles. On the one hand, a principle can be used to describe an operational cause and effect such as "bright things come forward and dull things recede". On the other hand, a principle can describe a high quality standard to strive for such as "unity is better than chaos" or "variation beats boredom" in a work of art. So, the word "principle" can be used for very different purposes.

Another way to think about a principle is that it is a way to express a value judgment about a composition. Any list of these effects may not be comprehensive, but there are some that are more commonly used (unity, balance, etc). When we say a painting has unity we are making a value judgment. Too much *unity* without *variety* is boring and too much variation without unity is chaotic.

The principles of design help you to carefully plan and organize the elements of art so that you will hold interest and command attention. This is sometimes referred to as *visual impact*.

In any work of art there is a thought process for the arrangement and use of the elements of design. The artist who works with the principles of good composition will create a more interesting piece; it will be arranged to show a pleasing rhythm and movement. The center of interest will be strong and the viewer will not look away, instead, they will be drawn into the work. A good knowledge of composition is essential in producing good artwork. Some artists today like to bend or ignore these rules and by doing so are experimenting with different forms of expression. The following page explore important principles in composition.

Visual Balance

All works of art possess some form of visual balance – a sense of weighted clarity created in a composition. The artist arranges balance to set the dynamics of a composition. A really good example is in the work of Piet Mondrian, whose revolutionary paintings of the early twentieth century used non-objective balance instead of realistic subject matter to generate the visual power in his work. In the examples below you can see that where the white rectangle is placed makes a big difference in how the entire picture plane is activated.

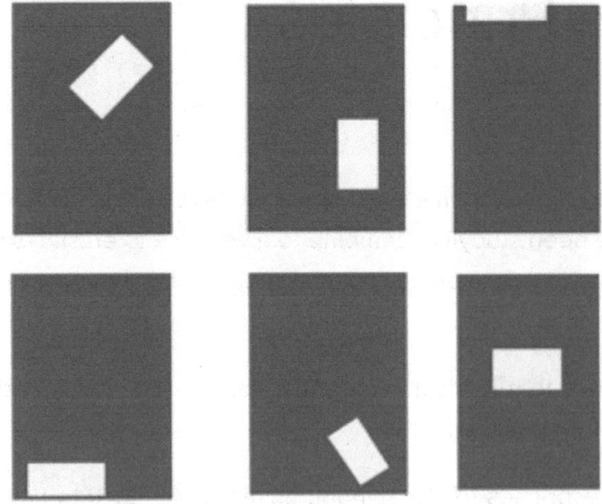

Image by Christopher Gildow. Used with permission.

The example on the top left is weighted toward the top, and the diagonal orientation of the white shape gives the whole area a sense of movement. The top middle example is weighted more toward the bottom, but still maintains a sense that the white shape is floating. On the top right, the white shape is nearly off the picture plane altogether, leaving most of the remaining area visually empty. This arrangement works if you want to convey a feeling of loftiness or simply direct the viewer's eyes to the top of the composition. The lower left example is perhaps the least dynamic: the white shape is resting at the bottom, mimicking the horizontal bottom edge of the ground. The overall sense here is restful, heavy and without any dynamic character. The bottom middle composition is weighted decidedly toward the bottom right corner, but again, the diagonal orientation of the white shape leaves some sense of movement. Lastly, the lower right example places the white shape directly in the middle on a horizontal axis. This is visually the most stable, but lacks any sense of movement. Refer to these six diagrams when you are determining the visual weight of specific artworks.

There are three basic forms of visual balance:

- Symmetrical
- Asymmetrical
- Radial

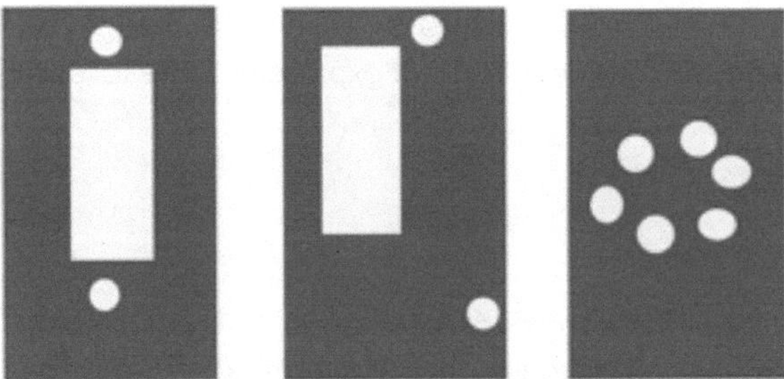

Examples of Visual Balance. Left: Symmetrical. Middle: Asymmetrical. Right: Radial. Image by Christopher Gildow. Used with permission.

Symmetrical balance is the most visually stable, and characterized by an exact—or nearly exact—compositional design on either (or both) sides of the horizontal or vertical axis of the picture plane. Symmetrical compositions are usually dominated by a central anchoring element. There are many examples of symmetry in the natural world that reflect an aesthetic dimension. The Moon Jellyfish fits this description; ghostly lit against a black background, but absolute symmetry in its design.

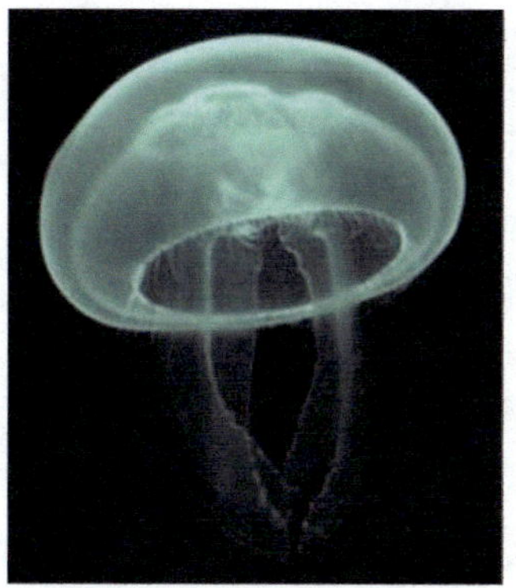

Moon Jellyfish, (detail). Digital image by Luc Viator, licensed by Creative Commons

But symmetry's inherent stability can sometimes preclude a static quality. View the Tibetan scroll painting to see the implied movement of the central figure Vajrakilaya. The visual busyness of the shapes and patterns surrounding the figure are balanced by their compositional symmetry, and the wall of flame behind Vajrakilaya tilts to the right as the figure itself tilts to the left. Tibetan scroll paintings use the symmetry of the figure to symbolize their power and spiritual presence.

Spiritual paintings from other cultures employ this same balance for similar reasons. Sano di Pietro's 'Madonna of Humility', painted around 1440, is centrally positioned, holding the Christ child and forming a triangular design, her head the apex and her flowing gown making a broad base at the bottom of the picture. Their halos are visually reinforced with the heads of the angels and the arc of the frame.

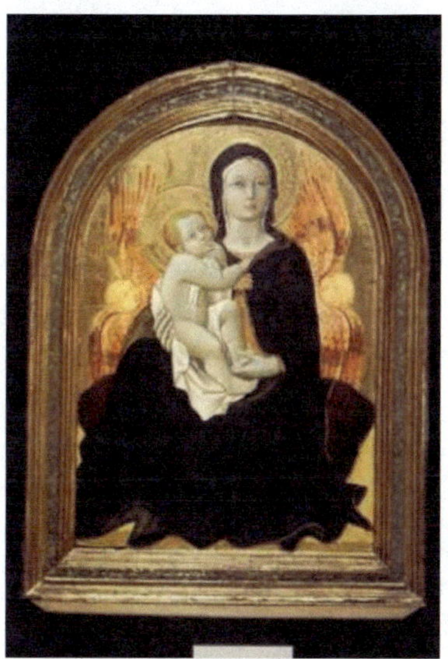

Sano di Peitro, Madonna of Humility, c.1440, tempera and tooled gold and silver on panel. Brooklyn Museum, New York. Image is in the public domain

The use of symmetry is evident in three-dimensional art, too. A famous example is the *Gateway Arch* in St. Louis, Missouri (below). Commemorating the westward expansion of the United States, its stainless steel frame rises over 600 feet into the air before gently curving back to the ground. Another example is Richard Serra's *Tilted Spheres* (also below). The four massive slabs of steel show a concentric symmetry and take on an organic dimension as they curve around each other, appearing to almost hover above the ground.

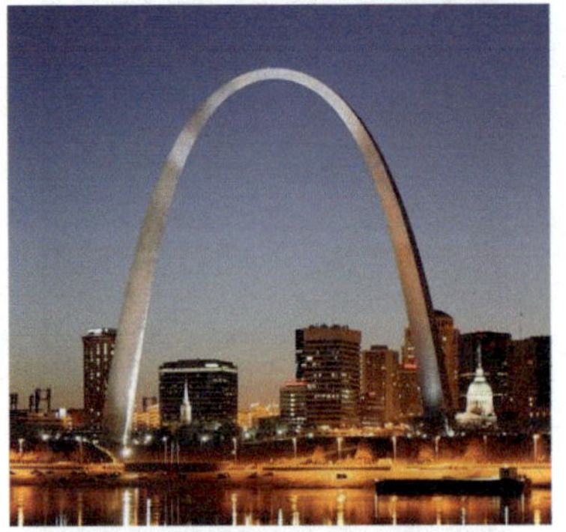

Eero Saarinen, Gateway Arch, 1963-65, stainless steel, 630' high. St. Louis, Missouri. Image Licensed through Creative Commons

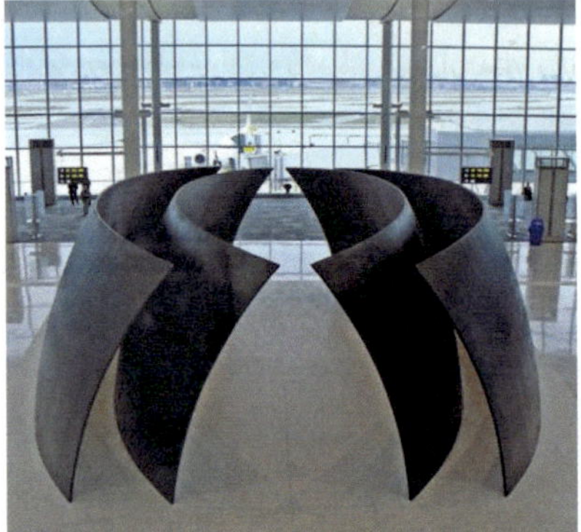

Richard Serra, Tilted Spheres, 2002 – 04, Cor-ten steel, 14' x 39' x 22'. Pearson International Airport, Toronto, Canada. Image Licensed through Creative Commons

Asymmetry uses compositional elements that are offset from each other, creating a visually unstable balance. Asymmetrical visual balance is the most dynamic because it creates a more complex design construction. A graphic poster from the 1930s shows how offset positioning and strong contrasts can increase the visual effect of the entire composition.

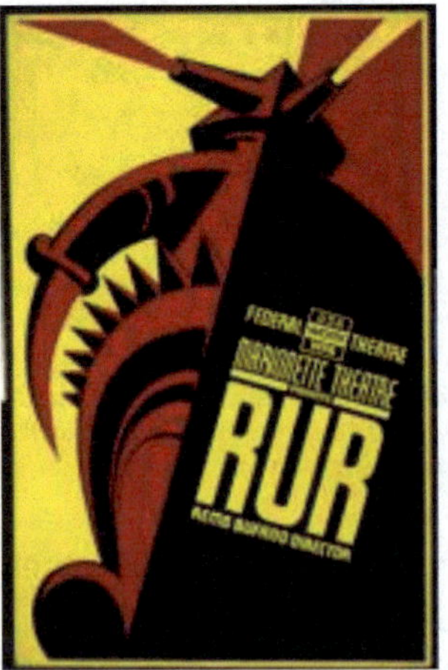

Poster from the Library of Congress archives. Image is in the public domain

Claude Monet's *Still Life with Apples and Grapes* from 1880 (below) uses asymmetry in its design to enliven an otherwise mundane arrangement. First, he sets the whole composition on the diagonal, cutting off the lower left corner with a dark triangle.

The arrangement of fruit appears haphazard, but Monet purposely sets most of it on the top half of the canvas to achieve a lighter visual weight. He balances the darker basket of fruit with the white of the tablecloth, even placing a few smaller apples at the lower right to complete the composition.

Monet and other Impressionist painters were influenced by Japanese woodcut prints, whose flat spatial areas and graphic color appealed to the artist's sense of design.

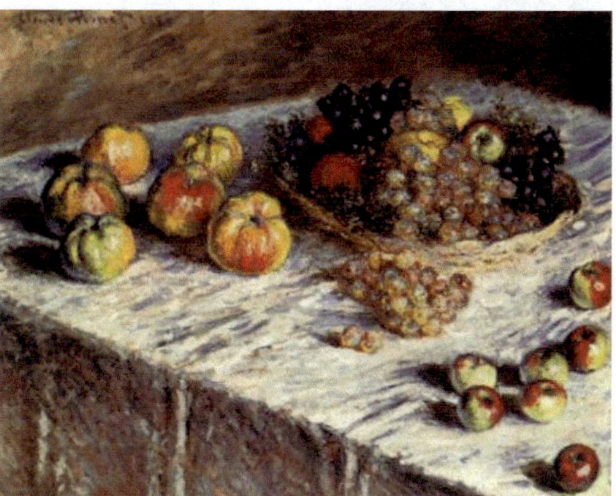

Claude Monet, Still Life with Apples and Grapes, 1880, oil on canvas. The Art Institute of Chicago. Licensed under Creative Commons

One of the best-known Japanese print artists is Ando Hiroshige. You can see the design strength of asymmetry in his woodcut *Shinagawa on the Tokaido* (below), one of a series of works that explores the landscape around the Takaido road. You can view many of his works through the hyperlink above.

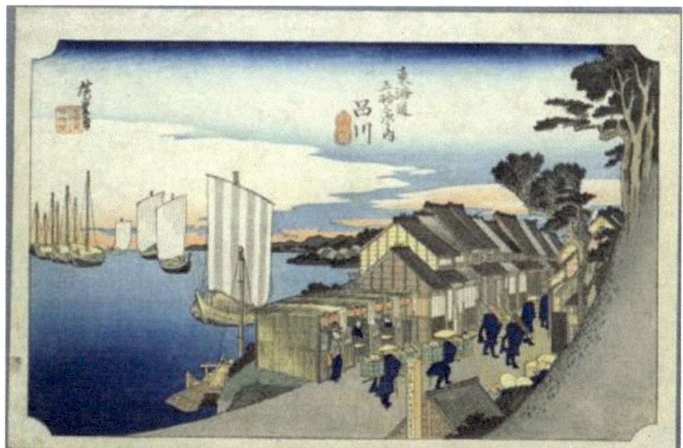

Hiroshige, Shinagawa on the Tokaido, ukiyo-e print, after 1832. Licensed under Creative Commons

In Henry Moore's *Reclining Figure* the organic form of the abstracted figure, strong lighting and precarious balance obtained through asymmetry make the sculpture a powerful example in three-dimensions.

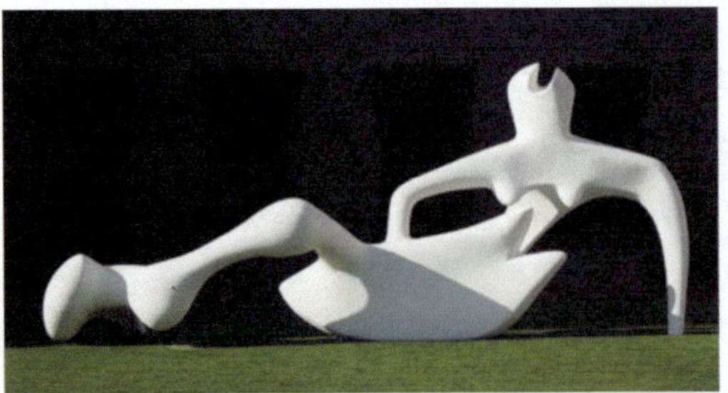

Henry Moore, Reclining Figure, 1951. Painted bronze. Fitzwilliam Museum, Cambridge. Photo by Andrew Dunn and licensed under Creative Commons

Radial balance suggests movement from the center of a composition towards the outer edge—or vise versa. Many times radial balance is another form of symmetry, offering stability and a point of focus at the center of the composition. Buddhist mandala paintings offer this kind of balance almost exclusively. Similar to the scroll painting we viewed previously, the image radiates outward from a central spirit figure. In the example below there are six of these figures forming a star shape in the middle. Here we have absolute symmetry in the composition, yet a feeling of movement is generated by the concentric circles within a rectangular format.

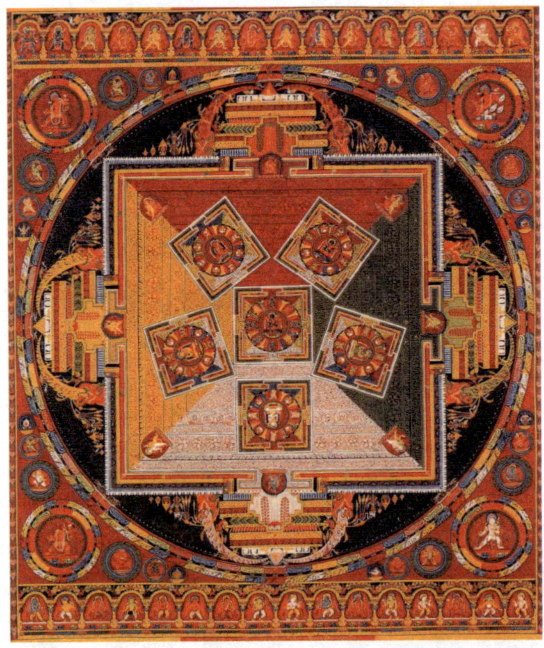

Tibetan Mandala of the Six Chakravartins, c. 1429-46. Central Tibet (Ngor Monestary). Image is in the public domain

Raphael's painting of Galatea, a sea nymph in Greek mythology, incorporates a double set of radial designs into one composition. The first is the swirl of figures at the bottom of the painting, the second being the four cherubs circulating at the top. The entire work is a current of figures, limbs and implied motion. Notice too the stabilizing classic triangle formed with Galatea's head at the apex and the other figures' positions inclined towards her. The cherub outstretched horizontally along the bottom of the composition completes the second circle.

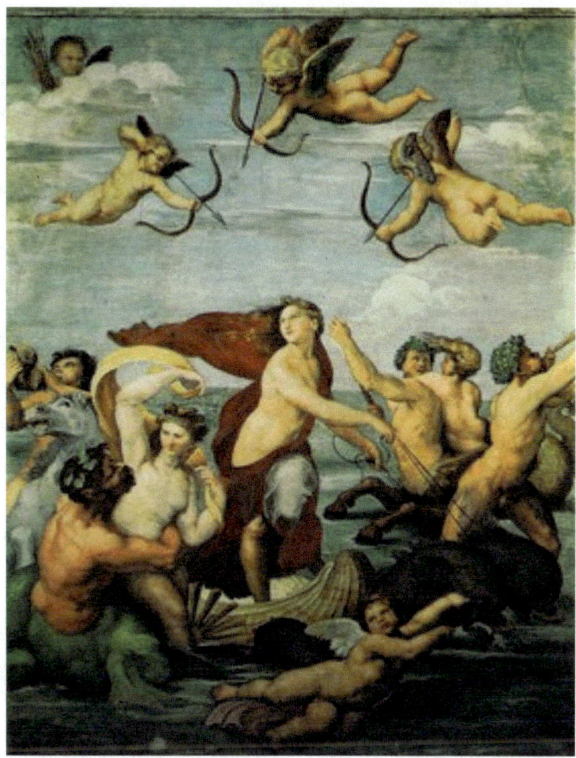

Raphael, Galatea, fresco, 1512. Villa Farnesina, Rome. Work is in the public domain

Within this discussion of visual balance, there is a relationship between the natural generation of organic systems and their ultimate form. This relationship is mathematical as well as aesthetic, and is expressed as the Golden Ratio:

- https://youtu.be/fmaVqkR0ZXg

Here is an example of the golden ratio in the form of a rectangle and the enclosed spiral generated by the ratios:

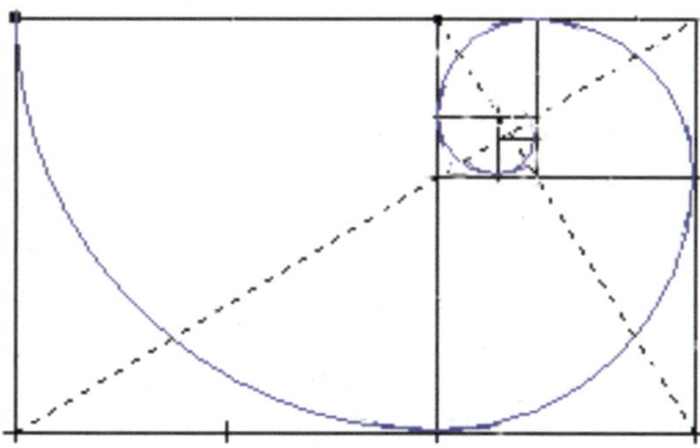

The golden ratio. Image from Wikipedia Commons and licensed through Creative Commons

The natural world expresses radial balance, manifest through the golden ratio, in many of its structures, from galaxies to tree rings and waves generated from dropping a stone on the water's surface. You can see this organic radial structure in some natural systems by comparing the satellite image of hurricane Isabel and a telescopic image of spiral galaxy M51 below.

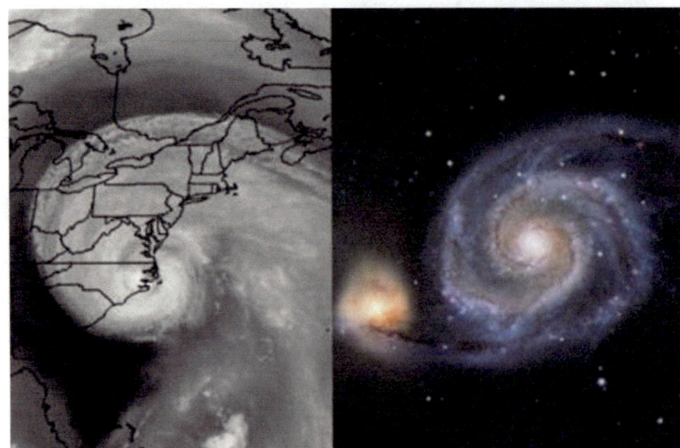

Images by the National Weather service and NASA. Images are in the public domain.

A snail shell, unbeknownst to its inhabitant, is formed by this same universal ratio, and, in this case, takes on the green tint of its surroundings.

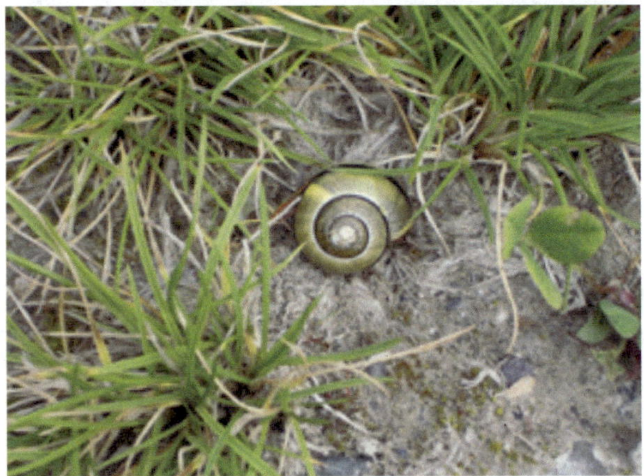

Image by Christopher Gildow. Used with permission.

Environmental artist Robert Smithson created *Spiral Jetty,* an earthwork of rock and soil, in 1970. The jetty extends nearly 1500 feet into the Great Salt Lake in Utah as a symbol of the interconnectedness of our selves to the rest of the natural world.

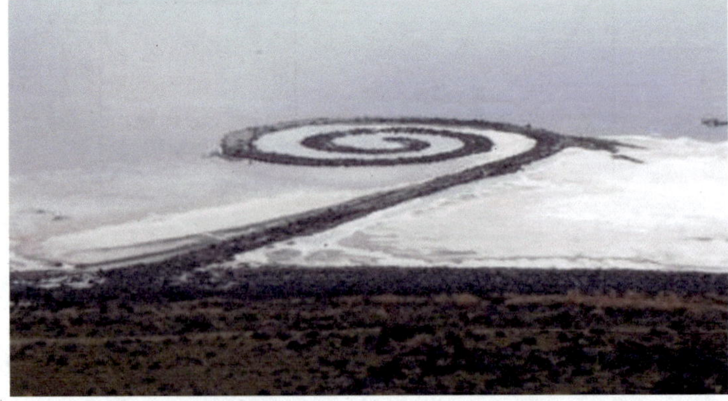

Robert Smithson, Spiral Jetty, 1970. Image by Soren Harward, CC BY-SA

Repetition

Repetition is the use of two or more like elements or forms within a composition. The systematic arrangement of a repeated shapes or forms creates **pattern.**

Patterns create **rhythm**, the lyric or syncopated visual effect that helps carry the viewer, and the artist's idea, throughout the work. A simple but stunning visual pattern, created in this photograph of an orchard by Jim Wilson for the New York Times, combines color, shape and direction into a rhythmic flow from left to right. Setting the composition on a diagonal increases the feeling of movement and drama.

The traditional art of Australian aboriginal culture uses repetition and pattern almost exclusively both as decoration and to give symbolic meaning to images. The *coolamon,* or carrying vessel pictured below, is made of tree bark and painted with stylized patterns of colored dots indicating paths, landscapes or animals. You can see how fairly simple patterns create rhythmic undulations across the surface of the work. The design on this particular piece indicates it was probably made for ceremonial use. We'll explore aboriginal works in more depth in the 'Other Worlds' module.

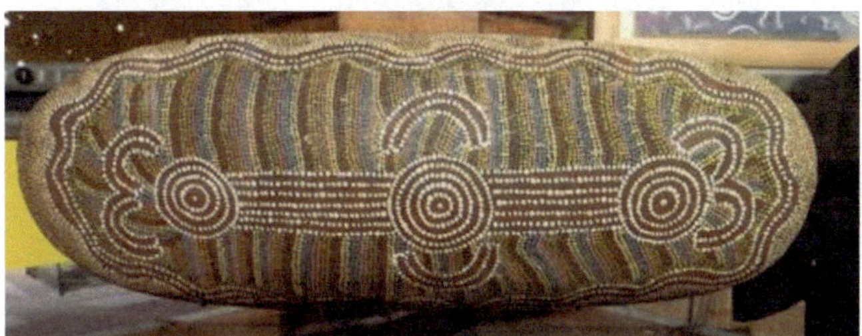

Australian aboriginal softwood coolamon with acrylic paint design. Licensed under Creative Commons

Rhythmic cadences take complex visual form when subordinated by others. Elements of line and shape coalesce into a formal matrix that supports the leaping salmon in Alfredo Arreguin's '*Malila Diptych*'. Abstract arches and spirals of water reverberate in the scales, eyes and gills of the fish. Arreguin creates two rhythmic beats here, that of the water flowing downstream to the left and the fish gracefully jumping against it on their way upstream.

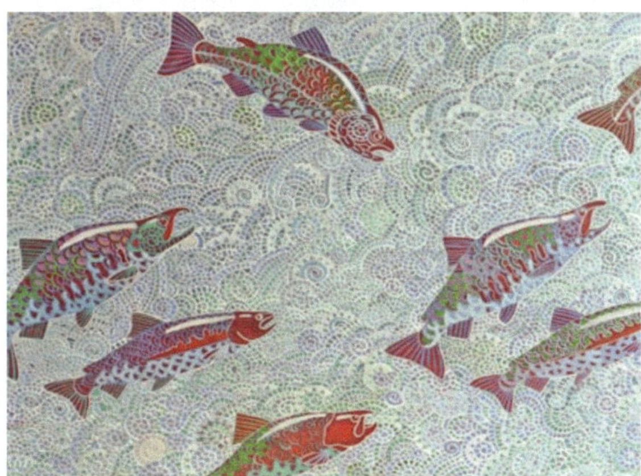

Alfredo Arreguin, Malila Diptych, 2003 (detail). Washington State Arts Commission. Digital Image by Christopher Gildow. Licensed under Creative Commons.

The textile medium is well suited to incorporate pattern into art. The warp and weft of the yarns create natural patterns that are manipulated through position, color and size by the weaver. The Tlingit culture of coastal British Columbia produce spectacular ceremonial blankets distinguished by graphic patterns and rhythms in stylized animal forms separated by a hierarchy of geometric shapes. The symmetry and high contrast of the design is stunning in its effect.

Scale and Proportion

Scale and proportion show the relative size of one form in relation to another. Scalar relationships are often used to create illusions of depth on a two-dimensional surface, the larger form being in front of the smaller one. The scale of an object can provide a focal point or emphasis in an image. In Winslow Homer's watercolor *A Good Shot, Adirondacks* the deer is centered in the foreground and highlighted to assure its place of importance in the composition. In comparison, there is a small puff of white smoke from a rifle in the left center background, the only indicator of the hunter's position. Click the image for a larger view.

Scale and proportion are incremental in nature. Works of art don't always rely on big differences in scale to make a strong visual impact. A good example of this is Michelangelo's sculptural masterpiece *Pieta* from 1499 (below). Here Mary cradles her dead son, the two figures forming a stable triangular composition. Michelangelo sculpts Mary to a slightly larger scale than the dead Christ to give the central figure more significance, both visually and psychologically.

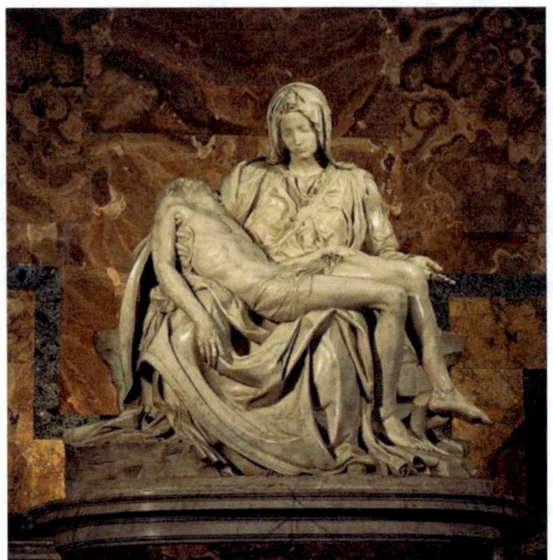

Michelangelo's Pieta, 1499, marble. St. Peter's Basilica, Rome. Licensed under GNU Free Documentation License and Creative Commons

When scale and proportion *are* greatly increased the results can be impressive, giving a work commanding space or fantastic implications. Rene Magritte's painting *Personal Values* constructs a room with objects whose proportions are so out of whack that it becomes an ironic play on how we view everyday items in our lives.

American sculptor Claes Oldenburg and his wife Coosje van Bruggen create works of common objects at enormous scales. Their *Stake Hitch* reaches a total height of more than 53 feet and links two floors of the Dallas Museum of Art. As big as it is, the work retains a comic and playful character, in part because of its gigantic size.

Emphasis

Emphasis—the area of primary visual importance—can be attained in a number of ways. We've just seen how it can be a function of differences in scale. Emphasis can also be obtained by isolating an area or specific subject matter through its location or color, value and texture. Main emphasis in a composition is usually supported by areas of lesser importance, a hierarchy within an artwork that's activated and sustained at different levels.

Like other artistic principles, emphasis can be expanded to include the main *idea* contained in a work of art. Let's look at the following work to explore this.

We can clearly determine the figure in the white shirt as the main emphasis in Francisco de Goya's painting *The Third of May, 1808* below. Even though his location is left of center, a candle lantern in front of him acts as a spotlight, and his dramatic stance reinforces his relative isolation from the rest of the crowd. Moreover, the soldiers with their aimed rifles create an implied line between them selves and the figure. There is a rhythm created by all the figures' heads—roughly all at the same level throughout the painting—that is continued in the soldiers' legs and scabbards to the lower right. Goya counters the horizontal emphasis by including the distant church and its vertical towers in the background.

In terms of the idea, Goya's narrative painting gives witness to the summary execution of Spanish resistance fighters by Napoleon's armies on the night of May 3, 1808. He poses the figure in the white shirt to imply a crucifixion as he faces his own death, and his compatriots surrounding him either clutch their faces in disbelief or stand stoically with him, looking their executioners in the eyes. While the carnage takes place in front of us, the church stands dark and silent in the distance. The genius of Goya is his ability to direct the narrative content by the emphasis he places in his composition.

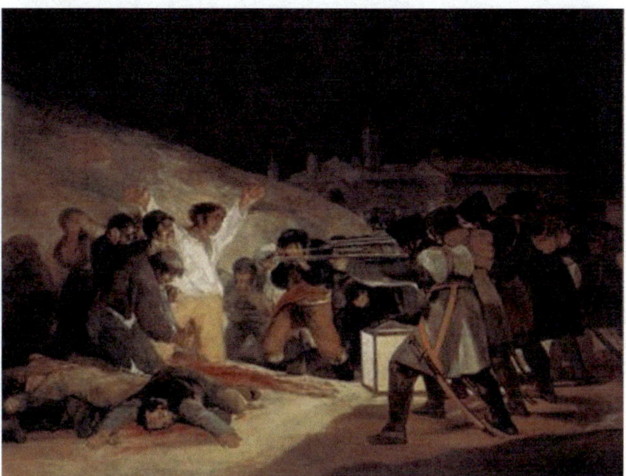

Francisco de Goya y Lucientes, The Third of May, 1808, 1814. Oil on canvas. The Prado Museum, Madrid. This image is in the public domain

A second example showing emphasis is seen in *Landscape with Pheasants*, a silk tapestry from nineteenth-century China. Here the main focus is obtained in a couple of different ways. First, the pair of birds are woven in *colored* silk, setting them apart visually from the gray landscape they inhabit. Secondly, their placement at the top of the outcrop of land allows them to stand out against the light background, their tail feathers mimicked by the nearby leaves. The convoluted treatment of the rocky outcrop keeps it in competition with the pheasants as a focal point, but in the end the pair of birds' color wins out.

A final example on emphasis, taken from *The Art of Burkina Faso* by Christopher D. Roy, University of Iowa, covers both design features and the idea behind the art. Many world cultures include artworks in ceremony and ritual. African *Bwa* Masks are large, graphically painted in black and white and usually attached to fiber costumes that cover the head. They depict mythic characters and animals or are abstract and have a stylized face with a tall, rectangular wooden plank attached to the top.* In any manifestation, the mask and the dance for which they are worn are inseparable. They become part of a community outpouring of cultural expression and emotion.

Time and Motion

One of the problems artists face in creating static (singular, fixed images) is how to imbue them with a sense of **time and motion**. Some traditional solutions to this problem employ the use of spatial relationships, especially perspective and atmospheric perspective. Scale and proportion can also be employed to show the passage of time or the illusion of depth and movement. For example, as something recedes into the background, it becomes smaller in scale and lighter in value. Also, the same figure (or other form) repeated in different places within the same image gives the effect of movement and the passage of time.

An early example of this is in the carved sculpture of Kuya Shonin. The Buddhist monk leans forward, his cloak seeming to move with the breeze of his steps. The figure is remarkably realistic in style, his head lifted slightly and his mouth open. Six small figures emerge from his mouth, visual symbols of the chant he utters.

Visual experiments in movement were first produced in the middle of the 19th century. Photographer Eadweard Muybridge snapped black and white sequences of figures and animals walking, running and jumping, then placing them side-by-side to examine the mechanics and rhythms created by each action.

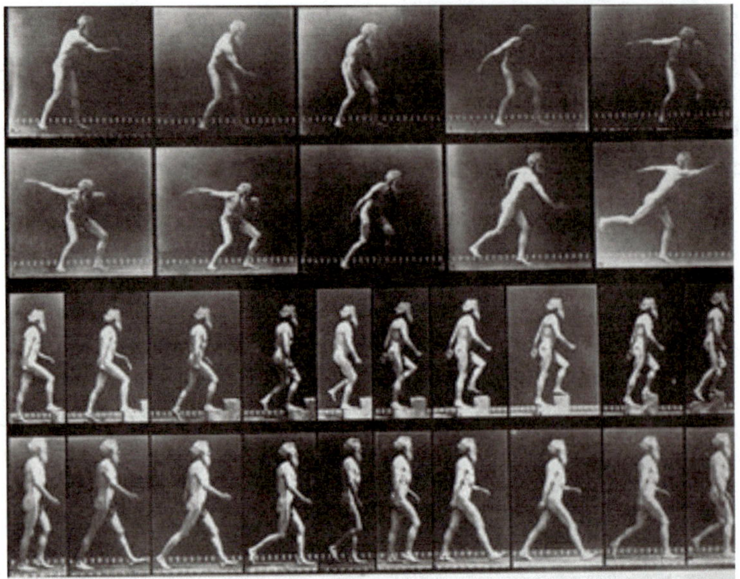

Eadweard Muybridge, sequences of himself throwing a disc, using a step and walking. Licensed through Creative Commons

In the modern era, the rise of cubism (please refer back to our study of 'space' in module 3) and subsequent related styles in modern painting and sculpture had a major effect on how static works of art depict time and movement. These new developments in form came about, in part, through the cubist's initial exploration of how to depict an object and the space around it by representing it from multiple viewpoints, incorporating all of them into a single image.

Marcel Duchamp's painting Nude Descending a Staircase from 1912 formally concentrates Muybridge's idea into a single image. The figure is abstract, a result of Duchamp's influence by cubism, but gives the viewer a definite feeling of movement from left to right. This work was exhibited at The Armory Show in New York City in 1913. The show was the first to exhibit modern art from the United States and Europe at an American venue on such a large scale. Controversial and fantastic, the Armory show became a symbol for the emerging modern art movement. Duchamp's painting is representative of the new ideas brought forth in the exhibition.

In three dimensions the effect of movement is achieved by imbuing the subject matter with a dynamic pose or gesture (recall that the use of diagonals in a composition helps create a sense of movement). Gian Lorenzo Bernini's sculpture of David from 1623 is a study of coiled visual tension and movement. The artist shows us the figure of David with furrowed brow, even biting his lip in concentration as he eyes Goliath and prepares to release the rock from his sling.

The temporal arts of film, video and digital projection by their definition show movement and the passage of time. In all of these mediums we watch as a narrative unfolds before our eyes. Film is essentially thousands of static images divided onto one long roll of film that is passed through a lens at a certain speed. From this apparatus comes the term *movies*.

Video uses magnetic tape to achieve the same effect, and digital media streams millions of electronically pixilated images across the screen. An example is seen in the work of Swedish Artist Pipilotti Rist. Her large-scale digital work Pour Your Body Out is fluid, colorful and absolutely absorbing as it unfolds across the walls.

Unity and Variety

Ultimately, a work of art is the strongest when it expresses an overall **unity** in composition and form, a visual sense that all the parts fit together; that the whole is greater than its parts. This same sense of unity is projected to encompass the idea and meaning of the work too. This visual and conceptual unity is sublimated by the **variety** of elements and principles used to create it. We can think of this in terms of a musical orchestra and its conductor: directing many different instruments, sounds and feelings into a single comprehendible symphony of sound. This is where the objective functions of line, color, pattern, scale and all the other artistic elements and principles yield to a more subjective view of the entire work, and from that an appreciation of the aesthetics and meaning it resonates.

We can view Eva Isaksen's work *Orange Light* below to see how unity and variety work together.

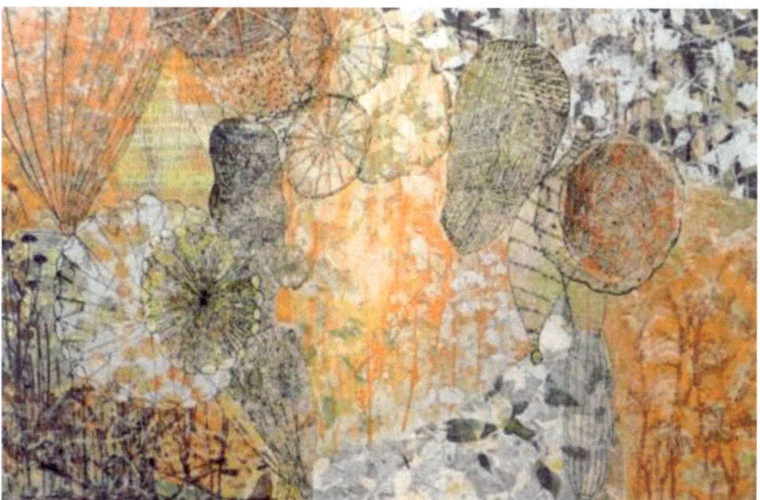

Eva Isaksen, Orange Light, 2010. Print and collage on canvas. 40" x 60." Permission of the artist

Isaksen makes use of nearly every element and principle including shallow space, a range of values, colors and textures, asymmetrical balance and different areas of emphasis. The unity of her composition stays strong by keeping the various parts in check against each other and the space they inhabit. In the end the viewer is caught up in a mysterious world of organic forms that float across the surface like seeds being caught by a summer breeze.

Types of Representation

Distinguish between representational (realistic), abstract, and nonrepresentational (or non-objective) imagery

LEARNING ACTIVITIES

The learning activities for this section include:

- Reading: Representational, Abstract, and Nonrepresentational Art

Take time to review and reflect on this activity in order to improve your performance on the assessment for this section.

Reading: Representational, Abstract, and Nonrepresentational Art

Abstract art exists on a continuum, from somewhat realistic representational work to fully nonrepresentational work.

KEY POINTS

- Representational art or figurative art represents objects or events in the real world.
- Romanticism, Impressionism, and Expressionism contributed to the emergence of abstract art in the nineteenth century.
- Even representational work is abstracted to some degree; entirely realistic art is elusive.

Term

- Verisimilitude: the property of seeming true, of resembling reality; has a resemblance to reality

Painting and sculpture can be divided into the categories of figurative (or representational) and abstract (which includes nonrepresentational art). Figurative art describes artworks—particularly paintings and sculptures–that are clearly derived from real object sources, and therefore are by definition representational. Since the arrival of abstract art in the early twentieth century, the term figurative has been used to refer to any form of modern art that retains strong references to the real world.

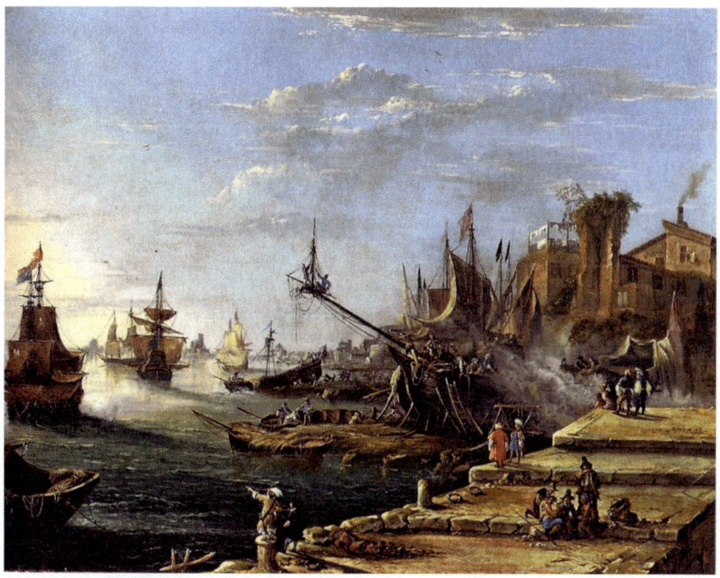

Johann Anton Eismann, Meerhaven. 17th c. Work is in the public domain

This figurative or representational work from the seventeenth century depicts easily recognizable objects–ships, people, and buildings. Artistic independence was advanced during the nineteenth century, resulting in the emergence of abstract art. Three movements that contributed heavily to the development of these were Romanticism, Impressionism, and Expressionism.

Abstraction indicates a departure from reality in depiction of imagery in art. Abstraction exists along a continuum; abstract art can formally refer to compositions that are derived (or abstracted) from a figurative or other natural source. It can also refer to nonrepresentational art and non-objective art that has no derivation from figures or objects.

Even art that aims for verisimilitude of the highest degree can be said to be abstract, at least theoretically, since perfect representation is likely to be exceedingly elusive. Artwork which takes liberties, altering for instance color and form in ways that are conspicuous, can be said to be partially abstract.

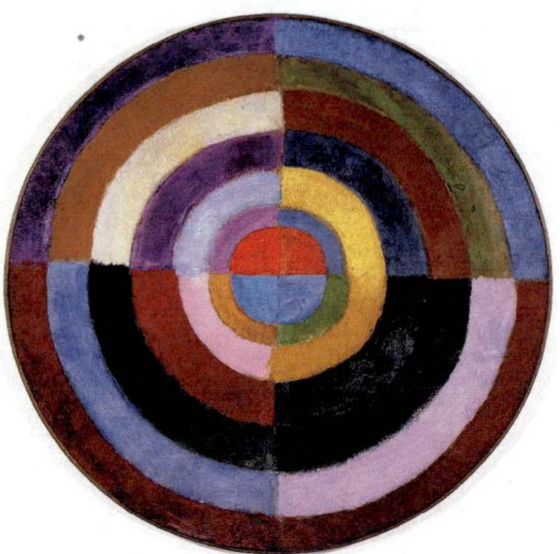

Robert Delaunay, Le Premier Disque, 1913. Work is in the public domain

Delaunay's work is a primary example of early abstract art. Nonrepresentational art refers to total abstraction, bearing no trace of any reference to anything recognizable. In geometric abstraction, for instance, one is unlikely to find references to naturalistic entities. Figurative art and total abstraction are almost mutually exclusive. But figurative and representational (or realistic) art often contains partial abstraction.

Putting It Together

This section began by defining formalism, which is an analytical way of looking at artwork and describing how its elements and principles of design work together to as a composition. It's also a way of discussing how the visual effects of composition can contribute to our understanding or interpretation of artwork.

Point, line, shape, space, color, and value are all elements of design. These basic building blocks of form are arranged using the principles of design. Principles act on elements as the various ways of organizing them in a composition.

Formalism allows anyone a way into an artwork without any prior knowledge of the artist or knowledge of deeper contexts that impacted how and why it was created.

Take another look at Picasso's *Guernica*.

With the knowledge of formalism you gained in this section, let's reconsider the question of how formalism can be applied to understanding its composition? First let's start with elements. What elements feel like they are strongly represented? Likely your answer is shape and value, and possibly implied line as well as space.

Which principles of design feel strongly engaged in this composition? It is an asymmetrical composition with considerable movement created by the repetition of directional triangular shapes. These bold shapes point and pull the viewer's eye around the composition.

What about the type of representation? Picasso at this point is engaged in semi-abstraction. Now that we have analyzed form through elements, principles, and type of representation, let's focus on how these contribute to interpreting meaning or feelings produced by these compositional choices. Visually the space is very active, almost to the point of visual discomfort. This combined with the subject matter affects how we feel, and ultimately the meaning we take away from experiencing the painting.

Visit the Museo Reina Sofia in Spain to learn more about the interpretations of Guernica and consider how these interpretations correlate with the formalist reading of its composition above.

CHAPTER 2: WHAT IS ART?

Why It Matters

Define "art" within the context of the ongoing discussion about its meaning (course level learning objective)

Introduction

As a thought experiment, imagine what a society without art would be like? How would buildings look? Could any kind of visual communication exist at all? It's a provocative question that quickly necessitates defining the boundaries of what does and does not constitute art. This mirrors the complexity of engaging in the ongoing definition of art.

Art is studied because "it is among the highest expressions of culture, embodying its ideals and aspirations, challenging its assumptions and beliefs, and creating new visions and possibilities for it to pursue" (Sayre, XVI). When we discuss contemporary art, we are typically referring to the practice of fine art, but prior to the Renaissance, art was defined within the realm of functional crafts, such as goldsmithing. The idea of autonomous art or art for art's sake developed later, over many eras.

Studying art leads to a greater understanding of our own cultural values and of the society that produced it. When colonizing forces of Europeans encountered African wood sculptural nkisi figures, primarily in what is now the Democratic Republic of the Congo, they considered them to be evidence of idolatry and witchcraft or opposition to the colonizing forces (Sayre 11–12). The figures were often pierced with nails as a symbolic gesture to initiate a desired goal, like protection from an enemy. The invading Europeans often destroyed the nkisi figures, which were sacred objects to the Congo people. We will return to this example at the end of the module.

Visit this link to see an example of a nkisi sculpture.

The material covered in this section will help you understand how we arrived at our contemporary understanding of art and how to begin engaging in the ongoing definition and discussion of art.

MODULE LEARNING OUTCOMES

- Recognize and summarize changing perceptions and definitions of art throughout history.
- Define aesthetics and some variables in how we perceive and assign value to art.
- Describe and discuss some contemporary theories in the definition of art.

How to study for the Performance Assessment (PA)

The PAs for this module are answering short essay questions that are designed to test your understanding of the learning outcomes (listed above) for this module. Read through the two performance assessments for this module BEFORE you begin the module content. I suggest printing them out, or making notes of the keywords in each question. Then, as you read through the module content take notes on the subjects or anything that you find relevant to the PA questions. Be sure to document the page or place in the content where you found each note, in case you need to return to that content, or need to ask me a specific question citing module content. Once you are ready to complete the PAs, you will have these notes to help you answer the questions thoughtfully.

OK, let's get started!

Work Cited

Sayre, Henry. *A World of Art*, Sixth edition. Boston: Prentice Hall, 2010. Print.

Art as a kind of communication and expression of culture

Recognize and summarize changing perceptions and definitions of art throughout history

LEARNING ACTIVITIES

The learning activities for this section include:

- Reading: Defining Art from the Medieval Period to Renaissance
- Reading: Defining Art from the Academy to Avant-garde
- Reading: Defining Art from Modernity to Globalization

Take time to review and reflect on each of these activities in order to improve your performance on the assessment for this section.

Reading: Defining Art from the Medieval Period to Renaissance

Medieval to Renaissance

We begin by considering the production and consumption of art from the Crusades through to the period of the Catholic Reformation. The focus is on art in medieval and Renaissance Christendom, but this does not imply that Europe was insular during this period. The period witnessed the slow erosion of the crusader states in the Holy Land, finally relinquished in 1291, and of the Greek Byzantine world until Constantinople fell to the Ottomans in 1453. Columbus made his voyage to the Americas in 1492. Medieval Christendom was well aware of its neighbors. Trade, diplomacy, and conquest connected Christendom to the wider world, which in turn had an impact on art.

Any notion of the humble medieval artist oblivious to anything beyond his own immediate environment must be dispelled. Artists and patrons were well aware of artistic developments in other countries. Artists travelled both within and between countries and on occasion even between continents. Such mobility was facilitated by the network of European courts, which were instrumental in the rapid spread of Italian Renaissance art. Europe-wide frameworks of philosophical and theological thought, reaching back to antiquity and governing religious art, applied – albeit with regional variations – throughout Europe.

Art, Visual Culture, and Skill

The term 'visual culture' is used here in preference to 'art' for the fundamental reason that the arts before 1600 were wide-ranging, including media today that we might deem within the realm of craft and not fine art. The Latin word 'ars' signified skilled work; it did not mean art as we might understand it today, but a craft activity demanding a high level of technical ability, including tapestry weaving, goldsmith's work, and embroidery. Literary statements of what constituted the arts during the medieval period are rare, particularly in northern Europe, but proliferate in the Renaissance. Giorgio Vasari (1511–74), the biographer of Italian artists, claimed in his famous book Le vite de' più eccelenti pittori, scultori e architettori (Lives of the Painters, Sculptors and Architects; first edition 1550 and revised 1568) that the architect Filippo Brunelleschi (1377–1446) was initially apprenticed to a goldsmith 'to the end that he might learn design' (Vasari, 1996 [1568], vol. 1, p. 326). According to Vasari, several other Italian Renaissance artists are supposed to have trained initially as goldsmiths, including the sculptors Ghiberti (1378–1455) and Verrocchio (1435–88), and the painters Botticelli (c.1445–1510) and Ghirlandaio (1448/49–94). The design skills necessary for goldsmiths' work were evidently a good foundation for future artistic success.

Medieval and Renaissance Visual Culture

The term 'visual culture' is also used for a second reason that is less to do with definition than with method. Including the various arts under the umbrella of 'visual culture' implies their inseparability from the visual rhetoric of power on the one hand, and the material culture of a society on the other. Before 1500 art was primarily part of the persuasive power and cultural identity of the church, ruler, city, institution, or the wealthy patron commissioning the artwork. In this sense, art might be considered alongside ceremonies, for example, as strategies conveying social meaning or magnificence, or as a demonstration of wealth and power by the patron commissioning the artwork to be made.

In later centuries art evolves into purely an aesthetic entity, prompting scrutiny for its own sake alone. The intent of the varied forms of art produced during the medieval and Renaissance period lie outside this definition. Objects were made that invited attentive scrutiny for their ingenuity in design, while at the same time fulfilling a variety of functions. No one in medieval times would have bothered to commission works of art unless they could assume that their contemporaries were vulnerable to their communicative power. For example, the wealthy lavished money on rich artifacts or dynastic portraits in part because these objects were a way of communicating their exclusiveness and social power to their contemporaries.

Artistic Quality

The fact that a work of art had a function did not mean that artistic quality was a matter of indifference. Some artists' guilds, such as the painters' guild of Tournai, south of Brussels, required candidates to submit a 'masterpiece' for examination by the guild in order to win the status of master. Those scrutinizing the masterpieces must have had a clear idea of the criteria of quality they were hoping for, even if these criteria were never set down in writing. The careful selection of artists even from far-flung locations, and the preference for one practitioner above another, shows that patrons too were quite capable of discriminating on the basis of artistic prowess. A work of art during the medieval and Renaissance period was expected to be of high quality as well as purposeful.

Artists and Patrons

Famously, in 1516, the renowned Renaissance artist Leonardo da Vinci (1452–1519) was invited to the French court of Francis I (ruled 1515–47), perhaps not so much for the work that he might produce at what was then an advanced age, as out of admiration and presumably for the prestige that the presence of such a renowned figure might endow on the French court. The advancement of artistic status is often associated with princely employment, for example by Martin Warnke in his seminal study of the court artist (Warnke, 1993, pp. 33–45). Given the example of Leonardo da Vinci, this appears to make sense. Maintained on a salary, a court artist was no longer a jobbing craftsman constantly on the lookout for work. Potentially, at least, he had access to projects demanding inventiveness and conferring honor, and time to lavish on his art and on study. Equally, however, court artists might be required to undertake mundane and routine work which they could not very well refuse. Court salaries were also often in arrears or not paid at all. In the same letter in which Leone Leoni described Charles V chatting with him for two to three hours at a time, he complains of his poverty, while carefully qualifying the complaint by claiming he serves the emperor for honor and cares for studying not moneymaking. The lot of the court artist might appear to fulfill aspirations for artistic status, but it certainly had its drawbacks.

Patterns of Artistic Employment: Workshop, Guild, and Court Employment

The pattern of artistic employment in the medieval period and the Renaissance varied. Traditionally, craftsmen working on great churches would be employed in workshops on site, albeit often for some length of time; during the course of their career, such craftsmen might move several times from one project to another. Many other artists moved around in search of new opportunities of employment, even to the extent of accompanying a crusade. Artists working for European courts might travel extensively as well, not just within a country but from country to country and court to court: El Greco (1541–1614) moved between three different countries before finding employment not at the royal court in Spain but in the city of Toledo.

A fixed artist's workshop depended not only on local institutional and individual patronage, but often also on the willingness of clients from further afield to come to the artist rather than the artist traveling to work for clients.

A guild served three main functions: promoting the social welfare of its members, maintaining the quality of its products and protecting its members from competition. This usually meant defining quite carefully the materials and tools that a guild member was allowed to use to prevent activities that infringed the privileges of other guilds and for which they had not been trained, for example a carpenter producing wood sculpture.

It is the protection from competition that art historians have seen as eliminating artistic freedom, but it is worth pausing to wonder whether this view owes more to modern free-market economics than to the realities of fifteenth-century craft practices. In practice, it meant that domestic craftsmen enjoyed preferential membership rates, but in many artistic centers foreign craftsmen were clearly also welcomed so long as their work reflected favorably on the reputation of the guild.

As the debate about artistic status grew, the real disadvantage of the guild system for artists was not so much lack of freedom or profitability or even status so much as the connotations of manual craft attached to the guild system of apprenticeship as opposed to the 'liberal' training offered by the art academies.

We have here sought to indicate the range and richness of visual culture in medieval Christendom and the Renaissance.

Works Cited

Adamson, J.S.A. (1999) The Princely Courts of Europe: Ritual, Politics and Culture under the Ancien Régime 1500–1750, London, Weidenfeld & Nicolson.

Alberti, L.B. (1966 [1435]) On Painting (trans. J.R. Spencer), New Haven, CT and London, Yale University Press.

Arciszweska, B. and McKellar, E. (2004) Articulating British Classicism: New Approaches to Eighteenth-Century Architecture, Aldershot and Burlington, VT, Ashgate.

Bailey, C. (1987) 'Conventions of the eighteenth-century cabinet de tableaux: Blondel d'Azincourt's La première idée de la curiosité', Art Bulletin, vol. 69, no. 3, pp. 431–47.

Bailey, C. (2002) Patriotic Taste: Collecting Modern Art in Pre-Revolutionary Paris, New Haven, CT and London, Yale University Press.

Bailey, G.A. (1999) Art on the Jesuit Missions in Asia and Latin America, 1542–1773, Toronto and London, University of Toronto Press.

Barr, A.H. (1974 [1936]) Cubism and Abstract Art, New York, Museum of Modern Art (exhibition catalogue).

Baudelaire, C. (1981 [1859]) 'On photography' in Newhall, B. (ed.) Photography: Essays and Images, New York, Secker & Warburg, pp. 112–13.

Baxandall, M. (1971) Giotto and the Orators: Humanist Observers of Painting in Italy and the Discovery of Pictorial Composition 1350–1450, Oxford, Clarendon Press.

Baxandall, M. (1972) Painting and Experience in Fifteenth-Century Italy, Oxford, Clarendon Press.

Baxandall, M. (1980) The Limewood Sculptors of Renaissance Germany, New Haven, CT, Yale University Press.

Belting, H. (1994) Likeness and Presence: A History of the Image before the Era of Art, Chicago, IL and London, University of Chicago Press.

Benjamin, W. (1983) Charles Baudelaire: A Lyric Poet in the Era of High Capitalism, London, Verso.

Bergdoll, B. (2000) European Architecture 1750–1890, Oxford, Oxford University Press.

Bermingham, A. (2000) Learning to Draw: Studies in the Cultural History of a Polite and Useful Art, New Haven, CT and London, Yale University Press.

Blanning, T.C.W. (2002) The Culture of Power and the Power of Culture: Old Regime Europe 1660–1789, Oxford, Oxford University Press.

Bürger, P. (1984) Theory of the Avant-Garde, Manchester, Manchester University Press; Minneapolis, MN, University of Minnesota Press.

Clark, T.J. (1982) Image of the People. Gustave Courbet and the 1848 Revolution, London, Thames & Hudson.

Clark, T.J. (1984) The Painting of Modern Life: Paris in the Art of Manet and his Followers, London, Thames & Hudson.

Clayton, T. (1997) The English Print, 1688–1802, London and New Haven, CT, Yale University Press.

Connell, S.M. (1976) The Employment of Sculptors and Stonemasons in Venice in the Fifteenth Century (doctoral thesis), Warburg Institute, University of London.

Craske, M. (1997) Art in Europe 1700–1830: A History of the Visual Arts in an Era of Unprecedented Urban Economic Growth, Oxford, Oxford University Press.

Crown, P. (1990) 'British Rococo as social and political style', Eighteenth-Century Studies, vol. 23, no. 3, pp. 269–82.

Duchamp, M. (1975) The Essential Writings of Marcel Duchamp (ed. M. Sanouillet and E. Peterson), London, Thames & Hudson.

Edwards, S. (ed.) (1999) Art and its Histories: A Reader, New Haven, CT and London, Yale University Press.

Elias, N. (1983) The Court Society (trans. E. Jephcott), Oxford, Blackwell.

Gilbert, C. (1985) 'A statement of the aesthetic attitude around 1230', Hebrew University Studies in Literature and the Arts, vol. 13, no. 2, pp. 125–52.

Gordon, D. (2003) The Fifteenth-Century Italian Paintings, National Gallery Catalogues, London, Yale University Press.

Greenberg, C. (1961) Art and Culture: Critical Essays, Boston, MA, Beacon Press.

Greenberg, C. (1986 [1939]) 'Avant-garde and kitsch' in O'Brian, J. (ed.) Clement Greenberg: The Collected Essays and Criticism, vol. 1: Perceptions and Judgements, 1939–1944, Chicago, IL, Chicago University Press, pp. 5–22.

Greenberg, C. (1993 [1960]) 'Modernist painting' in O'Brian, J. (ed.) Clement Greenberg: The Collected Essays and Criticism, vol. 4: Modernism with a Vengeance, 1957–1969, Chicago, IL, Chicago University Press, pp. 85–100.

Habermas, J. (1989 [1962]) The Structural Transformation of the Public Sphere: An Inquiry into a Category of Bourgeois Society, Cambridge, MA, MIT Press.

Hardie, P. (1993) 'Ut Pictura Poesis? Horace and the visual arts' in Horace 2000: A Celebration for the Bi-millennium, London, Duckworth, pp. 120–39.

Harris, A.S. (2008) Seventeenth-Century Art and Architecture (2nd edn), London, Laurence King.

Harrison, C., Wood, P. and Gaiger, J. (eds) (1998) Art in Theory 1815–1900: An Anthology of Changing Ideas, Oxford, Blackwell.

Harvey, D. (2003) Paris: Capital of Modernity, London and New York, Routledge.

Haskell, F. (1980) Patrons and Painters: A Study in the Relations between Italian Art and Society in the Age of the Baroque, New Haven and London, Yale University Press.

Haskell, F. and Penny, N. (1981) Taste and the Antique: The Lure of Classical Sculpture 1500–1900, New Haven, CT and London, Yale University Press.

Hauser, A. (1962 [1951]) The Social History of Art. Vol. 2: Renaissance, Mannerism, Baroque; Vol. 3. Rococo, Classicism and Romanticism (2nd edn), London, Routledge.

Haynes, C. (2006) Pictures and Popery: Art and Religion in England, 1660–1760, Aldershot, Ashgate.

Hemingway, A. and Vaughan, W. (eds) (1998) Art in Bourgeois Society 1790–1850, Cambridge, Cambridge University Press.

Hills, H. (ed.) (2011) Rethinking the Baroque, Farnham, Ashgate.

Honour, H. (1968) Neo-classicism, Harmondsworth, Penguin.

Honour, H. (1979) Romanticism, Harmondsworth, Penguin.

Hyde, M. (2006) Making up the Rococo: François Boucher and his Critics, Los Angeles, CA and London, Getty Research Institute.

Irwin, D. (1997) Neoclassicism, London, Phaidon.

Langdon, H. (1998) Caravaggio: A Life, London, Chatto & Windus.

Lee, R. (1967) Ut Pictura Poesis: The Humanistic Theory of Painting, New York, W.W. Norton.

Levy, E. (2004) Propaganda and the Jesuit Baroque, Berkeley, CA and London, University of California Press.

Lichtenstein, J. (2008) The Blind Spot: An Essay on the Relations between Painting and Sculpture in the Modern Age, Los Angeles, CA, Getty Research Institute.

Lymberopoulou, A., Bracewell-Homer, P. and Robinson, J. (eds) (2012) Art & Visual Culture: A Reader, London, Tate Publishing in association with The Open University.

McClellan, A. (1994) Inventing the Louvre: Art, Politics, and the Origins of the Modern Museum in Eighteenth-Century Paris, Cambridge, Cambridge University Press.

McClellan, A. (1996) 'Watteau's dealer: Gersaint and the marketing of art in eighteenth-century Paris', Art Bulletin, vol. 78, no. 3, pp. 439–53.

Montias, J.M. (1982) Artists and Artisans in Delft: A Socio-economic Study of the Seventeenth Century, Princeton, NJ, Princeton University Press.

Montias, J.M. (2002) Art at Auction in 17th Century Amsterdam, Amsterdam, Amsterdam University Press.

Nash, S. (2007) 'No Equal in Any Land': André Beauneveu – Artist to the Courts of France and Flanders, London, Paul Holberton Publishing.

Nesbit, M. (1992) Atget's Seven Albums, New Haven, CT and London, Yale University Press.

Nesbit, M. (2000) Their Common Sense, London, Black Dog.

North, M. (1997) Art and Commerce in the Dutch Golden Age, New Haven, CT and London, Yale University Press.

North, M. and Ormrod, D. (1998) Art Markets in Europe, 1400–1800, Aldershot, Ashgate.

Nuttall, G. (2012) Lucchese Patronage and Purveying during the Regime of Paolo Guinigi, 1400–1430: Dino Rapondi, Lorenzo Trenta and Paolo Guinigi, unpublished PhD Thesis, Courtauld Institute of Art, University of London.

O'Brian, J. (ed.) (1986–95) Clement Greenberg: The Collected Essays and Criticism, 4 vols, Chicago, IL, Chicago University Press.

Paviot, J. (1990) 'La vie de Jan van Eyck selon les documents écrits', Revue des archéologues et historiens d'art de Louvain, vol. 23, pp. 83–93.

Pears, I. (1988) The Discovery of Painting: The Growth of Interest in the Arts in England 1680–1768, New Haven, CT and London, Yale University Press.

Plon, E. (1887) Les Maîtres italiens au service de la maison d'Autriche: Leone Leoni sculpteur de Charles-Quint et Pompeo Leoni, sculpteur de Philippe II, , Paris, Librairie Plon.

Pollock, G. (1988) Vision and Difference: Femininity, Feminism and the Histories of Art, London and New York, Routledge.

Pomian, K. (1990) Collectors and Curiosities: Paris and Venice, 1500–1800, Cambridge, Polity Press.

Posner, D. (1993) 'Concerning the "mechanical" parts of painting and the artistic culture of seventeenth-century France', Art Bulletin, vol. 75, no. 4, pp. 583–98.

Porter, D. (2010) The Chinese Taste in Eighteenth-Century England, Cambridge, Cambridge University Press.

Potts, A. (2000) The Sculptural Imagination: Figurative, Modernist, Minimalist, New Haven, CT and London, Yale University Press.

Prendergast, C. (1992) Paris and the Nineteenth Century, Oxford, Blackwell.

Prior, N. (2002) Museums and Modernity : Art Galleries and the Making of Modern Culture, Oxford, Berg.

Richardson C.M., Woods, K.W. and Franklin, M.W. (eds) (2007) Renaissance Art Reconsidered: An Anthology of Primary Sources, Oxford, Blackwell.

Rosenberg, H. (1970 [1940]) 'The fall of Paris' in The Tradition of the New, London, Paladin, pp. 185–94.

Roy, A. and Gordon, D. (2001) 'The Battle of San Romano', National Gallery Technical Bulletin, vol. 22, pp. 4–17.

Sandler, I. (1970) The Triumph of American Painting, Westport, CT, Praeger.

Schapiro, M. (1977) 'On the aesthetic attitude in Romanesque art' in Romanesque Art: Selected Papers, London, Chatto & Windus, pp. 1–27.

Schapiro, M. (1978 [1937]) 'Nature of abstract art' in Modern Art: 19th and 20th Centuries. Selected Papers, New York, George Braziller, pp. 185–211.

Scott, K. (1995) The Rococo Interior: Decoration and Social Spaces in Early Eighteenth-Century Paris, New Haven, CT and London, Yale University Press.

Sheehan, J.J. (2000) Museums in the German Art World from the End of the Old Regime to the Rise of Modernism, Oxford, Oxford University Press.

Sheriff, M. (1990) Fragonard: Art and Eroticism, Chicago, IL, University of Chicago Press.

Shiner, L. (2001) The Invention of Art: A Cultural History, Chicago, IL, University of Chicago Press.

Simmel, G. (1997 [1903]) 'The metropolis and mental life' in Frisby, D.P. and Featherstone, M. (eds) Simmel on Culture: Selected Writings, New York, Sage, pp. 174–85. Extract reprinted in Lymberopoulou, A., Bracewell-Homer, P. and Robinson, J. (eds) Art and Visual Culture: A Reader, London, Tate Publishing in association with The Open University, pp. 267–9.

Snodin, M. (ed.) (1984) Rococo: Art and Design in Hogarth's England, London, V&A (exhibition catalogue).

Snodin, M. and Llewellyn, N. (eds) (2009) Baroque, 1620–1800: Style in the Age of Magnificence, London, V&A (exhibition catalogue).

Stechow, W. (1989 [1966]) Northern Renaissance Art 1400–1600: Sources and Documents, Evanston, IL, Northwestern University Press.

Suger, Abbot (1979) On the Abbey Church of Saint-Denis and its Art Treasures (eds E. Panofsky and G. Panofsky-Soergel), Princeton, NJ, Princeton University Press.

Tomlinson, J.A. (1994) Francisco Goya y Lucientes, 1746–1828, London, Phaidon.

Trotsky, L. (1962 [1928/1906]) The Permanent Revolution; Results and Prospects, London, New Park.

Vasari, G. (1996) [1568] Lives of the Painters, Sculptors and Architects, 2 vols (trans. G. du C. de Vere; ed. D. Ekserdijian), London, Everyman.

Warnke, M. (1993) The Court Artist: On the Ancestry of the Modern Artist (trans. D. McLintock), Cambridge, Cambridge University Press (first published in German in 1985).

Wolff, J. (1985) 'The invisible flaneuse: women and the literature of modernity', Theory, Culture and Society, vol. 2, no. 3, pp. 37–46.

Wölfflin, H. (1950) Principles of Art History: The Problem of the Development of Style in Later Art, New York, Dover.

Wolters, W. (1967) 'Ein Hauptwerk der neiderländischen Skulptur in Venedig', Mitteillung des Kunsthistorischen Institutes in Florenz, vol. 13, nos 1–2, pp. 185–9.

Wolters, W. (1976) La scultura Veneziana gotica 1300–1460, 2 vols, Venice, Alfieri.

Reading: Defining Art from the Academy to Avant-Garde

Academy to Avant-Garde

We now consider the key developments in the definition of art between c.1600 and c.1850.

From Function to Autonomy

The most important idea for this purpose is the concept of art itself, which came to be defined in the way that we still broadly understand it today during the course of the centuries explored here.

This concept rests on a distinction between art, on the one hand, and craft, on the other. It assumes that a work of art is to be appreciated and valued for its own sake, whereas other types of artifacts serve a functional purpose. A significant step in this direction was made by a group of painters and sculptors who in 1563 set up an Accademia del Disegno (Academy of Design) in Florence in order to distinguish themselves from craftsmen organized in guilds. Their central claim was that the arts they practiced were 'liberal' or intellectual rather than 'mechanical' or practical. After 1600, academies of art were founded in cities throughout Europe, including Paris (1648) and London (1768). Most offered training in architecture as well as in painting and sculpture. A decisive shift took place in the mid eighteenth century, when the three 'arts of design' began to be classified along with poetry and music In a new category of 'fine arts' (a translation of the French term, 'beaux-arts'). Other arts, such as landscape gardening, were sometimes included in this category. Architecture was occasionally excluded on the grounds that it was useful as well as beautiful, but the fine arts were usually defined in terms broad enough to encompass it. One writer, for example, described them as 'the offspring of genius; they have nature for model, taste for master, pleasure for aim' (Jacques Lacombe, Dictionnaire Portatif des Beaux-Arts, 1753 (1st edn 1752), p. 40, as translated in Shiner, 2001, p. 88).

From the Sacred to the Courtly

To chart what these conceptual shifts meant in practice, we can borrow the categories elaborated by the cultural theorist Peter Bürger (1984, pp. 47–8), who outlines a long-term shift away from the functions that art traditionally served. Such functions continued to play an important role after 1600, especially in the seventeenth century, when academies were rare outside Italy and many artists still belonged to guilds. As in the medieval period, the primary function was religious (or, in Bürger's terminology, 'sacral'). The so-called Counter Reformation gave a great boost to Roman Catholic patronage of the arts, as the church sought to renew itself in the aftermath of the Protestant Reformation. It was in this context that the word 'propaganda' originated; it can be traced back to 1622 when Pope Gregory XV (reigned 1621–23) founded the Congregazio de Propaganda Fide (Congregation for the Propagation of Faith) in Rome. The commitment to spreading the faith that this organization embodied helped to shape art not just in Europe but in every part of the world reached by the Catholic Missions, notably Asia and the Americas, throughout the period explored here. The churches that rejected the authority of Rome also played a role in supporting 'sacral art', primarily architecture since their use of other art forms was limited by Protestant strictures against 'Popish' idolatry (see for example Levy, 2004; Bailey, 1999; Haynes, 2006). Even in Catholic countries, however, the religious uses of art slowly declined relative to secular ones. The seventeenth century is the last in western art history in which a major canonical figure like the Italian painter Michelangelo Merisi da Caravaggio (1571–1610) might still be a primarily religious artist.

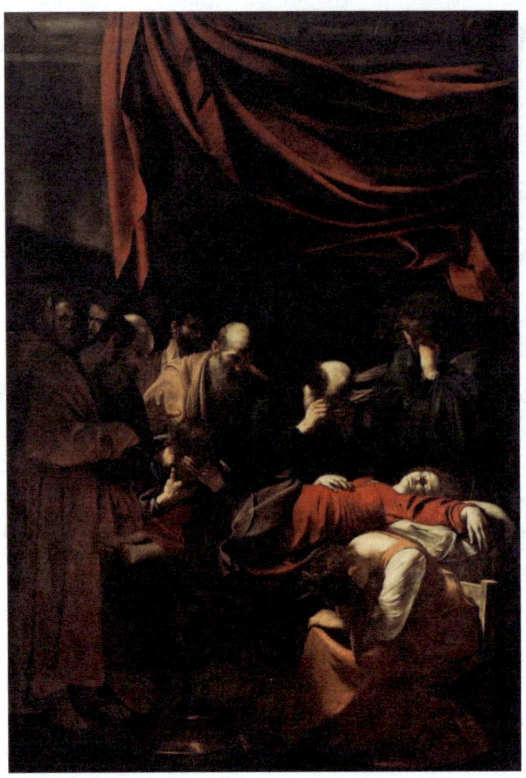

Michelangelo Merisi da Caravaggio, The Death of the Virgin, 1601–03, oil on canvas, 369 × 245 cm. Musée du Louvre, Paris. Photo: Web Gallery of Art, CC BY-SA. Work is in the public domain

Bürger's Functions of Art: the Courtly

By 1600, it was 'courtly art' (Bürger's second category) that increasingly prevailed in much of Europe. 'Courtly art' can be defined as consisting primarily of art actually produced at a royal or princely court, but also extending beyond it to include works of art that more generally promote the leisured lifestyle of an aristocratic elite. As in the Renaissance, artists served the needs of rulers by surrounding them with an aura of splendor and glory. In this context, art was integrated into the courtly or aristocratic way of life, as part of a culture of spectacle, which functioned to distinguish the nobles who frequented the court from other social classes and to legitimate the ruler's power in the eyes of the world (see for example, Elias, 1983; Adamson, 1999; Blanning, 2002). The consolidation of power in the hands of a fairly small number of European monarchs meant that their need for ideological justification was all the greater and so too were the resources they had at their disposal for the purpose. Exemplary in this respect is the French king Louis XIV (ruled 1643–1715), who harnessed the arts to the service of his own autocratic rule in the most conspicuous manner imaginable. From 1661 onwards, he employed the architects Louis Le Vau (1612/13–1670) and Jules Hardouin-Mansart (1648–1708), the painter Charles Le Brun (1619–90) and the landscape gardener André Le Nôtre (1613–1700), among many others, to create the vast and lavish palace of Versailles, not far from Paris. Every aspect of its design glorified the king, not least by celebrating the military exploits that made France the dominant power in Europe during his reign.

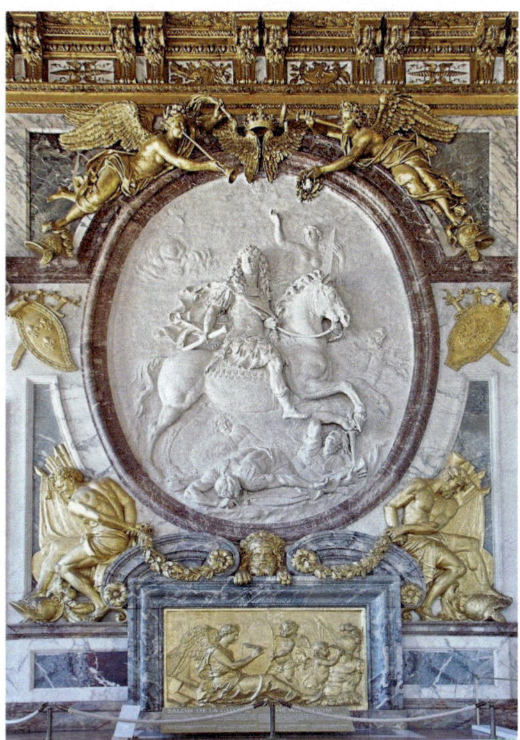

The Salon de la Guerre (War room), Château de Versailles, designed by Jules Hardouin-Mansart, showing plaster relief by Antoine Coysevox of Louis XIV trampling over his enemies, 1678–86. Photo: Jebulon. CCO

Bürger's Functions of Art: Bourgeois Art

By 1800, however, the predominant category was what Bürger calls 'bourgeois art'. His use of this term reflects his reliance on a broadly Marxist conceptual framework, which views artistic developments as being driven ultimately by social and economic change (Bürger, 1984, p. 47; Hemingway and Vaughan, 1998). Such art is bourgeois in so far as it owed its existence to the growing importance of trade and industry in Europe since the late medieval period, which gave rise to an increasingly large and influential wealthy middle class. Exemplary in this respect is seventeenth-century Dutch painting, the distinctive features and sheer profusion of which were both made possible by a large population of relatively affluent city-dwellers. In other countries, the commercialization of society and the urban development that went with it tended to take place more slowly. Britain, however, rapidly caught up with the Netherlands; by 1680, London was being transformed into a modern city characterized by novel uses of space as well as by new building types. Here too, artists produced images that were affordable and appealing to a middle-class audience; notable in this respect was William Hogarth (1697–1764), who began his career working in the comparatively cheap medium of engraving. Even his famous set of paintings Marriage A-la-Mode, which satirizes the manners and morals of fashionable society, was primarily intended as a model for prints to be made after them. Hogarth's work, like that of many other artists of the period, embodies a sense of didactic purpose, in accordance with the prevailing view that art should aim both to 'instruct and delight'.

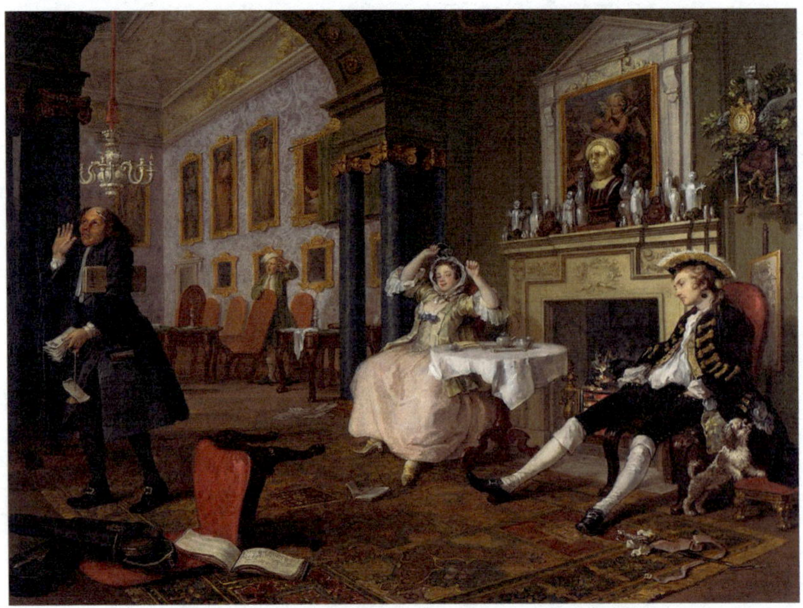

William Hogarth, Marriage A-la-Mode: 2, The Tête à Tête, circa 1743. Work is in the public domain.

What fundamentally distinguishes 'bourgeois art' from previous categories, however, is its lack of any actual function. Its defining feature, according to Bürger, is its autonomy, which he defines as 'art's independence from society' (Bürger, 1984, p. 35). As we have seen, a conception of 'fine art' as a category apart from everyday needs was formalized in the mid eighteenth century. What this meant in practice is best demonstrated by the case of easel painting, which had become the dominant pictorial form by 1600. Unlike an altarpiece or a fresco, this kind of picture has no fixed place; instead, its frame serves to separate it from its surroundings, allowing it to be hung in almost any setting. Its value lies not in any use as such, but in the ease with which it can be bought and sold (or what Marxists call its 'exchange value'). In taking the form of a commodity, easel-painting accords with the commercial priorities of bourgeois society, even though what appears within the frame may be far removed from these priorities. Art's previous functions did not simply vanish, however, not least because the nobility and its values retained considerable power and prestige.

Ultimately more important than such residual courtly functions, however, is the distinctly paradoxical way that art in bourgeois society at once preserves and transforms art's sacral functions. Autonomous art does not promote Christian beliefs and practices, as religious art traditionally did, but rather is treated by art lovers as itself the source of a special kind of experience, a rarefied or even spiritual pleasure. This type of pleasure is now called 'aesthetic', a word that was coined in 1735, by Alexander Baumgarten, though it was only towards the end of the eighteenth century that writers began to talk about their experience of art in such high-flown quasi-religious terms (for examples, see Shiner, 2001, pp. 135–6). What this boils down to is that art increasingly functioned during this period as a cult in its own right, sometimes referred to as the artwork's aura, one in which the artist of genius replaces God the creator as the source of meaning and value. This exalted conception of art consolidated the separation between the artist and the craftsman, which had motivated the foundation of the Florentine Academy some two centuries earlier.

From Patronage to the Public Sphere

Among the various approaches that have been applied to the study of art produced between c.1600 and c.1850, the dominant one in recent decades has been a concern to locate art in its historical context. Art historians who employ this kind of approach take account both of the institutional and commercial conditions in which works of art were produced and consumed and of the broader cultural, social, economic and political conditions of the period. Such an approach (known as the social history of art) represents a reaction against an older model of art history, which relied ultimately on a vague notion of the zeitgeist (or 'spirit of the age') as a means of explaining artistic developments. This older model of art history was closely associated with a focus on style, each style being assumed to reflect the spirit of a different age (Wölfflin, 1950, pp. 9–11, 233–4). It is now recognized that artistic practice within a period is invariably more diverse and complex than a style-based art history admits. Furthermore, rather than simply 'reflecting' or 'expressing' wider social forces, works of art are primarily shaped by the structures and values of the art world, but also connected to society at large in myriad subtle (and sometimes not so subtle) ways (Clark, 1982, pp. 9–20).

Patronage

In exploring artistic developments in the centuries with which we are concerned here, the first structure or institution to consider is that of patronage. As in the Renaissance, many artists worked for patrons, who commissioned them to execute works of art in accordance with their requirements. Patronage played an important role throughout the period, most obviously in the case of large-scale projects for a specific location that could not be undertaken without a commission. Exemplary in this respect is the work that the sculptor (and architect) Gian Lorenzo Bernini (1598–1680) carried out at St Peter's Basilica in Rome for a succession of popes from the 1620s onwards. Landscape gardening is another case in point. Artists also executed on commission for a patron works that, though not actually immoveable, involved too much risk to be executed 'on spec', in the hope that someone would come along and buy them after they were completed, either because they were large and expensive or because they did not make for easy viewing. Both considerations applied in the case of David's The Oath of the Horatii, a huge picture of a tragic subject painted in an uncompromising style, which was commissioned by the French state. An artist greatly in demand such as the sculptor Antonio Canova (1757–1822) would also tend to work on commission; in his case, the grandest patrons from across Europe sometimes waited for years to receive a statue by the master, even though he maintained (as both Bernini and Rubens also did) a large workshop to assist him in his labors.

Finally, portraiture was a genre that, with rare exceptions, such as the portrait of Omai by Sir Joshua Reynolds (1723–92), required a patron to commission an artist to take a likeness.

From Patronage to the Open Market

Nevertheless, the period after 1600 saw a shift away from patronage towards the open market. This shift accompanied the gradual decline of 'sacral' and 'courtly' art, both of which were normally executed on commission. Consider the case of Caravaggio's Death of the Virgin, an altarpiece commissioned for the church of Santa Maria della Scala in Rome in 1601. In the event, the resolutely human terms in which the painter depicted the subject and the unidealised treatment of the figures scandalized the monks responsible for the church. The painting was therefore put up for sale, exciting intense interest among artists, dealers and collectors; it was snapped up (at a high price) by the Duke of Mantua, on the advice of Rubens, who was then employed as the duke's court painter (Langdon, 1998, pp. 246–51, 317–18). Thus a functional religious artifact was transformed into a secular artwork, acclaimed as a masterpiece by a famous artist and sold to a princely collector, for whom the possession of such a work was a matter of personal prestige. The comparable transformation of courtly art in response to the market can be illustrated by reference to another picture immediately displaced from the location for which it was painted. In 1721, the Flemish-born artist Antoine Watteau (1684–1721) painted a large canvas as a shop sign for his friend, the Parisian art dealer Edme Gersaint. It shows the kind of elegant figures that the artist typically painted, but here, rather than engaging in aristocratic leisure and dalliance in a park-like setting, they are scrutinizing items for sale in an art dealer's shop; a portrait of Louis XIV is being packed away into a case, as if to mark the passing of the era of grand courtly art. Rapidly sold to a wealthy (though not aristocratic) collector, Gersaint's Shop Sign exemplifies the way that Watteau repackaged courtly ideals for the market to reach a wider audience. The painting also shows how art collecting became a refined pastime for the social elite, in which art dealers played a crucial role (McClellan, 1996).

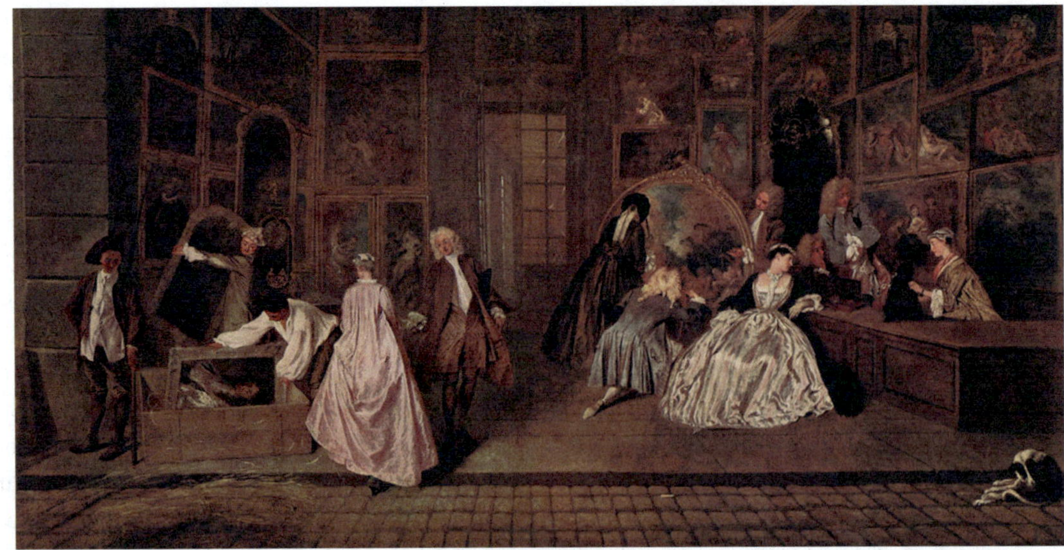

Antoine Watteau, Gersaint's Shop Sign, 1720–21, oil on canvas, 151 × 306 cm. Schloss Charlottenburg, Berlin. Work is in the public domain.

As these two examples demonstrate, more market-oriented structures and practices emerged in countries such as Italy and France from the end of the Renaissance onwards (see Haskell, 1980; Pomian, 1990; Posner, 1993; North and Ormrod, 1998). However, the tendency towards commercialization is even more striking elsewhere: for example, in the growth of large-scale speculative building in late seventeenth-century London. As already noted, the emergence of 'bourgeois art' (as distinct from architecture) is best exemplified by the Netherlands, where most artists produced small easel paintings for sale. This model of artistic practice went hand in hand with the rise of art dealers and other features of the modern art world, such as public auctions and sale catalogues (see Montias, 1982; North, 1997; Montias, 2002). In important respects, the Dutch case remains idiosyncratic, but nevertheless the genres of painting that dominated in this context – that is, portraiture, landscape, scenes of everyday life and still life – soon became the most popular and successful elsewhere in Europe too. It was not just subject matter that counted, however; increasing emphasis was also placed on the distinctive brushwork of the individual artist and on the skills of connoisseurship that both dealers and collectors needed in order to recognize and appreciate the 'hand' of each 'master' and, of course, to distinguish genuine works from misattributed ones and outright forgeries. Exemplary in this respect is the work of Rembrandt; it was thanks above all to his exceptionally broad and hence highly distinctive handling of paint that he came to be generally regarded as the greatest of all post-Renaissance artists by the mid nineteenth century. As a result of these developments, painting increasingly tended to overshadow other art forms, especially tapestry, which lost its previous high status with the decline of courtly art.

Habermas and the Public Sphere

The emergence of a recognizably modern art world between 1600 and 1850 formed part of the development of the 'public sphere', as it has been defined by the philosopher Jürgen Habermas. Habermas argues that the late seventeenth century onwards saw a shift away from 'representational culture', which embodied and displayed the power of the ruler and nobility, as courtly art traditionally did. It was replaced by a new urban culture, the 'bourgeois public sphere', which was brought into existence by private individuals, that is, middle-class people like merchants and lawyers, who came together to exchange news and ideas, giving rise to new cultural institutions, such as newspapers, clubs, lending libraries and public theatres (Habermas, 1989 [1962]; Blanning, 2002). A pioneering role in this respect was played by London as a consequence of the limited power of the monarch, which meant that the court dominated culture much less than it did in France at the same time. Public interest in art grew rapidly during the eighteenth century, aided by an expanding print culture, which allowed the circulation of high-art images to an ever larger audience (see Pears, 1988; Clayton, 1997). In both London and Paris, large audiences also attended the exhibitions that began to be held during the middle decades of the century. The first public museums were established around the same time. Most were royal and princely collections opened up to the public, whether as a benevolent gesture on the ruler's part or, in the case of the Louvre, by the French Revolutionary government in 1793 (McClellan, 1994; Sheehan, 2000; Prior, 2002). However, it was a charitable bequest from an art dealer that led to the creation of the first public art museum in Britain; housed in a building designed for the purpose by the architect Sir John Soane (1753–1837), Dulwich College Picture Gallery opened to the public in 1817.

The Art Museum and the Painting of Current Events

With the establishment of the art museum, the autonomy of art gained its defining institution. In a museum, a work of art could be viewed purely for its own sake, without reference to its traditional functions. Nevertheless, as indicated above, art's autonomy was far from complete. From around 1800 onwards, for example, the public sphere also opened up the possibility that artists might try to bridge the gap dividing art from society by independently producing works that engaged with current events, as the French painter Théodore Géricault (1791–1824) did in his vast picture, The Raft of the Medusa. This and comparable works by other French artists, notably Liberty Leading the People by Eugène Delacroix (1798–1863), which was painted just after the July Revolution of 1830, are often seen as having inaugurated a new tradition of politically committed modern or 'avant-garde' art, which came to the fore towards the end of the nineteenth century. However, it was during this period that the French military term 'avant garde' (meaning a section of an army that goes ahead of the rest) came to be applied to works of art. It was first used in this sense in a text published in 1825 under the name of the Utopian Socialist Henri de Saint-Simon, who argued that artists could help to transform society by spreading 'new ideas among men' (Harrison et al., 1998, p. 40). Although he does not seem to have had any specific type of art in mind, his emphasis on its role as a means of communication makes it plausible to apply the term to works such as The Raft of the Medusa and Liberty Leading the People, which convey a political message on a large scale and to striking effect.

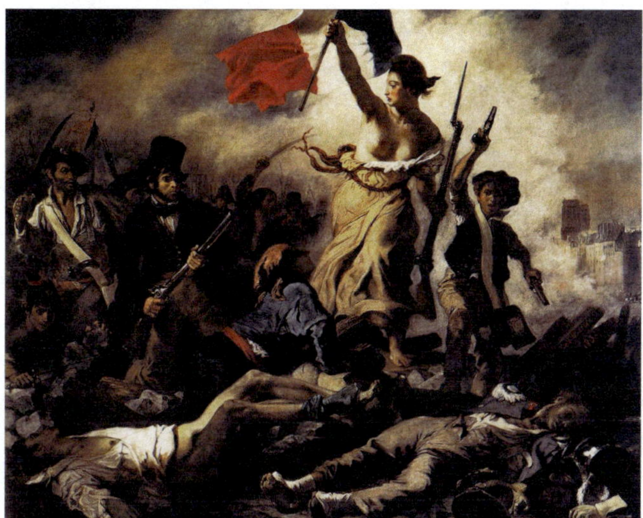

Eugène Delacroix, Liberty Leading the People, 1830, oil on canvas, 260 × 325 cm. Musée du Louvre, Paris. Work is in the public domain.

For present purposes, however, what is important about these two paintings is the way that they depended on the institutions of the public sphere. Rather than being commissioned by a patron, each was intended first and foremost for display at the official art exhibition in Paris known as the Salon. Both, moreover, were bought by the state for the Luxembourg museum, which was founded in 1818 to house modern French art (though, in Géricault's case, not until several years later). Indeed Delacroix may have painted his picture in the hope or even the expectation that this would happen, since two of the artist's works had already entered the museum. It should also be noted that such ambitious and challenging works were very much the exception, even in France and much more so in other countries where the state did not support living artists in the same way. Most of them earned a living by catering to the demands of the market, typically by specializing in a particular genre, such as portraiture. In this respect, the first half of the nineteenth century is continuous with the previous two centuries, during which high-status works by celebrated artists also constituted only a small part of the broad field of visual culture. Rather than tracing a single narrative of art's development from the establishment of the academies to the beginnings of the avant-garde, it is important to be aware of its diversity and complexity throughout western Europe during this period.

Works Cited

Adamson, J.S.A. (1999) The Princely Courts of Europe: Ritual, Politics and Culture under the Ancien Régime 1500–1750, London, Weidenfeld & Nicolson.

Alberti, L.B. (1966 [1435]) On Painting (trans. J.R. Spencer), New Haven, CT and London, Yale University Press.

Arciszweska, B. and McKellar, E. (2004) Articulating British Classicism: New Approaches to Eighteenth-Century Architecture, Aldershot and Burlington, VT, Ashgate.

Bailey, C. (1987) 'Conventions of the eighteenth-century cabinet de tableaux: Blondel d'Azincourt's La première idée de la curiosité', Art Bulletin, vol. 69, no. 3, pp. 431–47.

Bailey, C. (2002) Patriotic Taste: Collecting Modern Art in Pre-Revolutionary Paris, New Haven, CT and London, Yale University Press.

Bailey, G.A. (1999) Art on the Jesuit Missions in Asia and Latin America, 1542–1773, Toronto and London, University of Toronto Press.

Barr, A.H. (1974 [1936]) Cubism and Abstract Art, New York, Museum of Modern Art (exhibition catalogue).

Baudelaire, C. (1981 [1859]) 'On photography' in Newhall, B. (ed.) Photography: Essays and Images, New York, Secker & Warburg, pp. 112–13.

Baxandall, M. (1971) Giotto and the Orators: Humanist Observers of Painting in Italy and the Discovery of Pictorial Composition 1350–1450, Oxford, Clarendon Press.

Baxandall, M. (1972) Painting and Experience in Fifteenth-Century Italy, Oxford, Clarendon Press.

Baxandall, M. (1980) The Limewood Sculptors of Renaissance Germany, New Haven, CT, Yale University Press.

Belting, H. (1994) Likeness and Presence: A History of the Image before the Era of Art, Chicago, IL and London, University of Chicago Press.

Benjamin, W. (1983) Charles Baudelaire: A Lyric Poet in the Era of High Capitalism, London, Verso.

Bergdoll, B. (2000) European Architecture 1750–1890, Oxford, Oxford University Press.

Bermingham, A. (2000) Learning to Draw: Studies in the Cultural History of a Polite and Useful Art, New Haven, CT and London, Yale University Press.

Blanning, T.C.W. (2002) The Culture of Power and the Power of Culture: Old Regime Europe 1660–1789, Oxford, Oxford University Press.

Bürger, P. (1984) Theory of the Avant-Garde, Manchester, Manchester University Press; Minneapolis, MN, University of Minnesota Press.

Clark, T.J. (1982) Image of the People. Gustave Courbet and the 1848 Revolution, London, Thames & Hudson.

Clark, T.J. (1984) The Painting of Modern Life: Paris in the Art of Manet and his Followers, London, Thames & Hudson.

Clayton, T. (1997) The English Print, 1688–1802, London and New Haven, CT, Yale University Press.

Connell, S.M. (1976) The Employment of Sculptors and Stonemasons in Venice in the Fifteenth Century (doctoral thesis), Warburg Institute, University of London.

Craske, M. (1997) Art in Europe 1700–1830: A History of the Visual Arts in an Era of Unprecedented Urban Economic Growth, Oxford, Oxford University Press.

Crown, P. (1990) 'British Rococo as social and political style', Eighteenth-Century Studies, vol. 23, no. 3, pp. 269–82.

Duchamp, M. (1975) The Essential Writings of Marcel Duchamp (ed. M. Sanouillet and E. Peterson), London, Thames & Hudson.

Edwards, S. (ed.) (1999) Art and its Histories: A Reader, New Haven, CT and London, Yale University Press.

Elias, N. (1983) The Court Society (trans. E. Jephcott), Oxford, Blackwell.

Gilbert, C. (1985) 'A statement of the aesthetic attitude around 1230', Hebrew University Studies in Literature and the Arts, vol. 13, no. 2, pp. 125–52.

Gordon, D. (2003) The Fifteenth-Century Italian Paintings, National Gallery Catalogues, London, Yale University Press.

Greenberg, C. (1961) Art and Culture: Critical Essays, Boston, MA, Beacon Press.

Greenberg, C. (1986 [1939]) 'Avant-garde and kitsch' in O'Brian, J. (ed.) Clement Greenberg: The Collected Essays and Criticism, vol. 1: Perceptions and Judgements, 1939–1944, Chicago, IL, Chicago University Press, pp. 5–22.

Greenberg, C. (1993 [1960]) 'Modernist painting' in O'Brian, J. (ed.) Clement Greenberg: The Collected Essays and Criticism, vol. 4: Modernism with a Vengeance, 1957–1969, Chicago, IL, Chicago University Press, pp. 85–100.

Habermas, J. (1989 [1962]) The Structural Transformation of the Public Sphere: An Inquiry into a Category of Bourgeois Society, Cambridge, MA, MIT Press.

Hardie, P. (1993) 'Ut Pictura Poesis? Horace and the visual arts' in Horace 2000: A Celebration for the Bi-millennium, London, Duckworth, pp. 120–39.

Harris, A.S. (2008) Seventeenth-Century Art and Architecture (2nd edn), London, Laurence King.

Harrison, C., Wood, P. and Gaiger, J. (eds) (1998) Art in Theory 1815–1900: An Anthology of Changing Ideas, Oxford, Blackwell.

Harvey, D. (2003) Paris: Capital of Modernity, London and New York, Routledge.

Haskell, F. (1980) Patrons and Painters: A Study in the Relations between Italian Art and Society in the Age of the Baroque, New Haven and London, Yale University Press.

Haskell, F. and Penny, N. (1981) Taste and the Antique: The Lure of Classical Sculpture 1500–1900, New Haven, CT and London, Yale University Press.

Hauser, A. (1962 [1951]) The Social History of Art. Vol. 2: Renaissance, Mannerism, Baroque; Vol. 3. Rococo, Classicism and Romanticism (2nd edn), London, Routledge.

Haynes, C. (2006) Pictures and Popery: Art and Religion in England, 1660–1760, Aldershot, Ashgate.

Hemingway, A. and Vaughan, W. (eds) (1998) Art in Bourgeois Society 1790–1850, Cambridge, Cambridge University Press.

Hills, H. (ed.) (2011) Rethinking the Baroque, Farnham, Ashgate.

Honour, H. (1968) Neo-classicism, Harmondsworth, Penguin.

Honour, H. (1979) Romanticism, Harmondsworth, Penguin.

Hyde, M. (2006) Making up the Rococo: François Boucher and his Critics, Los Angeles, CA and London, Getty Research Institute.

Irwin, D. (1997) Neoclassicism, London, Phaidon.

Langdon, H. (1998) Caravaggio: A Life, London, Chatto & Windus.

Lee, R. (1967) Ut Pictura Poesis: The Humanistic Theory of Painting, New York, W.W. Norton.

Levy, E. (2004) Propaganda and the Jesuit Baroque, Berkeley, CA and London, University of California Press.

Lichtenstein, J. (2008) The Blind Spot: An Essay on the Relations between Painting and Sculpture in the Modern Age, Los Angeles, CA, Getty Research Institute.

Lymberopoulou, A., Bracewell-Homer, P. and Robinson, J. (eds) (2012) Art & Visual Culture: A Reader, London, Tate Publishing in association with The Open University.

McClellan, A. (1994) Inventing the Louvre: Art, Politics, and the Origins of the Modern Museum in Eighteenth-Century Paris, Cambridge, Cambridge University Press.

McClellan, A. (1996) 'Watteau's dealer: Gersaint and the marketing of art in eighteenth-century Paris', Art Bulletin, vol. 78, no. 3, pp. 439–53.

Montias, J.M. (1982) Artists and Artisans in Delft: A Socio-economic Study of the Seventeenth Century, Princeton, NJ, Princeton University Press.

Montias, J.M. (2002) Art at Auction in 17th Century Amsterdam, Amsterdam, Amsterdam University Press.

Nash, S. (2007) 'No Equal in Any Land': André Beauneveu – Artist to the Courts of France and Flanders, London, Paul Holberton Publishing.

Nesbit, M. (1992) Atget's Seven Albums, New Haven, CT and London, Yale University Press.

Nesbit, M. (2000) Their Common Sense, London, Black Dog.

North, M. (1997) Art and Commerce in the Dutch Golden Age, New Haven, CT and London, Yale University Press.

North, M. and Ormrod, D. (1998) Art Markets in Europe, 1400–1800, Aldershot, Ashgate.

Nuttall, G. (2012) Lucchese Patronage and Purveying during the Regime of Paolo Guinigi, 1400–1430: Dino Rapondi, Lorenzo Trenta and Paolo Guinigi, unpublished PhD Thesis, Courtauld Institute of Art, University of London.

O'Brian, J. (ed.) (1986–95) Clement Greenberg: The Collected Essays and Criticism, 4 vols, Chicago, IL, Chicago University Press.

Paviot, J. (1990) 'La vie de Jan van Eyck selon les documents écrits', Revue des archéologues et historiens d'art de Louvain, vol. 23, pp. 83–93.

Pears, I. (1988) The Discovery of Painting: The Growth of Interest in the Arts in England 1680–1768, New Haven, CT and London, Yale University Press.

Plon, E. (1887) Les Maîtres italiens au service de la maison d'Autriche: Leone Leoni sculpteur de Charles-Quint et Pompeo Leoni, sculpteur de Philippe II, , Paris, Librairie Plon.

Pollock, G. (1988) Vision and Difference: Femininity, Feminism and the Histories of Art, London and New York, Routledge.

Pomian, K. (1990) Collectors and Curiosities: Paris and Venice, 1500–1800, Cambridge, Polity Press.

Posner, D. (1993) 'Concerning the "mechanical" parts of painting and the artistic culture of seventeenth-century France', Art Bulletin, vol. 75, no. 4, pp. 583–98.

Porter, D. (2010) The Chinese Taste in Eighteenth-Century England, Cambridge, Cambridge University Press.

Potts, A. (2000) The Sculptural Imagination: Figurative, Modernist, Minimalist, New Haven, CT and London, Yale University Press.

Prendergast, C. (1992) Paris and the Nineteenth Century, Oxford, Blackwell.

Prior, N. (2002) Museums and Modernity : Art Galleries and the Making of Modern Culture, Oxford, Berg.

Richardson C.M., Woods, K.W. and Franklin, M.W. (eds) (2007) Renaissance Art Reconsidered: An Anthology of Primary Sources, Oxford, Blackwell.

Rosenberg, H. (1970 [1940]) 'The fall of Paris' in The Tradition of the New, London, Paladin, pp. 185–94.

Roy, A. and Gordon, D. (2001) 'The Battle of San Romano', National Gallery Technical Bulletin, vol. 22, pp. 4–17.

Sandler, I. (1970) The Triumph of American Painting, Westport, CT, Praeger.

Schapiro, M. (1977) 'On the aesthetic attitude in Romanesque art' in Romanesque Art: Selected Papers, London, Chatto & Windus, pp. 1–27.

Schapiro, M. (1978 [1937]) 'Nature of abstract art' in Modern Art: 19th and 20th Centuries. Selected Papers, New York, George Braziller, pp. 185–211.

Scott, K. (1995) The Rococo Interior: Decoration and Social Spaces in Early Eighteenth-Century Paris, New Haven, CT and London, Yale University Press.

Sheehan, J.J. (2000) Museums in the German Art World from the End of the Old Regime to the Rise of Modernism, Oxford, Oxford University Press.

Sheriff, M. (1990) Fragonard: Art and Eroticism, Chicago, IL, University of Chicago Press.

Shiner, L. (2001) The Invention of Art: A Cultural History, Chicago, IL, University of Chicago Press.

Simmel, G. (1997 [1903]) 'The metropolis and mental life' in Frisby, D.P. and Featherstone, M. (eds) Simmel on Culture: Selected Writings, New York, Sage, pp. 174–85. Extract reprinted in Lymberopoulou, A., Bracewell-Homer, P. and Robinson, J. (eds) Art and Visual Culture: A Reader, London, Tate Publishing in association with The Open University, pp. 267–9.

Snodin, M. (ed.) (1984) Rococo: Art and Design in Hogarth's England, London, V&A (exhibition catalogue).

Snodin, M. and Llewellyn, N. (eds) (2009) Baroque, 1620–1800: Style in the Age of Magnificence, London, V&A (exhibition catalogue).

Stechow, W. (1989 [1966]) Northern Renaissance Art 1400–1600: Sources and Documents, Evanston, IL, Northwestern University Press.

Suger, Abbot (1979) On the Abbey Church of Saint-Denis and its Art Treasures (eds E. Panofsky and G. Panofsky-Soergel), Princeton, NJ, Princeton University Press.

Tomlinson, J.A. (1994) Francisco Goya y Lucientes, 1746–1828, London, Phaidon.

Trotsky, L. (1962 [1928/1906]) The Permanent Revolution; Results and Prospects, London, New Park.

Vasari, G. (1996) [1568] Lives of the Painters, Sculptors and Architects, 2 vols (trans. G. du C. de Vere; ed. D. Ekserdijian), London, Everyman.

Warnke, M. (1993) The Court Artist: On the Ancestry of the Modern Artist (trans. D. McLintock), Cambridge, Cambridge University Press (first published in German in 1985).

Wolff, J. (1985) 'The invisible flaneuse: women and the literature of modernity', Theory, Culture and Society, vol. 2, no. 3, pp. 37–46.

Wölfflin, H. (1950) Principles of Art History: The Problem of the Development of Style in Later Art, New York, Dover.

Wolters, W. (1967) 'Ein Hauptwerk der niederländischen Skulptur in Venedig', Mitteilung des Kunsthistorischen Institutes in Florenz, vol. 13, nos 1–2, pp. 185–9.

Wolters, W. (1976) La scultura Veneziana gotica 1300–1460, 2 vols, Venice, Alfieri.

Reading: Defining Art from Modernity to Globalization

Modernity to Globalization

This section addresses art and architecture from around 1850 up to the present.

During this period, art changed beyond recognition. The various academies still held sway in Europe. It is true that the hierarchy of the genres was breaking down and the classical ideal was becoming less convincing.

What counted as art in much of the nineteenth century remained pretty stable. Whether in sculpture, painting, drawing or printmaking, artworks represented recognizable subjects in a credible human-centered space. To be sure, subjects became less high-flown, compositional effects often deliberately jarring and surface handling more explicit. There were plenty of academicians and commentators who believed these changes amounted to the end of civilization, but from today's perspective they seem like small shifts of emphasis.

In contrast, art in the first part of the twentieth century underwent a rapid gear change. Art historians agree that during this time artists began to radically revise picture making and sculpture. With the invention of photography and it being employed as the dominant conveyor of realism, painting undergoes a period of experimentation. Painters flattened out pictorial space, broke with conventional viewpoints and discarded local color. ('Local color' is the term used for the color things appear in the world. From the early twentieth century, painters began to experiment with non-local color.) Sculptors began to leave the surface of their works in a rough, seemingly unfinished state; they increasingly created partial figures and abandoned plinths or, alternatively, inflated the scale of their bases. Architects abandoned revivalist styles and rich ornamentation. To take one often cited example from painting, while the art of Paul Cézanne (1839–1906) is based on a recognizable motif, say a landscape, when looking at these paintings we get the distinct impression that the overall organization of the colors and structural elements matters as much or more than the scene depicted. To retain fidelity to his sense impressions, Cézanne is compelled to find a new order and coherence internal to the canvas. Frequently this turns into incoherence as he tries to manage the tension between putting marks on a flat surface and his external observation of space.

In fifteen years some artists would take this problem – the recognition that making art involved attention to its own formal conditions that are not reducible to representing external things – through Cubism to a fully abstract art. Conventionally, this story is told as a heroic progression of 'movements' and 'styles', each giving way to the next in the sequence: Post-Impressionism, Fauvism, Cubism, Futurism, Dada, Constructivism, Surrealism... Each changing of the guard is perceived as an advance and almost a necessary next step on the road to some preset goal. This rapid turnover of small groups and personal idioms can seem bewildering and, in fact, this is a minimal version of this story. Whether they sought new expressive resources, novel ways of conveying experience or innovative techniques for representing the modern world, modern artists turned their backs on the tried and tested forms of mimetic resemblance. But what counted as art changed too. Bits of the everyday world began to be incorporated into artworks – as collage or montage in two-dimensional art forms; in construction and assemblage in three-dimensional ones. The inclusion of found materials played a fundamental role in modern art. The use of modern materials and technologies – steel, concrete, photography – did something similar. Some artists abandoned easel painting or sculpture to make direct interventions in the world through the production of usable things, whether chairs or illustrated news magazines. Not all artists elected to work with these new techniques and materials, and many carried on in the traditional ways or attempted to adapt them to new circumstances.

Autonomy and Modernity

Broadly speaking, there are two different ways of thinking about modern art, or two different versions of the story. One way is to view art as something that can be practiced (and thought of) as an activity radically separate from everyday life or worldly concerns. From this point of view, art is said to be 'autonomous' from society – that is, it is believed to be self-sustaining and self-referring. One particularly influential version of this story suggests that modern art should be viewed as a process by which features extraneous to a particular branch of art would be progressively eliminated, and painters or sculptors would come to concentrate on problems specific to their domain. Another way of thinking about modern art is to view it as responding to the modern world, and to see modern artists immersing themselves in the conflicts and challenges of society. That is to say, some modern artists sought ways of conveying the changing experiences generated in Europe by the twin processes of commercialization (the commodification of everyday life) and urbanization. From this point of view, modern art is a way of reflecting on the transformations that created what we call, in a sort of shorthand, 'modernity'.

Greenberg and Autonomy

While it has its roots in the nineteenth century, the approach to modern art as an autonomous practice is particularly associated with the ideas of the English critics Roger Fry (1866–1934) and Clive Bell (1881–1964), the critic Clement Greenberg (1909–94) and the New York Museum of Modern Art's director Alfred H. Barr (1902–81). For a period this view largely became the common sense of modern art (O'Brian, 1986–95, 4 vols; Barr, 1974 [1936]). This version of modernism is itself complex. The argument presumes that art is self-contained and artists are seen to grapple with technical problems of painting and sculpture, and the point of reference is to artworks that have gone before. This approach can be described as 'formalist' (paying exclusive attention to formal matters), or, perhaps more productively drawing on a term employed by the critic Meyer Schapiro (1904–96), as 'internalist' (a somewhat less pejorative way of saying the same thing) (Schapiro, 1978 [1937]).

Rather than cloaking artifice, modern art, such as that made by Wassily Kandinsky (1866–1944) drew attention to the conventions, procedures and techniques supposedly 'inherent' in a given form of art. Modern art set about 'creating something valid solely on its own terms' (Ibid., p. 8). For painting, this meant turning away from illusion and story-telling to concentrate on the features that were fundamental to the practice – producing aesthetic effects by placing marks on a flat, bounded surface. For sculpture, it entailed arranging or assembling forms in space.

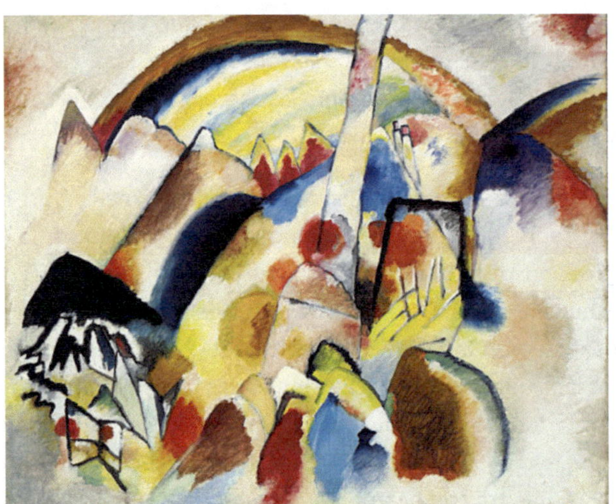

Wassily Kandinsky, Landscape with Red Spots, 1913. Work is in the public domain.

It important to understand that the account of autonomous art, however internalist it may seem, developed as a response to the social and political conditions of modern societies. In his 1939 essay 'Avant-garde and kitsch', Greenberg suggested that art was in danger from two linked challenges: the rise of the dictators (Stalin, Mussolini, Hitler and Franco) and the commercialized visual culture of modern times (the kitsch, or junk, of his title). Dictatorial regimes turned their backs on ambitious art and curried favor with the masses by promoting a debased form of realism that was easy to comprehend. Seemingly distinct from art made by dictatorial fiat, the visual culture of liberal capitalism pursued instant, canned entertainment that would appeal to the broadest number of paying customers. This pre-packaged emotional distraction was geared to easy, unchallenging consumption. Kitsch traded on sentimentality, common-sense values and flashy surface effects. The two sides of this pincer attack ghettoized the values associated with art. Advanced art, in this argument, like all human values, faced an imminent danger. Greenberg argued that, in response to the impoverished culture of both modern capitalist democracy and dictatorship, artists withdrew to create novel and challenging artworks that maintained the possibility for critical experience and attention. He claimed that this was the only way that art could be kept alive in modern society. In this essay, Greenberg put forward a left-wing sociological account of the origins of modernist autonomy; others came to similar conclusions from positions of cultural despair or haughty disdain for the masses.

The period from around 1850 onwards has been tumultuous: it has been regularly punctuated by revolutions, wars and civil wars, and has witnessed the rise of nation states, the growth and spread of capitalism, imperialism and colonialism, and decolonization. Sometimes artists tried to keep their distance from the historical whirlwind, at other moments they flung themselves into the eye of the storm. Even the most abstract developments and autonomous trends can be thought of as embedded in this historical process. Modern artists could be cast in opposition to repressive societies, or mass visual culture in the west, by focusing on themes of personal liberty and individual defiance. The New York School championed by Greenberg coincided with this political situation and with the high point of US mass cultural dominance – advertising, Hollywood cinema, popular music and the rest. In many ways, the work of this group of abstract painters presents the test case for assessing the claim that modern art offers a critical alternative to commercial visual culture. It could seem a plausible argument, but the increasing absorption of modern art into middle-class museum culture casts an increasing doubt over these claims. At the same time, the figurative art that was supposed to have been left in the hands of the dictators continued to be made in a wide variety of forms. If figurative art had been overlooked by critics during the high point of abstract art, it made a spectacular comeback with Pop Art.

The Emergence of Modern Art in Paris

Let's take a step back to the middle of the nineteenth century and consider the emergence of modern art in Paris. The new art that developed with Gustave Courbet (1819–77), Manet and the Impressionists entailed a self-conscious break with the art of the past. These modern artists took seriously the representation of their own time. In place of allegorical figures in togas or scenes from the Bible, modern artists concerned themselves with the things around them. When asked to include angels in a painting for a church, Courbet is said to have replied 'I have never seen angels. Show me an angel and I will paint one.' But these artists were not just empirical recording devices. The formal or technical means employed in modern art are jarring and unsettling, and this has to be a fundamental part of the story. A tension between the means and the topics depicted, between surface and subject, is central to what this art was. Nevertheless, we miss something crucial if we do not attend to the artists' choices of subjects. Principally, these artists sought the signs of change and novelty – multiple details and scenarios that made up contemporary life. This meant they paid a great deal of attention to the new visual culture associated with commercialized leisure.

Greenberg contrasted the mainstream of modern art, concerned with autonomous aesthetic experience and formal innovation, with what he called 'dead ends' – directions in art that he felt led nowhere. Even when restricted to the European tradition, this marginalized much of the most significant art made in interwar Europe – Dada, Constructivism and Surrealism (Greenberg, 1961). The groups of artists producing this art – usually referred to collectively as the 'avant-garde' or the 'historical avant-garde' – wanted to fuse art and life, and often based their practice on a socialist rejection of bourgeois culture (see, in particular, Bürger, 1984). From their position in western Europe, the Dadaists mounted an assault on the irrationalism and violence of militarism and the repressive character of capitalist culture; in collages, montages, assemblages and performances, they created visual juxtapositions aimed at shocking the middle-class audience and intended to reveal connections hidden behind everyday appearances. The material for this was drawn from mass-circulation magazines, newspapers and other printed ephemera. The Constructivists participated in the process of building a new society in the USSR, turning to the creation of utilitarian objects (or, at least, prototypes for them). The Surrealists combined ideas from psychoanalysis and Marxism in an attempt to unleash those forces repressed by mainstream society; the dream imagery is most familiar, but experiments with found objects and collage were also prominent. These avant-garde groups tried to produce more than refined aesthetic experiences for a restricted audience; they proffered their skills to help to change the world. In this work the cross-over to visual culture is evident;

communication media and design played an important role. Avant-garde artists began to design book covers, posters, fabrics, clothing, interiors, monuments and other useful things. They also began to merge with journalism by producing photographs and undertaking layout work. In avant-garde circles, architects, photographers and artists mixed and exchanged ideas. For those committed to autonomy of art, this kind of activity constitutes a denial of the shaping conditions of art and betrayal of art for propaganda, but the avant-garde were attempting something else – they sought a new social role for art. One way to explore this debate is by switching from painting and sculpture to architecture and design.

Responses to the Modern World

Marcel Duchamp (1887–1968), who is now seen as one of the most important artists of the twentieth century, occupies an important place in destabilization of the art object. Duchamp started out as a Cubist, but broke with the idea of art as a matter of special visual experience and turned his attention to puns and perceptual or conceptual conundrums (Duchamp, 1975). These activities brought him into the orbit of Dada in Paris and New York, but this was probably nothing more than a convenient alliance. Duchamp played games with words and investigated the associations of ordinary objects. He also messed around with gender conventions, inventing a female alter ego called Rrose Sélavy – a pun on 'Eros, c'est la vie' or 'Eros is life'. Critics and other artists have particularly focused on the strain of his work known as the 'readymades'. From 1914, Duchamp began singling out ordinary objects, such as a bottle rack, for his own attention and amusement and that of a few friends. Sometimes he altered these things in some small way, adding words and a title or joining them with something else in a way that shifted their meaning; with Bicycle Wheel, he attached an inverted bike wheel to a wooden stool – he seems to have been particularly interested in the shadow play this object created. We can see this odd object among the clutter of Duchamp's studio on West 67th Street in the photograph by Henri-Pierre Roche. He called these altered everyday things 'assisted readymades'.

Duchamp was interested in interrogating the mass-produced objects created by his society and the common-sense definitions and values that such things accrued. Mischievously, he probed the definitions and values of his culture for a small group of like-minded friends. It isn't at all clear that any of this was meant to be art; in fact, he explicitly posed the idea of making 'works' that could not be thought of as 'art' (Nesbit, 2000). Nevertheless, artists in the late 1950s and the 1960s became fascinated with this legacy and began to think of art as something the artist selected or posited, rather than something he or she composed or made. According to this idea, the artist could designate anything as art; what was important was the way that this decision allowed things to be perceived in a new light. This was to lead to a fundamentally different conception of art practice.

* https://youtu.be/MRv20I13vqM

With the breakup of the hegemony of the New York School, artists began to look at those features of modern art that had been left out of the formalist story. During this period, Duchamp came to replace Picasso or Matisse as the touchstone for young artists, but he was just one tributary of what became a torrent. Perhaps most significantly, painting and anything we might straightforwardly recognize as sculpture began to take a back seat. A host of experimental forms and new media came to prominence: performance art, video, works made directly in or out of the landscape, installations, photography and a host of other forms and practices. These works often engaged with the representation of modernity and the shifting pattern of world power relations we call 'globalization'.

National, International, Cosmopolitan

Whether holding itself apart from the visual culture of modernity or immersed in it, modern art developed not in the world's most powerful economy (Britain), but in the places that were most marked by 'uneven and combined development': places where explosive tensions between traditional rural societies and the changes wrought by capitalism were most acute (Trotsky, 1962 [1928/1906]). In these locations, people only recently out of the fields encountered the shocks and pleasures of grand-metropolitan cities. As the sociologist of modernity Georg Simmel (1858–1918) suggested: 'the city sets up a deep contrast with small-town and rural life with reference to the social foundations of psychic life'. In contrast to the over-stimulation of the senses in the city, Simmel thought that in the rural situation 'the rhythm of life and sensory mental imagery flows more slowly, more habitually, and more evenly' (Simmel, 1997 [1903], p. 175). This situation applies first of all to Paris (see Clark, 1984; Harvey,

2003; Prendergast, 1992). In Paris, the grand boulevards and new palaces of commercial entertainment went hand in hand with the 'zone', a vast shanty town ringing the city that was occupied by workers and those who eked out a precarious life. Whereas the Impressionists concentrated on the bourgeois city of bars, boulevards and boudoirs, the photographer Eugène Atget (1857–1927) represented the Paris that was disappearing – the medieval city with its winding alleys and old iron work – or those working-class quarters composed of cheap lodgings and traders recycling worn-out commodities (Nesbit, 1992; see also Benjamin, 1983). This clash of ways of life generated different ways of inhabiting and viewing the city with class and gender at their core. Access to the modern city and its representations was more readily available to middle-class men than to those with less social authority, whether they were working people, women or minority ethnic or religious groups (Wolff, 1985, pp. 37–46; Pollock, 1988, pp. 50–90).

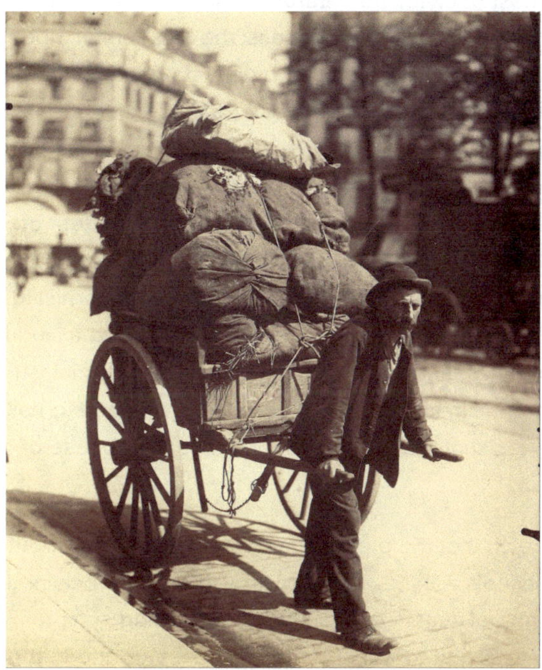

Eugène Atget, Chiffonier (Ragpicker), c. 1899–1901. Work is in the public domain.

Contradictions

Before the Second World War, the alternative centers of modernism were also key sites of uneven and combined development: Berlin, Budapest, Milan, Moscow and Prague. In these places, large-scale industry was created by traditional elites in order to develop the production capacities required to compete militarily with Britain. Factory production was plopped down into largely agrarian societies, generating massive shocks to social equilibrium. In many ways, Moscow is the archetypal version of this pattern of acute contradictions. Before the 1917 Revolution, Moscow was the site of enormous and up-to-date factories, including the world's largest engineering plant, but was set in a sea of peasant backwardness. This is one reason that Vladimir Lenin described Russia as the weakest link in the international-capitalist chain.

This set of contradictions put a particular perception of time at the center of modern art. Opposition to the transformations of society that were underway could be articulated in one of two ways, and in an important sense both were fantasy projections: on the one hand, artists looked to societies that were seen as more 'primitive' as an antidote to the upheavals and shallow glamour of capitalism. On the other hand, they attempted a leap into the future. Both perspectives – Primitivism and Futurism – entailed a profound hostility to the world as it had actually developed, and both orientations were rooted in the conditions of an uneven and combined world system.

The vast urban centers – Paris, Berlin, and Moscow – attracted artists, chancers, intellectuals, poets and revolutionaries. The interchange between people from different nations bred a form of cultural internationalism. In interwar Paris, artists from Spain, Russia, Mexico, Japan and a host of other places rubbed shoulders. Modernist artists attempted to transcend parochial and local conditions and create a formal 'language' valid beyond time and place, and 'the school of Paris' or the 'international modern movement' signified a commitment to a culture more capacious and vibrant than anything the word 'national' could contain. The critic Harold Rosenberg (1906–78) stated this theme explicitly. Rejecting the idea that 'national life' could be a source of inspiration, he suggested that the modernist culture of Paris, was a 'no-place' and a 'no-time' and only Nazi tanks returned the city to France by wiping out modernist internationalism (Rosenberg, 1970 [1940]).

A Move to New York

'No-place' then shifted continent. Perhaps for the only time in its history, after the Second World War modernism was positioned at the heart of world power – when a host of exiles from European fascism and war relocated in New York. American abstract art was centered on New York and a powerful series of institutions: the Museum of Modern Art, Peggy Guggenheim's gallery Art of This Century and a host of small independent galleries run by private dealers (including Betty Parsons, Samuel Koontz and Sidney Janis). In the main, these artists, such as Jackson Pollock (1912–56), Mark Rothko (1903–70), Arshile Gorky (1904–48), Robert Motherwell (1915–91) and Barnett Newman (1905–70), and associated critics (Greenberg and Rosenberg) were formed during the 1930s in the circles of the New York Left: they were modernist internationalists opposed to US parochialism in art and politics. After the war, they retained this commitment to an international modern art, while the politics drained away or was purged in the Cold War. The period of US hegemony in modern art coincided with the optimum interest in autonomous form and pure 'optical' experience. This was the time when artists working in the modernist idiom were least interested in articulating epochal changes and most focused on art as an act of individual realization and a singular encounter between the viewer and the artwork. At the same time, these artists continued to keep their distance from mainstream American values and mass culture. Some champions of autonomous art are inclined to think art came to a shuddering halt with the end of the New York School. Alternatively, we can see Conceptual Art as initiating or reinvigorating a new phase of modern art that continues in the global art of today.

It should be apparent from this brief sketch that the predominant ways of thinking about modern art have focused on a handful of international centers and national schools – even when artists and critics proclaim their allegiance to internationalism. The title of Irving Sandler's book The Triumph of American Painting is one telling symptom (Sandler, 1970). There is a story about geopolitics – about the relationship between the west and the rest – embedded in the history of modern art. These powerful forms of modernism cannot be swept aside, but increasingly critics and art historians are paying attention to other stories; to the artworks made in other places and in other ways, and which were sidelined in the dominant accounts of art's development. A focus on art in a globalized art world leads to revising the national stories told about modernism. This history is currently being recast as a process of global interconnections rather than an exclusively western-centered chronicle, and commentators are becoming more attentive to encounters and interchanges between westerners and people from what has helpfully been called the 'majority world', in art as in other matters. This term – majority world – was used by the Bangladeshi photographer Shahidul Alam, to describe what the term 'third world' had once designated. We use it here to characterize those people and places located outside centers of western affluence and power; they constitute the vast majority of the world's inhabitants and this reminds us that western experience is a minority condition and not the norm.

The Local and the Global

The reality is not that the majority world will be transformed into a high-tech consumer paradise. In fact, inequality is increasing across the world. What is referred to as globalization is the most recent phase of uneven and combined development. The new clash of hypermodern and traditional forms of economic activity and social life are taking place side by side; megacities spring up alongside the 'planet of slums', and communication technologies play an important role in this clash of space and time. Recent debates on globalization and art involve a rejection of modernist internationalism; instead, artists and art historians are engaged with local conditions of artistic production and the way these mesh in an international system of global art making. Modern art is currently being remade and rethought as a series of much more varied responses to contemporaneity around the world. Artists now draw on particular local experiences, and also on forms of representation from popular traditions. Engagement with Japanese popular prints played an important role in Impressionism, but in recent years this sort of cultural crossing has undergone an explosion.

Drawing local image cultures into the international spaces of modern art has once more shifted the character of art. The paradox is that the cultural means that are being employed – video art, installation, large color photographs and so forth – seem genuinely international. Walk into many of the large exhibitions around the globe and you will see artworks referring to particular geopolitical conditions, but employing remarkably similar conventions and techniques. This cosmopolitanism risks underestimating the real forces shaping the world; connection and mobility for some international artists goes hand in hand with uprootedness and the destruction of habitat and ways of life for others.

Conclusion

This overview has provided examples of the shifting perceptions and definitions of art across time. The first part demonstrated the changing role of the artist and diverse types of art in the medieval and Renaissance periods. The second part outlined the evaluation of art in the academies, issues of style, and changes to patronage, where art and its consumption became increasingly part of the public sphere during the period 1600 to 1850. The last part addressed the way in which artists broke from all conventions and the influence of globalization on art production, in the period 1850 to the present.

Works Cited

Adamson, J.S.A. (1999) The Princely Courts of Europe: Ritual, Politics and Culture under the Ancien Régime 1500–1750, London, Weidenfeld & Nicolson.

Alberti, L.B. (1966 [1435]) On Painting (trans. J.R. Spencer), New Haven, CT and London, Yale University Press.

Arciszweska, B. and McKellar, E. (2004) Articulating British Classicism: New Approaches to Eighteenth-Century Architecture, Aldershot and Burlington, VT, Ashgate.

Bailey, C. (1987) 'Conventions of the eighteenth-century cabinet de tableaux: Blondel d'Azincourt's La première idée de la curiosité', Art Bulletin, vol. 69, no. 3, pp. 431–47.

Bailey, C. (2002) Patriotic Taste: Collecting Modern Art in Pre-Revolutionary Paris, New Haven, CT and London, Yale University Press.

Bailey, G.A. (1999) Art on the Jesuit Missions in Asia and Latin America, 1542–1773, Toronto and London, University of Toronto Press.

Barr, A.H. (1974 [1936]) Cubism and Abstract Art, New York, Museum of Modern Art (exhibition catalogue).

Baudelaire, C. (1981 [1859]) 'On photography' in Newhall, B. (ed.) Photography: Essays and Images, New York, Secker & Warburg, pp. 112–13.

Baxandall, M. (1971) Giotto and the Orators: Humanist Observers of Painting in Italy and the Discovery of Pictorial Composition 1350–1450, Oxford, Clarendon Press.

Baxandall, M. (1972) Painting and Experience in Fifteenth-Century Italy, Oxford, Clarendon Press.

Baxandall, M. (1980) The Limewood Sculptors of Renaissance Germany, New Haven, CT, Yale University Press.

Belting, H. (1994) Likeness and Presence: A History of the Image before the Era of Art, Chicago, IL and London, University of Chicago Press.

Benjamin, W. (1983) Charles Baudelaire: A Lyric Poet in the Era of High Capitalism, London, Verso.

Bergdoll, B. (2000) European Architecture 1750–1890, Oxford, Oxford University Press.

Bermingham, A. (2000) Learning to Draw: Studies in the Cultural History of a Polite and Useful Art, New Haven, CT and London, Yale University Press.

Blanning, T.C.W. (2002) The Culture of Power and the Power of Culture: Old Regime Europe 1660–1789, Oxford, Oxford University Press.

Bürger, P. (1984) Theory of the Avant-Garde, Manchester, Manchester University Press; Minneapolis, MN, University of Minnesota Press.

Clark, T.J. (1982) Image of the People. Gustave Courbet and the 1848 Revolution, London, Thames & Hudson.

Clark, T.J. (1984) The Painting of Modern Life: Paris in the Art of Manet and his Followers, London, Thames & Hudson.

Clayton, T. (1997) The English Print, 1688–1802, London and New Haven, CT, Yale University Press.

Connell, S.M. (1976) The Employment of Sculptors and Stonemasons in Venice in the Fifteenth Century (doctoral thesis), Warburg Institute, University of London.

Craske, M. (1997) Art in Europe 1700–1830: A History of the Visual Arts in an Era of Unprecedented Urban Economic Growth, Oxford, Oxford University Press.

Crown, P. (1990) 'British Rococo as social and political style', Eighteenth-Century Studies, vol. 23, no. 3, pp. 269–82.

Duchamp, M. (1975) The Essential Writings of Marcel Duchamp (ed. M. Sanouillet and E. Peterson), London, Thames & Hudson.

Edwards, S. (ed.) (1999) Art and its Histories: A Reader, New Haven, CT and London, Yale University Press.

Elias, N. (1983) The Court Society (trans. E. Jephcott), Oxford, Blackwell.

Gilbert, C. (1985) 'A statement of the aesthetic attitude around 1230', Hebrew University Studies in Literature and the Arts, vol. 13, no. 2, pp. 125–52.

Gordon, D. (2003) The Fifteenth-Century Italian Paintings, National Gallery Catalogues, London, Yale University Press.

Greenberg, C. (1961) Art and Culture: Critical Essays, Boston, MA, Beacon Press.

Greenberg, C. (1986 [1939]) 'Avant-garde and kitsch' in O'Brian, J. (ed.) Clement Greenberg: The Collected Essays and Criticism, vol. 1: Perceptions and Judgements, 1939–1944, Chicago, IL, Chicago University Press, pp. 5–22.

Greenberg, C. (1993 [1960]) 'Modernist painting' in O'Brian, J. (ed.) Clement Greenberg: The Collected Essays and Criticism, vol. 4: Modernism with a Vengeance, 1957–1969, Chicago, IL, Chicago University Press, pp. 85–100.

Habermas, J. (1989 [1962]) The Structural Transformation of the Public Sphere: An Inquiry into a Category of Bourgeois Society, Cambridge, MA, MIT Press.

Hardie, P. (1993) 'Ut Pictura Poesis? Horace and the visual arts' in Horace 2000: A Celebration for the Bi-millennium, London, Duckworth, pp. 120–39.

Harris, A.S. (2008) Seventeenth-Century Art and Architecture (2nd edn), London, Laurence King.

Harrison, C., Wood, P. and Gaiger, J. (eds) (1998) Art in Theory 1815–1900: An Anthology of Changing Ideas, Oxford, Blackwell.

Harvey, D. (2003) Paris: Capital of Modernity, London and New York, Routledge.

Haskell, F. (1980) Patrons and Painters: A Study in the Relations between Italian Art and Society in the Age of the Baroque, New Haven and London, Yale University Press.

Haskell, F. and Penny, N. (1981) Taste and the Antique: The Lure of Classical Sculpture 1500–1900, New Haven, CT and London, Yale University Press.

Hauser, A. (1962 [1951]) The Social History of Art. Vol. 2: Renaissance, Mannerism, Baroque; Vol. 3. Rococo, Classicism and Romanticism (2nd edn), London, Routledge.

Haynes, C. (2006) Pictures and Popery: Art and Religion in England, 1660–1760, Aldershot, Ashgate.

Hemingway, A. and Vaughan, W. (eds) (1998) Art in Bourgeois Society 1790–1850, Cambridge, Cambridge University Press.

Hills, H. (ed.) (2011) Rethinking the Baroque, Farnham, Ashgate.

Honour, H. (1968) Neo-classicism, Harmondsworth, Penguin.

Honour, H. (1979) Romanticism, Harmondsworth, Penguin.

Hyde, M. (2006) Making up the Rococo: François Boucher and his Critics, Los Angeles, CA and London, Getty Research Institute.

Irwin, D. (1997) Neoclassicism, London, Phaidon.

Langdon, H. (1998) Caravaggio: A Life, London, Chatto & Windus.

Lee, R. (1967) Ut Pictura Poesis: The Humanistic Theory of Painting, New York, W.W. Norton.

Levy, E. (2004) Propaganda and the Jesuit Baroque, Berkeley, CA and London, University of California Press.

Lichtenstein, J. (2008) The Blind Spot: An Essay on the Relations between Painting and Sculpture in the Modern Age, Los Angeles, CA, Getty Research Institute.

Lymberopoulou, A., Bracewell-Homer, P. and Robinson, J. (eds) (2012) Art & Visual Culture: A Reader, London, Tate Publishing in association with The Open University.

McClellan, A. (1994) Inventing the Louvre: Art, Politics, and the Origins of the Modern Museum in Eighteenth-Century Paris, Cambridge, Cambridge University Press.

McClellan, A. (1996) 'Watteau's dealer: Gersaint and the marketing of art in eighteenth-century Paris', Art Bulletin, vol. 78, no. 3, pp. 439–53.

Montias, J.M. (1982) Artists and Artisans in Delft: A Socio-economic Study of the Seventeenth Century, Princeton, NJ, Princeton University Press.

Montias, J.M. (2002) Art at Auction in 17th Century Amsterdam, Amsterdam, Amsterdam University Press.

Nash, S. (2007) 'No Equal in Any Land': André Beauneveu – Artist to the Courts of France and Flanders, London, Paul Holberton Publishing.

Nesbit, M. (1992) Atget's Seven Albums, New Haven, CT and London, Yale University Press.

Nesbit, M. (2000) Their Common Sense, London, Black Dog.

North, M. (1997) Art and Commerce in the Dutch Golden Age, New Haven, CT and London, Yale University Press.

North, M. and Ormrod, D. (1998) Art Markets in Europe, 1400–1800, Aldershot, Ashgate.

Nuttall, G. (2012) Lucchese Patronage and Purveying during the Regime of Paolo Guinigi, 1400–1430: Dino Rapondi, Lorenzo Trenta and Paolo Guinigi, unpublished PhD Thesis, Courtauld Institute of Art, University of London.

O'Brian, J. (ed.) (1986–95) Clement Greenberg: The Collected Essays and Criticism, 4 vols, Chicago, IL, Chicago University Press.

Paviot, J. (1990) 'La vie de Jan van Eyck selon les documents écrits', Revue des archéologues et historiens d'art de Louvain, vol. 23, pp. 83–93.

Pears, I. (1988) The Discovery of Painting: The Growth of Interest in the Arts in England 1680–1768, New Haven, CT and London, Yale University Press.

Plon, E. (1887) Les Maîtres italiens au service de la maison d'Autriche: Leone Leoni sculpteur de Charles-Quint et Pompeo Leoni, sculpteur de Philippe II, , Paris, Librairie Plon.

Pollock, G. (1988) Vision and Difference: Femininity, Feminism and the Histories of Art, London and New York, Routledge.

Pomian, K. (1990) Collectors and Curiosities: Paris and Venice, 1500–1800, Cambridge, Polity Press.

Posner, D. (1993) 'Concerning the "mechanical" parts of painting and the artistic culture of seventeenth-century France', Art Bulletin, vol. 75, no. 4, pp. 583–98.

Porter, D. (2010) The Chinese Taste in Eighteenth-Century England, Cambridge, Cambridge University Press.

Potts, A. (2000) The Sculptural Imagination: Figurative, Modernist, Minimalist, New Haven, CT and London, Yale University Press.

Prendergast, C. (1992) Paris and the Nineteenth Century, Oxford, Blackwell.

Prior, N. (2002) Museums and Modernity : Art Galleries and the Making of Modern Culture, Oxford, Berg.

Richardson C.M., Woods, K.W. and Franklin, M.W. (eds) (2007) Renaissance Art Reconsidered: An Anthology of Primary Sources, Oxford, Blackwell.

Rosenberg, H. (1970 [1940]) 'The fall of Paris' in The Tradition of the New, London, Paladin, pp. 185–94.

Roy, A. and Gordon, D. (2001) 'The Battle of San Romano', National Gallery Technical Bulletin, vol. 22, pp. 4–17.

Sandler, I. (1970) The Triumph of American Painting, Westport, CT, Praeger.

Schapiro, M. (1977) 'On the aesthetic attitude in Romanesque art' in Romanesque Art: Selected Papers, London, Chatto & Windus, pp. 1–27.

Schapiro, M. (1978 [1937]) 'Nature of abstract art' in Modern Art: 19th and 20th Centuries. Selected Papers, New York, George Braziller, pp. 185–211.

Scott, K. (1995) The Rococo Interior: Decoration and Social Spaces in Early Eighteenth-Century Paris, New Haven, CT and London, Yale University Press.

Sheehan, J.J. (2000) Museums in the German Art World from the End of the Old Regime to the Rise of Modernism, Oxford, Oxford University Press.

Sheriff, M. (1990) Fragonard: Art and Eroticism, Chicago, IL, University of Chicago Press.

Shiner, L. (2001) The Invention of Art: A Cultural History, Chicago, IL, University of Chicago Press.

Simmel, G. (1997 [1903]) 'The metropolis and mental life' in Frisby, D.P. and Featherstone, M. (eds) Simmel on Culture: Selected Writings, New York, Sage, pp. 174–85. Extract reprinted in Lymberopoulou, A., Bracewell-Homer, P. and Robinson, J. (eds) Art and Visual Culture: A Reader, London, Tate Publishing in association with The Open University, pp. 267–9.

Snodin, M. (ed.) (1984) Rococo: Art and Design in Hogarth's England, London, V&A (exhibition catalogue).

Snodin, M. and Llewellyn, N. (eds) (2009) Baroque, 1620–1800: Style in the Age of Magnificence, London, V&A (exhibition catalogue).

Stechow, W. (1989 [1966]) Northern Renaissance Art 1400–1600: Sources and Documents, Evanston, IL, Northwestern University Press.

Suger, Abbot (1979) On the Abbey Church of Saint-Denis and its Art Treasures (eds E. Panofsky and G. Panofsky-Soergel), Princeton, NJ, Princeton University Press.

Tomlinson, J.A. (1994) Francisco Goya y Lucientes, 1746–1828, London, Phaidon.

Trotsky, L. (1962 [1928/1906]) The Permanent Revolution; Results and Prospects, London, New Park.

Vasari, G. (1996) [1568] Lives of the Painters, Sculptors and Architects, 2 vols (trans. G. du C. de Vere; ed. D. Ekserdijian), London, Everyman.

Warnke, M. (1993) The Court Artist: On the Ancestry of the Modern Artist (trans. D. McLintock), Cambridge, Cambridge University Press (first published in German in 1985).

Wolff, J. (1985) 'The invisible flaneuse: women and the literature of modernity', Theory, Culture and Society, vol. 2, no. 3, pp. 37–46.

Wölfflin, H. (1950) Principles of Art History: The Problem of the Development of Style in Later Art, New York, Dover.

Wolters, W. (1967) 'Ein Hauptwerk der niederländischen Skulptur in Venedig', Mitteillung des Kunsthistorischen Institutes in Florenz, vol. 13, nos 1–2, pp. 185–9.

Wolters, W. (1976) La scultura Veneziana gotica 1300–1460, 2 vols, Venice, Alfieri.

Purposes of Art

Explain the difference between non-motivated functions and motivated functions as purposes of art

LEARNING ACTIVITIES

The learning activities for this section include:

- Reading: Purpose of Art

Take time to review and reflect on this activity in order to improve your performance on the assessment for this section.

Reading: Purpose of Art

Art has had a great number of different functions throughout its history, making its purpose difficult to abstract or quantify to any single concept. This does not imply that the purpose of art is "vague" but that it has had many unique, different reasons for being created. Some of the functions of art are provided in the outline below. The different purposes of art may be grouped according to those that are non-motivated and those that are motivated (Lévi-Strauss).

Non-motivated Functions of Art

The non-motivated purposes of art are those that are integral to being human, transcend the individual, or do not fulfill a specific external purpose. In this sense, art, as creativity, is something humans must do by their very nature (i.e., no other species creates art), and is therefore beyond utility.

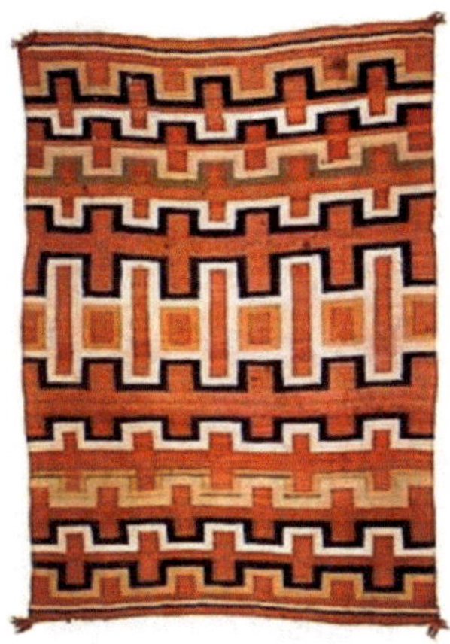

A Navajo rug made circa 1880

1. *Basic human instinct for harmony, balance, rhythm.* Art at this level is not an action or an object, but an internal appreciation of balance and harmony (beauty), and therefore an aspect of being human beyond utility.

> Imitation, then, is one instinct of our nature. Next, there is the instinct for 'harmony' and rhythm, meters being manifestly sections of rhythm. Persons, therefore, starting with this natural gift developed by degrees their special aptitudes, till their rude improvisations gave birth to Poetry. —Aristotle

2. *Experience of the mysterious.* Art provides a way to experience one's self in relation to the universe. This experience may often come unmotivated, as one appreciates art, music or poetry.

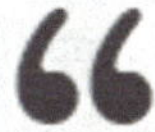

> The most beautiful thing we can experience is the mysterious. It is the source of all true art and science. —Albert Einstein

3. *Expression of the imagination.* Art provides a means to express the imagination in nongrammatic ways that are not tied to the formality of spoken or written language. Unlike words, which come in sequences and each of which have a definite meaning, art provides a range of forms, symbols and ideas with meanings that are malleable.

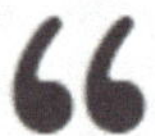

> Jupiter's eagle [as an example of art] is not, like logical (aesthetic) attributes of an object, the concept of the sublimity and majesty of creation, but rather something else – something that gives the imagination an incentive to spread its flight over a whole host of kindred representations that provoke more thought than admits of expression in a concept determined by words. They furnish an aesthetic idea, which serves the above rational idea as a substitute for logical presentation, but with the proper function, however, of animating the mind by opening out for it a prospect into a field of kindred representations stretching beyond its ken. —Immanuel Kant

4. *Ritualistic and symbolic functions.* In many cultures, art is used in rituals, performances and dances as a decoration or symbol. While these often have no specific utilitarian (motivated) purpose, anthropologists know that they often serve a purpose at the level of meaning within a particular culture. This meaning is not furnished by any one individual, but is often the result of many generations of change, and of a cosmological relationship within the culture.

> Most scholars who deal with rock paintings or objects recovered from prehistoric contexts that cannot be explained in utilitarian terms and are thus categorized as decorative, ritual or symbolic, are aware of the trap posed by the term "art."
> —Silva Tomaskova

Motivated Functions of Art

Motivated purposes of art refer to intentional, conscious actions on the part of the artists or creator. These may be to bring about political change, to comment on an aspect of society, to convey a specific emotion or mood, to address personal psychology, to illustrate another discipline, to (with commercial arts) to sell a product, or simply as a form of communication.

1. *Communication.* Art, at its simplest, is a form of communication. As most forms of communication have an intent or goal directed toward another individual, this is a motivated purpose. Illustrative arts, such as scientific illustration, are a form of art as communication. Maps are another example. However, the content need not be scientific. Emotions, moods and feelings are also communicated through art.

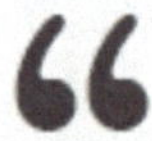

> [Art is a set of] artifacts or images with symbolic meanings as a means of communication. —Steve Mithen

2. *Art as entertainment*. Art may seek to bring about a particular emotion or mood, for the purpose of relaxing or entertaining the viewer. This is often the function of the art industries of Motion Pictures and Video Games.

3. *The Avante-Garde. Art for political change.* One of the defining functions of early twentieth-century art has been to use visual images to bring about political change. Art movements that had this goal—Dadaism, Surrealism, Russian constructivism, and Abstract Expressionism, among others—are collectively referred to as the avante-garde arts.

> By contrast, the realistic attitude, inspired by positivism, from Saint Thomas Aquinas to Anatole France, clearly seems to me to be hostile to any intellectual or moral advancement. I loathe it, for it is made up of mediocrity, hate, and dull conceit. It is this attitude which today gives birth to these ridiculous books, these insulting plays. It constantly feeds on and derives strength from the newspapers and stultifies both science and art by assiduously flattering the lowest of tastes; clarity bordering on stupidity, a dog's life. —André Breton (Surrealism)

4. *Art as a "tree zone,"* removed from the action of the social censure. Unlike the avant-garde movements, which wanted to erase cultural differences in order to produce new universal values, contemporary art has enhanced its tolerance towards cultural differences as well as its critical and liberating functions (social inquiry, activism, subversion, deconstruction...), becoming a more open place for research and experimentation.

5. *Art for social inquiry, subversion, and/or anarchy.* While similar to art for political change, subversive or deconstructivist art may seek to question aspects of society without any specific political goal. In this case, the function of art may be simply to criticize some aspect of society.

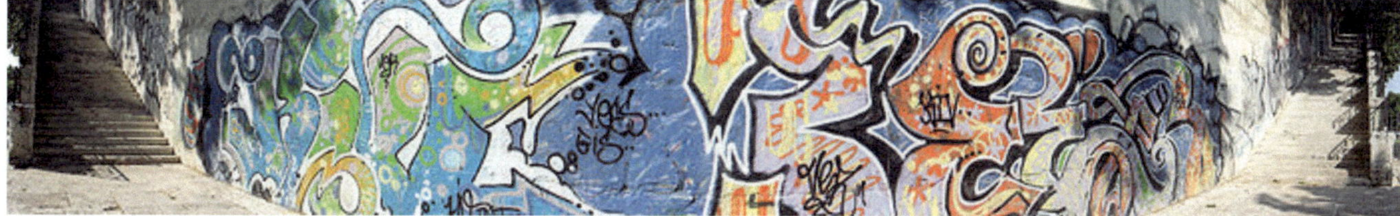

Spray-paint graffiti on a wall in Rome

Graffiti art and other types of street art are graphics and images that are spray-painted or stenciled on publicly viewable walls, buildings, buses, trains, and bridges, usually without permission. Certain art forms, such as graffiti, may also be illegal when they break laws (in this case vandalism).

6. *Art for social causes.* Art can be used to raise awareness for a large variety of causes. A number of art activities were aimed at raising awareness of autism, cancer, human trafficking, and a variety of other topics, such as ocean conservation, human rights in Darfur, murdered and missing Aboriginal women, elder abuse, and pollution. Trashion, using trash to make fashion, practiced by artists such as Marina DeBris is one example of using art to raise awareness about pollution.

7. *Art for psychological and healing purposes.* Art is also used by art therapists, psychotherapists and clinical psychologists as art therapy. The Diagnostic Drawing Series, for example, is used to determine the personality and emotional functioning of a patient. The end product is not the principal goal in this case, but rather a process of healing, through creative acts, is sought. The resultant piece of artwork may also offer insight into the troubles experienced by the subject and may suggest suitable approaches to be used in more conventional forms of psychiatric therapy.

8. *Art for propaganda or commercialism.* Art is often utilized as a form of propaganda, and thus can be used to subtly influence popular conceptions or mood. In a similar way, art that tries to sell a product also influences mood and emotion. In both cases, the purpose of art here is to subtly manipulate the viewer into a particular emotional or psychological response toward a particular idea or object.

9. *Art as a fitness indicator.* It has been argued that the ability of the human brain by far exceeds what was needed for survival in the ancestral environment. One evolutionary psychology explanation for this is that the human brain and associated traits (such as artistic ability and creativity) are the human equivalent of the peacock's tail. The purpose of the male peacock's extravagant tail has been argued to be to attract females. According to this theory superior execution of art was evolutionarily important because it attracted mates.

The functions of art described above are not mutually exclusive, as many of them may overlap. For example, art for the purpose of entertainment may also seek to sell a product (i.e. a movie or video game).

Aesthetics

Define aesthetics within the scope of an art experience

LEARNING ACTIVITIES

The learning activities for this section include:

- Reading: Art and the Aesthetic Experience

Take time to review and reflect on this activity in order to improve your performance on the assessment for this section.

Reading: Art, Aesthetics, and Beauty

Art and the Aesthetic Experience

Beauty is something we perceive and respond to. It may be a response of awe and amazement, wonder and joy, or something else. It might resemble a "peak experience" or an epiphany. It might happen while watching a sunset or taking in the view from a mountaintop—the list goes on. Here we are referring to a kind of experience, an *aesthetic response that is a response to the thing's representational qualities*, whether it is man-made or natural (Silverman). The subfield of philosophy called aesthetics is devoted to the study and theory of this experience of the beautiful; in the field of psychology, aesthetics is studied in relation to the physiology and psychology of perception.

Aesthetic analysis is a careful investigation of the qualities which belong to objects and events that evoke an aesthetic response. The aesthetic response is the thoughts and feelings initiated because of the character of these qualities and the particular ways they are organized and experienced perceptually (Silverman).

The aesthetic experience that we get from the world at large is different than the art-based aesthetic experience. It is important to recognize that we are not saying that the natural wonder experience is bad or lesser than the art world experience; we are saying it is different. What is different is the constructed nature of the art experience. The art experience is a type of aesthetic experience that also includes aspects, content, and context of our humanness. When something is made by a human— we know that there is some level of commonality and/or communal experience.

Why aesthetics is only the beginning in analyzing an artwork

We are also aware that beyond sensory and formal properties, all artwork is informed by its specific time and place or the specific historical and cultural milieu it was created in (Silverman). For this reason we analyze artwork through not only aesthetics, but also, historical and cultural contexts.

How we engage in aesthetic analysis

Often the feelings or thoughts evoked as a result of contemplating an artwork are initially based primarily upon what is actually seen in the work. The first aspects of the artwork we respond to are its sensory properties, its formal properties, and its technical properties (Silverman). Color is an example of a sensory property. Color is considered a kind of form and how form is arranged is a formal property. What medium (e.g., painting, animation, etc.) the artwork is made of is an example of a technical property. These will be discussed further in the next module. As Dr. Silverman, of California State University explains, the sequence of questions in an aesthetic analysis could be: what do we actually see? How is what is seen organized? And, what emotions and ideas are evoked as a result of what has been observed?

Works Cited

Silverman, Ronald. *Learning About Art: A Multicultural Approach*. California State University, 2001. Web. 24, June 2008.

Perception and Value

Define aesthetics and some variables in how we assign value to art

The learning activities for this section include:

- Reading: Art and the Aesthetic Experience
- Reading: Value Judgment

Take time to review and reflect on this activity in order to improve your performance on the assessment for this section.

Reading: Value Judgment

How We Assign Value to Art

The word art is often used to apply judgments of value, as in expressions like "that meal was a work of art" (implying that the cook is an artist) or "the art of deception" (the advanced, praiseworthy skill of deceiving). It is this use of the word as a measure of high value that gives the term its flavor of subjectivity.

Does It Have to Be Visually Pleasing or Not?

Making judgments of value requires a basis for criticism. At the simplest level, deciding whether an object or experience is be considered art is a matter of finding it to be either attractive or repulsive. Though perception is always colored by experience, and is necessarily subjective, it is commonly understood that what is not somehow visually pleasing cannot be art. However, "good" art is not always or even regularly visually pleasing to a majority of viewers. In other words, an artist's prime motivation need not be the pursuit of a pleasing arrangement of form. Also, art often depicts terrible images made for social, moral, or thought-provoking reasons.

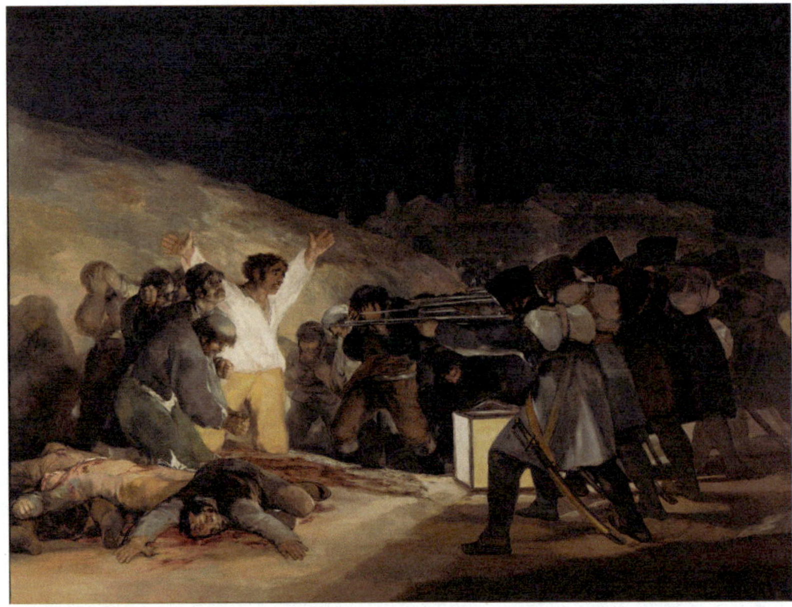
Francisco de Goya, El Tres de Mayo. Image is in the public domain.

For example, the painting pictured above, by Francisco Goya, depicts the Spanish shootings on the third of May, 1808. It is a graphic depiction of a firing squad executing several pleading civilians. Yet at the same time, the horrific imagery demonstrates Goya's keen artistic ability in composition and execution, and it produces fitting social and political outrage. Thus, the debate continues as to what mode of aesthetic satisfaction, if any, is required to define "art." The revision of what is popularly conceived of as being visually pleasing allows for a re-invigoration of and a new appreciation for the standards of art itself.

Art is often intended to appeal to and connect with human emotion. It can arouse aesthetic or moral feelings, and can be understood as a way of communicating these feelings. Art may be considered an exploration of the human condition or what it is to be human.

Factors Involved in the Judgment of Art

Seeing a rainbow often inspires an emotional reaction like delight or joy. Visceral responses such as disgust show that sensory detection is reflexively connected to facial expressions and to behaviors like the gag reflex. Yet disgust can often be a learned or cultural response, too; as Darwin pointed out, seeing a smear of soup in a man's beard is disgusting even though neither soup nor beards are themselves disgusting.

Artistic judgments may be linked to emotions or, like emotions, partially embodied in our physical reactions. Seeing a sublime view of a landscape may give us a reaction of awe, which might manifest physically as increased heart rate or widened eyes. These unconscious reactions may partly control, or at least reinforce, our judgment in the first place that the landscape is sublime.

Likewise, artistic judgments may be culturally conditioned to some extent. Victorians in Britain often saw African sculpture as ugly, but just a few decades later, those same audiences saw those sculptures as being beautiful. Evaluations of beauty may well be linked to desirability, perhaps even to sexual desirability. Thus, judgments of art can become linked to judgments of economic, political, or moral value. In a contemporary context, one might judge a Lamborghini to be beautiful partly because it is desirable as a status symbol, or we might judge it to be repulsive partly because it signifies for us over-consumption and offends our political or moral values.

Judging the value of an artwork is often partly intellectual and interpretative. It is what a thing means or symbolizes for us that is often what we are judging. Assigning value to artwork is often a complex negotiation of our senses, emotions, intellectual opinions, will, desires, culture, preferences, values, subconscious behavior, conscious decision, training, instinct, sociological institutions, and other factors. Watch the video below to hear discussion on these factors in value judgement.

- https://youtu.be/8-5DTsl1V5k

Watch this video on the artwork titled *The Physical Impossibility of Death in the Mind of Someone Living* by Damien Hirst. Consider the complexity of the interpretative experience of art and how value is assigned to an artwork.

- https://youtu.be/uDuzy-t7GDA

The Ongoing Definition of Art

Describe and discuss some contemporary theories in the definition of art.

LEARNING ACTIVITIES

The learning activities for this section include:

- Reading: Defining Art

Take time to review and reflect on this activity in order to improve your performance on the assessment for this section.

Reading: Defining Art

We have explored how the definition art has changed throughout history and the many complex factors that can be at play in assigning value to art. Despite this difficulty, ongoing discussion around the definition of art continues to evolve within our often complex, globally engaged society.

Some Contemporary Theories Defining Art

Many have argued that it is a mistake to even try to define art or beauty, that they have no essence, and so can have no definition.

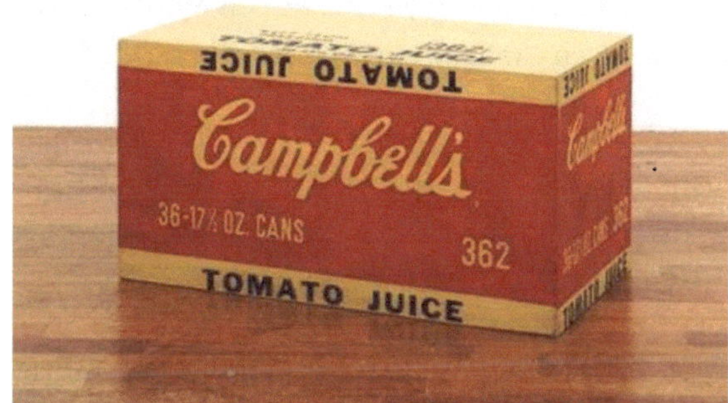

Campbell's Tomato Juice Box, 1964, Andy Warhol, Synthetic polymer paint and silkscreen ink on wood, 10 inches x 19 inches x 9 1/2 inches (25.4 x 48.3 x 24.1 cm), Museum of Modern Art, New York. © 2007 Andy Warhol Foundation / Fair Use

Andy Warhol exhibited wooden sculptures of Brillo Boxes as art.

One contemporary approach is to say that "art" is basically a sociological category that whatever art schools and museums, and artists get away with is considered art regardless of formal definitions. This **institutional theory** of art has been championed by George Dickie. Most people did not consider a store-bought urinal or a sculptural depiction of a Brillo Box to be art until Marcel Duchamp and Andy Warhol (respectively) placed them in the context of art (e.g., the art gallery), which then provided the association of these objects with the values that define art.

Proceduralists often suggest that it is the process by which a work of art is created or viewed that makes it, art, not any inherent feature of an object, or how well received it is by the institutions of the art world after its introduction to society at large. For John Dewey, for instance, if the writer intended a piece to be a poem, it is one whether other poets acknowledge it or not. Whereas if exactly the same set of words was written by a journalist, intending them as shorthand notes to help him write a longer article later, these would not be a poem.

Leo Tolstoy, on the other hand, claims that what makes something art or not is how it is experienced by its audience **(audience or viewer context)**, not by the intention of its creator.

Functionalists, like Monroe Beardsley argue that whether a piece counts as art depends on what function it plays in a particular context. For instance, the same Greek vase may play a non-artistic function in one context (carrying wine), and an artistic function in another context (helping us to appreciate the beauty of the human figure).

Contemporary Disputes about the Definition of Art

Philosopher David Novitz has argued that disagreements about the definition of art are rarely the heart of the problem, rather that "the passionate concerns and interests that humans vest in their social life" are "so much a part of all classificatory disputes about art" (Novitz, 1996). According to Novitz, classificatory disputes are more often disputes about our values and where we are trying to go with our society than they are about art. For example, when the Daily Mail criticized Damien Hirst and Tracey Emin's work by arguing "For 1,000 years art has been one of our great civilising forces. Today, pickled sheep and soiled beds threaten to make barbarians of us all" they are not advancing a definition or theory about art, but questioning the value of Hirst's and Emin's work. On the other hand, Thierry de Duve argues that disputes about the definition of art are a necessary consequence of Marcel Duchamp's presentation of a readymade as a work of art.

Controversy around Conceptual Art

The work of the French artist Marcel Duchamp from the 1910s and 1920s paved the way for the conceptual artists, providing them with examples of prototypically conceptual works (the readymades, for instance) that defied previous categorizations of art. Conceptual art emerged as a movement during the 1960s. The first wave of the "conceptual art" movement extended from approximately 1967 to 1978. Early "concept" artists like Henry Flynt, Robert Morris, and Ray Johnson influenced the later, widely accepted movement of conceptual artists like Dan Graham, Hans Haacke, and Douglas Huebler.

More recently, the "Young British Artists" (YBAs), led by Damien Hirst, came to prominence in the 1990s and their work is seen as conceptual, even though it relies very heavily on the art object to make its impact. The term is used in relation to them on the basis that the object is not the artwork, or is often a found object, which has not needed artistic skill in its production. Tracey Emin is seen as a leading YBA and a conceptual artist, even though she has denied that she is, and has emphasized her personal emotional expression.

Recent Examples of Conceptual Art

- 1991: Charles Saatchi funds Damien Hirst and the next year in the Saatchi Gallery exhibits his *The Physical Impossibility of Death in the Mind of Someone Living*, a shark in formaldehyde in a vitrine.
- 1993: Vanessa Beecroft holds her first performance in Milan, Italy, using young girls to act as a second audience to the display of her diary of food.
- 1999: Tracey Emin is nominated for the Turner Prize. Part of her exhibit is *My Bed*, her dishevelled bed, surrounded by detritus such as condoms, blood-stained knickers, bottles and her bedroom slippers.
- 2001: Martin Creed wins the Turner Prize for *The Lights Going On and Off*, an empty room where the lights go on and off.
- 2002: Miltos Manetas confronts the Whitney Biennial with his Whitneybiennial.com.
- 2005: Simon Starling wins the Turner Prize for *Shedboatshed*, a wooden shed which he had turned into a boat, floated down the Rhine and turned back into a shed again.

The Stuckist group of artists, founded in 1999, proclaimed themselves "pro-contemporary figurative painting with ideas and anti-conceptual art, mainly because of its lack of concepts." They also called it pretentious, "unremarkable and boring" and on July 25, 2002, in a demonstration, deposited a coffin outside the White Cube gallery, marked "The Death of Conceptual Art". In 2003, the Stuckism International Gallery exhibited a preserved shark under the title A Dead Shark Isn't Art, clearly referencing the Damien Hirst work

In 2002, Ivan Massow, the Chairman of the Institute of Contemporary Arts branded conceptual art "pretentious, self-indulgent, craftless" and in "danger of disappearing up its own arse …". Massow was consequently forced to resign. At the end of the year, the Culture Minister, Kim Howells, an art school graduate, denounced the Turner Prize as "cold, mechanical, conceptual bullshit".

In October 2004, the Saatchi Gallery told the media that "painting continues to be the most relevant and vital way that artists choose to communicate." Following this, Charles Saatchi began to sell prominent works from his YBA (Young British Artists) collection.

Disputes about New Media

Computer games date back as far as 1947, although they did not reach much of an audience until the 1970s. It would be difficult and odd to deny that computer and video games include many kinds of art (bearing in mind, of course, that the concept "art" itself is, as indicated, open to a variety of definitions). The graphics of a video game constitute digital art, graphic art, and probably video art; the original soundtrack of a video game clearly constitutes music. However it is a point of debate whether the video game as a whole should be considered a piece of art of some kind, perhaps a form of interactive art.

Film critic Roger Ebert, for example, has gone on record claiming that video games are not art, and for structural reasons will always be inferior to cinema, but then, he admits his lack of knowledge in the area when he affirmed that he "will never play a game when there is a good book to be read or a good movie to be watched.". Video game designer Hideo Kojima has argued that playing a videogame is not art, but games do have artistic style and incorporate art. Video game designer Chris Crawford argues that video games are art. Esquire columnist Chuck Klosterman also argues that video games are art. Tadhg Kelly argues that play itself is not art and that fun is a constant required for all games so the art in games is the art of location and place rather than interaction.

Putting It Together

During earlier eras, the definition of art was aligned with craftsmanship and guilds, but as societies changed, so too, did the meaning and purpose of art. Over time, art evolved beyond practical and religious functions and became an autonomous expression of the artist's creative process and of the surrounding culture.

Aesthetics is concerned with how we perceptually engage in the changing and complex concepts of beauty and the sublime (Ocvirk, 6).

Exploring the definition of art is an act of critical thinking. Critical thinking is creative thinking, and the critical-thinking process often requires a belief in the question, rather than an expectation of hard truths or answers. Through active questioning, exploration, and trial and error, we uncover multiple valid perspectives.

Consider the example of the nkisi figures introduced at the beginning of this module. Recall how that misunderstanding of visual culture was representative of the larger confrontation and oppression of African societies by Europeans. Consider also, in the final example of video games, how the introduction of new media keeps alive the ongoing debate about what is art.

Works Cited

Ocvirk, Stinson, Wigg, Bone, Cayton. *Art Fundamentals, Theory and Practice*, 12 Edition. New York: McGraw Hill, 2013. Print.

Sayre, Henry. *A World of Art*, Sixth edition. Boston: Prentice Hall, 2010. Print.

CHAPTER 3: CONTEXT AND PERSPECTIVE

Why It Matters

Recognize essential concepts in methods of visual analysis (course level learning objective)

Introduction

Contexts are the circumstances and background that form the setting for any kind of communication, including art, and the interpretation of its meaning(s). All artworks exist in multiple contexts. Considering different contexts can form analytical lenses through which to view and interpret an artwork.

An example of the first and most basic level of context is the time and place an artwork was created. A less discussed, but equally important, context is how or where we encounter an artwork, and how that affects our interpretation. This is part of the viewer context. Consider this photograph taken during the Spanish Civil War, *The Falling Soldier*, by highly regarded documentary photographer Robert Capa.

From its first release it was provocative, because it was assumed to be the first photograph of someone being shot at the moment of the bullet's impact and possibly the moment of death. Its authenticity continues to be hotly debated. When the photo was first seen in the European magazine *Vu* in 1936, it was accompanied by other photographs depicting the suffering of people during the Spanish Civil War. However, when *LIFE* magazine reprinted it in 1937 for an American audience, it was part of a two-page magazine spread adjacent to an ad for Vitalis, a men's hair product. How might this odd juxtaposition have affected the way American audiences interpreted the photo's meaning compared with their European counterparts?

In this module you'll learn more about context and perspective and their role in the interpretation of art.

Module Learning Outcomes

- Define 3 basic types of perspective and how they impact interpretations of an artwork
- Recognize different types of context and how contextual information can broaden our understanding of art
- Recognize and describe six different critical modalities that art critics use to analyze and interpret artwork
- Analyze and discuss artwork in relation to two different cultures; explain how those two cultures are linked from a wider, global perspective
- Recognize what a symbol is and differentiate how semiotics and iconography are used to decipher symbols in artwork and other types of visual culture

How to Study for the Performance Assessment (PA)

The PA for this module involves answering short essay questions that are designed to test your understanding of the Learning Outcomes for this module. Read through the performance assessment for this module BEFORE you begin the module content. I suggest printing it out, or making notes on the keywords/concepts in each PA question. A concept example is: contextual information. In the first PA question, you need to be able to discern what contextual information is to successfully answer the question. Use what you noted on the PA as a study guide. As you read through the module content, take notes on the subjects or anything that you find relevant to the PA questions. Be sure to document the page or place in the content where you found each note, in case you need to return to that content, or need to ask me a specific question citing module content. Once you are ready to complete the PA, you will have these notes to help you answer the questions thoughtfully.

OK, let's get started!

Video: Art and Context

As we look at art and artworks, there are a number of factors that influence and affect what we see. This section is about drawing out, looking at, and discussing some of these factors.

- https://youtu.be/2aUFB9hQncQ

Perspective

Define 3 basic types of perspective and how they impact interpretations of an artwork.

LEARNING ACTIVITIES

The learning activities for this section include:

- Reading: Perspective

Take time to review and reflect on this activity in order to improve your performance on the assessment for this section.

Reading: Perspective

Is seeing also understanding?

The physiological processes that come together to form our vision, or sight capabilities, are a component of the larger complex process of how we 'see' or comprehend the world. Consider the statement by Henry Sayre, "Everything you see is filtered through a long history of fears, prejudices, desires, emotions, customs, and beliefs." Our understanding of visual culture, including art, is dynamic, informed by our prior experiences and identities.

We live in a time of unprecedented saturation of visual culture, exponentially increased by the ease of digital communication. The term ocularcentrism has been used to describe the dominance of the visual in contemporary Western life (Rose 3). But does seeing necessarily equal understanding? Consider Sayre's example in questioning visual information, as to what colored stripe is at the top and bottom of the American flag (16)? As our national symbol, we assume we have a thorough understanding of it because we've seen it so frequently. However- not only seeing, but remembering what we have seen is often inaccurate, and can be more of a creative interpretive process than we may recognize.

To be able to engage artwork at a deeper level, beyond passive looking, it is necessary to develop a breadth of understanding in art history, methods of visual analysis, and specific descriptive language. To communicate how visual art affects you it is necessary to understand vocabulary, phrases, and concepts that allow you to think critically about visual images (Sayre 19). In the prior module you learned the terms and meanings of the language of form, the elements and principles of design. This module builds on that by considering perspective, context, and other methods of visual analysis beyond formalism.

Perspective

Perspective is a point-of-view. In a way it is regarding something through a specific filter. Each perspective or filter has unique characteristics that direct how something is considered. For example, if you were analyzing an artwork in regards to gender, an aspect of identity, you might consider how being male, female, or transgendered might contribute to the experience of an artwork. Context or contextual knowledge relates to perspective, in that all perspectives are shaped by the circumstances around them that constitute a kind of background they form within.

3 Basic Types of Perspective

Cultural Perspective

Culture is a complex concept that encompasses the ways that social life effects and informs our experiences. To quote Stuart Hall:

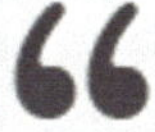

"Culture, it is not so much a set of things- novels and paintings, or TV programs or comics- as a process, a set of practices. Primarily culture is concerned with the production and exchange of meanings- the 'giving and taking of meaning' between members in a society or group... Thus culture depends on its participants interpreting meaning- fully what is around them, and 'making sense' of the world, in broadly similar ways (Rose 2)."

It could be said that growing up in America contributes to an 'American worldview'. We each may have variations to this, but unless you were raised outside of the United States, you are strongly (consciously or unconsciously) influenced by an American perspective. This is an example of cultural perspective. Where in the United States you were raised might also contribute contextually to this, as many regions of the country are unique and form a specific kind of background.

Representations, in whatever form they take, contribute to 'made meanings' of culture, specifically as visual culture. As Gillian Rose points out- these representations, whether they are high art or advertisements, are not transparent windows on the world, rather- they interpret the world (Rose 2). When we select and take in specific kinds of representations there is an exchange of meaning that goes two ways. We participate in constructing culture by selecting and elevating certain forms of representations, and that specific visual culture we experience has the power to influence our personal view on life.

Historical Perspective

As time passes, scholarship and research occur and many people become aware of a particular artwork, art form, art style, etc. Recognition may increase (and sometimes decreases). Vincent Van Gogh is an example here—totally unappreciated while he was alive, he's recognized worldwide as a notable painter. Other examples might be the negative attitudes towards jazz music or hip-hop in the mid-twentieth century. These currents of recognition often spring from institutions like museums, academic writing and journals, college art classes, and art history as a field of study.

Personal Perspective

Personal perspectives are formed by the layered aspects that form our individual identities. This could be any number of defining aspects such as, gender, class, race, where you were born and raised, education, aspects of family, group affiliations, etc., and the list goes on. These aspects form our unique biographical experiences that constitute our identities and color our personal point of view or the way we interpret our life experiences.

You may find that your personal response to art and artworks will change as you learn more about design, art making, and the history of art in general. Knowledge and/or education about art usually helps us appreciate and understand it.

Sweeping judgments based purely on a personal emotional response can be colored with bias and often come from having little knowledge of a subject or artwork or the larger cultural context. These are habits of thinking that inhibit a critical understanding of things that are new to us like artwork. In general, it's a good idea to take a generous stance to art forms or artworks we don't like or don't understand or just don't connect to.

WORKS CITED

Rose, Gillian. *Visual Methodologies: An Introduction to Researching Visual Materials*. Los Angeles: Sage Publications, 2012. Print.

Sayre, Henry. *A World of Art*, Sixth edition. Boston: Prentice Hall, 2010. Print.

Subjective vs. Objective Analysis

Define the terms "subjective" and "objective" in relation to seeing images

LEARNING ACTIVITIES

The learning activities for this section include:

- Reading: How We See: Objective and Subjective Means

Take time to review and reflect on this activity in order to improve your performance on the assessment for this section.

Reading: How We See: Objective and Subjective Means

Up until now we've been looking at artworks through the most immediate of visual effects: what we see in front of our eyes. Now we can begin to break down some barriers to finding specific meaning in art, including those of different styles and cultures. To help in this journey we need to learn the difference between looking at something in an objective way versus subjectively.

To look objectively is to get an unbiased overview of our field of vision. Subjective seeing speaks more to understanding. When we use the term "*I see*" we communicate that we understand what something means. There are some areas of learning, particularly psychology and biology, that help form the basis of understanding how we see. For example, the fact that humans perceive flat images as having a "reality" to them is very particular. In contrast, if you show a dog an image of another dog, they neither growl nor wag their tail, because they are unable to perceive flat images as containing any meaning. So you and I have actually developed the ability to "see" and read specific meanings into images.

In essence, there is more to seeing than meets the eye. We need to take into account a cultural component in how we perceive images and that we do so in subjective ways. Seeing is partly a result of cultural conditioning and biases. For example, when many of us from industrialized cultures see a parking lot, we can pick out each car immediately, while others from remote tribal cultures (who are not familiar with parking lots) cannot.

Context

Recognize different types of context and how contextual information can broaden our understanding of art.

LEARNING ACTIVITIES

The learning activities for this section include:

- Reading: Context

Take time to review and reflect on each of these activities in order to improve your performance on the assessment for this section.

Reading: Context

Contextual Information

Specific to artwork, context consists of all of the things about the artwork that might have influenced the artwork or the maker (artist) but which are not actually part of the artwork. Contextual information can deepen and/or improve our understanding of an artwork. With some additional contextual information about the time, the culture, and the maker/artist of an artwork, we can become more informed. All artworks exist in a context—more accurately, all artworks exist in multiple contexts.

Historical context

Time is the most basic and first context we consider. When we say, "When in time?" the question is also related to where in time.

Artist Context

Though this kind of context is often ignored in more recent trends of visual research, the context for the artist or creator includes:

- Their culture (where they grew up; family values; etc.).
- Their place; geography (e.g., city, rural, home, traveling).
- Their personal perspective or "worldview," aspects unique to their identity.

Viewing context

Context also has to do with the viewing experience.The context of display or where we encounter an image or artwork is crucial to the meanings it accrues (Rose 127). Consider, how is the experience viewing a masterwork, like a painting by Caravaggio, hanging in a museum versus seeing a digital representation of the same painting on a personal computer in one's home— different? You go to a museum specifically with the intention to view artwork. Are their specific social practices you engage in a museum that impact your experience? For example, we typically comport ourselves quietly in a museum, looking intently as we move from one artwork to the next. Presumably, this social practice is intended to encourage contemplation.There are also texts on the walls of museums like an artwork's title, and sometimes captions. Reading these may direct our experience of the artwork. Being in front of the actual work, rather than a copy, imbues the work with certain aura as the object the artist actually touched and created. At home, we are in a more casual setting without specific conventions of behavior. Though we are looking at the same artwork, we know we are looking at a copy. The context of where and how an image or artwork is received can impact what affect it has on us.

WORKS CITED

Rose, Gillian. Visual Methodologies: An Introduction to Researching Visual Materials. Los Angeles: Sage Publications, 2012. Print.

Critical Modalities

Recognize and describe six different critical modalities that art critics use to analyze and interpret artwork

LEARNING ACTIVITIES

The learning activities for this section include:

- Reading: Critical Modalities

Take time to review and reflect on this activity in order to improve your performance on the assessment for this section.

Reading: Critical Modalities

Introduction

From the first forms of art criticism in ancient Greece, the discussion of meaning in art has taken many directions. The professional art critic is one of the gatekeepers who, through their writing, endorse or reject particular kinds of art, whether in style, artistic ability, or message. In fact, a study of the different ways to look at art can tell us much about changing times and philosophies: the role of aesthetics, economics, and other cultural issues have a lot to do with the origin of these philosophical positions. Of course, none of them is completely true—they're simply different types of discourse. People approach meaning from different perspectives. The artworks sit silent while all around them the voices change. We are in a time when there are several, sometimes greatly conflicting, ways of thinking about meaning in art. Here are six different critical modalities art critics use as compasses to interpreting meaning:

Structural Criticism

We started this course with a discussion of what art *is*. That discussion was actually based on one of the ways to look at art: what is known as**structuralism**. Structuralism is based on the notion that our concept of reality is expressed through language and related systems of communication. On a larger scale, visualize culture as a structure whose foundation is language, speech and other forms of communication. When this approach is applied to the visual arts, the world of art becomes a collective human construction, where a single work needs to be judged within the framework supported by the whole structure of art. This structure is still based in language and knowledge and how we communicate ideas. I often use the example of the word "cowboy".

In your head: visualize a cowboy: then describe what you saw. What gender was your person? What race was this person? Now let's apply those answers to historical fact. The fact is that upwards of 60 percent of the historical cowboys in the United States were black slaves freed after the Civil War. Did you see your cowboy as white?

Your idea of cowboy might have come from film, which is an extremely different form of reality. The structural idea manifests itself when we look for meaning in art based on any preconceived ideas about it we already have in our mind. These preconceptions (or limitations) are shaped by language, social interaction and other cultural experiences.

Deconstructive Criticism

Deconstruction goes one step further and posits that any work of art can have many meanings attached to it, none of which is limited by a particular language or experience outside the work itself. In other words, the critic must reveal (deconstruct) the structured world in order to knock out any underpinnings of stereotypes, preconceptions, or myths that get in the way of true meaning. Taking the perspective of a deconstructive critic, we would view a portrait of Marilyn Monroe by pop artist Andy Warhol as an imaginary construct of what is real. As a popular culture icon, Marilyn Monroe the movie star was ubiquitous: in film, magazines, television and photographs. But Marilyn Monroe the person committed suicide in 1962 at the height of her stardom. In truth, the bright lights and celebrity of her Hollywood persona eclipsed the real Marilyn, someone who was troubled, confused and alone. Warhol's many portraits of her —each one made from the same publicity photograph —perpetuate the myth and cult of celebrity.

Formalist Criticism

Formalism is what we engaged in when we looked at the elements and principles of art. Formalism doesn't really care about what goes on outside the actual space of the work, but finds meaning in its use of materials. One of the champions of the formalist approach was Clement Greenberg. His writing stresses "medium specificity": the notion there is inherent meaning in the way materials are used to create the artwork. As is relates to painting and works on paper, the result is a focus on the two-dimensional surface. This is contrary to its traditional use as a platform for the illusion of depth. Formalism allows a more reasoned discussion of abstract and nonrepresentational art because we can approach them on their own terms, where the subject matter becomes the medium instead of something it represents. This is a good way to approach artworks from cultures we are not familiar with, though it has the tendency to make them purely decorative and devalue any deeper meaning. It also allows a kind of training in visual seeing, so it is still used in all studio arts and art appreciation courses.

Greenberg was a strong defender of the Abstract Expressionist style of painting that developed in the United States after World War 2. He referred to it as "pure painting" because of its insistence on the act of painting, eventually releasing it from its ties to representation.

Ideological Criticism

Ideological criticism is most concerned with the relationship between art and structures of power. It infers that art is embedded in a social, economic, and political structure that determines its final meaning. Born of the writings of Karl Marx, ideological criticism translates art and artifacts as symbols that reflect political ideals and reinforce one version of reality over another. A literal example of this perspective would view the *Lincoln Memorial* in Washington, D.C. as a testament to a political system that oppressed people because of race yet summoned the political will to set them free in the process of ending a Civil War.

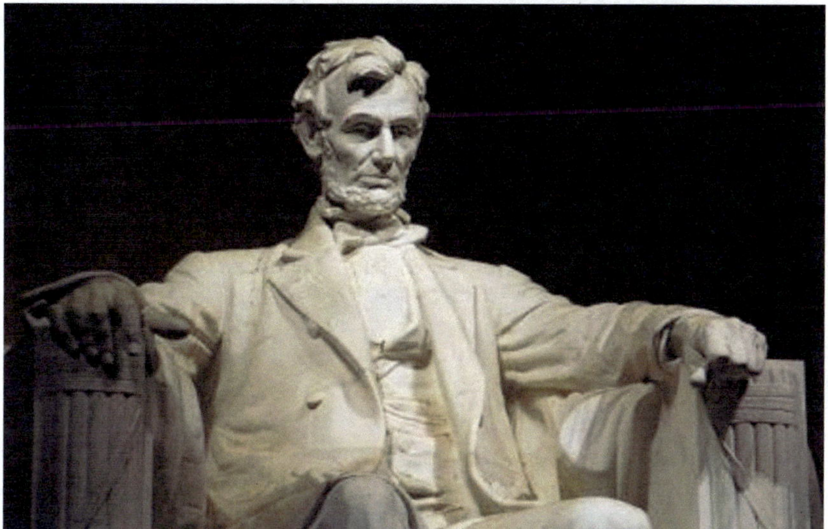

The Lincoln Memorial, Washington, D.C. Photo by Jeff Kubina and licensed through Creative Commons

In contrast, Ernst Ludwig Kirchner's painting *Franzi in Front of a Carved Chair* (below) from 1910 is also considered a symbol of artistic (hence, political) freedom. His Expressionist art – with its strong, sometimes arbitrary colors and rough approach to forms, was denounced by Nazi Germany as being "degenerate." The Degenerate Art Show of 1937 was a way for the German political establishment to label modern art as something evil and corrupt. Hitler's regime was only interested in heroic, representational and idealistic images, something Kirchner was rebelling *against*. Kirchner and other Expressionist artists were marginalized and many of their works destroyed by the authorities.

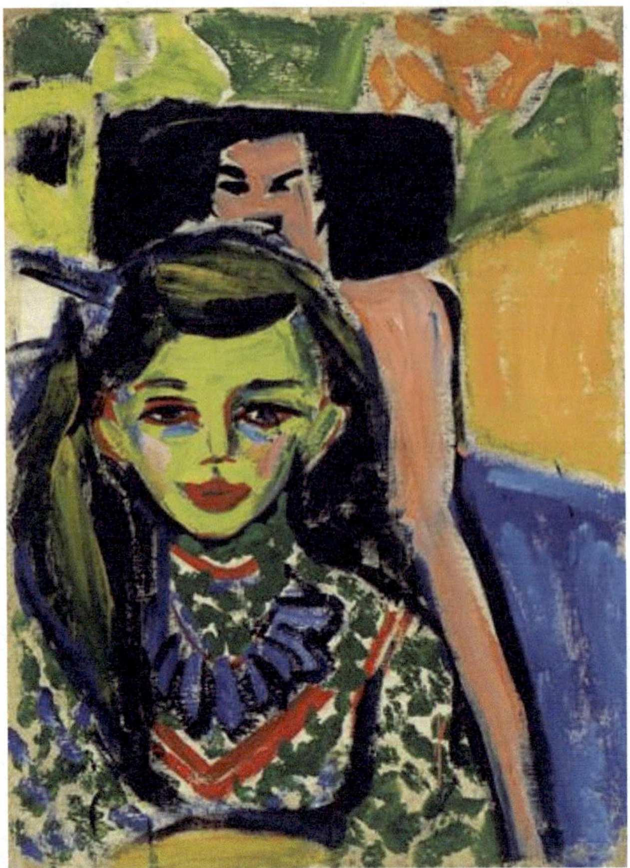

Ernst Ludwig Kirchner, Franzi In Front of A Carved Chair, 1910, oil on canvas, Thyssen-Bornemisza Museum, Madrid. This work is in the public domain

Psychoanalytic Criticism

Psychoanalytic criticism is the way we should look at artwork if we feel it is only about personal expression. The purest form of this criticism ranks the work of untrained and mentally ill artists as being just as important as any other art. It is in this way that the artist "inside" is more important than any other reason the art happens or the effect the art has. When discussing Vincent van Gogh you will often hear people allude to his mental state more than his actual artwork, experience, or career. This is a good example of psychoanalytic criticism. One of the problems in this type of criticism is that the critic is usually discussing issues the artist themselves may be totally unaware of (or deny).

Feminist Criticism

Feminist Criticism began in the 1970s as a response to the neglect of women artists over time and in historical writings. This form of criticism is specific to viewing art as an example of gender bias in historical western European culture, and views all work as a manifestation of this bias. Feminist criticism created whole movements in the art world (specifically performance based art), and has changed over the last few years to include all underrepresented groups. Examples of feminist art include Judy Chicago's large-scale installation *The Dinner Party* and the work of Nancy Spero.

In reality, all of these critical modalities hold some truth. Art is a multifaceted medium that contains influences from most all the characteristics of the culture it was created in, and some that transcend cultural environments. These modalities, along with the different levels of meaning we explored in this module, help us to unravel some of the mysteries inherent in works of art, and bring us closer to seeing how art expresses feelings, ideas and experiences that we all share. In our search it is important to be aware of all the issues involved, take aspects of each critical position depending upon the work being viewed, the environment (and context) you're seeing it in, and make up our own mind.

Cultural and World Perspective

Analyze and discuss artwork in relation to two different cultures; explain how those two cultures are linked from a wider, global perspective

<table>
<tr><td align="center">LEARNING ACTIVITIES</td></tr>
<tr><td>

The learning activities for this section include:

- Reading: Crossing cultures: The artwork of Kehinde Wiley

</td></tr>
</table>

Take time to review and reflect on this activity in order to improve your performance on the assessment for this section.

Reading: Crossing Cultures, the artwork of Kehinde Wiley

Coming across a Kehinde Wiley painting in a museum is an unforgettable experience. All at once you recognize visual conventions of historical European oil painting, including the theatrical poses of power, mixed with opulent patterns, the obsessive rendering of the texture and folds of fabric, and the rendering of lush light and color. Yet these portraits are also as clearly contemporary, as they are echoes from the past. In this, past and present collide into a moment that is both melodious and a cacophony you cannot turn away from. As Roberta Smith of the New York Times explains, "You can love or hate Kehinde Wiley's bright, brash, history-laden, kitsch-tinged portraits of confident, even imperious young black men and women. But it is hard to ignore them…"

As Wiley, an African-American raised in Los Angeles, explained in a 2015 interview with NPR's Audie Cornish,

"What I wanted to do was to look at the powerlessness that I felt as — and continue to feel at times — as a black man in the American streets. I know what it feels like to walk through the streets, knowing what it is to be in this body, and how certain people respond to that body. This dissonance between the world that you know, and then what you mean as a symbol in public, that strange, uncanny feeling of having to adjust for … this double consciousness."

Through-out history the power to be seen or not seen, to control your image, images that would likely outlast you, has been dominated by the wealthy and powerful. The type of historical paintings Wiley is mimicking were created primary at the behest and patronage of wealthy and powerful European men. Speaking of patrons of painting during the Renaissance, anthropologist Levi-Strauss explained it as, "…immense fortunes were being amassed in Florence and elsewhere, and rich Italian merchants looked upon painters as agents, who allowed them to confirm their possession of all that was beautiful and desirable in the world (Berger 86)." John Berger goes further in suggesting that the art of any period serves the idealogical interests of the ruling class (86). Africans, indigenous people, and the institutions of slavery and colonization that were unfolding globally when many of these traditional European master works were created, were rare subject matter. The dominance of Western art in art history has habituated us to expect the visual conventions of these paintings. To see bodies of African descent, in essence, inhabit scenes of European royalty or history painting creates a conflicted reaction of both familiarity and tension.

Wiley exploits the tropes of art history and provocatively flips our expectations of visual conventions, scenes and narratives only represented by white bodies, are replaced with the supple bodies of black or brown youths (Guzman). More recently he has expanded the portraits beyond where he began in Brooklyn, New York, to a contemporary global interplay with art historic traditions, by using men and women from Africa, Brazil, Israel, Palestine as portrait subjects (Guzman).

Works Cited

Berger, John. *Ways of Seeing*. London: British Broadcasting Services and Penguin Books, 1972. Print

Guzman, Alissa. *Kehinde Wiley's "Politics of Perception"*. Hyperallergic, 22 April 2015. Web. 21 August 2015.

Smith, Roberta. *Review: 'Kehinde Wiley: A New Republic' at the Brooklyn Museum*. New York Times, 19 February 2015. Web. 21 August 2015.

The Exquisite Dissonance of Kehinde Wiley. National Public Radio, 22 May 2015. Web. 21 August 2015.

Symbolism

Recognize what a symbol is and and differentiate how semiotics and iconography are used to decipher symbols in artwork and other types of visual culture.

<table><tr><td>LEARNING ACTIVITIES</td></tr><tr><td>

The learning activities for this section include:

- Reading: Analyzing Symbols

</td></tr></table>

Take time to review and reflect on each of these activities in order to improve your performance on the assessment for this section.

Reading: Analyzing Symbols

Iconography

Iconography was developed by art historian Erwin Panofsky, as a means of expanding beyond formal analysis, and focusing on analyzing subject matter in artwork, specifically symbols whose meaning is understood by a people or culture in that specific time (Rose 202, Sayre 32). For example, in the Western world we are familiar with what a Buddha statue looks like, but most Western people likely have no idea that the position of the hands in the statue carries symbolic meaning (Sayre 33). If you are a Buddhist however, you would read a specific meaning into the hand gesture and position. Symbolic meanings in artwork may also be lost over time even within the culture that created them (Sayre 35).

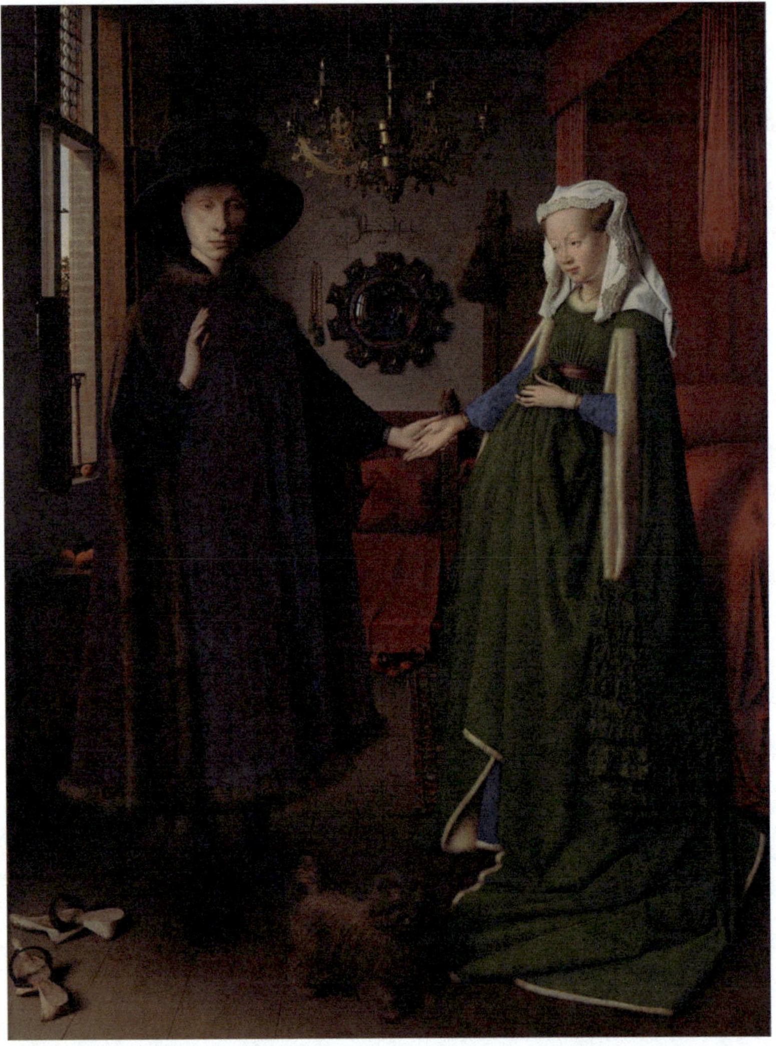

Jan van Eyck, Arnolfini Portrait, 1434, oil on canvas. Work is in the public domain.

Jan van Eyck's painting, *Giovanni Arnolfini and his wife Giovanna Cenami*, from 1434, is often used as a prototype example for iconographic analysis, and the conflicts that arise within it. As a painter, Van Eyck was revered for his incredible ability to mimic realism and the effects of light. The painting's many symbols, some of Christian origin, have been a source of some debate. It was widely accepted as a painting representing a marriage, but recent controversy suggests it is more a record of engagement than a wedding portrait. In van Eyck's time, a woman laying her hands in the palm of a male, as she so conspicuously does in the painting, was understood to be an agreement to wed (Sayre 35). Above the mirror in the center of the background are the words "Jan van Eyck has been here, 1434." To contemporary ears this almost sounds like a bit of playful graffiti, but it also clearly establishes the painter as a witness to the event being painted (Sayre 35).

Additional resources:

- More on Jan van Eyck
- Image of Giovanni Arnolfini and his wife Giovanna Cenami
- A recent article on the Arnolfini wedding portrait

Iconography shares similarities to semiotics in interpreting signs (in semiotics signs can be symbols) on both a denotive and connotative level. Iconography is typically used in analyzing works from the past, as Gillian Rose notes, typically Western figurative images from the 16th through 18th centuries (202). While semiotics is more often used to analyze more contemporary visual culture, like advertising.

Artists continue to use symbolic visual language. Though artist Jean-Michele Basquiat's life and career were tragically cut short by a drug overdose, he developed a rich vocabulary of symbolism that mixed private and public meanings. Using his neo-expressionist style he drew inspiration from prominent African Americans, such as Dizzy Gillespie, Muhammad Ali, and Sugar Ray Robinson (Rosenberg). As Sayre points out, central to his personal iconography was a three pointed crown, a symbol he related to himself, but also his African American heroes (37). He was familiar with the *Symbol Sourcebook: An Authoritative Guide to International Graphic Symbols*, by Henry Dreyfuss, and was drawn to the section on "hobo signs," in particular the "X" which within the hobo culture was a signal that a place was okay (Sayre 37). Of course, the 'X' is a common symbol with multiple meanings. An "X" could be used to mark a spot and constitute its importance, or in essence, to eliminate something by crossing it out. And, according to Sayre, this is often the difficult and ambiguous position Basquiat's African American heroes found themselves in, in 20th century America (37). In his 1982 painting *Charles the First*, Charles is a reference to both Charlie Parker and Charles I of England, who was beheaded by Protestants (Sayre 37). Included in the painting is the text, "Most kings get their head cut off."

Additional resources:

- Read more on Jean-Michele Basquiat
- Examples of his use of symbolism
- A more in-depth reading "Iconographic Analysis" by Marjorie Munsterberg

Semiotics

The formalism you practiced in module two is focused on compositional analysis by being descriptive. Semiotics offers another way of analyzing images, be they found in artwork or another type of visual culture, like advertising. Semiotics is the study of signs. In semiotics the basic unit is the sign. Signs are representations that have meanings beyond what they literally represent. Signs can come in visual or auditory form- as in language or sounds. Signs are everywhere, not just in art. Semiotics offers a way to break an image into its constituent parts- its signs, and trace how they relate to each other, and other systems of meaning (Rose 105).

Signified and Signifier

In semiotics the image itself is the focus and the most important site of meaning (Rose 108). The signs in an image are analyzed into two parts, the signified and signifier. The signified is the concept or thing the representation stands in for. The signifier is the representation. For example, in a photograph with a baby in it— the baby is the signifier, and the signified could be youth, or the future, or some other association that we make with the representation of a baby.

Icon, index, symbol

There are three basic types of signs: icon, index, and symbol. Icons bear a very close visual relationship to the thing they represent. An icon of a woman might be a photograph of an actual woman. An indexical sign points to the thing it represents or bears some relationship to the thing it represents, but is one step removed. An example of an indexical sign of a woman is the simple illustration of a woman that you find on restrooms designated for women. A symbol is arbitrary, and bears no relation to the thing it represents. An example of a symbol for women is the circle/cross shape that signifies the female gender.

Female gender symbol

A short video on Semiotics and the Icon/Index/Symbol distinctions:

- https://youtu.be/rEgxTKUP_WI

Another example of a symbol is the American flag. If you were raised in America, you are taught that it stands for the country America and national pride, and possibly other meanings like freedom, but how the flag looks is arbitrary. It could just as easily have taken on some other graphic representation, and still have been coded with those meanings, just like the flags of other countries share a similar national significance in those other cultures.

Denotative and Connotative meanings

Signs can have denotative, or literal meaning, and connotative meanings that are in addition to their literal meaning. Signs exist in relationship to other signs. Signs also connect to wider systems of meaning that are conventionalized meanings shared by particular groups of people or cultures (Rose 128). This is referred to as codes. Because signs can often be polysemic, or have multiples meanings, unpacking their meanings fully can be very complex. It is accepted, however, that within specific groups/ cultures, and particular times, there are often preferred or dominant readings of signs that are interpreted in ways intended to retain the institutional/political/idealogical order imprinted on them for that time (Rose 133).

Advertisers make design choices with transference in mind. They intend for specific meanings to be transferred from one sign to another. Think of how often you have seen a new car ad where the car and some kind sexualized representation of a woman are paired together. What is the intended transference of meaning between these two signs, the car and the woman? Consider how focus groups are used to figure out what will be the most effective tactic to use in selling a product to the target consumer. Focus groups are a way of researching the target consumer's codes. What signs will they pay attention to and interpret in such a way that will ultimately manufacture desire for that product?

Steps in Conducting a Basic Semiotic Analysis:

- Decide what the signs are.
- Decide what they signify 'in themselves'.
- Consider how they relate to other signs.
- Explore their connections to wider systems of meaning, from codes to ideologies.

Consider these questions in relation to this 2009 Levis Ad for their "Go Forth" campaign directed by Cary Fukunaga for Portland's Weiden+Kennedy Advertising Agency.

- https://youtu.be/_uBsV8wAEhw

Styles of dress are kinds of signs. In Western culture we consider the suit to be a visual signal for business. In connection, people who work in white collar jobs are sometimes referred to informally as "suits." In the ad there is a man in a suit, presumably a white collar worker. We might infer by other signs like the limousine that he is wealthy or powerful. How does the treatment of the man in the suit compare with the other figures who appear in the ad? The neon sign of the word "America" is partially submerged. What does this signify? Through out the ad their are loud banging sounds. What do these auditory signs signify? Considering the signs in this ad, what do you think Levi's wants you to associate with their brand and products?

Works Cited

Rose, Gillian. *Visual Methodologies: An Introduction to Researching Visual Materials*. Los Angeles: Sage Publications, 2012. Print.

Rosenberg, Bonnie. *Jean-Michele Basquiat, American Painter*. The Art Story. Web. 18 August 2015.

Sayre, Henry. *A World of Art, Sixth edition*. Boston: Prentice Hall, 2010. Print.

Reading: Iconographic Analysis

Read "Iconographic Analysis" by Marjorie Munsterberg: http://www.saylor.org/site/wp-content/uploads/2011/04/Iconographic-Analysis.pdf

Putting It Together

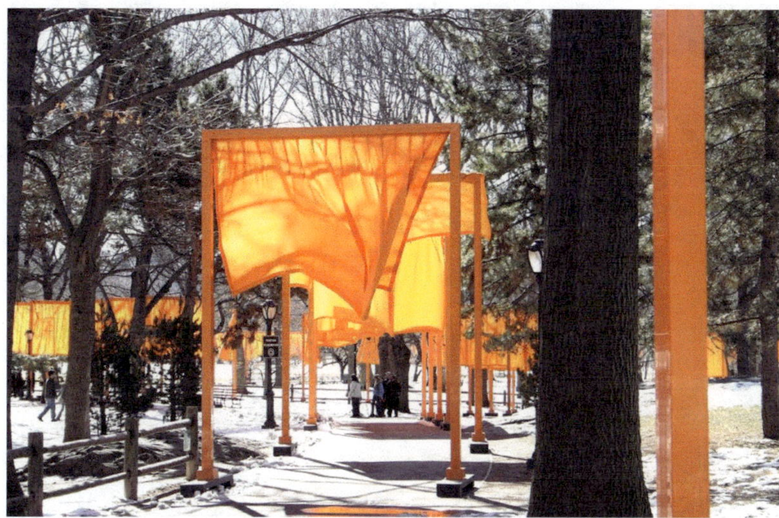
Christo, The Gates, New York City

All communication, including art as a form of visual culture, takes place in multiple contexts. In the beginning we discussed Robert Capa's photograph, *The Falling Soldier*, and how the context of its viewing in America might have impacted what American viewers took away from the photograph. Now let's use the knowledge of different contexts to analyze a more recent artwork, the 2005 installation in Central Park, New York, titled *The Gates*, by artists Christo and Jeanne-Claude. At the time of its unveiling, many people pointed out the similarities to the Fushimi Inari shrine in Kyoto, Japan (Jennifer Lee, "Nostalgia Draped in Orange: Remembering 'The Gates,'" nytimes.com).

When questioned about this in 2008, Christo acknowledged knowing about the Japanese shrine, but quickly pointed out it was not his inspiration for *The Gates*. His claim demonstrates the artist's perspective. However, if Japanese (or other) viewers had previously experienced the Inari Shrine, their experience of The Gates would have been much different from most American viewers' (Sayre, 3). Despite Christo's perspective on his own work, there is still a contextual difference for the American viewer versus the Japanese viewer of the same artwork.

Consider what unique aspects of your life (age, race, gender, geography, economic status, etc.) form contexts that influence how and where you encounter art and how you interpret those experiences of art.

Works Cited

Lee, Jennifer. "Nostalgia Draped in Orange: Remembering 'The Gates.'" *New York Times*. 2008. Web. 31 May 2015.

Sayre, Henry. *A World of Art*, Sixth edition. Boston: Prentice Hall, 2010. Print.

CHAPTER 4: PERIODS IN ART HISTORY

Why It Matters

Identify and explain the periods of art history; identify and discuss period artworks (course level learning objective)

Introduction

We now embark on studying art in historical context. Consider this statement by James W. Loewen about the importance of studying American history:

> Even when an event seems to be new, the causes of the acts and feelings are deeply embedded in the past. Thus, to understand an event—an election, an act of terror, a policy decision about the environment, whatever—we must start in the past (11).

In this sense, artwork can be taken to resemble a kind of event. To develop a deep understanding of art, we must consider it within the trajectory of history and within the most basic contexts—time and place. How is an artwork from one period of history an affirmation, rejection, or some more nuanced continuation of what came before it? Watch this video of a posthumous installation of a work by Felix Gonzalez-Torres, *Candies (Portrait of Ross in L.A.)*:

- https://youtu.be/37bSb-aQ4BM

At the end of this module we will discuss how this art installation is not only emblematic of a specific time and place, but it is also part of the continuum of art history. Consider these questions as you work through this section: How do artworks build on what came before them? How and why did Marcel Duchamp's "readymades" represent a kind of seismic shift in the world of art? Can they be considered as "events" that had a profound impact on what kinds of things are considered art today? How is this installation by Gonzalez-Torres a product of the time in which it was created?

Works Cited

Loewen, James. *Teaching What Really Happened*. New York: Teacher's College Press, 2010. Print.

MODULE LEARNING OUTCOMES

- Identify and describe key characteristics and defining events of art from prehistory
- Identify and describe key characteristics and defining events of art from the Age of Faith
- Identify and describe key characteristics and defining events of art from the Renaissance through Baroque periods
- Identify and describe key characteristics and defining events of art from the eighteenth and nineteenth centuries
- Identify and describe key characteristics and defining events of art from the twentieth century to the present
- Compare and contrast two works of art from a similar period
- Compare and contrast two works of art from different cultures and periods in terms of formal qualities, context, and

meaning
- Analyze a modern work of art and describe how it borrows from or is influenced by an earlier work of art

How to Study for the Performance Assessments (PA)

The PA in this module is answering short answer and short essay questions. Read through the PA for this module BEFORE you begin the module content. This module is the longest in the course so there are more questions on it than other modules. Due to this, I highly suggest you print the PA questions out so you can follow along and take notes as you read through the content related to each historical period. As you read through the module content, take notes on the subjects or anything that you find relevant to the PA questions. Be sure to document the page or place in the content where you found each note, in case you need to return to that content, or need to ask me a specific question citing module content. Once you are ready to complete the PA, you will have these notes to help you answer the questions thoughtfully.

OK, let's get started!

Key Characteristics of Art: Prehistory

Identify and describe key characteristics and defining events of art from prehistory

LEARNING ACTIVITIES

The learning activities for this section include:

- Reading: Prehistoric Art: Paleolithic Origins
- Reading: The Neolithic Revolution
- Reading: Ancient Near East
- Reading: Ancient Egypt
- Reading: Ancient Greece and Rome

Take time to review and reflect on each of these activities in order to improve your performance on the assessment for this section.

Reading: Prehistoric Art: Paleolithic Origins

Humans make art. We do this for many reasons and with whatever technologies are available to us. Extremely old, non-representational ornamentation has been found across Africa. The oldest firmly-dated example is a collection of 82,000 year old Nassarius snail shells found in Morocco that are pierced and covered with red ochre. Wear patterns suggest that they may have been strung beads. Nassarius shell beads found in Israel may be more than 100,000 years old and in the Blombos cave in South Africa, pierced shells and small pieces of ochre (red Haematite) etched with simple geometric patterns have been found in a 75,000-year-old layer of sediment.

The oldest known representational imagery comes from the Aurignacian culture of the Upper Paleolithic period. Archeological discoveries across a broad swath of Europe (especially Southern France, Northern Spain, and Swabia, in Germany) include over two hundred caves with spectacular Aurignacian paintings, drawings and sculpture that are among the earliest undisputed examples of representational image-making. The oldest of these is a 2.4-inch tall female figure carved out of mammoth ivory that was found in six fragments in the Hohle Fels cave near Schelklingen in southern Germany. It dates to 35,000 B.C.E. The caves at Chauvet-Pont-d'Arc (see the image below), Lascaux, Pech Merle, and Altamira contain the best known examples of prehistoric painting and drawing. Here are remarkably evocative renderings of animals and some humans that employ a complex mix of naturalism and abstraction. Archeologists that study Paleolithic (old stone age) era humans, believe that the paintings discovered in 1994, in the cave at Chauvet-Pont-d'Arc in the Ardèche valley in France, are more than 30,000 years old. The images found at Lascaux and Altamira are more recent, dating to approximately 15,000 B.C.E. The paintings at Pech Merle date to both 25,000 and 15,000 B.C.E.

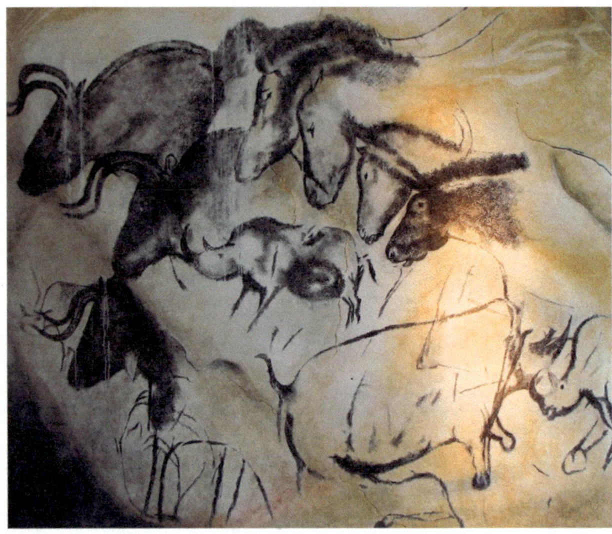

What can we really know about the creators of these paintings and what the images originally meant? These are questions that are difficult enough when we study art made only 500 years ago. It is much more perilous to assert meaning for the art of people who shared our anatomy but had not yet developed the cultures or linguistic structures that shaped who we have become. Do the tools of art history even apply? Here is evidence of a visual language that collapses the more than 1,000 generations that separate us, but we must be cautious. This is especially so if we want understand the people that made this art as a way to understand ourselves. The desire to speculate based on what we see and the physical evidence of the caves is wildly seductive.

The cave at Chauvet-Pont-d'Arc is over 1,000 feet in length with two large chambers. Carbon samples date the charcoal used to depict the two head-to-head Rhinoceroses (see the image above, bottom right) to between 30,340 and 32,410 years before 1995 when the samples were taken. The cave's drawings depict other large animals including horses, mammoths, musk ox, ibex, reindeer, aurochs, megaceros deer, panther, and owl (scholars note that these animals were not then a normal part of people's diet). Photographs show that the drawing shown above is very carefully rendered but may be misleading. We see a group of horses, rhinos and bison and we see them as a group, overlapping and skewed in scale. But the photograph distorts the way these animal figures would have been originally seen. The bright electric lights used by the photographer create a broad flat scope of vision; how different to see each animal emerge from the dark under the flickering light cast by a flame.

In a 2009 presentation at UC San Diego, Dr. Randell White, Professor of Anthropology at NYU, suggested that the overlapping horses pictured above might represent the same horse over time, running, eating, sleeping, etc. Perhaps these are far more sophisticated representations than we have imagined. There is another drawing at Chauvet-Pont-d'Arc that cautions us against ready assumptions. It has been interpreted as depicting the thighs and genitals of a woman but there is also a drawing of a bison and a lion and the images are nearly intertwined. In addition to the drawings, the cave is littered with the skulls and bones of cave bear and the track of a wolf. There is also a foot print thought to have been made by an eight-year-old boy.

Reading: The Neolithic Revolution

A Settled Life

When people think of the Neolithic era, they often think of Stonehenge, the iconic image of this early era. Dating to approximately 3000 B.C.E. and set on Salisbury Plain in England, it is a structure larger and more complex than anything built before it in Europe.

Stonehenge is an example of the cultural advances brought about by the Neolithic revolution—the most important development in human history. The way we live today, settled in homes, close to other people in towns and cities, protected by laws, eating food grown on farms, and with leisure time to learn, explore and invent is all a result of the Neolithic revolution, which occurred approximately 11,500-5,000 years ago. The revolution which led to our way of life was the development of the technology needed to plant and harvest crops and to domesticate animals.

Before the Neolithic revolution, it's likely you would have lived with your extended family as a nomad, never staying anywhere for more than a few months, always living in temporary shelters, always searching for food and never owning anything you couldn't easily pack in a pocket or a sack. The change to the Neolithic way of life was huge and led to many of the pleasures (lots of food, friends and a comfortable home) that we still enjoy today.

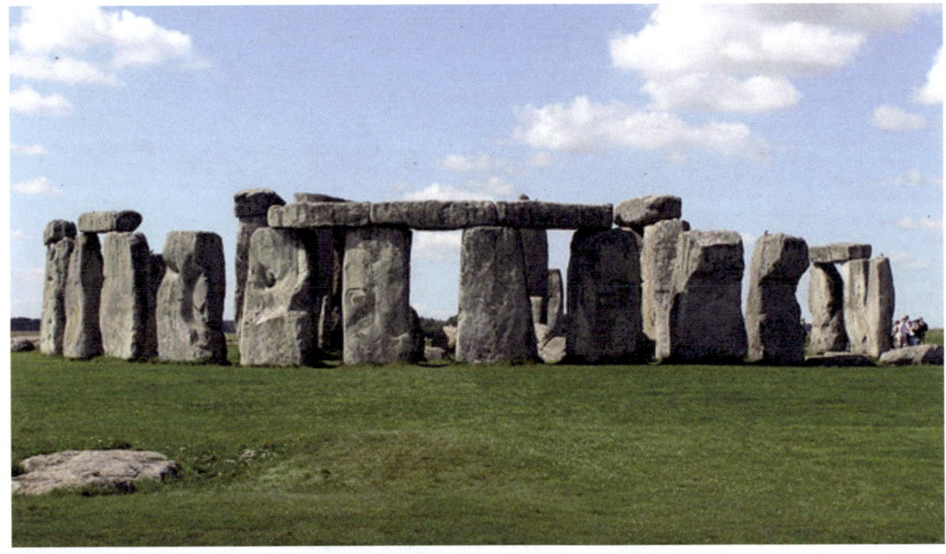

Stonehenge, c. 3,000 B.C.E., Salisbury Plain, England

Neolithic Art

The massive changes in the way people lived also changed the types of art they made. Neolithic sculpture became bigger, in part, because people didn't have to carry it around anymore; pottery became more widespread and was used to store food harvested from farms. This is when alcohol was invented and when architecture, and its interior and exterior decoration, first appears. In short, people settle down and begin to live in one place, year after year.

It seems very unlikely that Stonehenge could have been made by earlier, Paleolithic, nomads. It would have been a waste to invest so much time and energy building a monument in a place to which they might never return or might only return infrequently. After all, the effort to build it was extraordinary. Stonehenge is approximately 320 feet in circumference and the stones which compose the outer ring weigh as much as 50 tons; the small stones, weighing as much as 6 tons, were quarried from as far away as 450 miles. The use or meaning of Stonehenge is not clear, but the design, planning and execution could have only been carried out by a culture in which authority was unquestioned. Here is a culture that was able to rally hundreds of people to perform very hard work for extended periods of time. This is another characteristic of the Neolithic era.

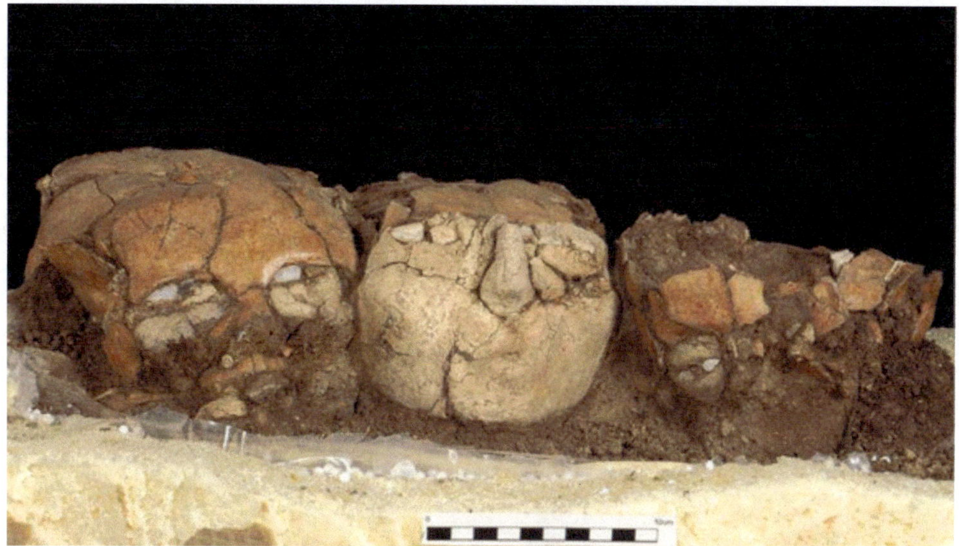

Skulls with plaster and shell from the Pre-Pottery Neolithic B, 6,000-7,000 B.C.E., found at the Yiftah'el archeological site in the Lower Galilee, Israel

Plastered Skulls

The Neolithic period is also important because it is when we first find good evidence for religious practice, a perpetual inspiration for the fine arts. Perhaps most fascinating are the plaster skulls found around the area of the Levant, at six sites, including Jericho in Israel. At this time in the Neolithic, c. 7000-6,000 B.C.E., people were often buried under the floors of homes, and in some cases their skulls were removed and covered with plaster in order to create very life-like faces, complete with shells inset for eyes and paint to imitate hair and moustaches.

The traditional interpretation of these the skulls has been that they offered a means of preserving and worshiping male ancestors. However, recent research has shown that among the sixty-one plastered skulls that have been found, there is a generous number that come from the bodies of women and children. Perhaps the skulls are not so much religious objects but rather powerful images made to aid in mourning lost loved ones. Neolithic peoples didn't have written language, so we may never know.[1]

[1] The earliest example of writing develops in Sumer in Mesopotamia in the late 4th millennium B.C.E. However, there are scholars that believe that earlier proto-writing developed during the Neolithic period.

- https://youtu.be/ld8kHvz1yN4

Reading: Ancient Near East

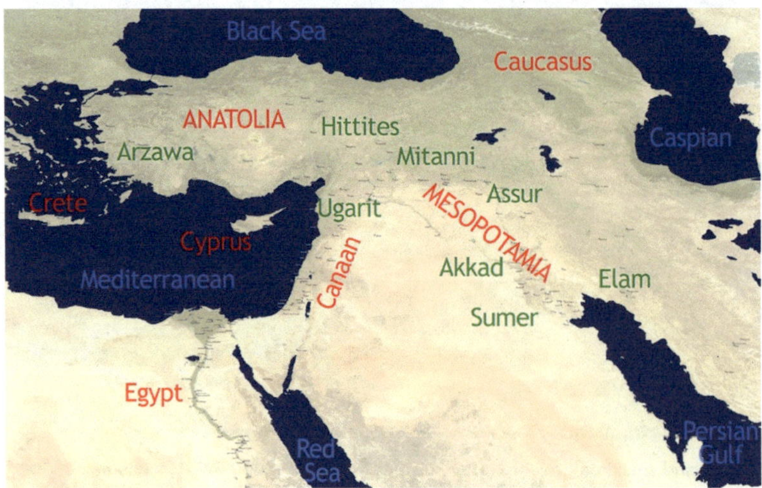

The Cradle of Civilization

Mesopotamia, the area between the Tigris and Euphrates Rivers (in modern day Iraq), is often referred to as the cradle of civilization because it is the first place where complex urban centers grew. The history of Mesopotamia, however, is inextricably tied to the greater region, which is comprised of the modern nations of Egypt, Iran, Syria, Jordan, Israel, Lebanon, the Gulf states and Turkey. We often refer to this region as the Near or Middle East.

What's in a Name?

Why is this region named this way? What is it in the middle of or near to? It is the proximity of these countries to the West (to Europe) that led this area to be termed "the *near* east." Ancient Near Eastern Art has long been part of the history of Western art, but history didn't have to be written this way. It is largely because of the West's interests in the Biblical "Holy Land" that ancient Near Eastern materials have been be regarded as part of the Western canon of the history of art.

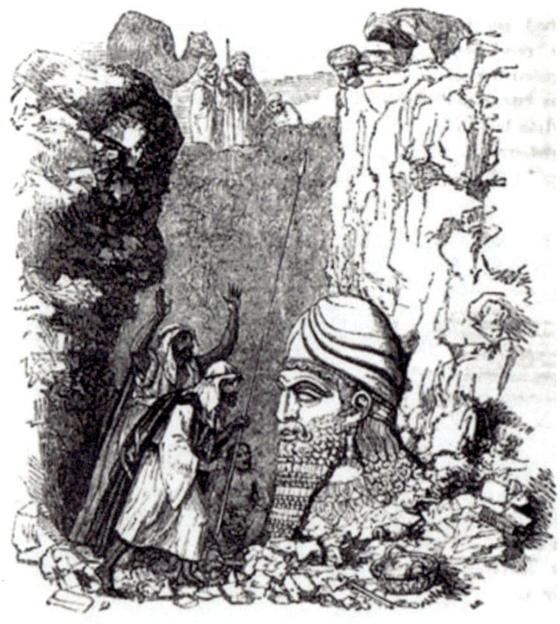

Discovery of the Colossal Head.

The Land of the Bible

An interest in finding the locations of cities mentioned in the Bible (such as Nineveh and Babylon) inspired the original English and French nineteenth century archaeological expeditions to the Near East. These sites were discovered and their excavations revealed to the world a style of art which had been lost.

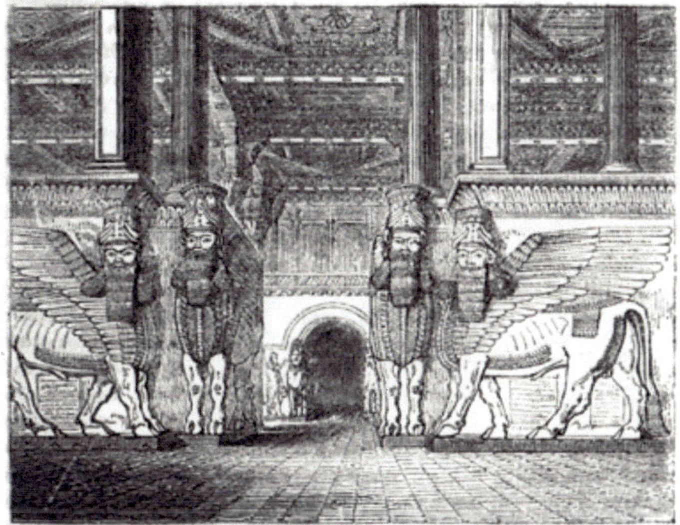

Entrance to Nineveh Court.

Illustrations from: Sir Austen Henry Layard, The Nineveh Court in the Crystal Palace, 1854

The excavations inspired *The Nineveh Court* at the 1851 World's Fair in London and a style of decorative art and architecture called Assyrian Revival. Ancient Near Eastern art remains popular today; in 2007 a 2.25 inch high, early 3rd millennium limestone sculpture, the *Guennol Lioness*, was sold for 57.2 million dollars, the second most expensive piece of sculpture sold at that time.

A Complex History

The history of the Ancient Near East is complex and the names of rulers and locations are often difficult to read, pronounce and spell. Moreover, this is a part of the world which today remains remote from the West culturally while political tensions have impeded mutual understanding. However, once you get a handle on the general geography of the area and its history, the art reveals itself as uniquely beautiful, intimate and fascinating in its complexity.

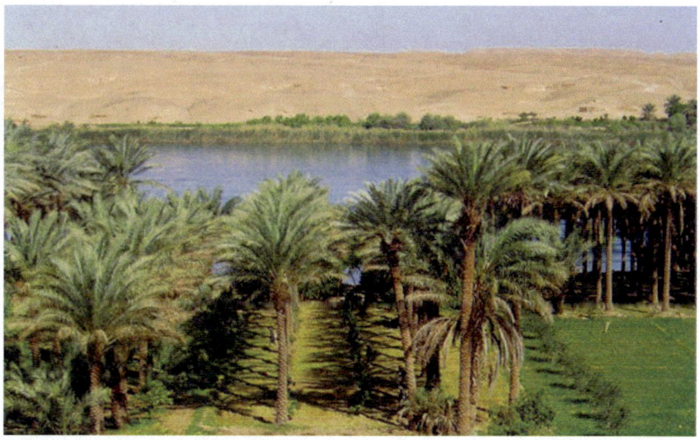

The Euphrates River in 2005

Geography and the Growth of Cities

Mesopotamia remains a region of stark geographical contrasts: vast deserts rimmed by rugged mountain ranges, punctuated by lush oases. Flowing through this topography are rivers and it was the irrigation systems that drew off the water from these rivers, specifically in southern Mesopotamia, that provided the support for the very early urban centers here.

The region lacks stone (for building) and precious metals and timber. Historically, it has relied on the long-distance trade of its agricultural products to secure these materials. The large-scale irrigation systems and labor required for extensive farming was managed by a centralized authority. The early development of this authority, over large numbers of people in an urban center, is really what distinguishes Mesopotamia and gives it a special position in the history of Western culture. Here, for the first time, thanks to ample food and a strong administrative class, the West develops a very high level of craft specialization and artistic production.

Sumerian Art

The region of southern Mesopotamia is known as Sumer, and it is in Sumer that we find some of the oldest known cities, including Ur and Uruk.

Uruk

Prehistory ends with Uruk, where we find some of the earliest written records. This large city-state (and it environs) was largely dedicated to agriculture and eventually dominated southern Mesopotamia. Uruk perfected Mesopotamian irrigation and administration systems.

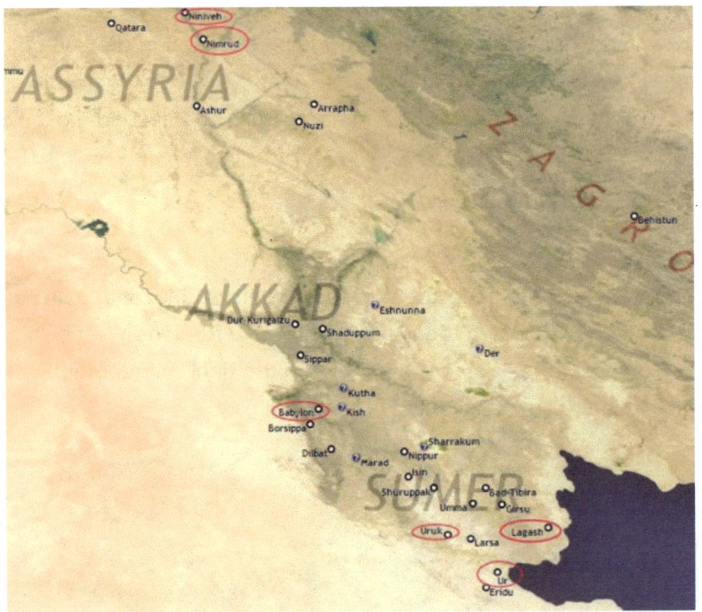

Uruk is circled in the region of Sumer.

An Agricultural Theocracy

Within the city of Uruk, there was a large temple complex dedicated to Innana, the patron goddess of the city. The City-State's agricultural production would be "given" to her and stored at her temple. Harvested crops would then be processed (grain ground into flour, barley fermented into beer) and given back to the citizens of Uruk in equal share at regular intervals.

The head of the temple administration, the chief priest of Innana, also served as political leader, making Uruk the first known theocracy.

We know many details about this theocratic administration because the Sumarians left numerous documents in cuneiform script.

These tablets made of dried mud and many were sealed in clay envelopes and signed using cylinder seals. A cylinder seals is a small pierced object like a long bead that is carved in reverse (intaglio) with a unique image and sometimes the name of the owner.

The seal was rolled over the soft clay of a tablet and functioned as a signature. The minute images on these seals use a system of symbolic representation that identifies the political status of the owner.

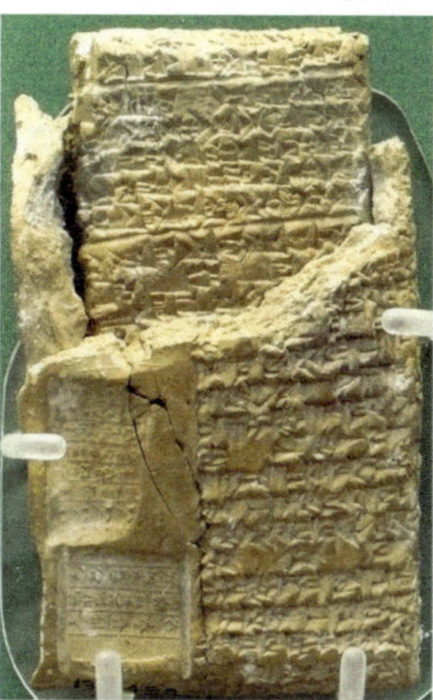

Cuneiform tablet (above), still in its clay case: legal case from Niqmepuh, King of Iamhad (Aleppo), 1720 B.C.E., 3.94 x 2" (British Museum)

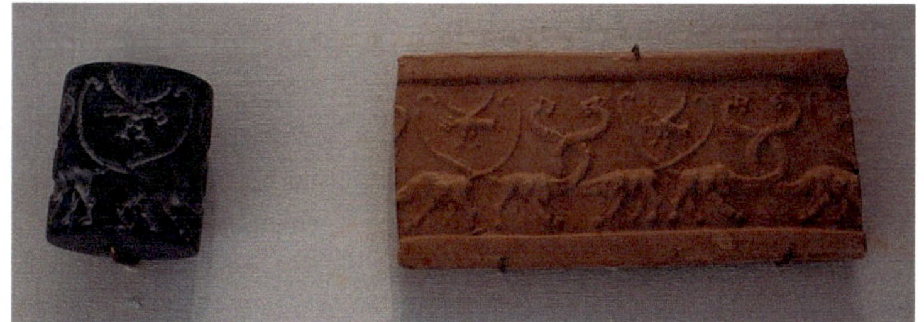

Lapis Lazuli Cylinder Seal with a modern impression, From Ur, southern Iraq, c. 2600 B.C.E. (British Museum)

Reading: Ancient Egypt

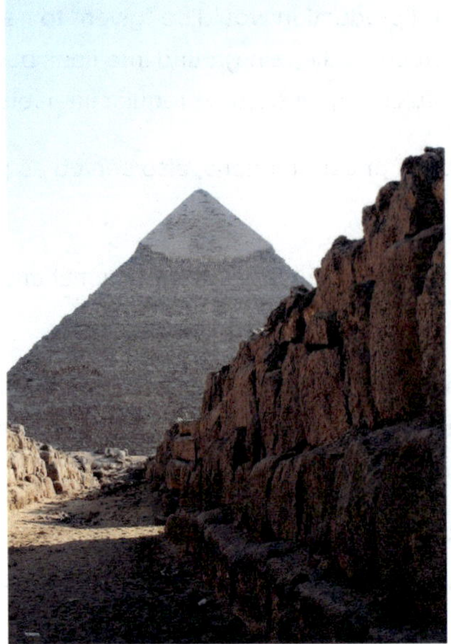

Pyramid of Khafre at Giza, c. 2520-2494 (right). Photo: Dr Amy Calvert, CC BY-NC

Egypt's impact on later cultures was immense. You could say that Egypt provided the building blocks for Greek and Roman culture, and, through them, influenced all of the Western tradition.

Today, Egyptian imagery, concepts, and perspectives are found everywhere; you will find them in architectural forms, on money, and in our day to day lives. Many cosmetic surgeons, for example, use the silhouette of Queen Nefertiti (whose name means "the beautiful one has come") in their advertisements.

This introduction will provide you with the primary filters to view and understand ancient Egypt.

Longevity

Ancient Egyptian civilization lasted for more than 3000 years and showed an incredible amount of continuity. That is more than 15 times the age of the United States, and consider how often our culture shifts; less than 10 years ago, there was no Facebook, Twitter, or Youtube.

While today we consider the Greco-Roman period to be in the distant past, it should be noted that Cleopatra VII's reign (which ended in 30 BCE) is closer to our own time than it was to that of the construction of the pyramids of Giza. It took humans nearly 4000 years to build something–anything–taller than the Great Pyramids. Contrast that span to the modern era; we get excited when a record lasts longer than a decade.

Consistency and Stability

Egypt's stability is in stark contrast to the Ancient Near East of the same period, which endured an overlapping series of cultures and upheavals with amazing regularity.

The earliest royal monuments, such as the Narmer Palette carved around 3100 B.C.E., display identical royal costumes and poses as those seen on later rulers, even Ptolemaic kings on their temples 3000 years later.

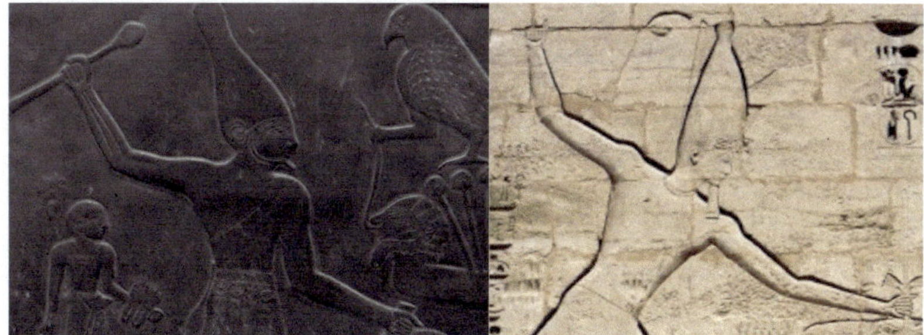

Palette of Narmer, c. 3000-2920 B.C.E. (left) and Ramses III smiting at Medinet Habu (1160 B.C.E.) (right)

A vast amount of Egyptian imagery, especially royal imagery that was governed by decorum (a sense of what was 'appropriate'), remained stupefyingly consistent throughout its history. This is why, especially to the untrained eye, their art appears extremely static—and in terms of symbols, gestures, and the way the body is rendered, it was. It was intentional. The Egyptians were aware of their consistency, which they viewed as stability, divine balance, and clear evidence of the correctness of their culture.

This consistency was closely related to a fundamental belief that depictions had an impact beyond the image itself—tomb scenes of the deceased receiving food, or temple scenes of the king performing perfect rituals for the gods—were functionally causing those things to occur in the divine realm. If the image of the bread loaf was omitted from the deceased's table, they had no bread in the Afterlife; if the king was depicted with the incorrect ritual implement, the ritual was incorrect and this could have dire consequences. This belief led to an active resistance to change in codified depictions.

The earliest recorded tourist graffiti on the planet came from a visitor from the time of Ramses II who left their appreciative mark at the already 1300-year-old site of the Step Pyramid at Saqqara, the earliest of the massive royal stone monuments. They were understandably impressed by the works of their ancestors and endeavored to continue that ancient legacy.

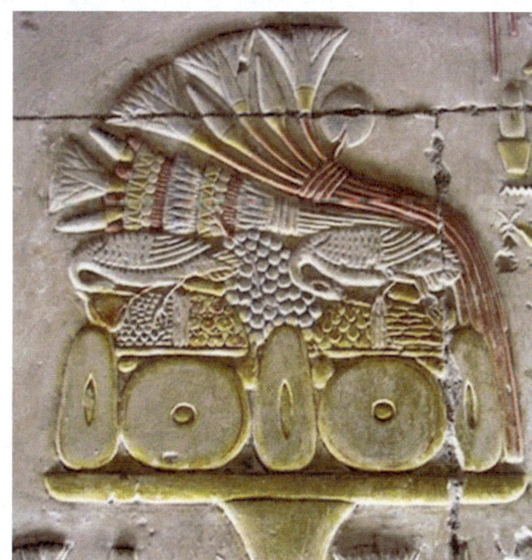

Painted raised relief offering table in the Temple of Seti I at Abydos (New Kingdom). Photo: Dr Amy Calvert, CC BY-NC

Geography

Egypt is a land of duality and cycles, both in topography and culture. The geography is almost entirely rugged, barren desert, except for an explosion of green that straddles either side of the Nile as it flows the length of the country. The river emerges from far to the south, deep in Africa, and empties into the Mediterranean sea in the north after spreading from a single channel into a fan-shaped system, known as a delta, at its northernmost section.

The influence of this river on Egyptian culture and development cannot be overstated—without its presence, the civilization would have been entirely different, and most likely entirely elsewhere. The Nile provided not only a constant source of life-giving water, but created the fertile lands that fed the growth of this unique (and uniquely resilient) culture.

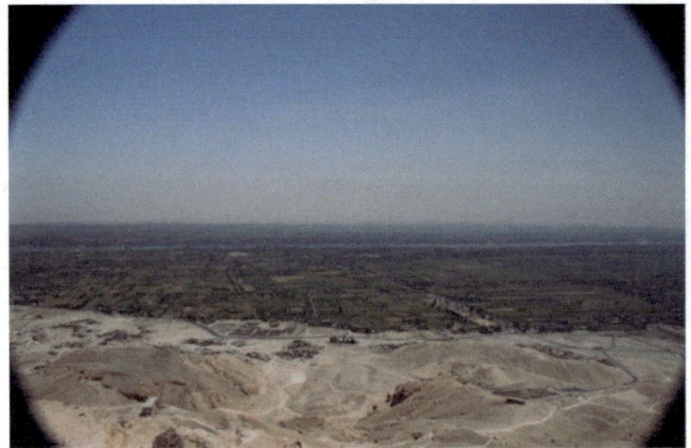

View from the high peak of the Theban hills showing the sharp delineation between the lush Valley and the barren desert. Photo: Dr Amy Calvert, CC BY-NC

Each year, fed by melting snows in the far-off headlands, the river overflowed its banks in an annual flood that covered the ground with a rich, black silt and produced incredibly fertile fields. The Egyptians referred to this as *Kemet*, the "black lands", and contrasted this dense, dark soil against the *Deshret*, the "red lands" of the sterile desert; the line between these zones was (and in most cases still is) a literal line. The visual effect is stark, appearing almost artificial in its precision.

Time—Cyclical and Linear

The annual inundation of the Nile was also a reliable, and measurable, cycle that helped form their concept of the passage of time. In fact, the calendar we use today is derived from one developed by the ancient Egyptians.

They divided the year into 3 seasons: *akhet* 'inundation', *peret* 'growing/emergence', and *shemw* 'harvest.' Each season was, in turn, divided into four 30-day months. Although this annual cycle, paired with the daily solar cycle that is so evident in the desert, led to a powerful drive to see the universe in cyclical time, this idea existed simultaneously with the reality of linear time.

These two concepts—the cyclical and the linear—came to be associated with two of their primary deities: Osiris, the eternal lord of the dead, and Re, the sun god who was reborn with each dawn.

Early Development: The Predynastic Period

The civilization of Egypt obviously did not spring fully formed from the Nile mud; although the massive pyramids at Giza may appear to the uninitiated to have appeared out of nowhere, they were founded on thousands of years of cultural and technological development and experimentation. 'Dynastic' Egypt—sometimes referred to as 'Pharaonic' (after 'pharaoh', the Greek title of the Egyptian kings derived from the Egyptian title *per aA*, 'Great House') which was the time when the country was largely unified under a single ruler, begins around 3100 B.C.E.

The period before this, lasting from about 5000 B.C.E. until unification, is referred to as Predynastic by modern scholars. Prior to this were thriving Paleolithic and Neolithic groups, stretching back hundreds of thousands of years, descended from northward migrating homo erectus who settled along the Nile Valley. During the Predynastic period, ceramics, figurines, mace heads, and other artifacts such as slate palettes used for grinding pigments, begin to appear, as does imagery that will become iconic during the Pharaonic era—we can see the first hints of what is to come.

Dynasties

It is important to recognize that the dynastic divisions modern scholars use were not used by the ancients themselves. These divisions were created in the first Western-style history of Egypt, written by an Egyptian priest named Manetho in the 3rd century

BCE. Each of the 33 dynasties included a series of rulers usually related by kinship or the location of their seat of power. Egyptian history is also divided into larger chunks, known as 'kingdoms' and 'periods', to distinguish times of strength and unity from those of change, foreign rule, or disunity.

Period	Dates
Old Kingdom (the 'pyramid age')	c. 2649 – 2150 B.C.E.
First Intermediate Period	c. 2150 – 2030 B.C.E.
Middle Kingdom	c. 2030 – 1640 B.C.E.
Second Intermediate Period (Northern Delta region ruled by Asiatics)	c. 1640 – 1540 B.C.E.
New Kingdom	c. 1550 – 1070 B.C.E.
Third Intermediate Period	c. 1070 – 713 B.C.E.
Late Period (a series from foreign dynasties, including Nubian, Libyan and Persian rulers)	c. 712 – 332 B.C.E.
Ptolemaic Period (ruled by Greco-Romans)	c. 332-30 B.C.E.

The Egyptians themselves referred to their history in relation to the ruler of the time. Years were generally recorded as the regnal dates (from the Latin regnum, meaning kingdom or rule) of the ruling king, so that with each new reign, the numbers began anew.

Later kings recorded the names of their predecessors in vast 'king-lists' on the walls of their temples and depicted themselves offering to the rulers who came before them—one of the best known examples is in the temple of Seti I at Abydos.

These lists were often condensed, with some rulers (such as the contentious and disruptive Akhenaten) and even entire dynasties omitted from the record; they are not truly history, rather they are a form of ancestor worship, a celebration of the consistency of kingship of which the current ruler was a part.

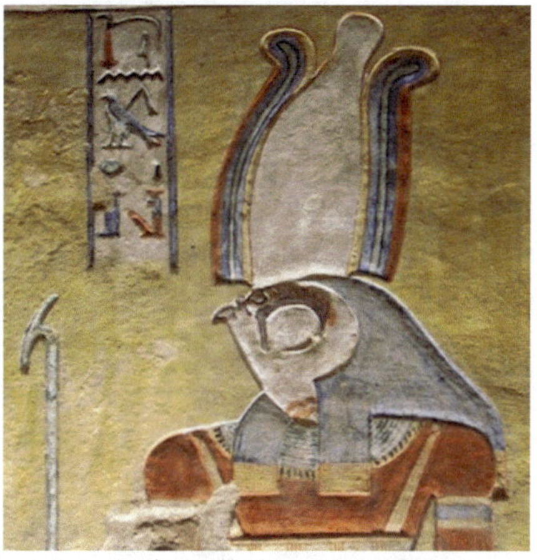

Horus in the tomb of Khaemwaset. Photo: Dr Amy Calvert, CC BY-NC

- https://youtu.be/cxs1d3N60UI
- https://youtu.be/ryycDVWXDvc

The Pharaoh—Not Just a King

Kings in Egypt were complex intermediaries that straddled the terrestrial and divine realms. They were, obviously, living humans, but upon accession to the throne, they also embodied the eternal office of kingship itself.

The ka, or spirit, of kingship was often depicted as a separate entity standing behind the human ruler. This divine aspect of the office of kingship was what gave authority to the human ruler.

The living king was associated with the god Horus, the powerful, virile falcon-headed god who was believed to bestow the throne to the first human king.

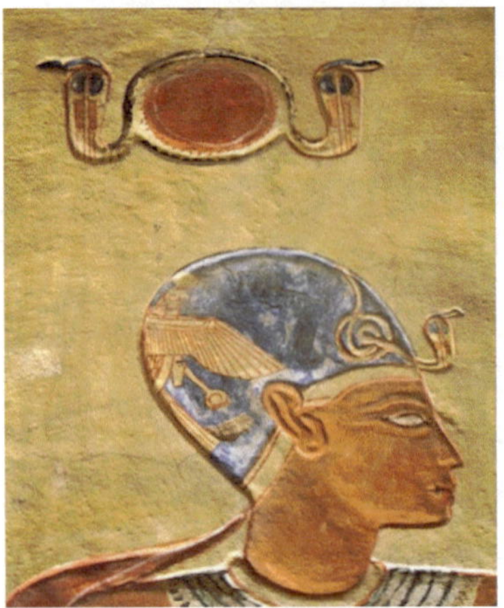

Horus is regularly shown guarding and guiding the living ruler; as in this image of a falcon (Horus) wrapped behind the head of Ramses III in the tomb of Khaemwaset (above). Photo: Dr Amy Calvert, CC BY-NC

Horus's immensely important father, Osiris, was the lord of the underworld. One of the original divine rulers of Egypt, this deity embodied the promise of regeneration. Cruelly murdered by his brother Seth, the god of the chaotic desert, Osiris was revived through the potent magic of his wife Isis.

Through her knowledge and skill, Osiris was able to sire the miraculous Horus, who avenged his father and threw his criminal uncle off the throne to take his rightful place.

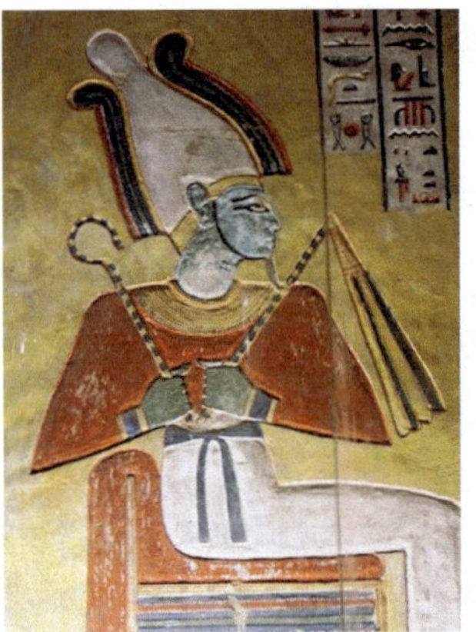

Osiris (above; from QV44 in the Valley of the Queens). Photo: Dr Amy Calvert, CC BY-NC

Osiris became ruler of the realm of the dead, the eternal source of regeneration in the Afterlife. Deceased kings were identified with this god, creating a cycle where the dead king fused with the divine king of the dead and his successor 'defeated' death to take his place on the throne as Horus.

Reading: Ancient Greece and Rome

Introduction

Classical Antiquity (or Ancient Greece and Rome) is a period of about 900 years, when ancient Greece and then ancient Rome (first as a Republic and then as an Empire) dominated the Mediterranean area, from about 500 B.C.E. – 400 C.E. We tend to lump ancient Greece and Rome together because the Romans adopted many aspects of Greek culture when they conquered the areas of Europe under Greek control (circa 145 – 30 B.C.E.).

Gods and Goddesses

For example, the Romans adopted the Greek pantheon of Gods and Godesses but changed their names—the Greek god of war was Ares, whereas the Roman god of war was Mars. The ancient Romans also copied ancient Greek art. However, the Romans often used marble to create copies of sculptures that the Greeks had originally made in bronze.

A Rational Approach

The ancient Greeks were the first Western culture that believed in finding rational answers to the great questions of earthly life. They assumed that there were consistent laws which governed the universe—how the stars move; the materials that compose the universe; mathematical laws that govern harmony and beauty, geometry and physics.

Both the Ancient Greeks and the Ancient Romans had enormous respect for human beings, and what they could accomplish with their minds and bodies. They were Humanists (a frame of mind which was re-born in the Renaissance). This was very different from the period following Classical Antiquity—the Middle Ages, when Christianity (with its sense of the body as sinful) came to dominate Western Europe.

When you imagine Ancient Greek or Roman sculpture, you might think of a figure that is nude, athletic, young, idealized, and with perfect proportions—and this would be true of Ancient Greek art of the Classical period (5th century B.C.E.) as well as much of Ancient Roman art.

Roman Copies of Ancient Greek Art

When we study ancient Greek art, so often we are really looking at ancient Roman art, or at least their copies of ancient Greek sculpture (or paintings and architecture for that matter).

Basically, just about every Roman wanted ancient Greek art. For the Romans, Greek culture symbolized a desirable way of life—of leisure, the arts, luxury and learning.

The Popularity of Ancient Greek Art for the Romans

Greek art became the rage when Roman generals began conquering Greek cities (beginning in 211 B.C.E.), and returned triumphantly to Rome not with the usual booty of gold and silver coins, but with works of art. This work so impressed the Roman elite that studios were set up to meet the growing demand for copies destined for the villas of wealthy Romans. The Doryphoros was one of the most sought after, and most copied Greek sculptures.

Bronze vs. Marble

For the most part, the Greeks created their free-standing sculpture in bronze, but because bronze is valuable and can be melted down and reused, sculpture was often recast into weapons. This is why so few ancient Greek bronze originals survive, and why we often have to look at ancient Roman copies in marble (of varying quality) to try to understand what the Greeks achieved.

Why Sculptures Are Often Incomplete or Reconstructed

To make matter worse, Roman marble sculptures were buried for centuries, and very often we recover only fragments of a sculpture that have to be reassembled. This is the reason you will often see that sculptures in museums include an arm or hand that are modern recreations, or that ancient sculptures are simply displayed incomplete.

The *Doryphoros (Spear-Bearer)* in the Naples museum is a Roman copy of a lost Greek original that we think was found, largely intact, in the provincial Roman city of Pompeii.

- https://youtu.be/EAR9RAMg9NY

The Canon

The idea of a canon, a rule for a standard of beauty developed for artists to follow, was not new to the ancient Greeks. The ancient Egyptians also developed a canon. Centuries later, during the Renaissance, Leonardo da Vinci investigated the ideal proportions of the human body with his Vitruvian Man. The ideal male nude has remained a staple of Western art and culture to this day, see, for example, of the work of Robert Mapplethorpe.

Polykleitos's idea of relating beauty to ratio was later summarized by Galen, writing in the second century,

> Beauty consists in the proportions, not of the elements, but of the parts, that is to say, of finger to finger, and of all the fingers to the palm and the wrist, and of these to the forearm, and of the forearm to the upper arm, and of all the other parts to each other.

Note: Recent scholarship suggests that the Doryphoros sculpture in the Naples museum may not have been found in a Palestra at Pompeii. See Warren G. Moon, ed., *Polykleitos, The Doryphoros and Tradition*, University of Wisconsin Press, 1995.

Key Characteristics of Art: Age of Faith

Identify and describe key characteristics and defining events of art from the Age of Faith

LEARNING ACTIVITIES

The learning activities for this section include:

- Reading: The Medieval and Byzantine Eras
- Reading: Early Christian Art
- Reading: Church Architecture
- Reading: Arts of the Islamic World: the Early Period
- Reading: Introduction to Mosque Architecture
- Reading: Romanesque
- Reading: Gothic Architecture
- Reading: Neo-Confucianism and Fan Kuan's Travelers by Streams and Mountains
- Reading: Shiva As Lord of the Dance (Nataraja)
- Reading: Classic Maya Portrait Stelae

Take time to review and reflect on each of these activities in order to improve your performance on the assessment for this section.

Reading: The Medieval and Byzantine Eras

The Dark Ages?

So much of what the average person knows, or thinks they know, about the Middle Ages comes from film and TV. When I polled a group of well-educated friends on Facebook, they told me that the word "medieval" called to mind *Monty Python and the Holy Grail*, *Blackadder*,*The Sword in the Stone*, lusty wenches, feasting, courtly love, the plague, jousting, and chain mail.

Perhaps someone who had seen (or better yet read) *The Name of the Rose* or *Pillars of the Earth* would add cathedrals, manuscripts, monasteries, feudalism, monks, and friars.

Petrarch, an Italian poet and scholar of the fourteenth century, famously referred to the period of time between the fall of the Roman Empire (circa 476) and his own day (circa 1330s) as the Dark Ages.

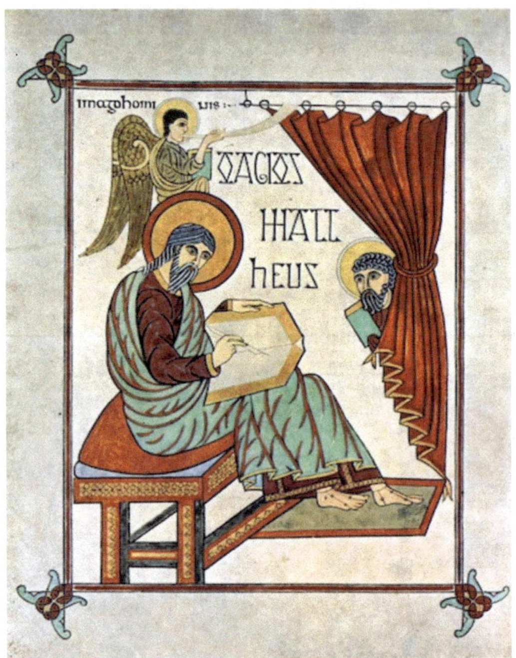

Matthew from the Lindisfarne Gospels, made on the island of Lindisfarne off the coast of England, late seventh century or early eighth century

Petrarch believed that the Dark Ages was a period of intellectual darkness due to the loss of the classical learning, which he saw as light. Later historians picked up on this idea and ultimately the term Dark Ages was transformed into Middle Ages. Broadly speaking, the Middle Ages is the period of time in Europe between the end of antiquity in the fifth century and the Renaissance, or rebirth of classical learning, in the fifteenth century and sixteenth centuries.

Characterizing the Middle Ages as a period of darkness falling between two greater, more intellectually significant periods in history is misleading. The Middle Ages was not a time of ignorance and backwardness, but rather a period during which Christianity flourished in Europe. Christianity, and specifically Catholicism in the Latin West, brought with it new views of life and the world that rejected the traditions and learning of the ancient world.

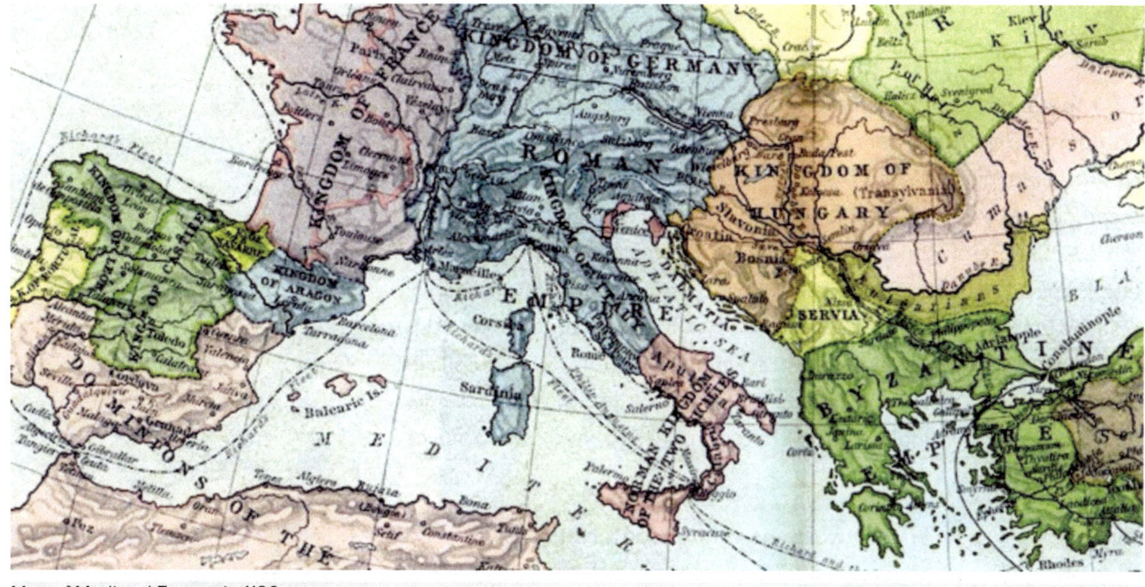
Map of Medieval Europe in 1190

Not So Dark After All

During this time, the Roman Empire slowly fragmented into many smaller political entities. The geographical boundaries for European countries today were established during the Middle Ages. This was a period that heralded the formation and rise of universities, the establishment of the rule of law, numerous periods of ecclesiastical reform and the birth of the tourism industry. Many works of medieval literature, such as the Canterbury Tales, the Divine Comedy, and The Song of Roland, are widely read and studied today.

The visual arts prospered during Middles Ages, which created its own aesthetic values. The wealthiest and most influential members of society commissioned cathedrals, churches, sculpture, painting, textiles, manuscripts, jewelry and ritual items from artists. Many of these commissions were religious in nature but medieval artists also produced secular art. Few names of artists survive and fewer documents record their business dealings, but they left behind an impressive legacy of art and culture.

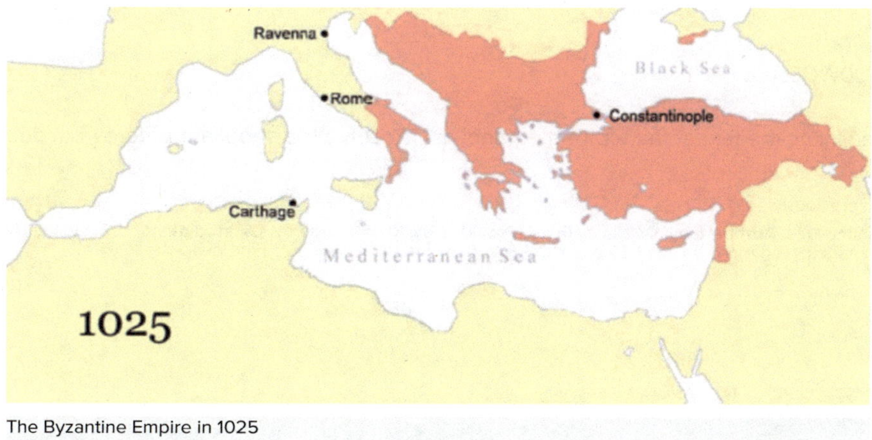

The Byzantine Empire in 1025

Byzantium

When I polled the same group of friends about the word "Byzantine", many struggled to come up with answers. Among the better ones were the song "Istanbul (Not Constantinople)" sung by They Might Be Giants, crusades, things that are too complex (like the tax code or medical billing), Hagia Sophia, the poet Yeats, mosaics, monks, and icons. Unlike Western Europe in the Middle Ages, the Byzantine Empire is not romanticized in television and film. In the medieval West, the Roman Empire fragmented, but in the Byzantine East, it remained a strong, centrally-focused political entity. Byzantine emperors ruled from Constantinople, which they thought of as the New Rome. Constantinople housed Hagia Sophia, the world's largest church until 1520, and was a major center of artistic production.

The Byzantine Empire experienced two periods of Iconoclasm (730-787 and 814-842), when images and image-making were problematic. Iconoclasm left a visible legacy on Byzantine art because it created limits on what artists could represent and how those subjects could be represented. Byzantine Art is broken into three periods. Early Byzantine or Early Christian art begins with the earliest extant Christian works of art c. 250 and ends with the end of Iconoclasm in 842. Middle Byzantine art picks up at the end of Iconoclasm and extends to the sack of Constantinople by Latin Crusaders in 1204. Late Byzantine art was made between the sack of Constantinople and the fall of Constantinople to the Ottoman Turks in 1453.

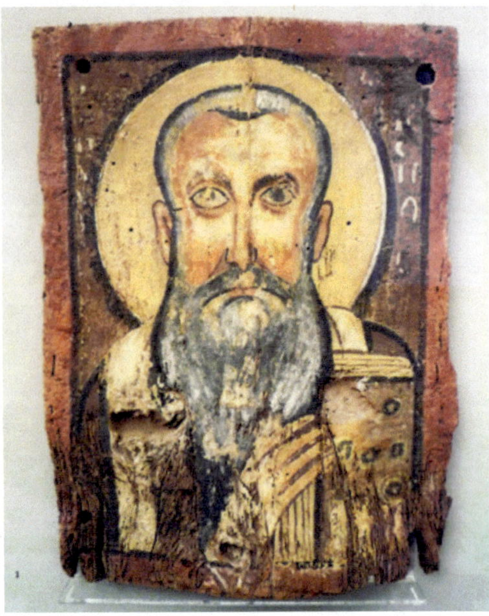

Apa Abraham, c. 590-600, watercolor on panel, Egyptian (Bode Museum, Berlin)

In the European West, medieval art is often broken into smaller periods. These date ranges vary by location:

c.500–800: Early Medieval Art
c.780–900: Carolingian Art
c.900–1000: Ottonian Art
c.1000–1200: Romanesque Art
c.1200–1400: Gothic Art

- https://youtu.be/f7J0WQsajX8

The British Museum translates the text at the top of the panel as: "Receive the suppliant before you, despite his sinfulness."

Reading: Early Christian Art

The beginnings of an identifiable Christian art can be traced to the end of the second century and the beginning of the third century. Considering the Old Testament prohibitions against graven images, it is important to consider why Christian art developed in the first place. The use of images will be a continuing issue in the history of Christianity. The best explanation for the emergence of Christian art in the early church is due to the important role images played in Greco-Roman culture.

As Christianity gained converts, these new Christians had been brought up on the value of images in their previous cultural experience and they wanted to continue this in their Christian experience. For example, there was a change in burial practices in the Roman world away from cremation to inhumation. Outside the city walls of Rome, adjacent to major roads, catacombs were dug into the ground to bury the dead. Families would have chambers or cubicula dug to bury their members. Wealthy Romans would also have sarcophagi or marble tombs carved for their burial. The Christian converts wanted the same things. Christian catacombs were dug frequently adjacent to non-Christian ones, and sarcophagi with Christian imagery were apparently popular with the richer Christians.

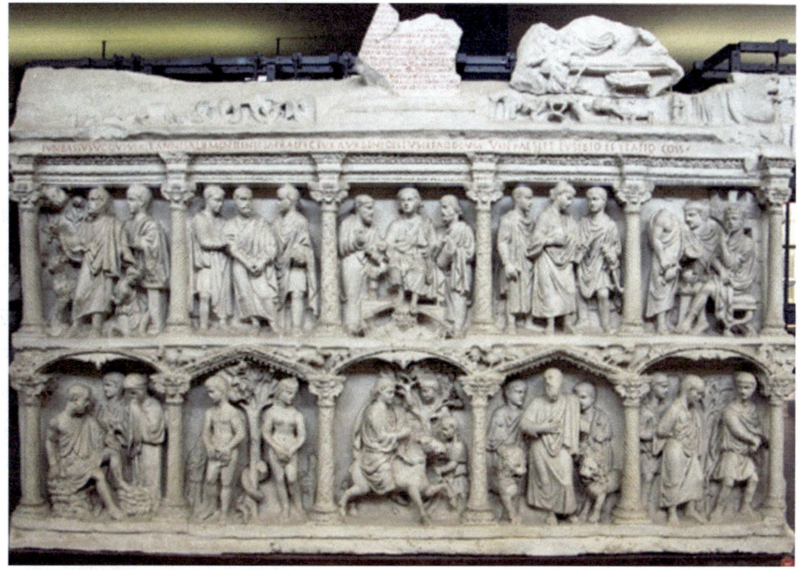

Junius Bassus Sarcophagus

Junius Bassus, a Roman praefectus urbi or high ranking government administrator, died in 359 C.E. Scholars believe that he converted to Christianity shortly before his death accounting for the inclusion of Christ and scenes from the Bible. (Photograph above shows a plaster cast of the original.)

Themes of Death and Resurrection (Borrowed from the Old Testament)

A striking aspect of the Christian art of the third century is the absence of the imagery that will dominate later Christian art. We do not find in this early period images of the Nativity, Crucifixion, or Resurrection of Christ, for example. This absence of direct images of the life of Christ is best explained by the status of Christianity as a mystery religion. The story of the Crucifixion and Resurrection would be part of the secrets of the cult.

While not directly representing these central Christian images, the theme of death and resurrection was represented through a series of images, many of which were derived from the Old Testament that echoed the themes. For example, the story of Jonah—being swallowed by a great fish and then after spending three days and three nights in the belly of the beast is vomited out on dry ground—was seen by early Christians as an anticipation or prefiguration of the story of Christ's own death and resurrection. Images of Jonah, along with those of Daniel in the Lion's Den, the Three Hebrews in the Firey Furnace, Moses Striking the Rock, among others, are widely popular in the Christian art of the third century, both in paintings and on sarcophagi.

All of these can be seen to allegorically allude to the principal narratives of the life of Christ. The common subject of salvation echoes the major emphasis in the mystery religions on personal salvation. The appearance of these subjects frequently adjacent to each other in the catacombs and sarcophagi can be read as a visual litany: save me Lord as you have saved Jonah from the belly of the great fish, save me Lord as you have saved the Hebrews in the desert, save me Lord as you have saved Daniel in the Lion's den, etc.

One can imagine that early Christians—who were rallying around the nascent religious authority of the Church against the regular threats of persecution by imperial authority—would find great meaning in the story of Moses of striking the rock to provide water for the Israelites fleeing the authority of the Pharaoh on their exodus to the Promised Land.

Christianity's Canonical Texts and the New Testament

One of the major differences between Christianity and the public cults was the central role faith plays in Christianity and the importance of orthodox beliefs. The history of the early Church is marked by the struggle to establish a canonical set of texts and the establishment of orthodox doctrine.

Questions about the nature of the Trinity and Christ would continue to challenge religious authority. Within the civic cults there were no central texts and there were no orthodox doctrinal positions. The emphasis was on maintaining customary traditions. One accepted the existence of the gods, but there was no emphasis on belief in the gods.

The Christian emphasis on orthodox doctrine has its closest parallels in the Greek and Roman world to the role of philosophy. Schools of philosophy centered around the teachings or doctrines of a particular teacher. The schools of philosophy proposed specific conceptions of reality. Ancient philosophy was influential in the formation of Christian theology. For example, the opening of the Gospel of John: "In the beginning was the word and the word was with God...," is unmistakably based on the idea of the "logos" going back to the philosophy of Heraclitus (ca. 535 – 475 BCE). Christian apologists like Justin Martyr writing in the second century understood Christ as the Logos or the Word of God who served as an intermediary between God and the World.

Early Representations of Christian and the Apostles

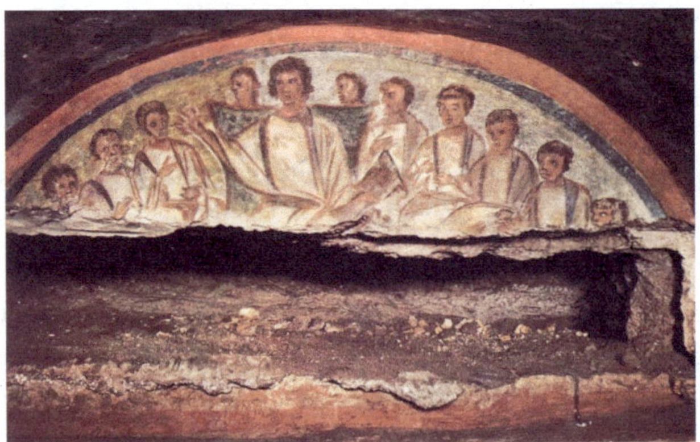
Christ, from the Catacomb of Domitilla

An early representation of Christ found in the Catacomb of Domitilla shows the figure of Christ flanked by a group of his disciples or students. Those experienced with later Christian imagery might mistake this for an image of the Last Supper, but instead this image does not tell any story. It conveys rather the idea that Christ is the true teacher.

Christ draped in classical garb holds a scroll in his left hand while his right hand is outstretched in the so-called *ad locutio* gesture, or the gesture of the orator. The dress, scroll, and gesture all establish the authority of Christ, who is placed in the center of his disciples. Christ is thus treated like the philosopher surrounded by his students or disciples.

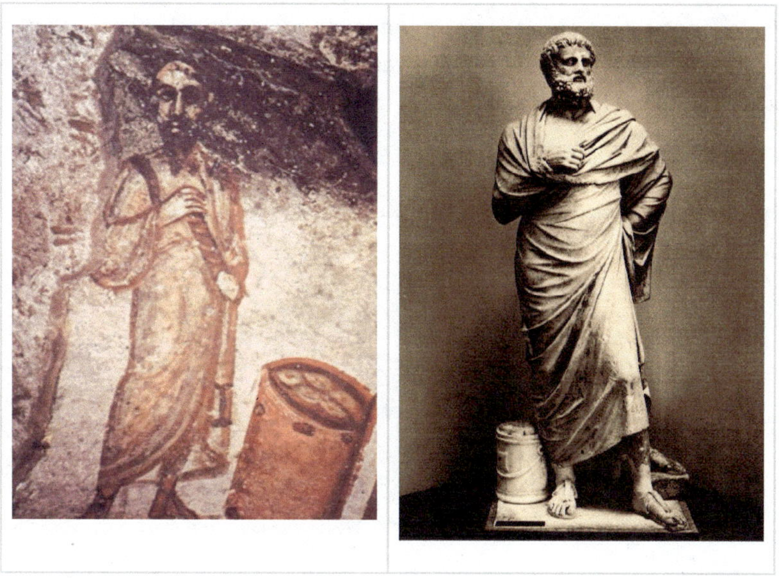

Comparably, an early representation of the apostle Paul, identifiable with his characteristic pointed beard and high forehead, is based on the convention of the philosopher, as exemplified by a Roman copy of a late fourth century B.C.E. portrait of the fifth century B.C.E. playwright Sophocles.

Reading: Church Architecture

Many of Europe's medieval cathedrals are museums in their own right, housing fantastic examples of craftsmanship and works of art. Additionally, the buildings themselves are impressive. Although architectural styles varied from place to place, building to building, there are some basic features that were fairly universal in monumental churches built in the Middle Ages, and the prototype for that type of building was the Roman basilica.

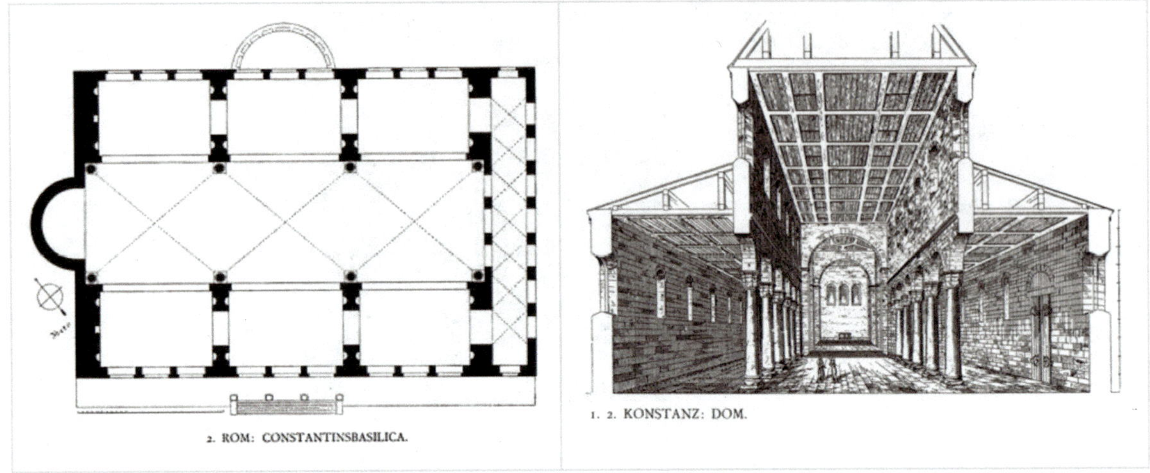

Prototype: The Ancient Roman Basilica

In ancient Rome, the basilica was created as a place for tribunals and other types of business. The building was rectangular in shape, with the long, central portion of the hall made up of the *nave*. Here the interior reached its fullest height. The nave was flanked on either side by a colonnade that delineated the side aisles, which were of a lower height than the nave. Because the side aisles were lower, the roof over this section was below the roofline of the nave, allowing for windows near the ceiling of the nave. This band of windows was called the *clerestory*. At the far end of the nave, away from the main door, was a semi-circular extension, usually with a half-dome roof. This area was the *apse*, and is where the magistrate or other senior officials would hold court.

Because this plan allowed for many people to circulate within a large, and awesome, space, the general plan became an obvious choice for early Christian buildings. The religious rituals, masses, and pilgrimages that became commonplace by the Middle Ages were very different from today's services, and to understand the architecture it is necessary to understand how the buildings were used and the components that made up these massive edifices.

The Medieval Church

Plan Although medieval churches are usually oriented east to west, they all vary slightly. When a new church was to be built, the patron saint was selected and the altar location laid out. On the saint's day, a line would be surveyed from the position of the rising sun through the altar site and extending in a westerly direction. This was the orientation of the new building.

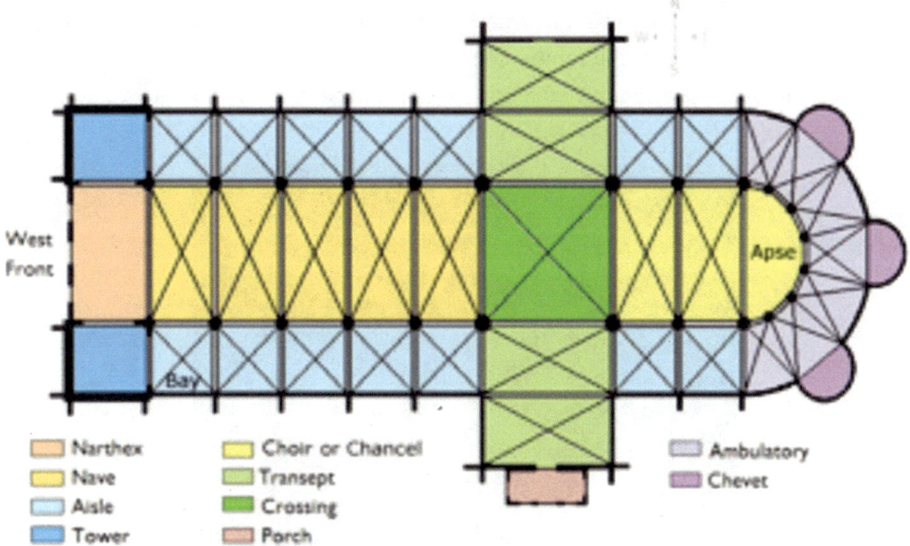

The entrance foyer is called the *narthex*, but this is not found in all medieval churches. Daily access may be through a door on the north or south side. The largest, central, western door may have been reserved for ceremonial purposes.

The Church Plan

Inside, you should imagine the interior space without the chairs or pews that we are used to seeing today. Unlike in a Roman basilica, the side aisles run behind a series of arches rather than columns. In very extensive buildings there may be two side aisles, with the ceiling of the outer one lower than the one next to the nave. This hierarchy of size and proportion extended to the major units of the plan – the *bays*. A bay is the square unit in the arcade defined by a vault, the section supported by consecutive pillars. Typically, the width of the nave was equal to two bays. The *vault* is the arched roof or ceiling, or a section of it.

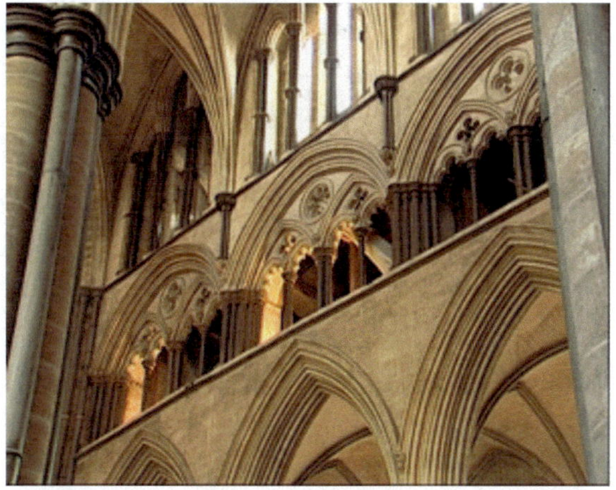
Salisbury Cathedral, view of the top of the nave arcade, above that the gallery, and above that, the windows of the clerestory.

The major arcade at the ground floor is topped by a second arcade, called the *gallery*, which is topped by the clerestory or a third arcade level. The arcade just below the clerestory is called the *triforium*. The nave was used for the procession of the clergy to the altar. The main altar was basically in the position of the basilican apse, although in some designs it is further forward. The area around the altar – the *choir* or *chancel* – was reserved for the clergy or monks, who performed services throughout the day.

The cathedrals and former monastery churches are much larger than needed for the local population. They expected and received numerous pilgrims who came to various shrines and altars within the church where they might pray to a supposed piece of the true cross, or a bone of a martyr, or the tomb of a king. The pilgrims entered the church and found their way to the chapel or altar of their desire—therefore, the side aisles made an efficient path for pilgrims to come and go without disrupting the daily services.

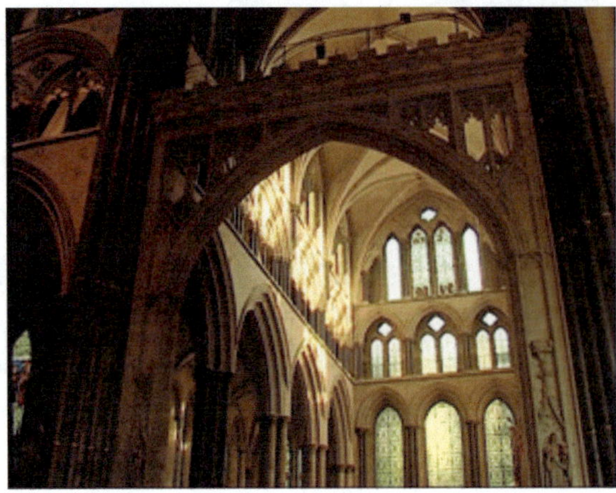

Transept Salisbury Cathedral

Development of this plan over time shows that very soon the apse was elongated, adding more room to the choir. Additionally, the termini of the aisles developed into small wings themselves, known as *transepts*. These were also extended, providing room for more tombs, more shrines, and more pilgrims.

The area where the axes of the nave and transepts meet is called, logically, the *crossing*.

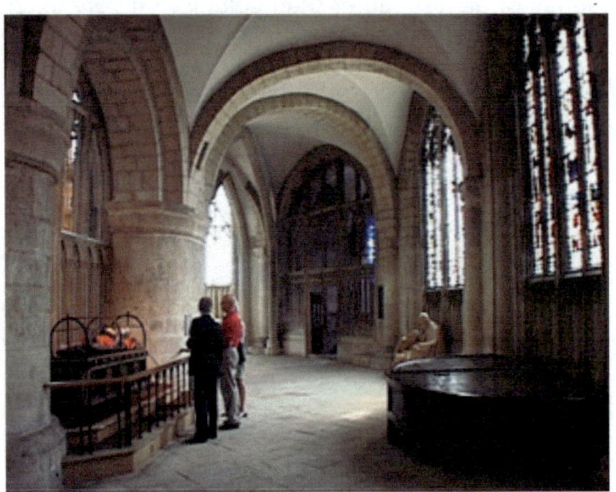

Ambulatory, Gloucester Cathedral

An aisle often surrounds the apse, running behind the altar. Called the *ambulatory*, this aisle accessed additional small chapels, called *radiating chapels* or *chevets*. Of course, there are many variations on these typical building blocks of medieval church design. Different regions had different tastes, greater or lesser financial power, more or less experienced architects and masons, which created the diversity of medieval buildings still standing today.

Reading: Arts of the Islamic World: the Early Period

Islamic Art: The Caliphates (Political/Religious Dynasties)

The umbrella term "Islamic art" casts a pretty big shadow, covering several continents and more than a dozen centuries. So to make sense of it, we first have to first break it down into parts. One way is by medium—say, ceramics or architecture—but this method of categorization would entail looking at works that span three continents. Geography is another means of organization, but modern political boundaries rarely match the borders of past Islamic states.

A common solution is to consider instead, the historical caliphates (the states ruled by those who claimed legitimate Islamic rule) or dynasties. Though these distinctions are helpful, it is important to bear in mind that these are not discrete groups that produced one particular style of artwork. Artists throughout the centuries have been affected by the exchange of goods and ideas and have been influenced by one another.

Umayyad (661–750)

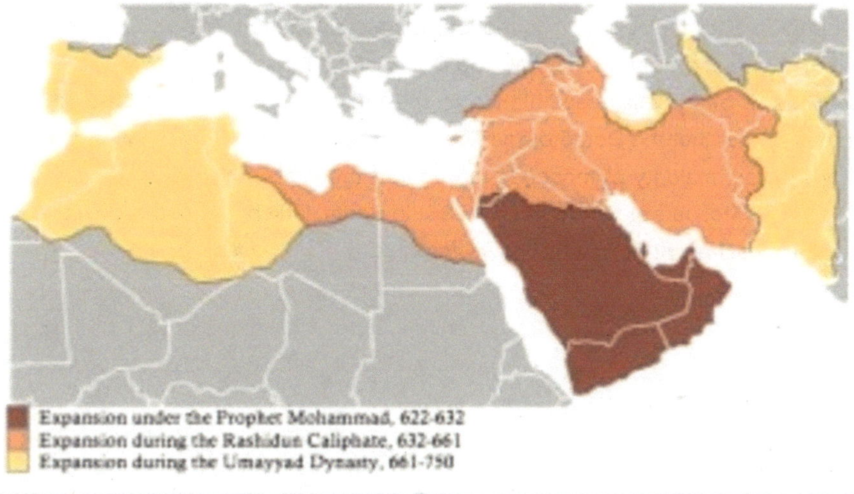

Map showing Islam expansion from 622 to 750

Four leaders, known as the Rightly Guided Caliphs, continued the spread of Islam immediately following the death of the Prophet. It was following the death of the fourth caliph that Mu'awiya seized power and established the Umayyad caliphate, the first Islamic dynasty. During this period, Damascus became the capital and the empire expanded West and East.

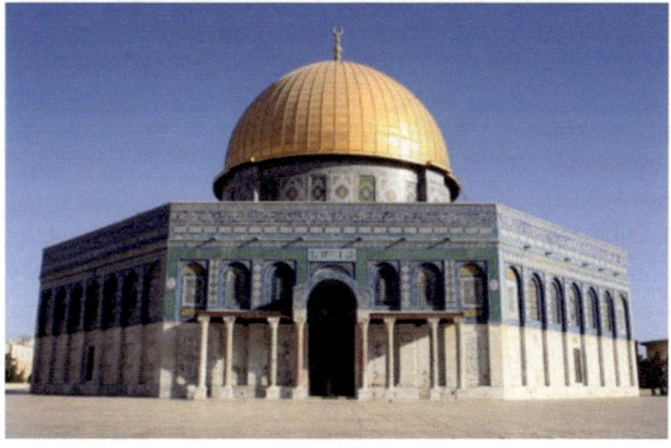

Dome of the Rock, 687, Jerusalem (photo: author)

The first years following the death of Muhammad were, of course, formative for the religion and its artwork. The immediate needs of the religion included places to worship (mosques) and holy books (Korans) to convey the word of God. So, naturally, many of the first artistic projects included ornamented mosques where the faithful could gather and Korans with beautiful calligraphy. Because Islam was still a very new religion, it had no artistic vocabulary of its own, and its earliest work was heavily influenced by older styles in the region. Chief among these sources were the Coptic tradition of present-day Egypt and Syria, with its scrolling vines and geometric motifs, Sassanian metalwork and crafts from what is now Iraq with their rhythmic, sometimes abstracted qualities, and naturalistic Byzantine mosaics depicting animals and plants.

These elements can be seen in the earliest significant work from the Umayyad period, the most important of which is the Dome of the Rock in Jerusalem. This stunning monument Incorporates Coptic, Sassanian, and Byzantine elements in its decorative program and remains a masterpiece of Islamic architecture to this day.

Remarkably, just one generation after the religion's inception, Islamic civilization had produced a magnificent, if singular, monument. While the Dome of the Rock is

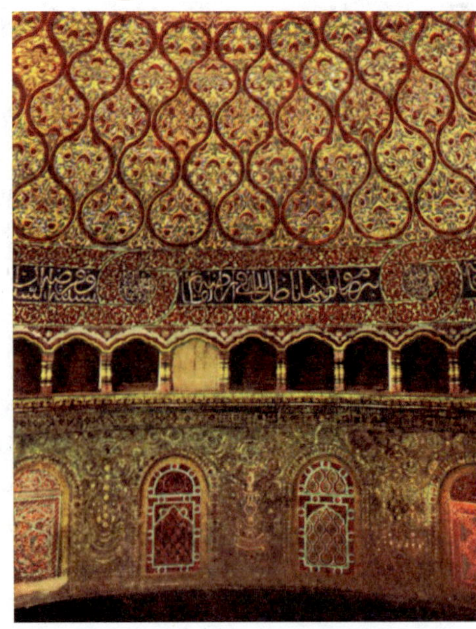
Interior of the base of the dome, Dome of the Rock

considered an influential work, it bears little resemblance to the multitude of mosques created throughout the rest of the caliphate. It is important to point out that the Dome of the Rock is not a mosque. A more common plan, based on the house of the Prophet, was used for the vast majority of mosques throughout the Arab peninsula and the Maghreb. Perhaps the most remarkable of these is the Great Mosque of Córdoba (784-786) in Spain, which, like the Dome of the Rock, demonstrates an integration of the styles of the existing culture in which it was created.

Abbasid (750–1258)

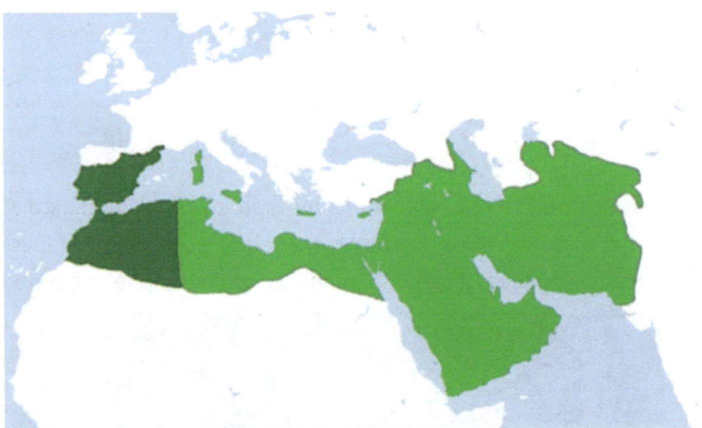
Abbasid Caliphate (light and dark green) at its greatest extent, c. 850. Territories in dark green were lost early on.

The Abbasid revolution in the mid-eighth century ended the Umayyad dynasty, resulted in the massacre of the Umayyad caliphs (a single caliph escaped to Spain, prolonging Umayyad work after dynasty) and established the Abbasid dynasty in 750. The new caliphate shifted its attention eastward and established cultural and commercial capitals at Baghdad and Samarra.

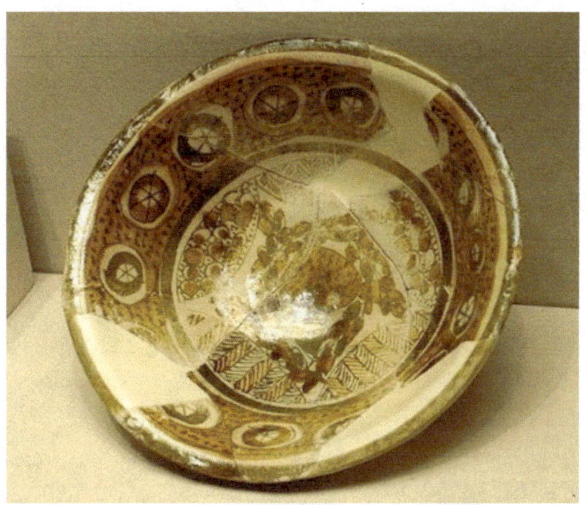

Bowl, 9th century, Susa, Iran, Earthenware, metal lustre overglaze decoration, opaque glaze

The Umayyad dynasty produced little of what we would consider decorative arts (like pottery, glass, metalwork), but under the Abbasid dynasty production of decorative stone, wood and ceramic objects flourished. Artisans in Samarra developed a new method for carving surfaces that allowed for curved, vegetal forms (called arabesques) which became widely adopted. There were also developments in ceramic decoration. The use of luster painting (which gives ceramic ware a metallic sheen) became popular in surrounding regions and was extensively used on tile for centuries. Overall, the Abbasid epoch was an important transitional period that disseminated styles and techniques to distant Islamic lands.

The Abbasid empire weakened with the establishment and growing power of semi-autonomous dynasties throughout the region, until Baghdad was finally overthrown in 1258. This dissolution signified not only the end of a dynasty, but marked the last time that the Arab-Muslim empire would be united as one entity.

Reading: Introduction to Mosque Architecture

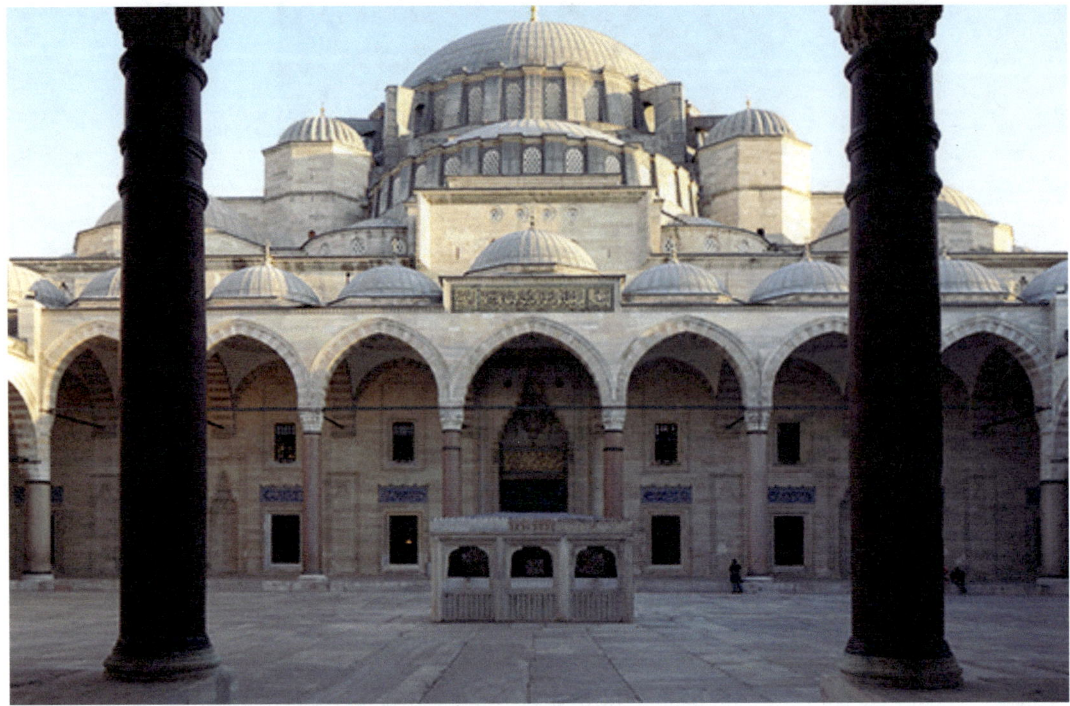

Mimar Sinan, courtyard of the Süleymaniye Mosque, İstanbul, 1558

From Indonesia to the United Kingdom, the mosque in its many forms is the quintessential Islamic building. The mosque, *masjid* in Arabic, is the Muslim gathering place for prayer. *Masjid* simply means "place of prostration." Though most of the five daily prayers prescribed in Islam can take place anywhere, all men are required to gather together at the mosque for the Friday noon prayer.

Mosques are also used throughout the week for prayer, study, or simply as a place for rest and reflection. The main mosque of a city, used for the Friday communal prayer, is called a *jami masjid*, literally meaning "Friday mosque," but it is also sometimes called a congregational mosque in English. The style, layout, and decoration of a mosque can tell us a lot about Islam in general, but also about the period and region in which the mosque was constructed.

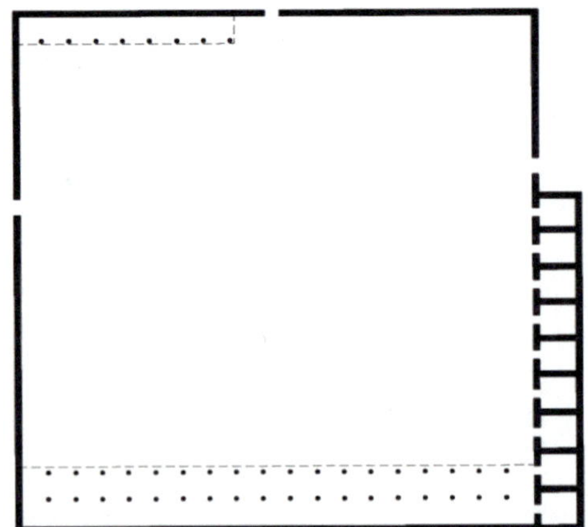

Diagram reconstruction of the Prophet's House, Medina, Saudi Arabia

The home of the Prophet Muhammad is considered the first mosque. His house, in Medina in modern-day Saudi Arabia, was a typical 7th-century Arabian style house, with a large courtyard surrounded by long rooms supported by columns. This style of mosque came to be known as a hypostyle mosque, meaning "many columns." Most mosques built in Arab lands utilized this style for centuries.

Common Features

The architecture of a mosque is shaped most strongly by the regional traditions of the time and place where it was built. As a result, style, layout, and decoration can vary greatly. Nevertheless, because of the common function of the mosque as a place of congregational prayer, certain architectural features appear in mosques all over the world.

Sahn (Courtyard)

The most fundamental necessity of congregational mosque architecture is that it be able to hold the entire male population of a city or town (women are welcome to attend Friday prayers, but not required to do so). To that end congregational mosques must have a large prayer hall. In many mosques this is adjoined to an open courtyard, called a *sahn*. Within the courtyard one often finds a fountain, its waters both a welcome respite in hot lands, and important for the ablutions (ritual cleansing) done before prayer.

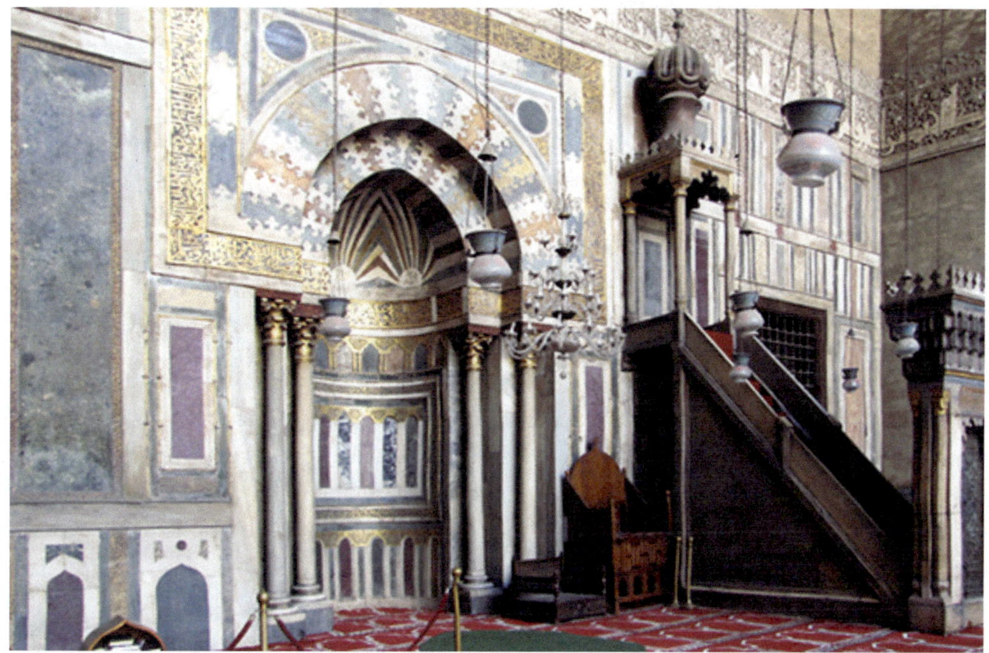

Mihrab and minbar, Mosque of Sultan Hassan, Cairo, 1356-63 (photo: Dave Berkowitz, CC BY)

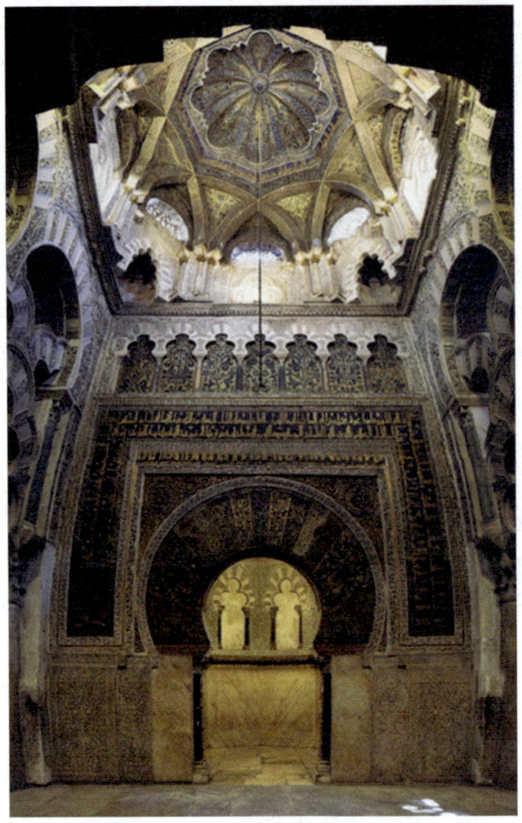

Mihrab, Great Mosque of Cordoba, c. 786 (photo: Bongo Vongo, CC BY-SA)

Mihrab (Niche)

Another essential element of a mosque's architecture is a *mihrab*—a niche in the wall that indicates the direction of Mecca, towards which all Muslims pray. Mecca is the city in which the Prophet Muhammad was born, and the home of the most important Islamic shrine, the Kaaba. The direction of Mecca is called the *qibla*, and so the wall in which the *mihrab* is set is called the *qibla* wall. No matter where a mosque is, its mihrab indicates the direction of Mecca (or as near that direction as science and geography were able to place it). Therefore, a *mihrab* in India will be to the west, while a one in Egypt will be to the east. A *mihrab* is usually a relatively shallow niche, as in the example from Egypt, above. In the example from Spain, shown right, the*mihrab*'s niche takes the form of a small room, this is more rare.

Minbar (Pulpit)

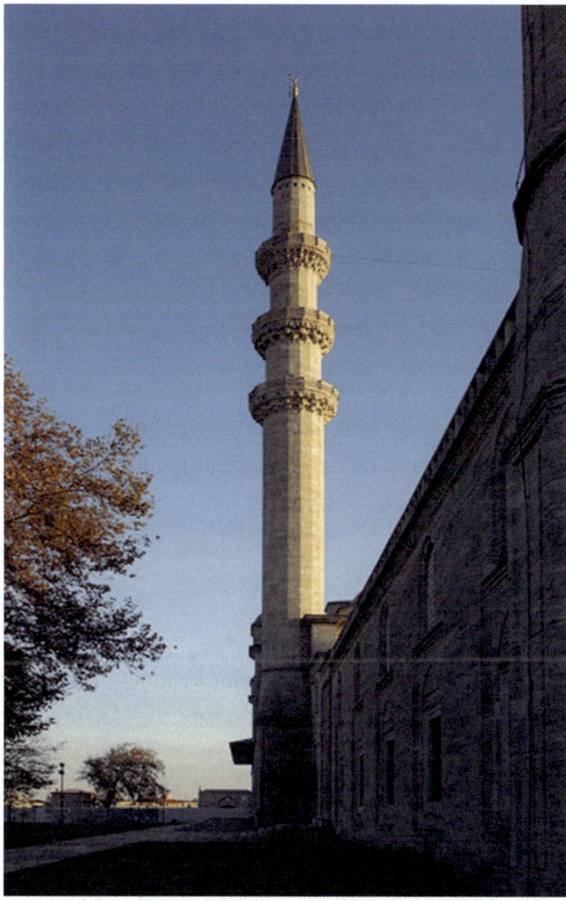

Mimar Sinan, Minaret, Süleymaniye Mosque, Istanbul, 1558

The *minbar* is often located on the *qibla* wall to the right of the *mihrab*. A *minbar* is a pulpit from which the Friday sermon is delivered. Simple *minbars* consist of a short flight of stairs, but more elaborate examples may enclose the stairway with ornate panels, doors, and a covered pulpit at the top.

Minaret (Tower)

One of the most visible aspects of mosque architecture is the *minaret*, a tower adjacent or attached to a mosque, from which the call to prayer is announced. Minarets take many different forms—from the famous spiral minaret of Samarra, to the tall, pencil minarets of Ottoman Turkey. Not solely functional in nature, the minaret serves as a powerful visual reminder of the presence of Islam.

Qubba (Dome)

Most mosques also feature one or more domes, called *qubba* in Arabic. While not a ritual requirement like the mihrab, a dome does possess significance within the mosque—as a symbolic representation of the vault of heaven. The interior decoration of a dome often emphasizes this symbolism, using intricate geometric, stellate, or vegetal motifs to create breathtaking patterns meant to awe and inspire. Some mosque types incorporate multiple domes into their architecture (as in the Ottoman Süleymaniye Mosque pictured at the top of the page), while others only feature one. In mosques with only a single dome, it is invariably found surmounting the qibla wall, the holiest section of the mosque. The Great Mosque of Kairouan, in Tunisia (not pictured) has three domes: one atop the *minaret*, one above the entrance to the prayer hall, and one above the *qibla* wall.

Because it is the directional focus of prayer, the *qibla* wall, with its *mihrab* and *minbar*, is often the most ornately decorated area of a mosque. The rich decoration of the *qibla* wall is apparent in this image of the *mihrab* and *minbar* of the Mosque of Sultan Hasan in Cairo, Egypt (see image higher on the page).

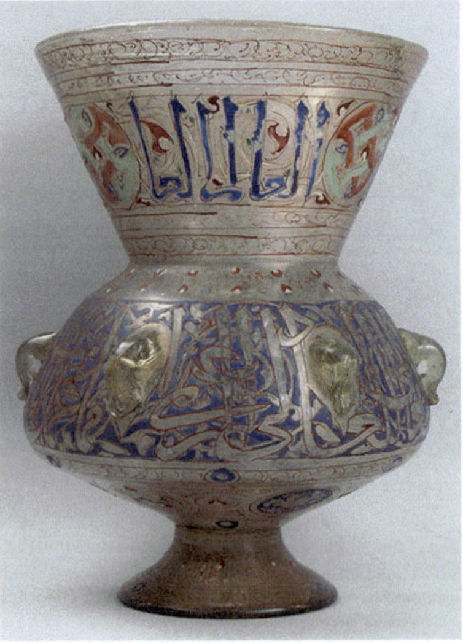

Mosque lamp, 14th century, Egypt or Syria, blown glass, enamel, gilding, 31.8 x 23.2 cm (Metropolitan Museum of Art)

Furnishings

There are other decorative elements common to most mosques. For instance, a large calligraphic frieze or a cartouche with a prominent inscription often appears above the *mihrab*. In most cases the calligraphic inscriptions are quotations from the *Qur'an*, and often include the date of the building's dedication and the name of the patron. Another important feature of mosque decoration are hanging lamps, also visible in the photograph of the Sultan Hasan mosque. Light is an essential feature for mosques, since the first and last daily prayers occur before the sun rises and after the sun sets. Before electricity, mosques were illuminated with oil lamps. Hundreds of such lamps hung inside a mosque would create a glittering spectacle, with soft light emanating from each, highlighting the calligraphy and other decorations on the lamps' surfaces. Although not a permanent part of a mosque building, lamps, along with other furnishings like carpets, formed a significant—though ephemeral—aspect of mosque architecture.

Mosque Patronage

Most historical mosques are not stand-alone buildings. Many incorporated charitable institutions like soup kitchens, hospitals, and schools. Some mosque patrons also chose to include their own mausoleum as part of their mosque complex. The endowment of charitable institutions is an important aspect of Islamic culture, due in part to the third pillar of Islam, which calls for Muslims to donate a portion of their income to the poor.

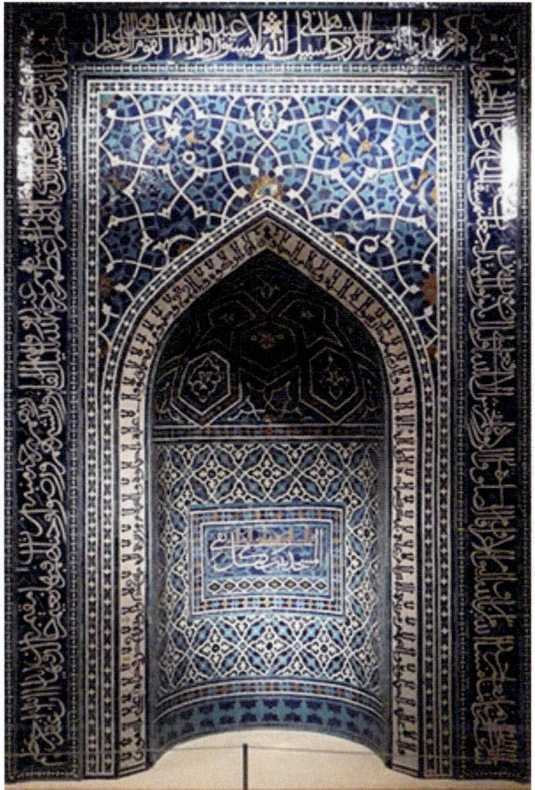

Mihrab, 1354–55, just after the Ilkhanid period, Madrasa Imami, Isfahan, Iran, polychrome glazed tiles, 343.1 x 288.7 cm (Metropolitan Museum of Art)

The commissioning of a mosque would be seen as a pious act on the part of a ruler or other wealthy patron, and the names of patrons are usually included in the calligraphic decoration of mosques. Such inscriptions also often praise the piety and generosity of the patron. For instance, the mihrab now at the Metropolitan Museum of Art, bears the inscription:

And he [the Prophet], blessings and peace be upon him, said: "Whoever builds a mosque for God, even the size of a sand-grouse nest, based on piety, [God will build for him a palace in Paradise]."

The patronage of mosques was not only a charitable act therefore, but also, like architectural patronage in all cultures, an opportunity for self-promotion. The social services attached the mosques of the Ottoman sultans are some of the most extensive of their type. In Ottoman Turkey the complex surrounding a mosque is called a *kulliye*. The *kulliye* of the Mosque of Sultan Suleyman, in Istanbul, is a fine example of this phenomenon, comprising a soup kitchen, a hospital, several schools, public baths, and a *caravanserai* (similar to a hostel for travelers). The complex also includes two mausoleums for Sultan Suleyman and his family members.

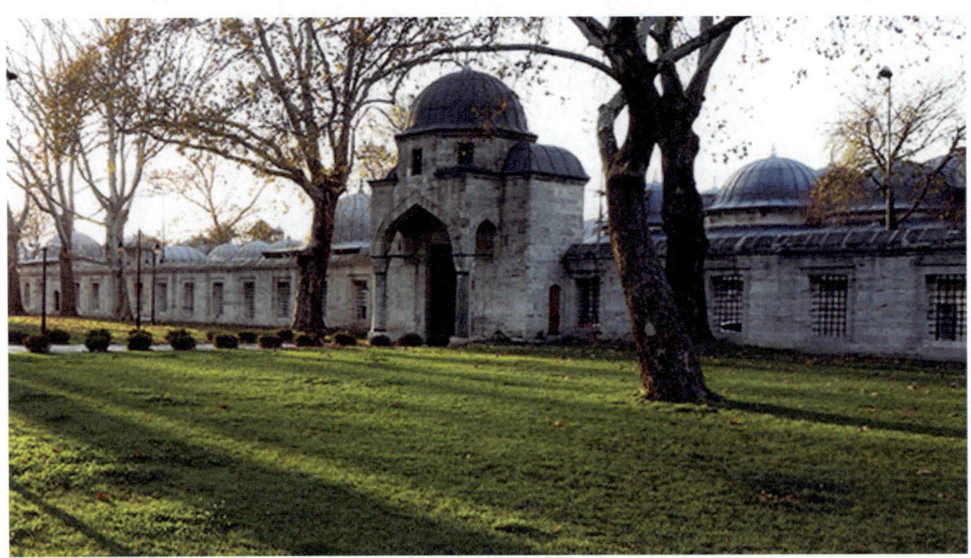

Kulliyesi (view of kitchens and caravanserai), Istanbul

Reading: Romanesque

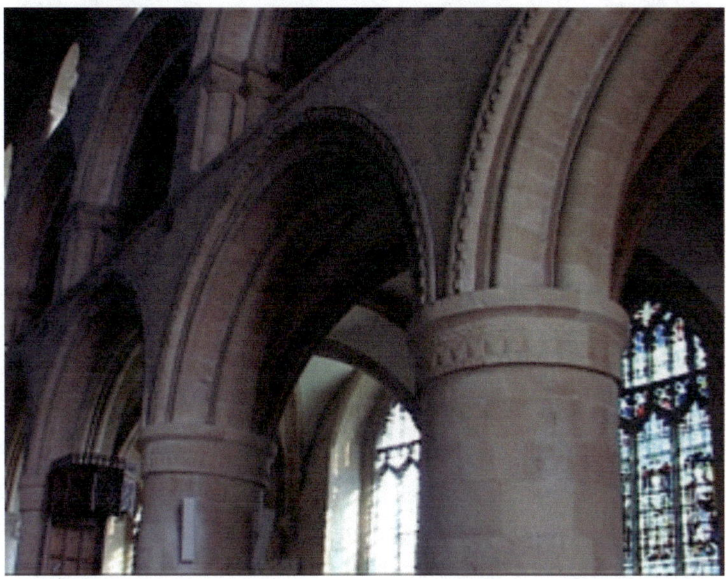

The name gives it away—Romanesque architecture is based on Roman architectural elements. It is the rounded Roman arch that is the literal basis for structures built in this style.

All through the regions that were part of the ancient Roman Empire are ruins of Roman aqueducts and buildings, most of them exhibiting arches as part of the architecture. (You may make the etymological leap that the two words are related, but the Oxford English Dictionary shows arch as coming from Latin *arcus*, which defines the shape, while *arch*-as in architect, archbishop and archenemy-comes from Greek *arkhos,* meaning chief. *Tekton* means builder.)

When Charlemagne was crowned Holy Roman Emperor in 800 C.E., Europe began to take its first steps out of the "Dark Ages" since the fall of Rome in the fifth century. The remains of Roman civilization were seen all over the continent, and legends of the great empire would have been passed down through generations. So when Charlemagne wanted to unite his empire and validate his reign, he began building churches in the Roman style—particularly the style of Christian Rome in the days of Constantine, the first Christian Roman emperor.

After a gap of around two hundred years with no large building projects, the architects of Charlemagne's day looked to the arched, or arcaded, system seen in Christian Roman edifices as a model. It is a logical system of stresses and buttressing, which was fairly easily engineered for large structures, and it began to be used in gatehouses, chapels, and churches in Europe. These early examples may be referred to as pre-Romanesque because, after a brief spurt of growth, the development of architecture again lapsed. As a body of knowledge was eventually re-developed, buildings became larger and more imposing. Examples of Romanesque cathedrals from the early Middle Ages (roughly 1000-1200) are solid, massive, impressive churches that are often still the largest structure in many towns.

In Britain, the Romanesque style became known as "Norman" because the major building scheme in the 11th and 12th centuries was instigated by William the Conqueror, who invaded Britain in 1066 from Normandy in northern France. (The Normans were the descendants of Vikings – Norse, or north men – who had invaded this area over a century earlier.) Durham and Gloucester Cathedrals and Southwell Minster are excellent examples of churches in the Norman, or Romanesque style.

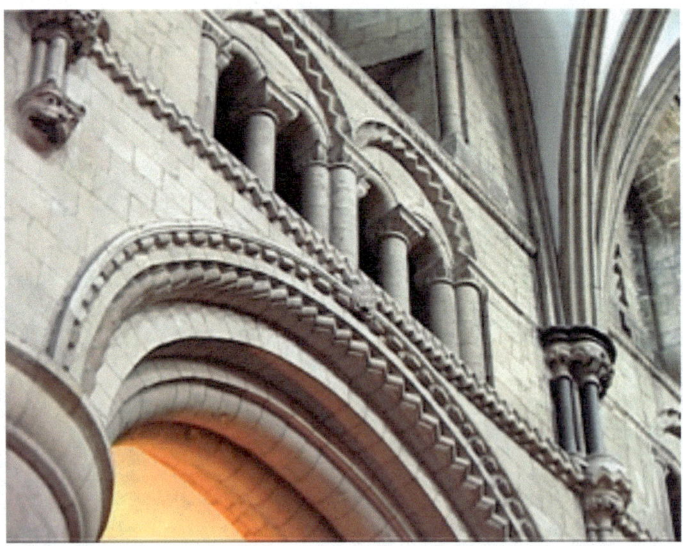

The arches that define the naves of these churches are well modulated and geometrically logical – with one look you can see the repeating shapes, and proportions that make sense for an immense and weighty structure. There is a large arcade on the ground level made up of bulky piers or columns. The piers may have been filled with rubble rather than being solid, carved stone. Above this arcade is a second level of smaller arches, often in pairs with a column between the two. The next higher level was again proportionately smaller, creating a rational diminution of structural elements as the mass of the building is reduced.

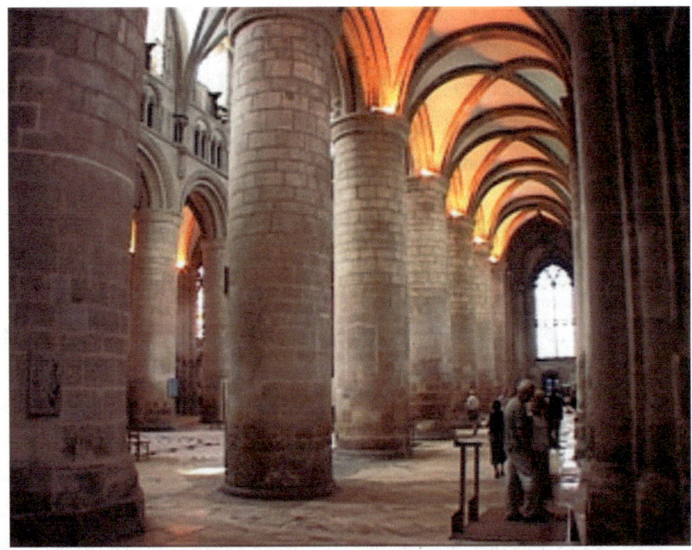

The decoration is often quite simple, using geometric shapes rather than floral or curvilinear patterns. Common shapes used include diapers – squares or lozenges – and chevrons, which were zigzag patterns and shapes. Plain circles were also used, which echoed the half-circle shape of the ubiquitous arches.

Early Romanesque ceilings and roofs were often made of wood, as if the architects had not quite understood how to span the two sides of the building using stone, which created outward thrust and stresses on the side walls. This development, of course, didn't take long to manifest, and led from barrel vaulting (simple, semicircular roof vaults) to cross vaulting, which became ever more adventurous and ornate in the Gothic.

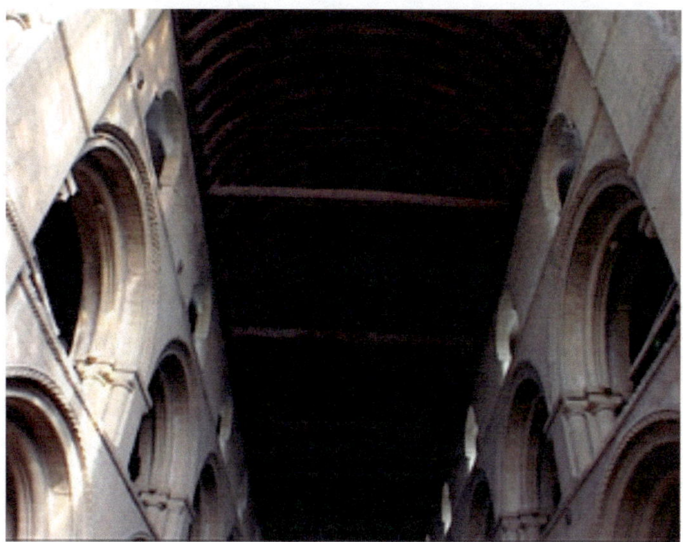

The third and fourth images on this page are from Gloucester Cathedral; all other images depict Southwell Minster.

Reading: Gothic Architecture

Forget the association of the word "Gothic" to dark, haunted houses, *Wuthering Heights,* or ghostly pale people wearing black nail polish and ripped fishnets. The original Gothic style was actually developed to bring sunshine into people's lives and especially into their churches. To get past the accrued definitions of the centuries, it's best to go back to the very start of the word Gothic, and to the style that bears the name.

The Goths were a so-called barbaric tribe who held power in various regions of Europe, between the collapse of the Roman Empire and the establishment of the Holy Roman Empire (so, from roughly the fifth to the eighth century). They were not renowned for great achievements in architecture. As with many art historical terms, "Gothic" came to be applied to a certain architectural style after the fact.

The style represented giant steps away from the previous, relatively basic building systems that had prevailed. The Gothic grew out of the Romanesque architectural style, when both prosperity and peace allowed for several centuries of cultural development and great building schemes. From roughly 1000 to 1400, several significant cathedrals and churches were built, particularly in Britain and France, offering architects and masons a chance to work out ever more complex problems and daring designs.

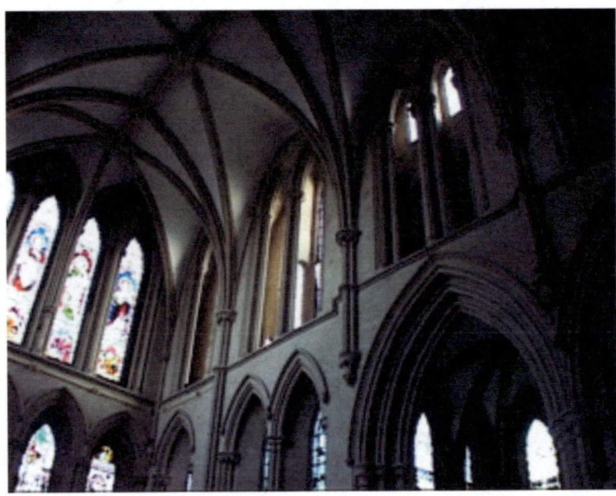

The most fundamental element of the Gothic style of architecture is the pointed arch, which was likely borrowed from Islamic architecture that would have been seen in Spain at this time. The pointed arch relieved some of the thrust, and therefore, the stress on other structural elements. It then became possible to reduce the size of the columns or piers that supported the arch.

So, rather than having massive, drum-like columns as in the Romanesque churches, the new columns could be more slender. This slimness was repeated in the upper levels of the nave, so that the gallery and clerestory would not seem to overpower the lower arcade. In fact, the column basically continued all the way to the roof, and became part of the vault.

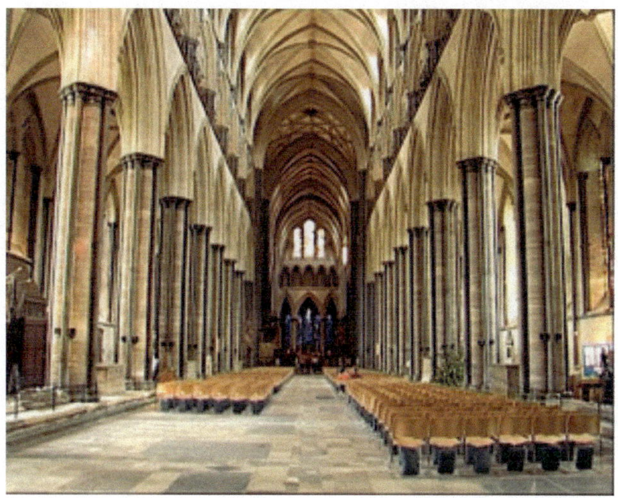

In the vault, the pointed arch could be seen in three dimensions where the ribbed vaulting met in the center of the ceiling of each bay. This ribbed vaulting is another distinguishing feature of Gothic architecture. However, it should be noted that prototypes for the pointed arches and ribbed vaulting were seen first in late-Romanesque buildings.

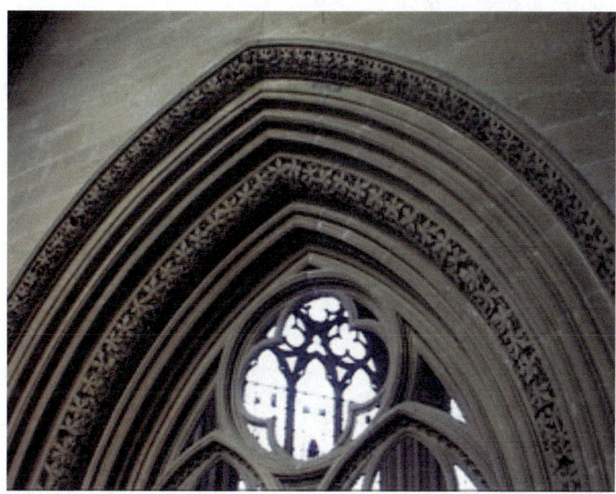

The new understanding of architecture and design led to more fantastic examples of vaulting and ornamentation, and the Early Gothic or Lancet style (from the twelfth and thirteenth centuries) developed into the Decorated or Rayonnant Gothic (roughly fourteenth century). The ornate stonework that held the windows—called *tracery*—became more florid, and other stonework even more exuberant.

The ribbed vaulting became more complicated and was crossed with *lierne* ribs into complex webs, or the addition of cross ribs, called *tierceron*. As the decoration developed further, the Perpendicular or International Gothic took over (fifteenth century). Fan vaulting decorated half-conoid shapes extending from the tops of the columnar ribs.

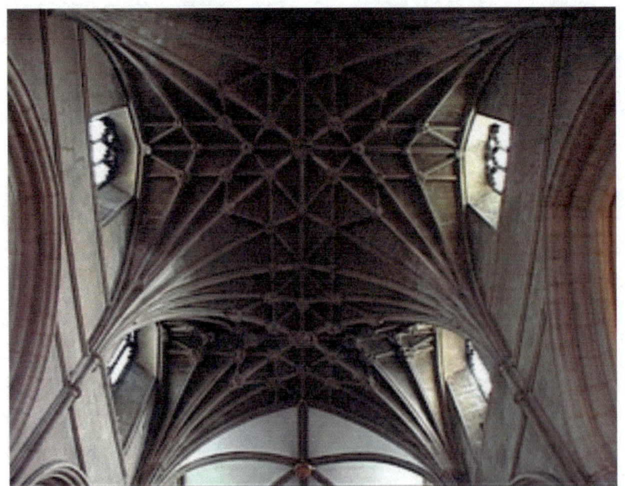

The slender columns and lighter systems of thrust allowed for larger windows and more light. The windows, tracery, carvings, and ribs make up a dizzying display of decoration that one encounters in a Gothic church. In late Gothic buildings, almost every surface is decorated. Although such a building as a whole is ordered and coherent, the profusion of shapes and patterns can make a sense of order difficult to discern at first glance.

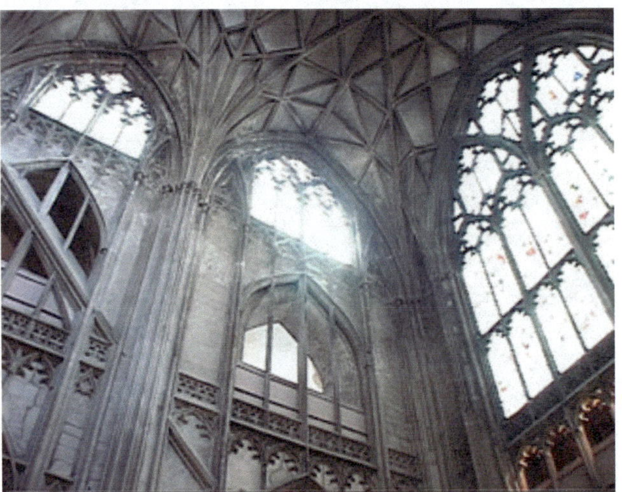

After the great flowering of Gothic style, tastes again shifted back to the neat, straight lines and rational geometry of the Classical era. It was in the Renaissance that the name Gothic came to be applied to this medieval style that seemed vulgar to Renaissance sensibilities. It is still the term we use today, though hopefully without the implied insult, which negates the amazing leaps of imagination and engineering that were required to build such edifices.

- https://youtu.be/w8QRG-Xc6oU
- https://youtu.be/dN5XRW7T0cc

Reading: Neo-Confucianism and Fan Kuan's Travelers by Streams and Mountains

Daoist mountain man, hermit, rustic, wine-lover—Fan Kuan has the reputation of having been truly unconventional. We know very little about this great artist, yet he painted the most majestic landscape painting of the early Song period. Everything about *Travelers by Streams and Mountains*, which is possibly the only surviving work by Fan Kuan, is an orderly statement reflecting the artist's worldview.

Landscape As a Subject in Its Own Right

Fan Kuan's masterpiece is an outstanding example of Chinese landscape painting. Long before Western artists considered landscape anything more than a setting for figures, Chinese painters had elevated landscape as a subject in its own right. Bounded by mountain ranges and bisected by two great rivers—the Yellow and the Yangzi—China's natural landscape has played an important role in the shaping of the Chinese mind and character. From very early times, the Chinese viewed mountains as sacred and imagined them as the abode of immortals. The term for landscape painting (shanshui hua) in Chinese is translated as "mountain water painting."

After a Period of Upheaval

During the tumultuous Five Dynasties period in the early 10th century (an era of political upheaval from 907–960 C.E., between the fall of the Tang Dynasty and the founding of the Song Dynasty, when five dynasties quickly succeeded one another in the north, and more than twelve independent states were established, mainly in the south), recluse scholars who fled to the mountains saw the tall pine tree as representative of the virtuous man. In the early Northern Song dynasty that followed, from the mid-10th to the mid-11th century, gnarled pine trees and other symbolic elements were transformed into a grand and imposing landscape style.

Fan Kuan, Travelers by Streams and Mountains, hanging scroll, ink on silk, c. 1000, 206.3 x 103.3 cm. (National Palace Museum, Taibei)

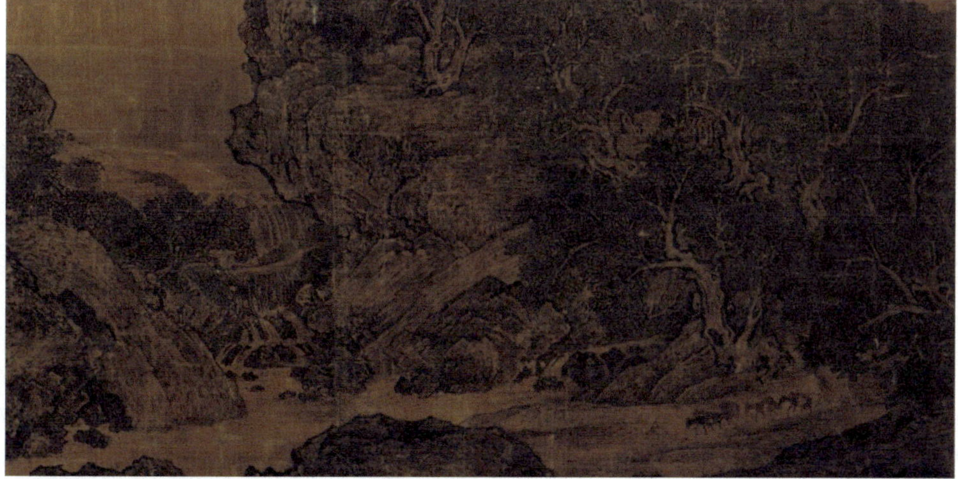

Fan Kuan, Travelers Among Mountains and Streams (detail)

Fan Kuan painted a bold and straightforward example of Chinese landscape painting. After the long period of political disunity (the Five Dynasties period), Fan Kuan lived as a recluse and was one of many poets and artists of the time who were disenchanted with human affairs. He turned away from the world to seek spiritual enlightenment. Through his painting *Travelers by Streams and Mountains*, Fan Kuan expressed a cosmic vision of man's harmonious existence in a vast but orderly universe. The Neo-Confucian search for absolute truth in nature as well as self-cultivation reached its climax in the 11th century and is demonstrated in this work. Fan Kuan's landscape epitomizes the early Northern Song monumental style of landscape painting. Nearly seven feet in height, the hanging scroll composition presents universal creation in its totality, and does so with the most economic of means.

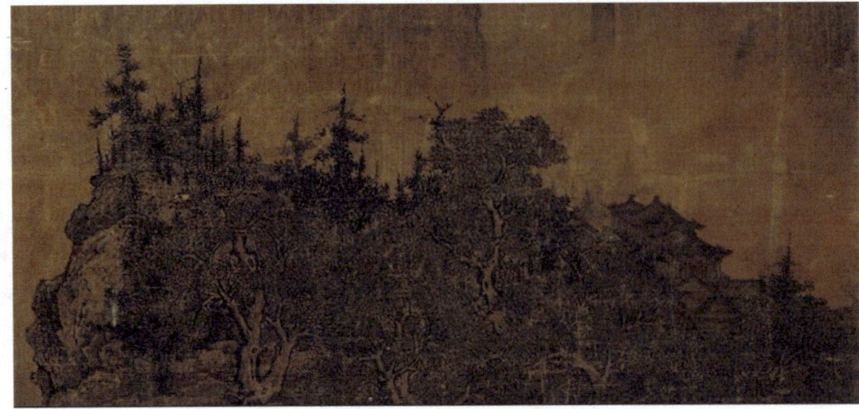

Fan Kuan, Travelers Among Mountains and Streams (detail)

Immense boulders occupy the foreground and are presented to the viewer at eye level. Just beyond them one sees crisp, detailed brushwork describing rocky outcroppings, covered with trees. Looking closely, one sees two men driving a group of donkeys loaded with firewood and a temple partially hidden in the forest. In the background a central peak rises from a mist-filled chasm and is flanked by two smaller peaks. This solid screen of gritty rock takes up nearly two-thirds of the picture. The sheer height of the central peak is accentuated by a waterfall plummeting from a crevice near the summit and disappearing into the narrow valley.

Fan Kuan, Travelers Among Mountains and Streams (detail)

The mountain form accurately captures the geological traits of southern Shaanxi and northwestern Henan provinces—thick vegetation grows only at the top of the bare steep-sided cliffs in thick layers of fine-grained soil known as loess. The mountains are triangular with deep crevices. In the painting they are conceived frontally and additively. To model the mountains, Fan Kuan used incisive thickening-and-thinning contour strokes, texture dots and ink wash. Strong, sharp brushstrokes depict the knotted trunks of the large trees. Notice the detailed brushwork that delineates the foliage and the fir trees silhouetted along the upper edge of the ledge in the middle distance.

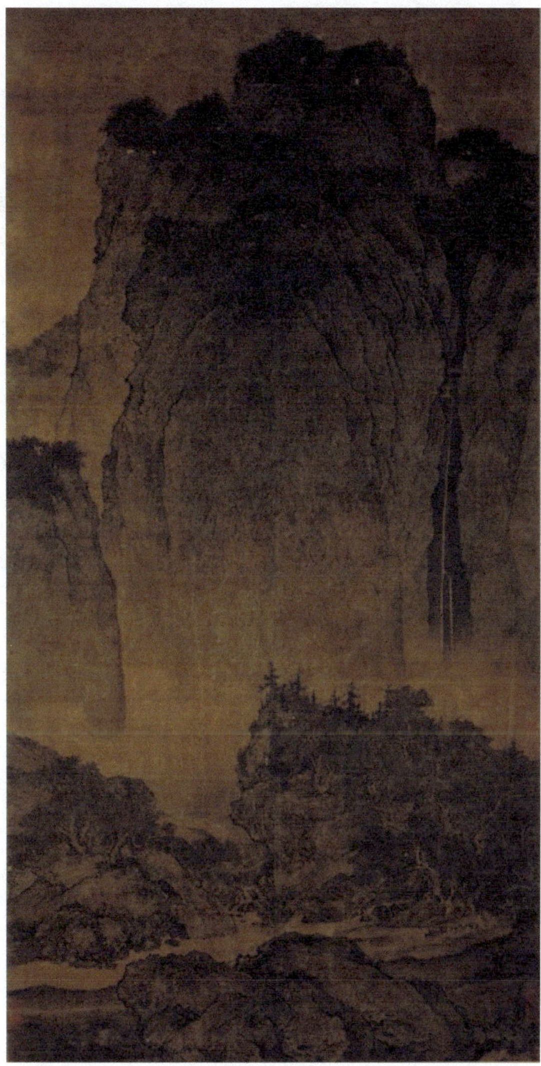

To convey the sheer size of the landscape depicted in *Travelers by Streams and Mountains*, Fan Kuan relied on suggestion rather than description. The gaps between the three distances act as breaks between changing views. Note the boulders in the foreground, the tree-covered rock outcropping in the middle, and the soaring peaks in the background. The additive images do not physically connect; they are comprehended separately. The viewer is invited to imagine himself roaming freely, yet one must mentally jump from one distance to the next.

The unsurpassed grandeur and monumentality of Fan Kuan's composition is expressed through the skillful use of scale. Fan Kuan's landscape shows how the use of scale can dramatically heighten the sense of vastness and space. Diminutive figures are made visually even smaller in comparison to the enormous trees and soaring peaks. They are overwhelmed by their surroundings. Fan Kuan's signature is hidden among the leaves of one of the trees in the lower right corner.

Neo-Confucianism

The development of Monumental landscape painting coincided with that of Neo Confucianism a reinterpretation of Chinese moral philosophy. It was Buddhism that first introduced, from India, a system of metaphysics and a coherent worldview more advanced than anything known in China. With Buddhist thought, scholars in the 5th and 6th centuries engaged in philosophical discussions of truth and reality, being and non-being, substantiality and nonsubstantiality. Beginning in the late Tang and early Northern Song (960-1127), Neo-Confucian thinkers rebuilt Confucian ethics using Buddhist and Daoist metaphysics. Chinese philosophers found it useful to think in terms of complimentary opposites, interacting polarities— inner and outer, substance and function, knowledge and action. In their metaphysics they naturally employed the ancient *yin* and *yang* (*Yin:* feminine, dark, receptive, yielding, negative, and weak. *Yang*: masculine, bright, assertive, creative, positive, and strong.) The interaction of these complementary poles was viewed as integral to the processes that generate natural order.

Central to understanding Neo-Confucian thought is the conceptual pair of *li* and *qi*. *Li* is usually translated as principles. It can be understood as principles that underlie all phenomena. *Li* constitutes the underlying pattern of reality. Nothing can exist if there is no li for it. This applies to human conduct and to the physical world. *Qi* can be characterized as the vital force and substance of which man and the universe are made. *Qi* can also be conceived of as energy, but energy which occupies space. In its most refined form it occurs as mysterious ether, but condensed it becomes solid metal or rock.

Not As the Human Eye Sees

The Neo-Confucian theory of observing things in the light of their own principles (*li*) clearly resonates in the immense splendor of Fan Kuan's masterpiece. Northern Song landscape painters did not paint as the human eye sees. By seeing things not through the human eye, but in the light of their own principles (*li*), Fan Kuan was able to organize and present different aspects of a landscape within a single composition—he does this with a constantly shifting viewpoint. In his masterful balance of *li* and *qi*, Fan Kuan created a microcosmic image of a moral and orderly universe.

Fan Kuan looked to nature and carefully studied the world around him. He expressed his own response to nature. As Fan Kuan sought to describe the external truth of the universe visually, he discovered at the same time an internal psychological truth. The bold directness of Fan's painting style was thought to be a reflection of his open character and generous disposition. His grand image of the beauty and majesty of nature reflects Fan Kuan's humble awe and pride.

Reading: Shiva As Lord of the Dance (Nataraja)

A Sacred Object out of Context

The art of medieval India, like the art of medieval Europe, was primarily in the service of religion. The devotee's spiritual experience was enhanced by meditation inspired by works of art and architecture. Just as the luminous upper chapel of the Sainte Chapelle dazzled and overwhelmed worshipers in France, the looming bronze statues of Shiva and Parvati in, for example, the inner halls of the Meenakshi Temple in Madurai, in south India would have awed a Hindu devotee.

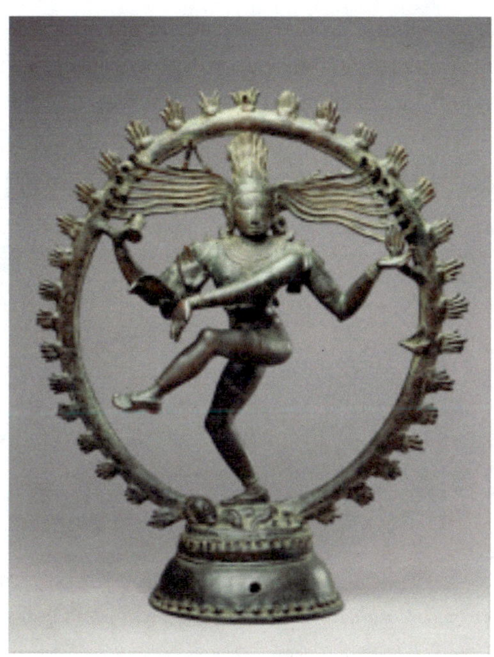

Shiva As Lord of the Dance (Nataraja), c. 11th century, Copper alloy, Chola period, 68.3 x 56.5 cm (The Metropolitan Museum of Art)

It's important to keep in mind that the bronze *Shiva As Lord of the Dance* ("Nataraja"—nata meaning dance or performance, and raja meaning king or lord), is a sacred object that has been taken out of its original context—in fact, we don't even know where this particular sculpture was originally venerated. In the intimate spaces of the Florence and Herbert Irving South Asian Galleries in the Metropolitan Museum of Art, the Shiva Nataraja is surrounded by other metal statues of Hindu gods including the Lords Vishnu, Parvati, and Hanuman. It is easy to become absorbed in the dark quiet of these galleries with its remarkable collection of divine figures, but it is important to remember that this particular statue was intended to be movable, which explains its moderate size and sizeable circular base, ideal for lifting and hoisting onto a shoulder.

Made for Mobility

From the 11th century and onwards, Hindu devotees carried these statues in processional parades as priests followed chanting prayers and bestowing blessings on people gathered for this purpose. Sometimes the statues would be adorned in resplendent red and green clothes and gold jewelry to denote the glorious human form of the gods. In these processions The *Shiva Nataraja* may have had its legs wrapped with a white and red cloth, adorned with flowers, and surrounded by candles. In a religious Hindu context, the statue is the literal embodiment of the divine. When the worshiper comes before the statue and begins to pray, faith activates the divine energy inherent in the statue, and at that moment, Shiva is present.

A Bronze Shiva

Shiva constitutes a part of a powerful triad of divine energy within the cosmos of the Hindu religion. There is Brahma, the benevolent creator of the universe; there is Vishnu, the sagacious preserver; then there is Shiva, the destroyer. "Destroyer" in this sense is not an entirely negative force, but one that is expansive in its impact. In Hindu religious philosophy all things must come to a natural end so they can begin anew, and Shiva is the agent that brings about this end so that a new cycle can begin.

The Metropolitan Museum's *Shiva Nataraja* was made some time in the eleventh century during the Chola Dynasty (9th–13th centuries C.E.) in south India, in what is now the state of Tamil Nadu. One of the longest lasting empires of south India, the Chola Dynasty heralded a golden age of exploration, trade, and artistic development. A great area innovation within the arts of the Chola period was in the field of metalwork, particularly in bronze sculpture. The expanse of the Chola empire stretched southeast towards Sri Lanka and gave the kingdom access to vast copper reserves that enabled the proliferation of bronze work by skilled artisans.

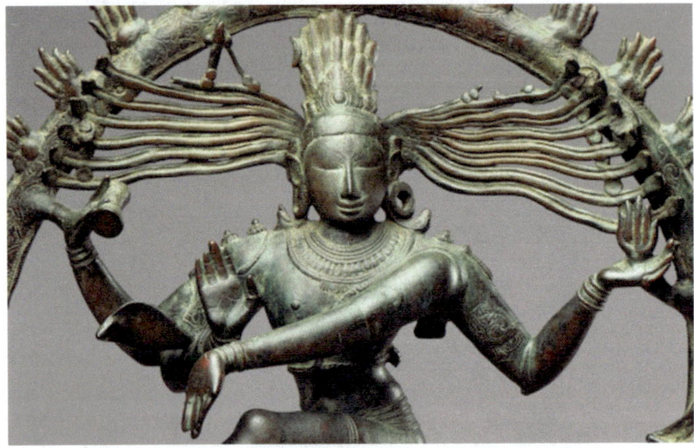

A Dance within the Cosmic Circle of Fire

During this period a new kind of sculpture is made, one that combines the expressive qualities of stone temple carvings with the rich iconography possible in bronze casting. This image of Shiva is taken from the ancient Indian manual of visual depiction, the *Shilpa Shastras* (The Science or Rules of Sculpture), which contained a precise set of measurements and shapes for the limbs and proportions of the divine figure. Arms were to be long like stalks of bamboo, faces round like the moon, and eyes shaped like almonds or the leaves of a lotus. The *Shastras* were a primer on the ideals of beauty and physical perfection within ancient Hindu ideology.

Here, Shiva embodies those perfect physical qualities as he is frozen in the moment of his dance within the cosmic circle of fire that is the simultaneous and continuous creation and destruction of the universe. The ring of fire that surrounds the figure is the encapsulated cosmos of mass, time, and space, whose endless cycle of annihilation and regeneration moves in tune to the beat of Shiva's drum and the rhythm of his steps.

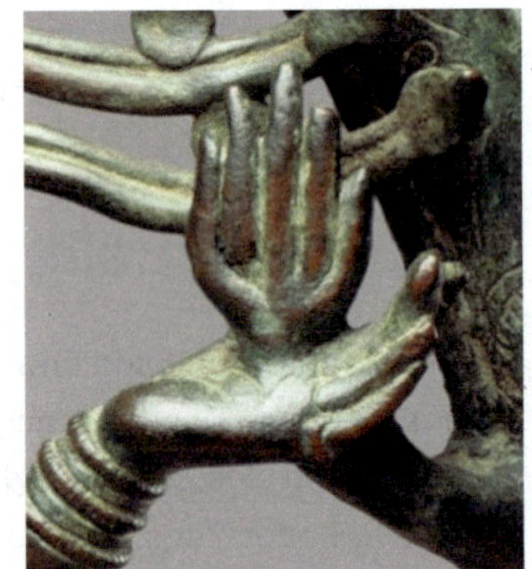

In his upper right hand he holds the *damaru*, the drum whose beats syncopate the act of creation and the passage of time.

His lower right hand with his palm raised and facing the viewer is lifted in the gesture of the *abhaya mudra*, which says to the supplicant, "Be not afraid, for those who follow the path of righteousness will have my blessing."

Shiva's lower left hand stretches diagonally across his chest with his palm facing down towards his raised left foot, which signifies spiritual grace and fulfillment through meditation and mastery over one's baser appetites.

In his upper left hand he holds the *agni* (image right), the flame of destruction that annihilates all that the sound of the*damaru* has drummed into existence.

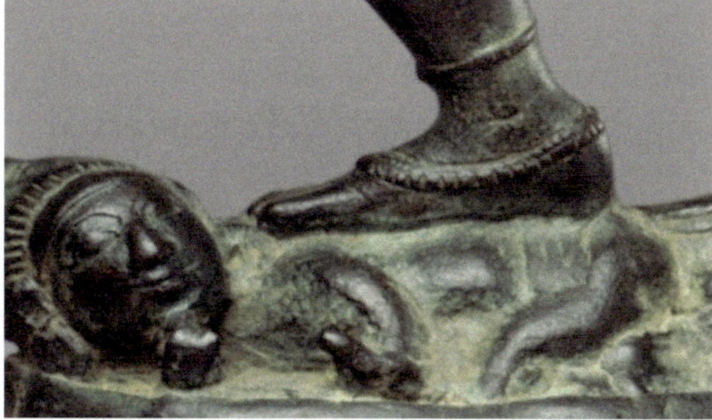

Shiva's right foot stands upon the huddled dwarf, the demon Apasmara, the embodiment of ignorance.

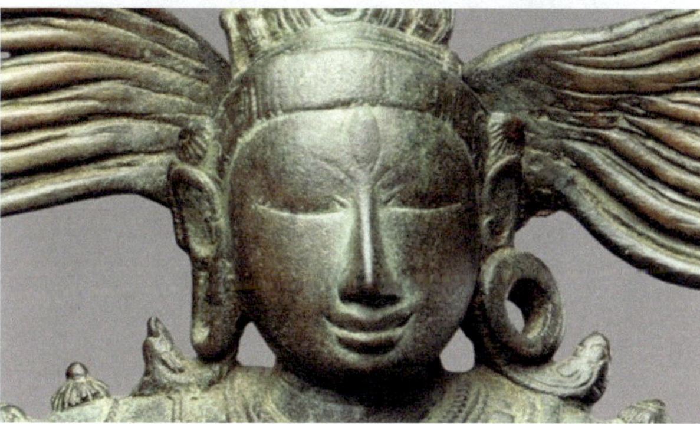

Shiva's hair, the long hair of the yogi, streams out across the space within the halo of fire that constitutes the universe. Throughout this entire process of chaos and renewal, the face of the god remains tranquil, transfixed in what the historian of South Asian art Heinrich Zimmer calls, "the mask of god's eternal essence."

Beyond Grace There Is Perfection

The supple and expressive quality of the dancing Shiva is one of the touchstones of South Asian, and indeed, world sculpture. When the French sculptor Auguste Rodin saw some photographs of the 11th century bronze Shiva Nataraja in the Madras Museum around 1915, he wrote that it seemed to him the "perfect expression of rhythmic movement in the world." In an essay he wrote that was published in 1921 he wrote that the Shiva Nataraja has "what many people cannot see—the unknown depths, the core of life. There is grace in elegance, but beyond grace there is perfection." The English philosopher Aldous Huxley said in an interview in 1961 that the Hindu image of god as a dancer is unlike anything he had seen in Western art. "We don't have anything that approaches the symbolism of this work of art, which is both cosmic and psychological."

The eloquent bronze statue of the *Shiva Nataraja*, despite the impact of its formal beauty on Rodin who knew little of its background, is incomplete without an understanding of its symbolism and religious significance. Bronzes of the Chola period such as *Shiva as Lord of the Dance (Nataraja)* arose out of a need to transmute the divine into a physical embodiment of beauty.

Reading: Classic Maya Portrait Stelae

Kings in Stone

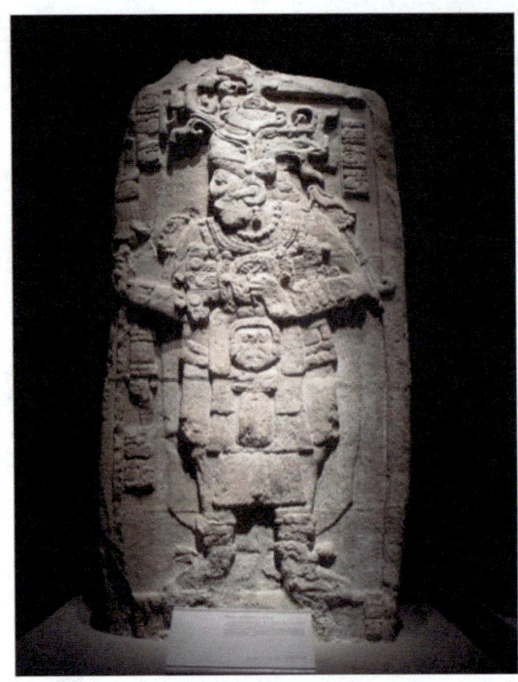

Stela 51, Calakmul, Campeche, Mexico (731 C.E.). A Maya ruler in ritual dress (Museo Nacional de Antropología, Mexico D.F.)

In 1839, American lawyer and amateur archaeologist John Lloyd Stephens and English artist Frederick Catherwood were the first outsiders to venture into the rainforests of Central America. They brought back their romanticized accounts and drawings of the remains of ancient Maya civilization to an eager England. In their publications, Stephens and Catherwood conveyed that they had uncovered the ruins of a great civilization that was uniquely American, one that had developed without contact with Egypt, India, or China.

Among the many strange and wonderful sites they encountered, it was the monuments that most aroused their interest and sparked their Victorian sensibility for engaging past civilizations. In regard to these hefty carved stones, Stephens penned the following excerpt:

Standing as they do in the depths of the forest, silent and solemn, strange in design, excellent in sculpture, rich in ornament . . . their uses and purposes and whole history so entirely unknown. . . .

Over the past thirty years, scholars have made substantial advances in understanding the 'uses and purposes' of Maya stone sculptures, and of the ancient peoples that produced them. This progress is due in no small part to developments in the decipherment of Maya hieroglyphics, which has escalated in recent decades. Epigraphers and art historians have labored to reconstruct the history and culture of the flourishing Classic period (c. 250-900 C.E.) expressed on the sculptures found throughout México, Honduras, Guatemala, El Salvador and Belize.

We now understand that the sculptors who chiseled these monuments were commissioned by privileged elites who lorded over vast city-states. These regional political and geographic partitions were dominated by singular powerful city-centers that vied for control of land and resources. Such cities were immense, and within them architects built grand pyramids and temples embellished with sculptures. Sculpted stone was an enduring record, and as early explorers witnessed, the remains of hundreds of carved monoliths still grace the ruins of these ancient Maya cities.

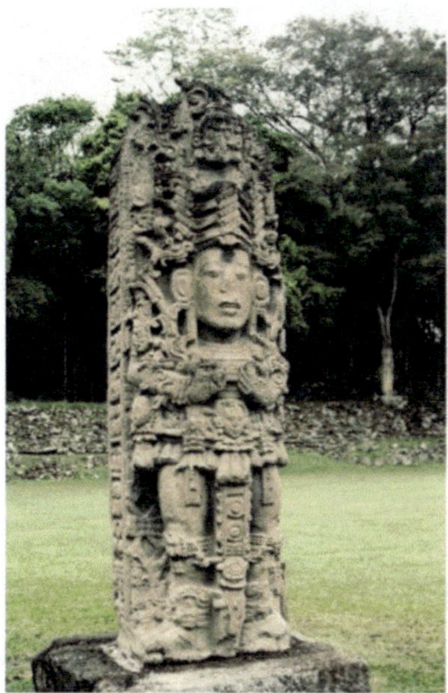

Stela A, Copán, Honduras, 731 C.E., Portrait of '18-Rabbit' of Copán.

A Medium for Political and Religious Rhetoric

The stone monuments over which Stephens and Catherwood marveled were crucial to the social and political cohesion of ancient Maya city-states. While small-scale art objects were cloistered behind the walls of privileged homes and courts, larger stone sculptures served as the principal medium for presenting political and religious rhetoric to the public.

The most vital and imposing format was the 'stela', an upright flat slab of stone worked in relief on one, two, or four faces. Their placement at the base of immense pyramids or in open plazas facing small stage-like platforms suggests that they were intended to be viewed by vast audiences in conjunction with other public spectacles. These lakam-tuun "banner stones," conveyed a broad and complex set of ideologies concerning royal history and politics, ceremonial activity, and calendrical reckoning. Their just-over human scale renders them ideal for presentations of engaging and awe-inspiring ruler portraits. In the tense political atmosphere of the Classic period, enduring images of powerful leaders ensured that the public recognized the authority of the ruler, the fortitude of his or her dynasty, and of the favor of deities.

Iconography and text carved onto stelae illuminated the king's visionary power. Contemporary notions of idealization prescribed that rulers appear youthful, handsome, and athletic. They wore a vast inventory of authoritative garb that included jade ornaments, various symbols of kingship, and an unwieldy, oversized headdress that must have been highly impractical for regular use. These figures act out one of a standard set of rites of passage: they wear battle garb to emphasize their military prowess, ritually let blood in offering to the deities, 'scatter' sacred substances with outstretched hands, or participate in ritual dance. Imagine trying to dance while balancing a headdress that is half your own height! Accompanying hieroglyphic texts elaborated on the life of the ruler and his ancestors.

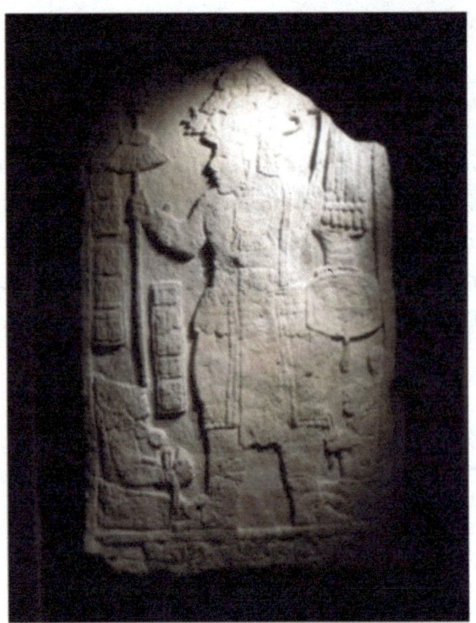

Stela 6, Aguateca, Guatemala. Portrait of King Tahn Te' K'inich (ruled 770-802 C.E.) in the garb of a warrior (Museo Chileno del Arte Precolombino, Santiago, Chile).

The Conquering Ruler

As regional conflicts became more frequent in 8th century, military themes on portrait stelae increased.

Stela 6 from Aguateca, Guatemala (right) exemplifies the archetype of the conquering ruler, responsible for defeating enemies and procuring captives for ritual sacrifice. Although the hieroglyphs on this monument are eroded, the portrait appears to depict King Tahn Te' K'inich (ruled 770-802 C.E.) as he brandishes a spear and shield and stands victoriously over two bound enemy captives.

Although Classic-period Maya stelae are no longer shrouded in mystery, numerous questions remain in regard to how they functioned. Perhaps most importantly, they provide only one side of the story, that of the ruler and of royal ideology. Stelae offer us little information regarding how they were received by the public, and we can only guess as to how effectively they impacted the common person. Although we know far more about ancient Maya stelae than Catherwood and Stephens ever imagined possible, the haze of mystery and intrigue through which they viewed these monuments has hardly evaporated.

Key Characteristics of Art: Renaissance through Baroque

Identify and describe key characteristics and defining events that shaped art from the Renaissance through Baroque periods

LEARNING ACTIVITIES

The learning activities for this section include:

- Reading: Florence in the Trecento (1300s)
- Reading: Florence in the Early Renaissance
- Video: Linear Perspective: Brunelleschi's Experiment
- Video: How One-Point Linear Perspective Works
- Video: Rogier van der Weyden, Deposition, c. 1435
- Reading: Toward the High Renaissance
- Reading: 1500–1600 End of the Renaissance and the Reformation
- Reading: The Baroque: Art, Politics, and Religion in Seventeenth-Century Europe

Take time to review and reflect on each of these activities in order to improve your performance on the assessment for this section.

Reading: Florence in the Trecento (1300s)

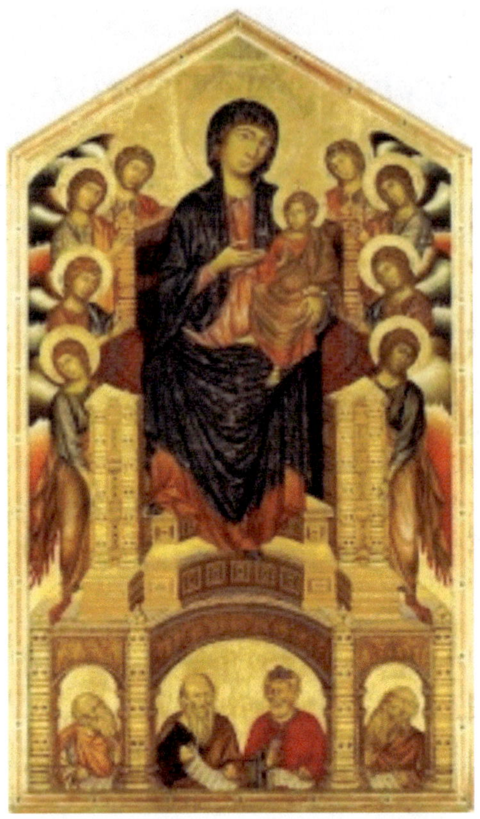

Cimabue, Santa Trinita Madonna (Madonna and Child Enthroned), 1280-90, tempera on panel (Galleria degli Uffizi, Florence)

A New Style Emerges

During the late thirteenth century, artists in a handful of Italian cities began to move away from the Italo-Byzantine style. The Roman artist Pietro Cavallini created frescoes and mosaics featuring solid, monumentalizing figures; the sculptor Nicola Pisano studied ancient Roman sculpture; Sienese artists seem to have broken new ground in exploring perspective.

Meanwhile, back in Florence, Cimabue's paintings showed more interest in depicting space and modeling figures with gradations of light and shade. These ideas spread as artists travelled throughout Italy and southern France in search of work, creating a network of artistic centers that all exerted influence on one another.

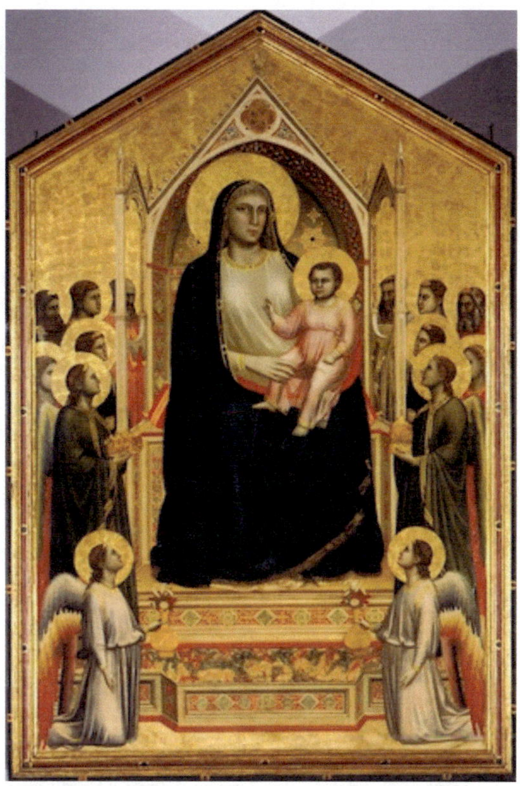

Giotto di Bondone, The Ognissanti Madonna, 1306-10, tempera on panel, 128 x 80 1/4″ or 325 x 204 cm (Galleria degli Uffizi, Florence)

Giotto

As the new century opened, the painter Giotto di Bondone observed many of these currents and forged them into something distinctively Florentine and enormously influential.

Where earlier works of art engage us with the embellished splendor of the heavenly, Giotto's paintings capture our attention by representing holy figures and stories as if in a majestic but earthly realm. Bold modeling of draperies and the bodies beneath them gives his figures greater volume and a sense of sculptural relief. Clever kinds of perspective create the illusion that a space is opening up in front of the viewer, as if we might be peering onto a stage.

Perhaps just as importantly, Giotto was a master of visual storytelling – a skill evident in his most important surviving project, the frescoes in the Arena Chapel in Padua (c. 1305). Here the monumentality of the figures, the quiet dignity of their movements, and the way architectural and landscape settings seem to echo the action all conjure up a solemn aura

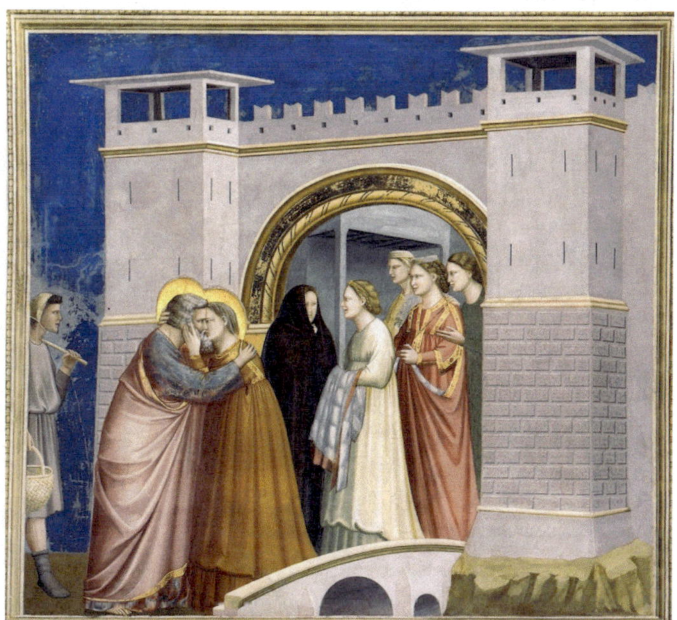

Giotto, Meeting at the Golden Gate, Arena (Scrovegni) Chapel, Padua, c. 1305.

of the sacred. Like many of the narrative paintings attributed to Giotto, the scenes use closely observed human gestures and careful composition to enhance the drama and emotion of the moment depicted.

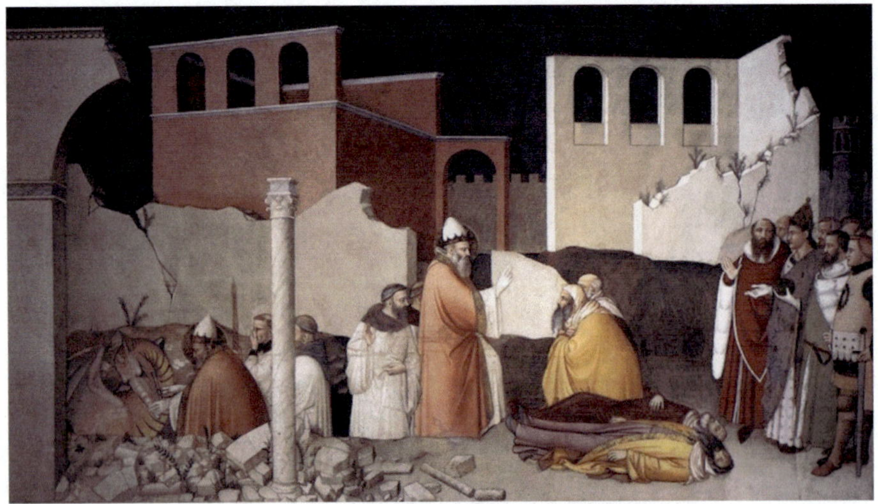

Maso di Banco, Pope Sylvester's Miracle, c. 1340 (Bardi Chape, Santa Croce, Florence)

Art After Giotto

Giotto had an enormous workshop full of students and assistants, making it hard to tell which works he painted and which were by his pupils. Even more confusingly, his style was so immediately influential that it is still difficult to say who his formal students were. What we do know is that, in the years immediately after his death, the artists who were the most "Giottesque" received the lion's share of the important commissions for new projects. The success of artists like Bernardo Daddi, Maso di Banco, and Taddeo Gaddi demonstrates that wealthy patrons were on board with Giotto's new vision for art.

Sometime around mid-century, though, certain artists began to drift from the clear, spare art of Giotto's school. Many experimented with visually crowded compositions or with complex subjects represented through elaborate symbols and schemes. Some even seem to have purposefully echoed the ornamental, formal art of the Italo-Byzantine period. This has led art historians to wonder whether these changes in style were caused by Florence's collective despair after the outbreak of the bubonic plague—a sickness that wiped out over half the city's population in one year alone (1348).

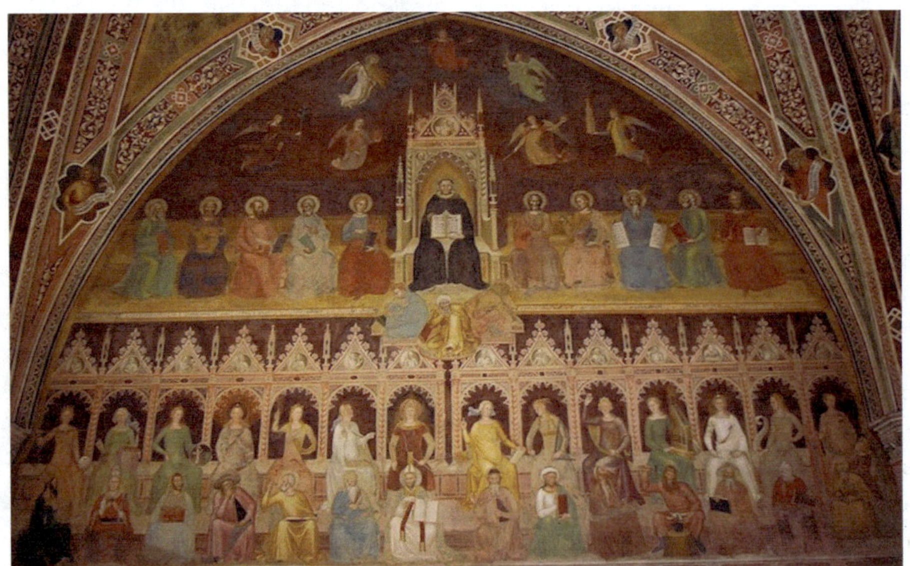

Andrea Bonaiuti, Triumph of St Thomas Aquinas, c. 1365-67, Guidalotti Chapel (Spanish Chapel) (Santa Maria Novella, Florence)

Most scholars now think the situation was more mixed than this theory might lead us to believe. In fact, late fourteenth-century art is hard to generalize. This is partly because no single workshop dominated the art of Florence as much as Giotto and his school had in previous decades. But it is also because artists of the time were skilled at adapting their own style to the specific tastes of each patron and to the context and function of each image.

Overall, however, Florentine art from 1348 to 1400 did not experience the same kind of major stylistic shift that characterized Giotto's years on the scene. Rather, the fundamental influence of Giotto continued into the early 1400s. In the end, the long fourteenth century was Giotto's century.

Reading: Florence in the Early Renaissance

Introduction

The Renaissance really gets going in the early years of fifteenth-century in Florence. In this period, which we call the Early Renaissance, Florence is not a city in the unified country of Italy, as it is now. Instead, Italy was divided into many city-states (Florence, Milan, Venice etc.), each with their own form of government.

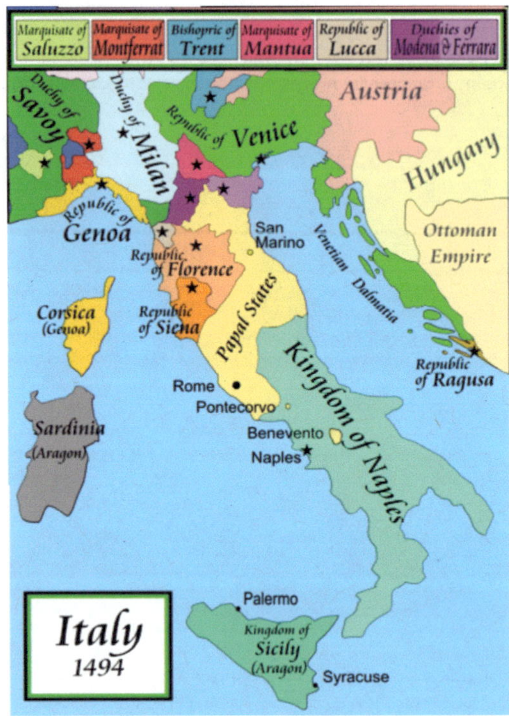

Now, we normally think of a Republic as a government where everyone votes for representatives who will represent their interests to the government (remember the pledge of allegiance: "and to the republic for which it stands..."). However, Florence was a Republic in the sense that there was a constitution which limited the power of the nobility (as well as laborers) and ensured that no one person or group could have complete political control (so it was far from our ideal of everyone voting, in fact a very small percentage of the population had the vote). Political power resided in the hands of middle-class merchants, a few wealthy families (such as the Medici, important art patrons who would later rule Florence) and the powerful guilds.

Rebirth of the Renaissance

So, why did the extraordinary rebirth of the Renaissance begin in Florence?

There are several answers to that question: Extraordinary wealth accumulated in Florence during this period among a growing middle and upper class of merchants and bankers. With the accumulation of wealth often comes a desire to use it to enjoy the pleasures of life—and not an exclusive focus on the hereafter.

Florence saw itself as the ideal city state, a place where the freedom of the individual was guaranteed, and where many citizens had the right to participate in the government (this must have been very different than living in the Duchy of Milan, for example, which was ruled by a succession of Dukes with absolute power) In 1400 Florence was engaged in a struggle with the Duke of Milan. The Florentine people feared the loss of liberty and respect for individuals that was the pride of their Republic.

Luckily for Florence, the Duke of Milan caught the plague and died in 1402. Then, between 1408 and 1414 Florence was threatened once again, this time by the King of Naples, who also died before he could successfully conquer Florence. And in

1423 the Florentine people prepared for war against the son of the Duke of Milan who had threatened them earlier. Again, luckily for Florence, the Duke was defeated in 1425. The Florentine citizens interpreted these military "victories" as signs of God's favor and protection. They imagined themselves as the "New Rome"—in other words, as the heirs to the Ancient Roman Republic, prepared to sacrifice for the cause of freedom and liberty.

Important! The Florentine people were very proud of their form of government in the early 15th century (as we are of our democracy). A republic is, after all, a place that respects the opinions of individuals, and we know that individualism was a very important part of the Humanism that thrived in Florence in the fifteenth century.

- https://youtu.be/6kUUJJV_MNA

Video: Linear Perspective: Brunelleschi's Experiement

- https://youtu.be/bkNMM8uiMww

Video: How One-Point Linear Perspective Works

- https://youtu.be/eOksHhQ8TLM

Video: Rogier van der Weyden, Deposition, c. 1435

- https://youtu.be/SLf_oAkngP4

Reading: Toward the High Renaissance

The High Renaissance is just that—the height of the Renaissance! When you think of the Renaissance, the names that come to mind are probably the artists of this period: Leonardo and Michelangelo, for instance. When many people think of the greatest work of art in the Western world, they think of Michelangelo's *Sistine Ceiling*. This is a period of big, ambitious projects.

What exactly is the High Renaissance, and how is it different from the Early Renaissance?

As the humanism of the Early Renaissance grows, a problem begins to develop. Have a look again at Fra Filippo Lippi's *Madonna and Child with Angels*. We see in this painting an image of the Madonna and Christ Child that has become so real, the figures so human, that we can hardly tell that these are spiritual figures (except for the faint shadow of a halo). On the other hand, as we have seen in the Middle Ages, if you want to make your figure spiritual then you sacrifice its realism.

It's almost as if there is this feeling in the Early Renaissance that if you want to be spiritual, then your painting can't look real, and if you want it to be real, then it loses some spirituality. It has to be one or the other. Well, Leonardo da Vinci comes along, and basically says—you don't have to make that choice. It's not either/or. Leonardo is able to create figures that are physical and real—just as real as Lippi's or Masaccio's figures and yet they have an undeniable and intense spirituality at the same time. So we can say that Leonardo unites the real and spiritual, or soul and substance.

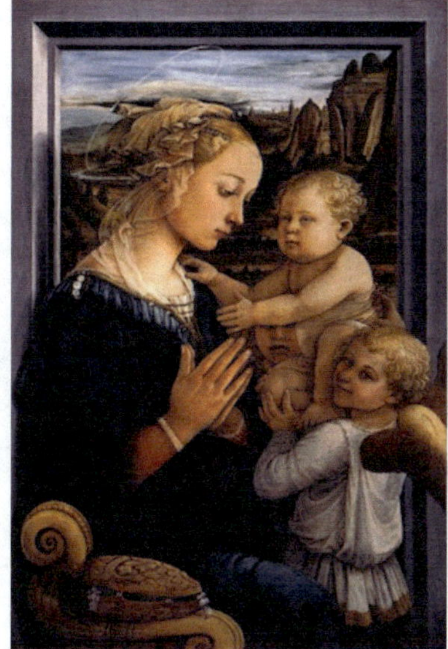

Fra Filippo Lippi, Madonna and Child with Two Angels, tempera on wood, ca. 1455–1466 (Galleria degli Uffizi, Florence)

The best way to see this is in this painting by Verrocchio, to whom Leonardo was apprenticed when he was young.

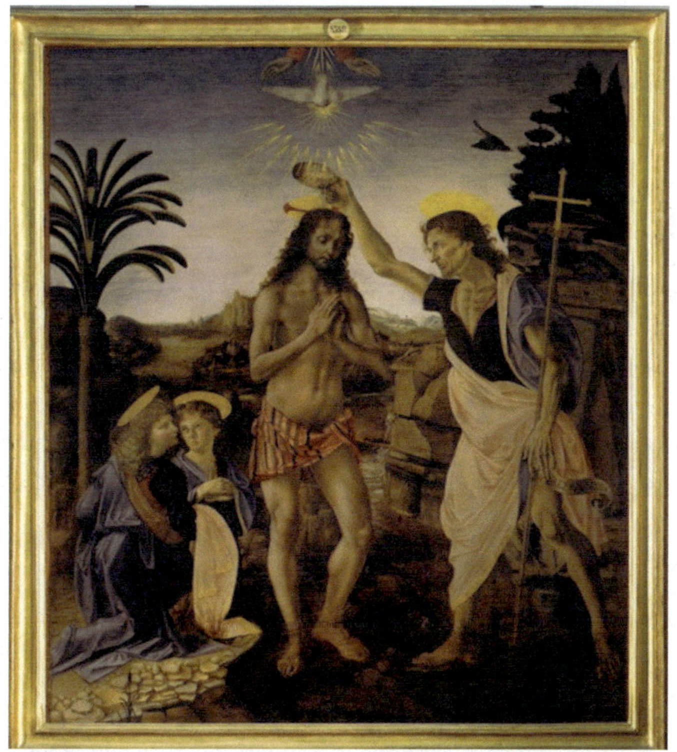

Andrea del Verrocchio (with Leonardo), Baptism of Christ, 1470-75, oil and tempera on panel, 70 3/4 x 59 3/4 inches or 180 x 152 cm (Galleria degli Uffizi, Florence)

Verocchio asked Leonardo to paint one of the angels in his painting of the *Baptism of Christ*, which we see here. Can you tell which angel is Leonardo's?

One angel should look more like a boy—that's the Early Renaissance angel (the one painted by Verrocchio) and the other angel should look like a High Renaissance angel, like a spiritual figure—truly like an angel sent by God from heaven (that's Leonardo's angel).

Can you tell which one is by Leonardo? Take a minute and look closely.

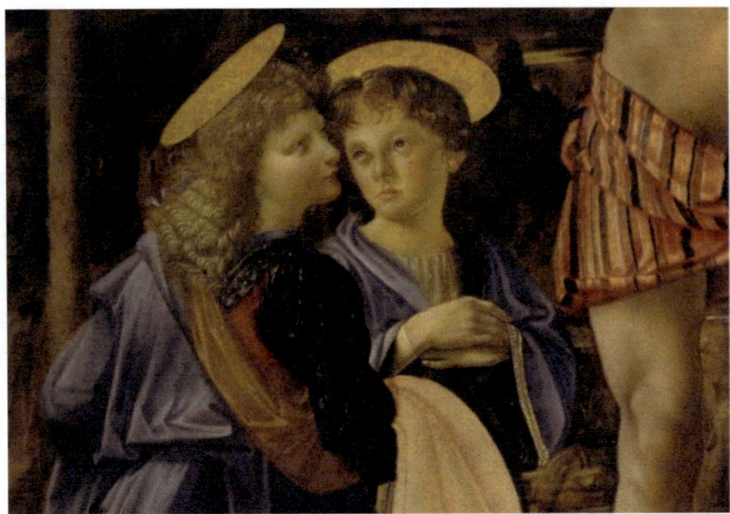

Detail. Andrea del Verrocchio (with Leonardo), Baptism of Christ, 1470-75, oil and tempera on panel, 70 3/4 x 59 3/4 inches or 180 x 152 cm (Galleria degli Uffizi, Florence)

(Answer: the angel on the left)

Leonardo's angel is ideally beautiful and moves in a graceful and complex way, twisting to the left but raising her head up and to the right. Figures that are elegant and ideally beautiful are a key characteristic of the High Renaissance.

Leonardo da Vinci

Leonardo's Early Life and Training

Leonardo was born illegitimate to a prominent Tuscan family of potters and notaries. He may have traveled from Vinci to Florence where his father worked for several powerful families including the Medici. At age seventeen, Leonardo reportedly apprenticed with the Florentine artist Verrocchio. Here, Leonardo gained an appreciation for the achievements of Giotto and Masaccio and in 1472 he joined the artists' guild, Compagnia di San Luca. Because of his family's ties, Leonardo benefited when Lorenzo de' Medici (the Magnificent) ruled Florence. By 1478 Leonardo was completely independent of Verrocchio and may have then met the exiled Ludovico Sforza, the future Duke of Milan, who would later commission the Last Supper.

Leonardo in Milan

Four years later, Leonardo arrived in Milan bearing a silver lyre (which he may have been able to play), a gift for the regent Ludovico from the Florentine ruler, Lorenzo the Magnificent. Ludovico sought to transform Milan into a center of humanist learning to rival Florence.

Leonardo flourished in this intellectual environment. He opened a studio, received numerous commissions, instructed students, and began to systematically record his scientific and artistic investigations in a series of notebooks. The archetypal "renaissance man," Leonardo was an unrivaled painter, an accomplished architect, an engineer, cartographer, and scientist (he was particularly interested in biology and physics). He was influenced by a variety of ancient texts including Plato's Timaeus, Ptolemy's Cosmography, and Vitruvius's On Architecture. Leonardo is credited with having assisted Luca Pacioli with his treatise, Divina Proportione (1509). Joining the practical and the theoretical, Leonardo designed numerous mechanical devices for battle, including a submarine, and even experimented with designs for flight.

In a now famous letter, Leonardo listed his talents to the Duke, focusing mostly on his abilities as a military engineer. The letter begins:

> Having until now sufficiently studied and examined the experiments of all those who claim to be experts and inventors of war machines, and having found that their machines do not differ in the least from those ordinarily in use, I shall make so bold, without wanting to cause harm to anyone, as to address myself to Your Excellency to divulge my secrets to him, and offer to demonstrate to him, at his pleasure, all the things briefly enumerated below.

In ten short paragraphs, Leonardo enumerated the service he could perform for the Duke — he said (among other things) that he could build bridges, tunnels, fortresses, and "make siege guns, mortars and other machines, of beautiful and practical shape, completely different from what is generally in use."

What might seem amazing to us is that it is not until the very last paragraph that Leonardo mentions art, and he mentions it so modestly! Here is what he wrote:

> In time of peace, I believe I am capable of giving you as much satisfaction as anyone, whether it be in architecture, for the construction of public or private buildings, or in bringing water from one place to another. Item, I can sculpt in marble, bronze or terracotta; while in painting, my work is the equal of anyone's.

Return to Florence, Then France

In 1489, Leonardo secured a long awaited contract with Ludovico and was honored with the title, "The Florentine Apelles," a reference to an ancient Greek painter revered for his great naturalism. Leonardo returned to Florence when Ludovico was deposed by the French King, Charles VII. While there, Leonardo would meet the Niccolò Machiavelli, author of The Prince and his future patron, François I. In 1516, after numerous invitations, Leonardo traveled to France and joined the royal court. Leonardo died on May 2, 1519 in the king's chateau at Cloux.

Leonardo's Death and the Changing Status of the Artist

> Finally, having grown old, he remained ill many months, and, feeling himself near to death, asked to have himself diligently informed of the teaching of the Catholic faith, and of the good way and holy Christian religion; and then, with many moans, he confessed and was penitent; and although he could not raise himself well on his feet, supporting himself on the arms of his friends and servants, he was pleased to take devoutly the most holy Sacrament, out of his bed. The King, who was wont often and lovingly to visit him, then came into the room; wherefore he, out of reverence, having raised himself to sit upon the bed, giving him an account of his sickness and the circumstances of it, showed withal how much he had offended God and mankind in not having worked at his art as he should have done. Thereupon he was seized by a paroxysm, the messenger of death; for which reason the King having risen and having taken his head, in order to assist him and show him favour, to then end that he might alleviate his pain, his spirit, which was divine, knowing that it could not have any greater honour, expired in the arms of the King. (Vasari)

This story is a good indication of the changing status of the artist. Leonardo, who spent the last years of his life in France working for King Francis I, was often visited by the King! Remember that the artist was considered only a skilled artisan in the Middle Ages and for much of the Early Renaissance.

In the High Renaissance, beginning with Leonardo, we find that artists are considered intellectuals, and that they keep company with the highest levels of society. Quite a change! All of this has to do with Humanism in the Renaissance of course, and the growing recognition of the achievement of great individuals (something virtually unheard of in the Middle Ages!). Artists in the Early Renaissance insisted that they should in fact be considered intellectuals because they worked with their brains as well as with their hands. They defended this position by pointing to the scientific tools that they used to make their work more naturalistic (scientific naturalism): the study of human anatomy, of mathematics and geometry, of linear perspective. These were clearly all intellectual pursuits!

Look closely at this self-portrait. Isn't it clear that Leonardo thought of himself as a thinker, a philosopher, an intellectual?

Leonardo's Naturalism

Ancient Greek physicians dissected cadavers. The early church's rejection of the science of the classical world, along with the possibility of bodily resurrection led to prohibitions against dissection. Both Leonardo and Michelangelo performed them — probably exclusively on the bodies of executed criminals. According to his own count, Leonardo dissected 30 corpses during his lifetime.

*   https://youtu.be/URcpchITNBY

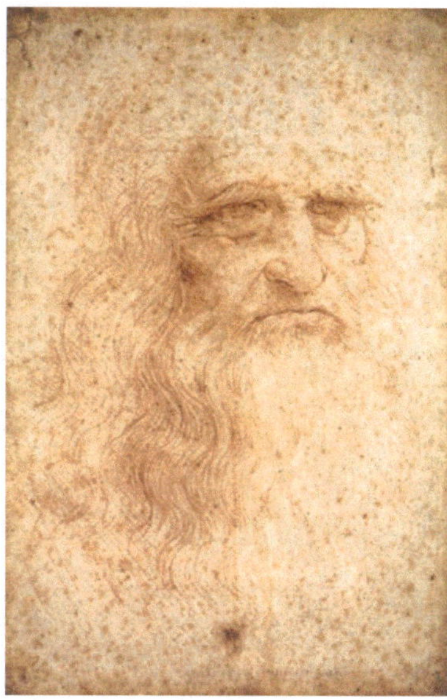

Leonardo da Vinci, Self-Portrait

Reading: 1500–1600 End of the Renaissance and the Reformation

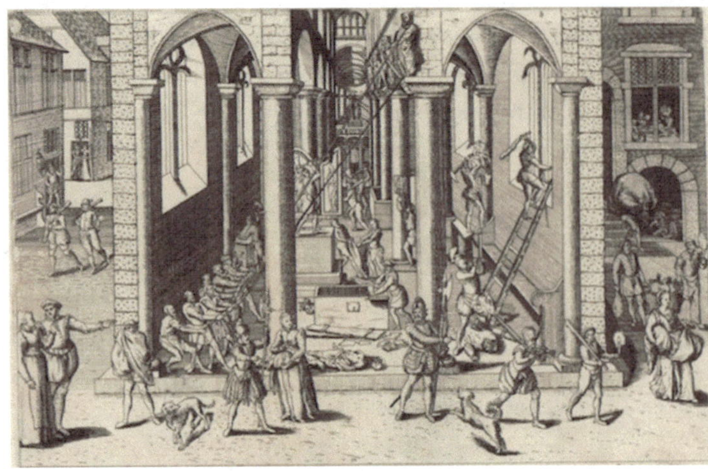

Frans Hogenberg, Iconoclasm 1566, 1566-70

A Challenge to the Church in Rome

In art history, the sixteenth century sees the styles we call the High Renaissance followed by Mannerism, and—at the end of the century—the emergence of the Baroque style. Naturally, these styles are all shaped by historical forces, the most significant being the Protestant Reformation's successful challenge to the spiritual and political power of the Church in Rome. For the history of art this has particular significance since the use (and abuse) of images was the topic of debate. In fact, many images were attacked destroyed during this period, a phenomenon called iconoclasm.

The Protestant Reformation

Today there many types of Protestant Churches. For example, Baptist is currently the largest denomination in the United States but there are many dozens more. How did this happen? Where did they all begin? To understand the Protestant Reform movement, we need to go back in history to the early 16th century when there was only one church in Western Europe—what we would now call the Roman Catholic Church—under the leadership of the Pope in Rome. Today, we call this "Roman Catholic" because there are so many other types of churches (ie Methodist, Baptist, Lutheran, Calvinist, Anglican—you get the idea).

The Church and the State

So, if we go back to the year 1500, the Church (what we now call the Roman Catholic Church) was very powerful (politically and spiritually) in Western Europe (and in fact ruled over significant territory in Italy called the Papal States). But there were other political forces at work too. There was the Holy Roman Empire (largely made up of German speaking regions ruled by princes, dukes and electors), the Italian city-states, England, as well as the increasingly unified nation states of France and Spain (among others). The power of the rulers of these areas had increased in the previous century and many were anxious to take the opportunity offered by the Reformation to weaken the power of the papacy (the office of the Pope) and increase their own power in relation to the Church in Rome and other rulers.

Keep in mind too, that for some time the church had been seen as an institution plagued by internal power struggles (at one point in the late 1300s and 1400s church was ruled by three Popes simultaneously). Popes and Cardinals often lived more like Kings than spiritual leaders. Popes claimed temporal (political) as well as spiritual power. They commanded armies, made political alliances and enemies, and, sometimes, even waged war. Simony (the selling of church offices) and nepotism (favoritism based on family relationships) were rampant. Clearly, if the Pope was concentrating on these worldly issues, there wasn't as much time left for caring for the souls of the faithful. The corruption of the Church was well known, and several attempts had been made to reform the Church (notably by John Wyclif and Jan Hus), but none of these efforts was successfully challenged Church practice until Martin Luther's actions in the early 1500s.

Martin Luther

Martin Luther was a German monk and Professor of Theology at the University of Wittenberg. Luther sparked the Reformation in 1517 by posting, at least according to tradition, his "95 Theses" on the door of the Castle Church in Wittenberg, Germany—these theses were a list of statements that expressed Luther's concerns about certain Church practices—largely the sale of indulgences, but they were based on Luther's deeper concerns with church doctrine. Before we go on, notice that Protestant contains the word "protest" and that reformation contains the word "reform" —this was an effort, at least at first, to protest some practices of the Catholic Church and to reform that Church.

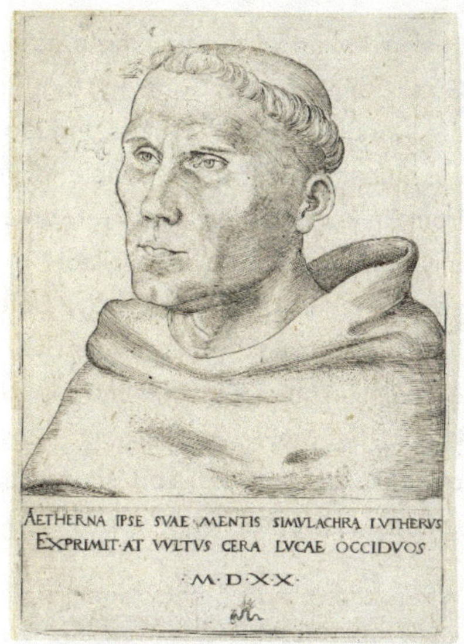

Lucas Cranach the Elder, Martin Luther, Bust in Three-Quarter View, 1520 (The Museum of Fine Arts, Houston)

Indulgences

The sale of indulgences was a practice where the church acknowledged a donation or other charitable work with a piece of paper (an indulgence), that certified that your soul would enter heaven more quickly by reducing your time in purgatory. If you committed no serious sins that guaranteed your place in hell, and you died before repenting and atoning for all of your sins, then your soul went to Purgatory—a kind of way-station where you finished atoning for your sins before being allowed to enter heaven.

Pope Leo X had granted indulgences to raise money for the rebuilding of St. Peter's Basilica in Rome. These indulgences were being sold by Johann Tetzel not far from Wittenberg, where Luther was Professor of Theology. Luther was gravely concerned about the way in which getting into heaven was connected with a financial transaction. But the sale of indulgences was not Luther's only disagreement with the institution of the Church.

Faith Alone

Martin Luther was very devout and had experienced a spiritual crisis. He concluded that no matter how "good" he tried to be, no matter how he tried to stay away from sin, he still found himself having sinful thoughts. He was fearful that no matter how many good works he did, he could never do enough to earn his place in heaven (remember that, according to the Catholic Church, doing good works, for example commissioning works of art for the Church, helped one gain entrance to heaven). This was a profound recognition of the inescapable sinfulness of the human condition. After all, no matter how kind and good we try to be, we all find ourselves having thoughts which are unkind and sometimes much worse. Luther found a way out of this problem when he read St. Paul, who wrote "The just shall live by faith" (Romans 1:17). Luther understood this to mean that those who go to heaven (the just) will get there by faith alone—not by doing good works. In other words, God's grace is something freely given to human beings, not something we can earn. For the Catholic Church on the other hand, human beings, through good works, had some agency in their salvation.

Scripture Alone

Luther (and other reformers) turned to the Bible as the only reliable source of instruction (as opposed to the teachings of the Church).

The invention of the printing press in the middle of the 15th century (by Gutenberg in Mainz, Germany) together with the translation of the Bible into the vernacular (the common languages of French, Italian, German, English, etc.) meant that it was possible for those that could read to learn directly from Bible without having to rely on a priest or other church officials. Before this time, the Bible was available in Latin, the ancient language of Rome spoken chiefly by the clergy. Before the printing press, books were handmade and extremely expensive. The invention of the printing press and the translation of the bible into the vernacular meant that for the first time in history, the Bible was available to those outside of the Church. And now, a direct relationship to God, unmediated by the institution of the Catholic Church, was possible.

When Luther and other reformers looked to the words of the Bible (and there were efforts at improving the accuracy of these new translations based on early Greek manuscripts), they found that many of the practices and teachings of the Church about how we achieve salvation didn't match

Gutenberg Bible (British Museum)

Christ's teaching. This included many of the Sacraments, including Holy Communion (also known as the Eucharist). According to the Catholic Church, the miracle of Communion is transubstantiation—when the priest administers the bread and wine, they change (the prefix "trans" means to change) their substance into the body and blood of Christ. Luther denied that anything changed during Holy Communion. Luther thereby challenged one of the central sacraments of the Catholic Church, one of its central miracles, and thereby one of the ways that human beings can achieve grace with God, or salvation.

The Counter-Reformation

The Church initially ignored Martin Luther, but Luther's ideas (and variations of them, including Calvinism) quickly spread throughout Europe. He was asked to recant (to disavow) his writings at the Diet of Worms (an unfortunate name for a council held by the Holy Roman Emperor in the German city of Worms). When Luther refused, he was excommunicated (in other words, expelled from the church). The Church's response to the threat from Luther and others during this period is called the Counter-Reformation ("counter" meaning against).

The Council of Trent

In 1545 the Church opened the Council of Trent to deal with the issues raised by Luther. The Council of Trent was an assembly of high officials in the Church who met (on and off for eighteen years) principally in the Northern Italian town of Trent for 25 sessions.

Selected Outcomes of the Council of Trent:

1. The Council denied the Lutheran idea of justification by faith. They affirmed, in other words, their Doctrine of Merit, which allows human beings to redeem themselves through Good Works, and through the sacraments.
2. They affirmed the existence of Purgatory and the usefulness of prayer and indulgences in shortening a person's stay in purgatory.
3. They reaffirmed the belief in transubstantiation and the importance of all seven sacraments

4.   They reaffirmed the authority of both scripture the teachings and traditions of the Church
5.   They reaffirmed the necessity and correctness of religious art (see below)

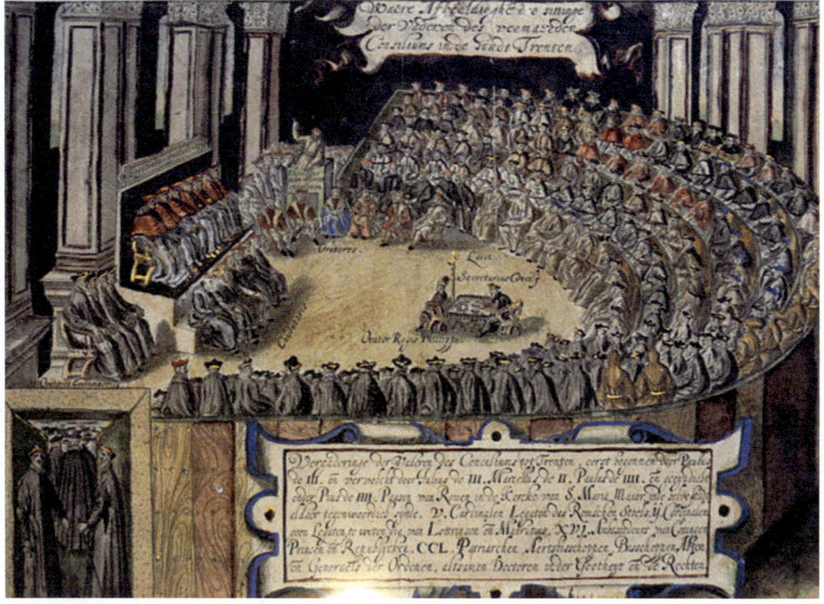

Session of the Council of Trent in Matthias Burglechner, "Tyrolischer Adler," vol.IX

The Council of Trent on Religious Art

At the Council of Trent, the Church also reaffirmed the usefulness of images—but indicated that church officials should be careful to promote the correct use of images and guard against the possibility of idolatry. The council decreed that images are useful "because the honour which is shown them is referred to the prototypes which those images represent" (in other words, through the images we honor the holy figures depicted). And they listed another reason images were useful, "because the miracles which God has performed by means of the saints, and their salutary examples, are set before the eyes of the faithful; that so they may give God thanks for those things; may order their own lives and manners in imitation of the saints; and may be excited to adore and love God, and to cultivate piety."

Violence

The Reformation was a very violent period in Europe, even family members were often pitted against one another in the wars of religion. Each side, both Catholics and Protestants, were often absolutely certain that they were in the right and that the other side was doing the devil's work.

The artists of this period—Michelangelo in Rome, Titian in Venice, Durer in Nuremberg, Cranach in Saxony—were impacted by these changes since the Church had been the single largest patron for artists. And now art was now being scrutinized in an entirely new way. The Catholic Church was looking to see if art communicated the stories of the Bible effectively and clearly (see Veronese's Feast in the House of Levi for more on this). Protestants on the other hand, for the most part lost the patronage of the Church and religious images (sculptures, paintings, stained glass windows etc) were destroyed in iconoclastic riots.

Other Developments

It is also during this period that the Scientific Revolution gained momentum and observation of the natural world replaced religious doctrine as the source of our understanding of the universe and our place in it. Copernicus up-ended the ancient Greek model of the heavens by suggesting that the sun was at the center of the solar system and that the planets orbited around it.

At the same time, exploration, colonization and (the often forced) Christianization of what Europe called the "new world" continued. By the end of the century, the world of the Europeans was a lot bigger and opinions about that world were more varied and more uncertain than they had been for centuries.

Reading: The Baroque: Art, Politics, and Religion in Seventeenth-Century Europe

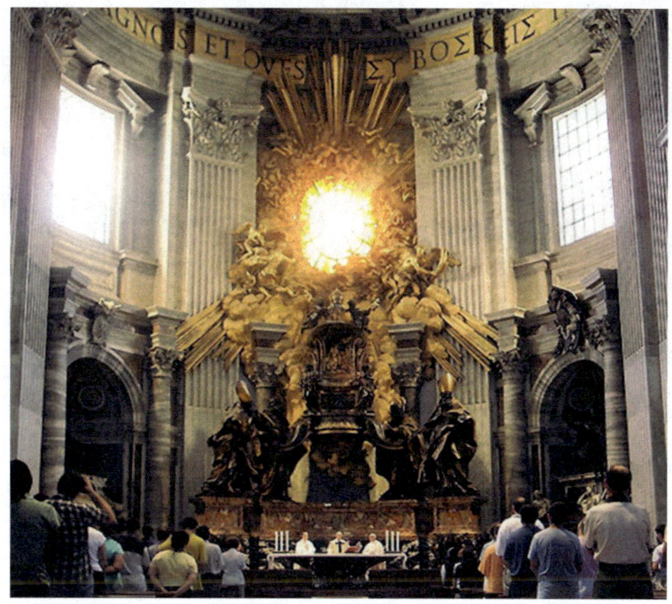

Gian Lorenzo Bernini, Cathedra Petri (or Chair of St. Peter), gilded bronze, gold, wood, stained glass, 1647-53 (apse of Saint Peter's Basilica, Vatican City, Rome)

Rome: From the "Whore of Babylon" to the Resplendent Bride of Christ

When Martin Luther tacked his 95 theses to the doors of Wittenburg Cathedral in 1517 protesting the Catholic Church's corruption, he initiated a movement that would transform the religious, political, and artistic landscape of Europe. For the next century, Europe would be in turmoil as new political and religious boundaries were determined, often through bloody military conflicts. Only in 1648, with the signing of the Treaty of Westphalia, did the conflicts between Protestants and Catholics subside in continental Europe.

Martin Luther focused his critique on what he saw as the Church's greed and abuse of power. He called Rome, the seat of papal power, "the whore of Babylon" decked out in finery of expensive art, grand architecture, and sumptuous banquets. The Church responded to the crisis in two ways: by internally addressing issues of corruption and by defending the doctrines rejected by the Protestants. Thus, while the first two decades of the 16th century were a period of lavish spending for the Papacy, the middle decades were a period of austerity. As one visitor to Rome noted in the 1560s, the entire city had become a convent. Piety and asceticism ruled the day.

By the end of the 16th century, the Catholic Church was once again feeling optimistic, even triumphant. It had emerged from the crisis with renewed vigor and clarity of purpose. Shepherding the faithful—instructing them on Catholic doctrines and inspiring virtuous behavior—took center stage. Keen to rebuild Rome's reputation as a holy city, the Papacy embarked on extensive building and decoration campaigns aimed at highlighting its ancient origins, its beliefs, and its divinely-sanctioned authority. In the eyes of faithful Catholics, Rome was not an unfaithful whore, but a pure bride, beautifully adorned for her union with her divine spouse.

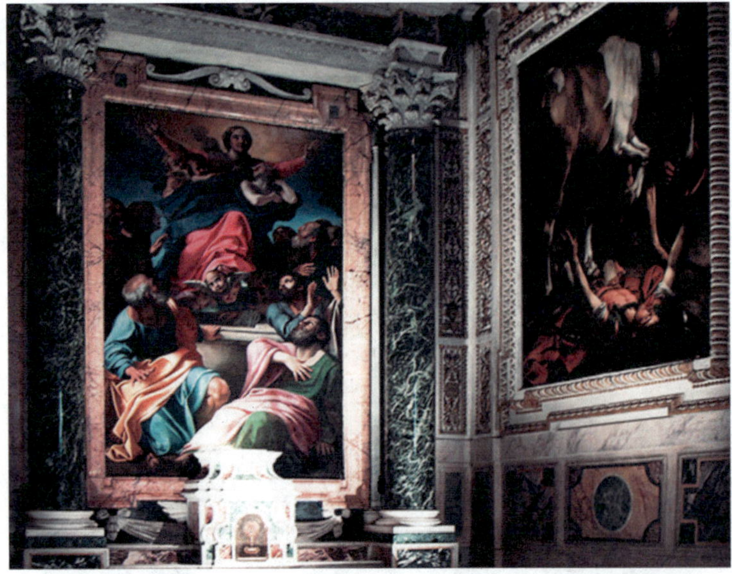

View of the Cerasi Chapel in Santa Maria del Popolo in Rome with Annibale Carracci's altarpiece, The Assumption of the Virgin, 1600-01, oil on canvas, 96 in × 61 inches and to the right, Caravaggio's Conversion of Saint Paul (Conversion of Saul), 1601, 91 in × 69 inches

The Art of Persuasion: to Instruct, to Delight, to Move

While the Protestants harshly criticized the cult of images, the Catholic Church ardently embraced the religious power of art. The visual arts, the Church argued, played a key role in guiding the faithful. They were certainly as important as the written and spoken word, and perhaps even more important, since they were accessible to the learned and the unlearned alike. In order to be effective in its pastoral role, religious art had to be clear, persuasive, and powerful. Not only did it have to instruct, it had to inspire. It had to move the faithful to feel the reality of Christ's sacrifice, the suffering of the martyrs, the visions of the saints.

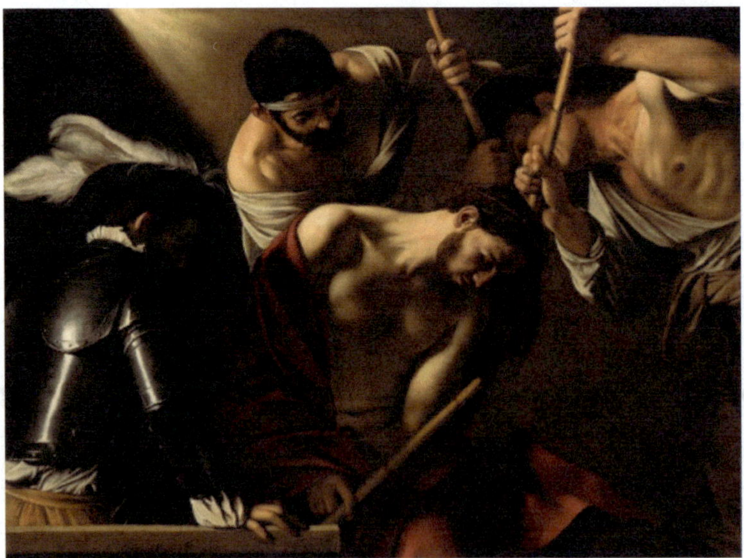

Caravaggio, The Crowning with Thorns, 1602-04, oil on canvas, 165.5 x 127 cm (Kunsthistorisches Museum, Vienna)

The Church's emphasis on art's pastoral role prompted artists to experiment with new and more direct means of engaging the viewer. Artists like Caravaggio turned to a powerful and dramatic realism, accentuated by bold contrasts of light and dark, and tightly-cropped compositions that enhance the physical and emotional immediacy of the depicted narrative. Other artists, like Annibale Carracci (who also experimented with realism), ultimately settled on a more classical visual language, inspired by the vibrant palette, idealized forms, and balanced compositions of the High Renaissance. Still others, like Giovanni Battista Gaulli, turned to daring feats of illusionism that blurred not only the boundaries between painting, sculpture, and architecture, but also those between the real and depicted worlds. In so doing, the divine was made physically present and palpable. Whether through shocking realism, dynamic movement, or exuberant ornamentation, seventeenth-century art is meant to impress. It aims to convince the viewer of the truth of its message by impacting the senses, awakening the emotions, and activating, even sharing the viewer's space.

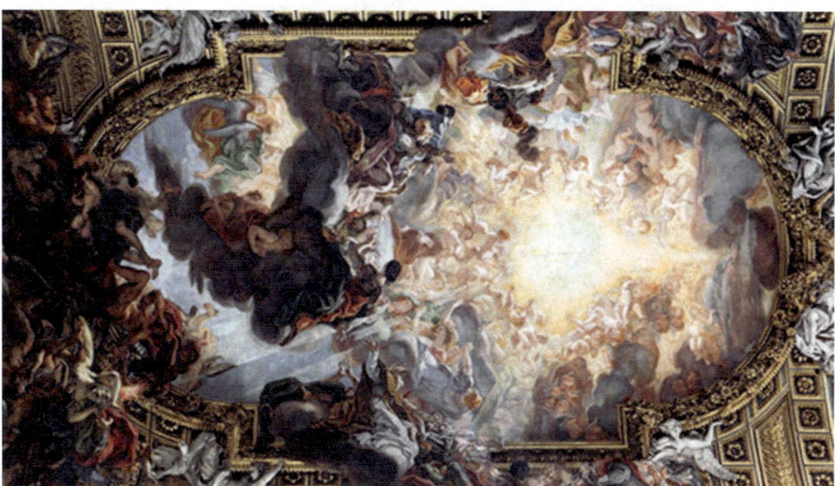

Giovanni Battista Gaulli, also known as il Baciccio, The Triumph of the Name of Jesus, Il Gesù ceiling fresco, 1672-1685

The Catholic Monarchs and Their Territories

The monarchs of Spain, Portugal, and France also embraced the more ornate elements of seventeenth century art to celebrate Catholicism. In Spain and its colonies, rulers invested vast resources on elaborate church facades, stunning, gold-covered chapels and tabernacles, and strikingly-realistic polychrome sculpture. In the Spanish Netherlands, where sacred art had suffered terribly as a result of the Protestant iconoclasm (the destruction of art), civic and religious leaders prioritized the adornment of churches as the region reclaimed its Catholic identity. Refurnishing the altars of Antwerp's churches kept Peter Paul Rubens' workshop busy for many years. Europe's monarchs also adopted this artistic vocabulary to proclaim their own power and status. Louis XIV, for example, commissioned the splendid buildings and gardens of Versailles as a visual expression of his divine right to rule.

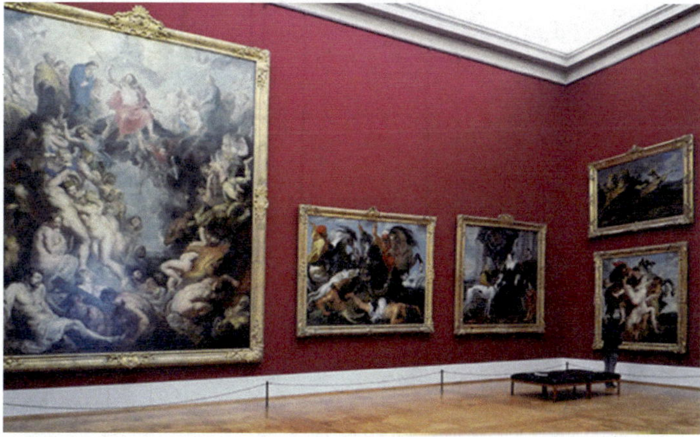

View of paintings by Peter Paul Rubens in the Alte Pinakothek, Munich

The Protestant North

In the Protestant countries, and especially in the newly-independent Dutch Republic (modern-day Holland), the artistic climate changed radically in the aftermath of the Reformation.

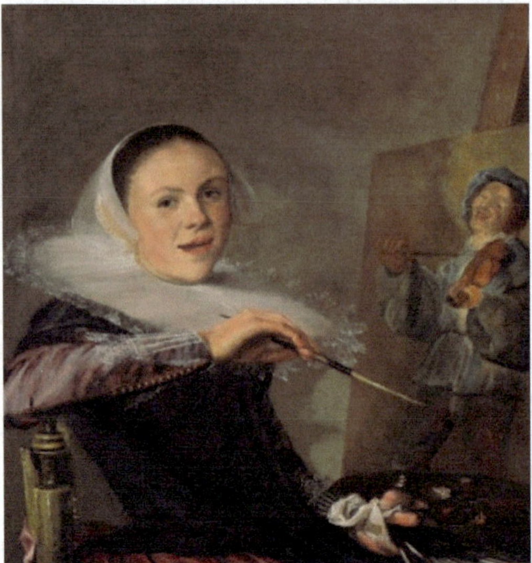

Judith Leyster, Self-Portrait, c. 1630, oil on canvas, 651 x 746 cm (National Gallery of Art, Washington)

Two of the wealthiest sources of patronage—the monarchy and the Church—were now gone. In their stead arose an increasingly prosperous middle class eager to express its status, and its new sense of national pride, through the purchase of art.

By the middle of the 17th century a new market had emerged to meet the artistic tastes of this class. The demand was now for smaller scale paintings suitable for display in private homes. These paintings included religious subjects for private contemplation, as seen in Rembrandt's poignant paintings and prints of biblical narratives, as well as portraits documenting individual likenesses.

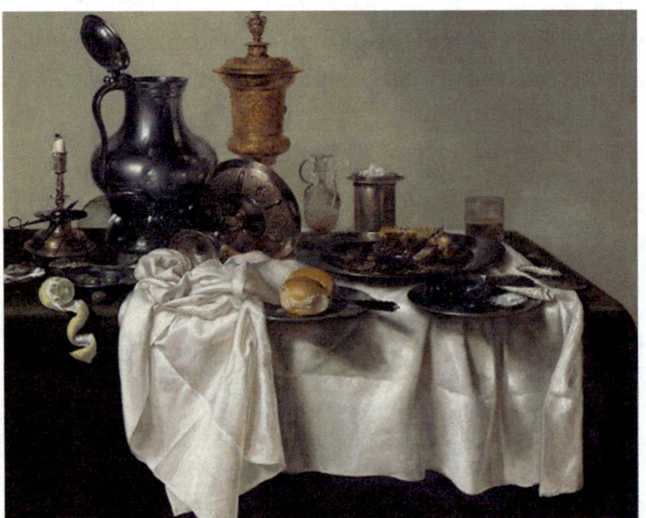

Willem Claesz Heda, Banquet Piece with Mince Pie, 1635, oil on canvas, 42 x 43-3/4 inches (National Gallery of Art, Washington)

But, the greatest change in the market was the dramatic increase in the popularity of landscapes, still-lifes, and scenes of everyday life (known as genre painting). Indeed, the proliferation of these subjects as independent artistic genres was one of the 17th century's most significant contributions to the history of Western art. In all of these genres, artists revealed a keen interest in replicating observed reality—whether it be the light on the Dutch landscape, the momentary expression on a face, or the varied textures and materials of the objects the Dutch collected as they reaped the benefits of their expanding mercantile empire. These works demonstrated as much artistic virtuosity and physical immediacy as the grand decorations of the palaces and churches of Catholic Europe.

"Baroque"—the Word, the Style, the Period

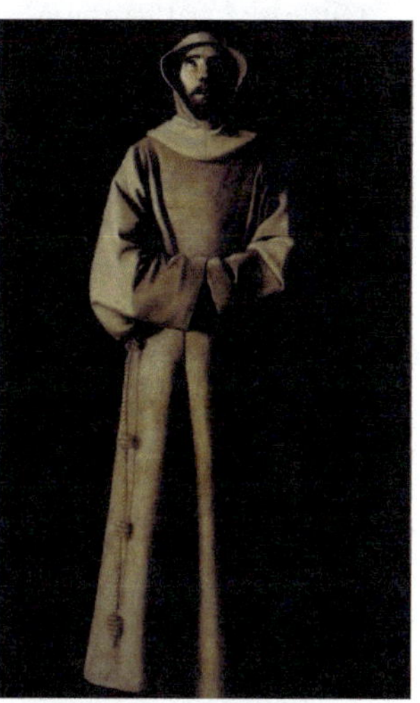

In the context of European history, the period from c. 1585 to c. 1700/1730 is often called the Baroque era. The word "baroque" derives from the Portuguese and Spanish words for a large, irregularly-shaped pearl ("barroco" and "barrueco," respectively). Eighteenth century critics were the first to apply the term to the art of the 17th century. It was not a term of praise. To the eyes of these critics, who favored the restraint and order of Neoclassicism, the works of Bernini, Borromini, and Pietro da Cortona appeared bizarre, absurd, even diseased—in other words, misshapen, like an imperfect pearl.

By the middle of the 19th century, the word had lost its pejorative implications and was used to describe the ornate and complex qualities present in many examples of 17th-century art, music and literature. Eventually, the term came to designate the historical period as a whole. In the context of painting, for example, the stark realism of Zurbaran's altarpieces, the quiet intimacy of Vermeer's domestic interiors, and restrained classicism of Poussin's landscapes are all "Baroque" (now with a capital "B" to indicate the historical period), regardless of the absence of the stylistic traits originally associated with the term.

Francisco de Zurbarán, Saint Francis of Assisi According to Pope Nicholas V's Vision, c. 1640, oil on canvas, 110.5 x 180.5 cm (Museum Nacional d'Art de Catalunya, Barcelona)

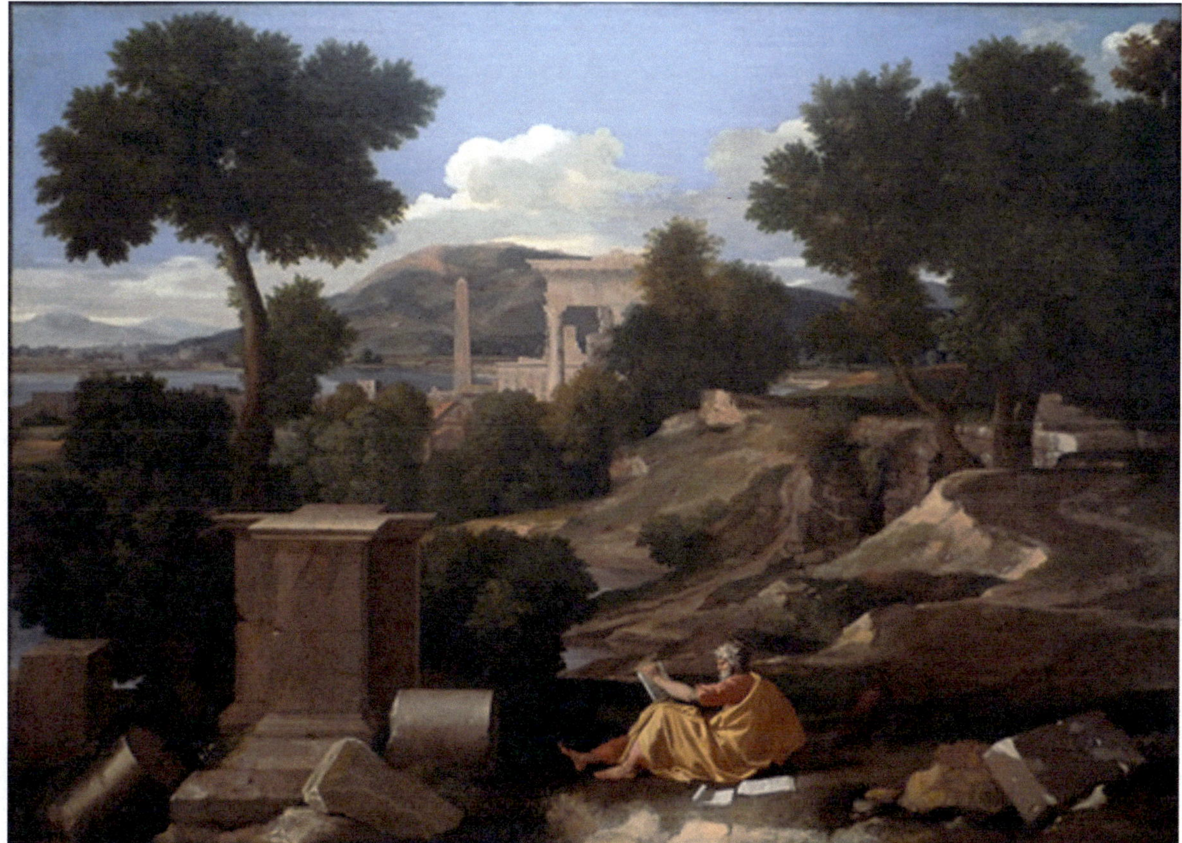

Nicolas Poussin, Landscape with St. John, 1640, oil on canvas, 39-1/2 x 53-5/8 inches (Art Institute of Chicago)

Scholars continue to debate the validity of this label, admitting the usefulness of having a label for this distinct historical period, while also acknowledging its limitations in characterizing the variety of artistic styles present in the 17th century.

Key Characteristics of Art: Eighteenth and Nineteenth Centuries

Identify and describe key characteristics of art from the eighteenth and nineteenth centuries

LEARNING ACTIVITIES

The learning activities for this section include:

- Reading: Fragonard's The Swing
- Reading: 1700–1800 Age of Enlightenment
- Reading: Neo-Classicism
- Reading: David's Death of Marat
- Reading: Romanticism in France Delacroix's Liberty Leading the People
- Video: Charles Barry and A.W.N. Pugin Palace of Westminster (Houses of Parliament)
- Reading: Hokusai's Under the Wave off Kanagawa (The Great Wave)
- Reading: Becoming Modern
- Reading: Early Photography
- Reading: Impressionism
- Reading: Nkisi Nkondi

Take time to review and reflect on each of these activities in order to improve your performance on the assessment for this section.

Reading: Fragonard's The Swing

The Beginnings of Rococo

In the early years of the 1700s, at the end of the reign of Louis XIV (who dies in 1715), there was a shift away from the classicism and "Grand Manner" (based on the art of Poussin) that had governed the art of the preceding 50 years, toward a new style that we call Rococo. Versailles was abandoned by the aristocracy, who once again took up residence in Paris. A shift away from the monarchy, toward the aristocracy characterizes this period.

What kind of lifestyle did the aristocracy lead during this period? Remember that the aristocracy had enormous political power as well as enormous wealth. Many chose leisure as a pursuit and became involved themselves in romantic intrigues. Indeed, they created a culture of luxury and excess that formed a stark contrast to the lives of most people in France. The aristocracy, only a small percentage of the population of France, owned over 90% of its wealth. A small, but growing middle class does not sit still with this for long (remember the French Revolution of 1789).

Fragonard's *The Swing*

As with most Rococo paintings, the subject of Fragonard's *The Swing* is not very complicated! Two lovers have conspired to get this older fellow to push the young lady in the swing while her lover hides in the bushes. Their idea is that as she goes up in the swing, she can part her legs, and he can get a perfect view up her skirt.

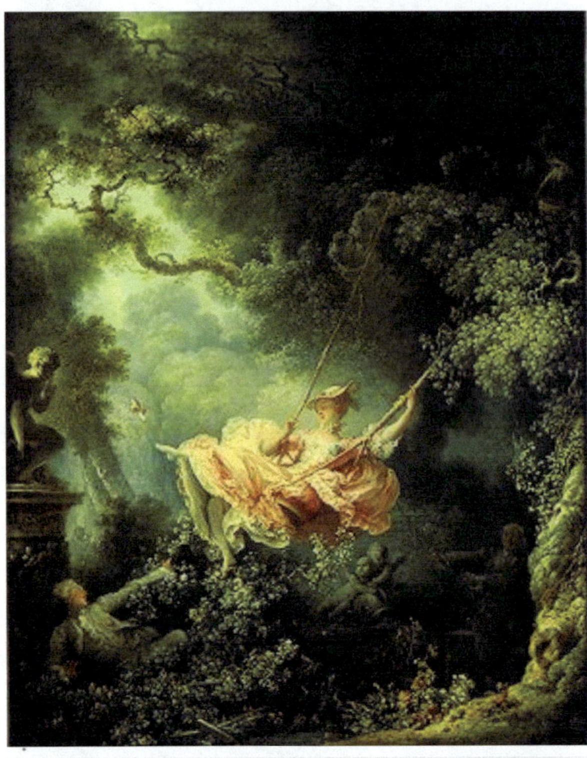

Jean-Honoré Fragonard, The Swing, oil on canvas, 1767 (Wallace Collection, London)

They are surrounded by a lush, overgrown garden. A sculptured figure to the left puts his fingers to his mouth, as though saying "hush," while another sculpture in the background has two cupid figures cuddled together. The colors are pastel — pale pinks and greens, and although we have a sense of movement and a prominent diagonal line — the painting lacks all of the seriousness of a baroque painting.

If you look really closely you can see the loose brushstrokes in the pink silk dress, and as she opens her legs, we get a glimpse of her garter belt. It was precisely this kind of painting that the philosophers of the Enlightenment were soon to condemn. They demanded a new style of art, one that showed an example of moral behavior, of human beings at their most noble.

- https://youtu.be/rVI5Sjm0xKl

Reading: 1700–1800 Age of Enlightenment

Scientific experiments like the one pictured here were offered as fascinating shows to the public in the mid-eighteenth century. In Joseph Wright of Derby's painting *A Philosopher Giving A Lecture at the Orrery* (1765), we see the demonstration of an orrery, a mechanical model of the solar system that was used to demonstrate the motions of the planets around the sun—making the universe seem almost like a clock.

In the center of the orrery is a gas light, which represents the sun (though the figure who stands in the foreground with his back to us block this from our view); the arcs represent the orbits of the planets. Wright concentrates on the faces of the figures to create a compelling narrative.

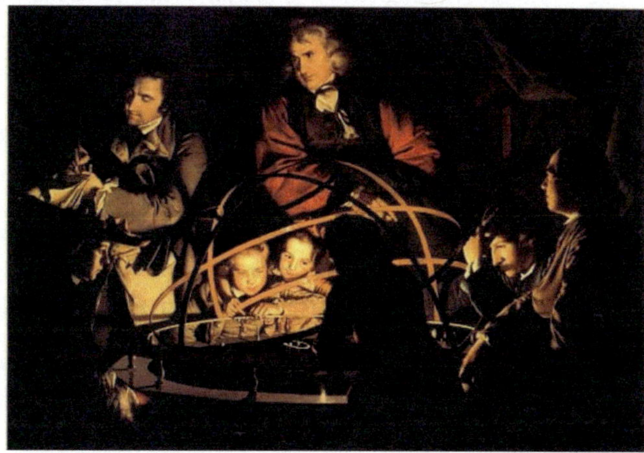

Wright of Derby, A Philosopher Giving A Lecture at the Orrery , 1765

With paintings like these, Wright invented a new subject: scenes of experiments and new machinery, and the beginnings of the Industrial Revolution (think cities, railroads, steam power, gas and then electric light, factories, machines, pollution). Wright's fascination with light, strange shadows, and darkness, reveals the influence of Baroque art.

Enlightenment

Toward the middle of the eighteenth century a shift in thinking occurred. This shift is known as the Enlightenment. You have probably already heard of some important Enlightenment figures, like Rousseau, Diderot and Voltaire. It is helpful I think to think about the word "enlighten" here—the idea of shedding light on something, illuminating it, making it clear.

The thinkers of the Enlightenment, influenced by the scientific revolutions of the previous century, believed in shedding the light of science and reason on the world, and in order to question traditional ideas and ways of doing things. The scientific revolution (based on empirical observation, and not on metaphysics or spirituality) gave the impression that the universe behaved according to universal and unchanging laws (think of Newton here). This provided a model for looking rationally on human institutions as well as nature.

Reason and Equality

Rousseau, for example, began to question the idea of the divine right of Kings. In *The Social Contract*, he wrote that the King does not, in fact, receive his power from God, but rather from the general will of the people. This, of course, implies that "the people" can also take away that power! The Enlightenment thinkers also discussed other ideas that are the founding principles of any democracy—the idea of the importance of the individual who can reason for himself, the idea of equality under the law, and the idea of natural rights. The Enlightenment was a period of profound optimism, a sense that with science and reason—and the consequent shedding of old superstitions—human beings and human society would improve.

You can probably tell already that the Enlightenment was anti-clerical; it was, for the most part, opposed to traditional Catholicism. Instead, the Enlightenment thinkers developed a way of understanding the universe called Deism—the idea, more or less, is that there is a God, but that this God is not the figure of the Old and New Testaments, actively involved in human affairs. He is more like a watchmaker who, once he makes the watch and winds it, has nothing more to do with it.

The Enlightenment, the Monarchy, and the Revolution

The Enlightenment encouraged criticism of the corruption of the monarchy (at this point King Louis XVI), and the aristocracy. Enlightenment thinkers condemned Rococo art for being immoral and indecent, and called for a new kind of art that would be moral instead of immoral, and teach people right and wrong.

Denis Diderot, Enlightenment philosopher, writer and art critic, wrote that the aim of art was "to make virtue attractive, vice odious, ridicule forceful; that is the aim of every honest man who takes up the pen, the brush or the chisel' (*Essai sur la peinture*).

These new ways of thinking, combined with a financial crisis (the country was literally bankrupt) and poor harvests left many ordinary French people both angry and hungry. In 1789, the French Revolution began. In its first stage, all the revolutionaries ask for is a constitution that would limit the power of the king.

Ultimately the idea of a constitution failed, and the revolution entered a more radical stage. In 1792, Louis XVI and his wife Marie Antoinette, were beheaded along with thousands of other aristocrats believed to be loyal to the monarchy.

Reading: Neo-Classicism

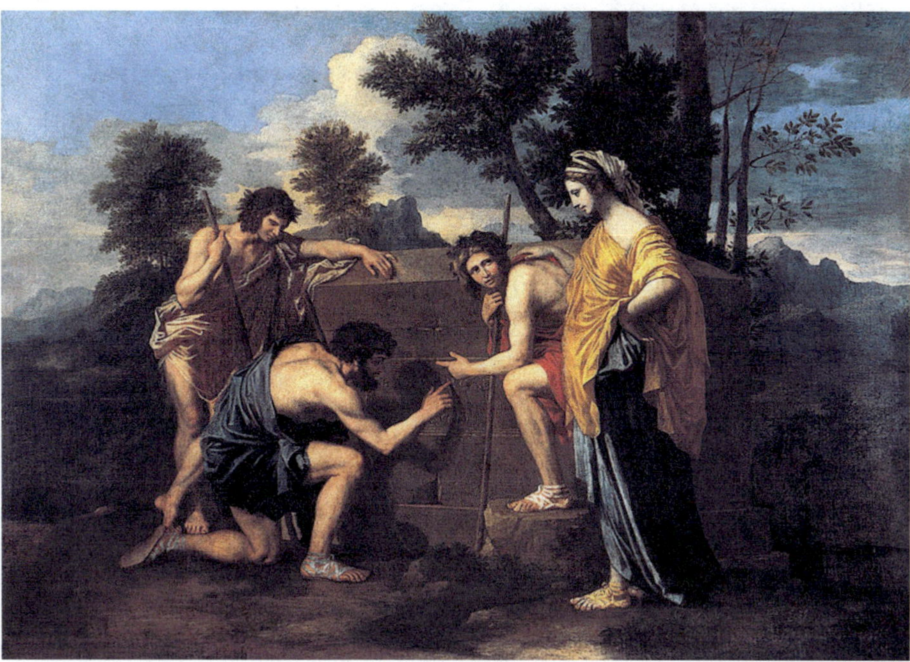

Nicolas Poussin, Et in Arcadia Ego, 1637-38, oil on canvas, 185 cm × 121 cm (72.8 in × 47.6 in) (Louvre)

In opposition to the frivolous sensuality of Rococo painters like Jean-Honoré Fragonard and François Boucher, the Neo-classicists looked to Nicolas Poussin for their inspiration. The decision to promote *Poussiniste* painting became an ethical consideration. They believed that strong drawing was rational, therefore morally better. They believed that art should be cerebral, not sensual.

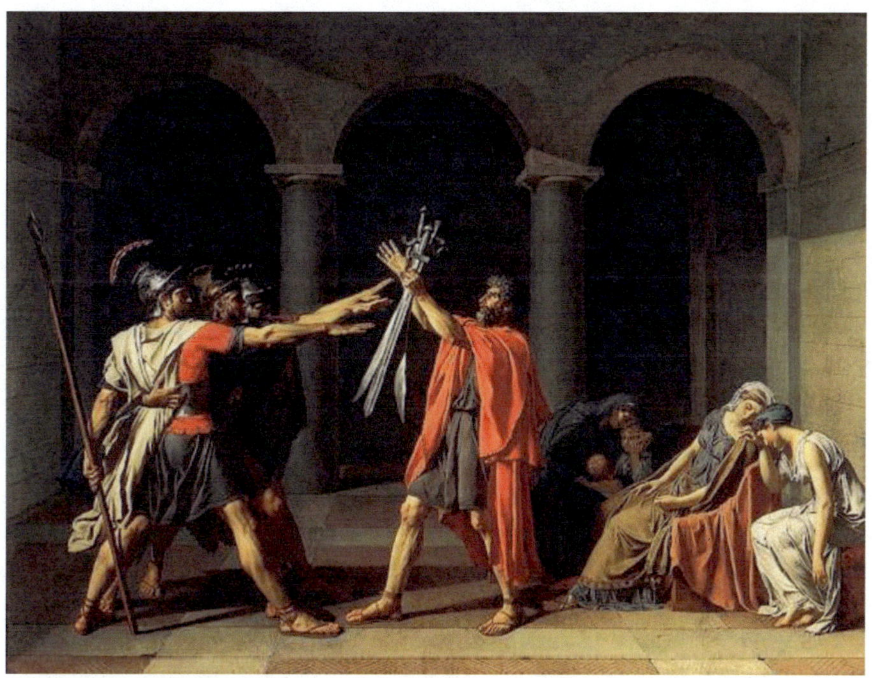

Jacques-Louis David, Oath of the Horatii, oil on canvas, 1784 (Musée du Louvre)

The Neo-classicists, such as Jacques-Louis David (pronounced *Da-VEED)*, preferred the well-delineated form—clear drawing and modeling (shading). Drawing was considered more important than painting. The Neo-classical surface had to look perfectly smooth—no evidence of brush-strokes should be discernable to the naked eye.

France was on the brink of its first revolution in 1789, and the Neo-classicists wanted to express rationality and sobriety that was fitting for their times. Artists like David supported the rebels through an art that asked for clear-headed thinking, self-sacrifice to the State (as in *Oath of the Horatii*) and an austerity reminiscent of Republican Rome.

Neo-classicism was a child of the Age of Reason (the Enlightenment), when philosophers believed that we would be able to control our destinies by learning from and following the Laws of Nature (the United States was founded on Enlightenment philosophy). Scientific inquiry attracted more attention. Therefore, Neo-classicism continued the connection to the Classical tradition because it signified moderation and rational thinking but in a new and more politically-charged spirit ("neo" means "new," or in the case of art, an existing style reiterated with a new twist.)

Neo-classicism is characterized by: clarity of form; sober colors; shallow space; strong horizontal and verticals that render that subject matter timeless, instead of temporal as in the dynamic Baroque works; and, Classical subject matter—or classicizing contemporary subject matter.

Reading: David's Death of Marat

By 1793, the violence of the Revolution dramatically increased until the beheadings at the Place de la Concorde became a constant, leading a certain Dr. Joseph Guillotine it invent a machine that would improve the efficiency of the ax and block and therefore make executions more humane. David was in thick of it. Early in the Revolution he had joined the Jacobins, a political club that would in time become the most rabid of the various rebel factions. Led by the ill-fated Georges Danton and the infamous Maximilien Robespierre, the Jacobins (including David) would eventually vote to execute Louis XVI and his Queen Marie Antionette who were caught attempting to escape across the border to the Austrian Empire.

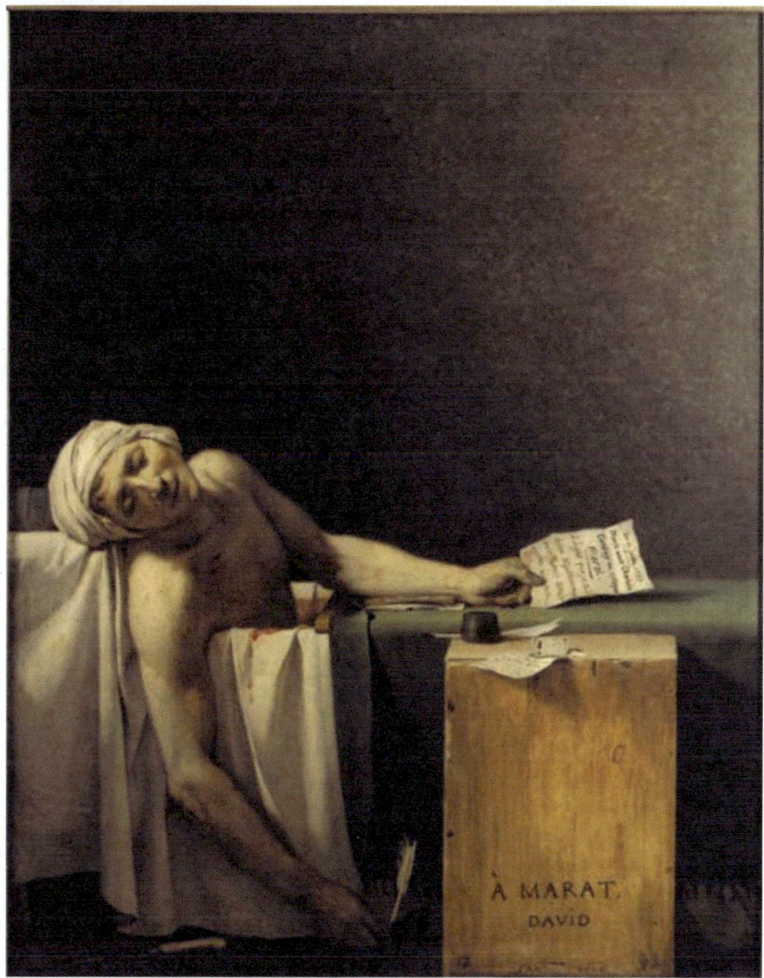

Jacques-Louis David, The Death of Marat, oil on canvas, 1793 (Royal Museum of Fine Arts, Brussels)

At the height of the Reign of Terror in 1793, David painted a memorial to his great friend, the murdered publisher, Jean Marat. As in his Death of Socrates, David substitutes the iconography (symbolic forms) of Christian art for more contemporary issues. The Death of Marat, 1793 an idealized image of David's slain friend is shown holding his murderess's (Charlotte Corday) letter of introduction.

The bloodied knife lays on the floor having opened a fatal gash that functions, as does Marat's very composition, as a reference to the entombment of Christ and a sort of secularized stigmata (reference to the wounds Christ is said to have received in his hands, feet and side while on the cross). Is David attempting now to find revolutionary martyrs to replace the saints of Catholicism (which had been outlawed)?

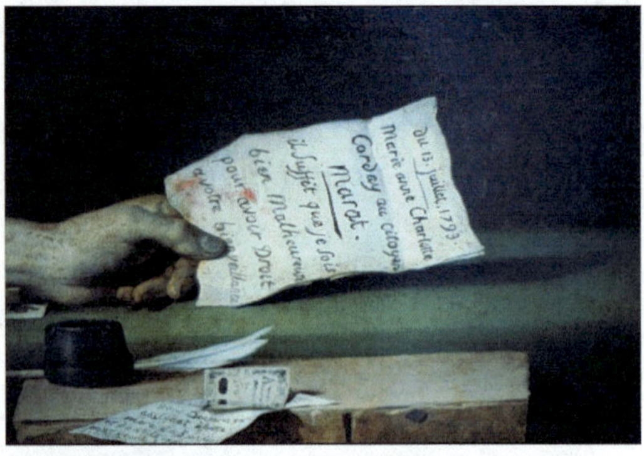

Jacques Louis David, The Death of Marat (detail), 1793 (Royal Museum of Fine Arts, Brussels)

By 1794 the Reign of Terror had run its course. The Jacobins had begun to execute not only captured aristocrats but fellow revolutionaries as well. Eventually, Robespierre himself would die and the remaining Jacobins were likewise executed or imprisoned. David escaped death by renouncing his activities and was locked in a cell in the former palace, the Louvre, until his eventual release by France's brilliant new ruler, Napoleon Bonaparte. This diminutive Corsican had been the youngest General in the French army and during the Revolution had become a national hero by waging a seemingly endless string of victorious military campaigns against the Austrians in Belgium and Italy. Eventually, Napoleon would control most of Europe, would crown himself Emperor, and would release David in recognition that the artist's talent could serve the ruler's purposes.

Reading: Romanticism in France Delacroix's Liberty Leading the People

The July Revolution

This painting was made in response to the political upheaval that would resulted in the overthrow of the reigning monarch, Charles X (brother of the beheaded Louis XVI). Charles X had restored the Bourbon throne after the fall of Napoleon and would himself be replaced by the restricted constitutional rule of Louis-Phillipe, the "citizen-king."

Delacroix's is a complex painting, full of historical reference, yet also full of the spectrum of human emotion—from grand heroism to angry despair—that is a central characteristic of French Romanticism. Note the complex interaction between areas that are brightly reflective and adjacent areas of dark shadow. The results are vivid contrasts which, like the rapid-fire brushwork, activates the surface and augments the painting's sense of movement and energy. Delacroix also breaks with the tradition of relying upon the painstakingly subtle modulation of color, and instead, applies

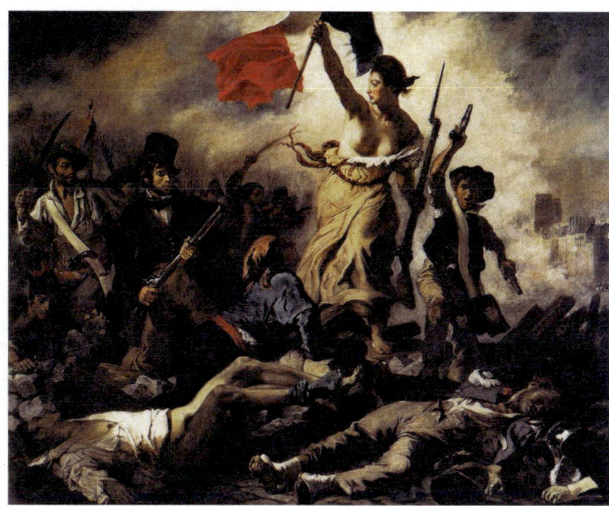

Eugène Delacroix, Liberty Leading the People, oil on canvas, 2.6 x 3.25m, 1830 (Musée du Louvre, Paris)

brilliant and shocking traces of pure pigment. See, for example, the notes of sharp primary colors, the blues, yellows and the especially powerful reds. Again, the effect is vivid and electrifying against the broad areas of brown and gray and this fits well with the subject. Liberty rushes forward over the debris of the barricades, by then a signifier of Parisian rebellion.

A Modern Nike

Prior to the late 19th century, the streets of this largely medieval city were the chaotic result of organic unplanned growth. Paris was a warren of tangled streets, some little more than narrow alleys that slowed travel, trade and troops, and could be easily blocked allowing revolutionaries to fortify entire sections of the city. It is upon these very barricades that Liberty, the personification of freedom (who the French call Marianne) stands. She holds the tri-color aloft. This is the banned flag of revolution and democracy.

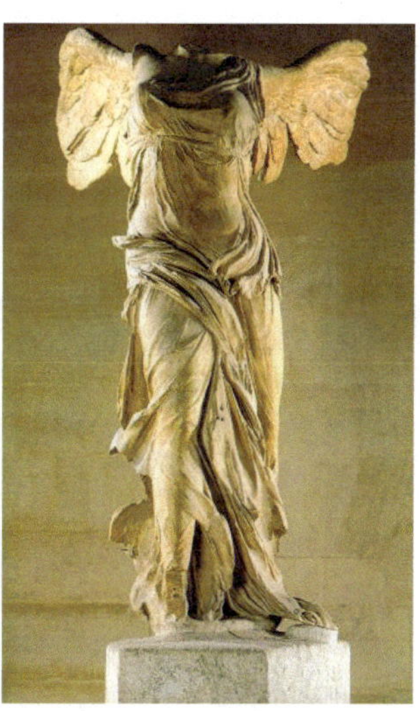

Nike of Samothrace, 220-190 B.C.E. (Louvre, Paris)

The wind spins her drapery around her hips alluding to classical statuary. Note that the spiraling costume of the great Hellenistic (late ancient Greek) sculpture, the Nike (victory) of Samothrace on view in the Musée de Louvre was found after the Delacroix was created but is a useful reference nevertheless. For what possible reason has Delacroix exposed Marianne's breasts? The answer lies in the figure not being an actual person but rather the embodiment of an idea in a human figure. Marianne is, of course, democracy. Democracy was born in Ancient Greece as Delacroix reminds us by his reference to ancient sculpture and his use of partial nudity. But there is a second reference here. During France's first revolution, the one that began in 1789, the newly created democratic state was sometimes depicted as an infant suckled by freedom, by Marianne, its mother.

Class Distinctions

Beside Marianne, we see a menacing crowd that dissolves into the smoke and the confusion of battle. But in the left middle ground, Delacroix depicts two figures with greater clarity. They stand together but represent very different social and economic positions. The man in the top hat, waistcoat and jacket is a member of the middle class. The second figure is less well off. He wears a white shirt and cap and is meant to represent a laborer, a member of the working or lower class. Delacroix's message is clear. The revolution unites these classes against the ruling aristocracy.

The Cost of Rebellion

In the foreground lay two dead bodies. The figure on the left is intended to enrage the viewer. To set the viewer firmly against the excesses of the king's troops. In this sense the painting is pure propaganda. The dead figure on the left is dressed in a long nightshirt that has been push up as his body was dragged into the street from his bedroom where, presumably, he had been shot. Delacroix is alluding to the despised practice of the royal troops who spread terror by murdering suspected revolutionary sympathizers in their beds and then dragging the bodies into the streets as a warning. The dead uniformed figure on the right is a royalist soldier. Here, Delacroix shows the enemy as vulnerable. If you look carefully at the buildings at the right you will see the battle joined and in the distance, the great Gothic cathedral, Notre Dame de Paris, a symbol of the King's power but which is now triumphantly flying the tricolor.

Video: Charles Barry and A.W.N. Pugin Palace of Westminster (Houses of Parliament)

- https://youtu.be/7oBUlo5R5qg

Reading: Hokusai's Under the Wave off Kanagawa (The Great Wave)

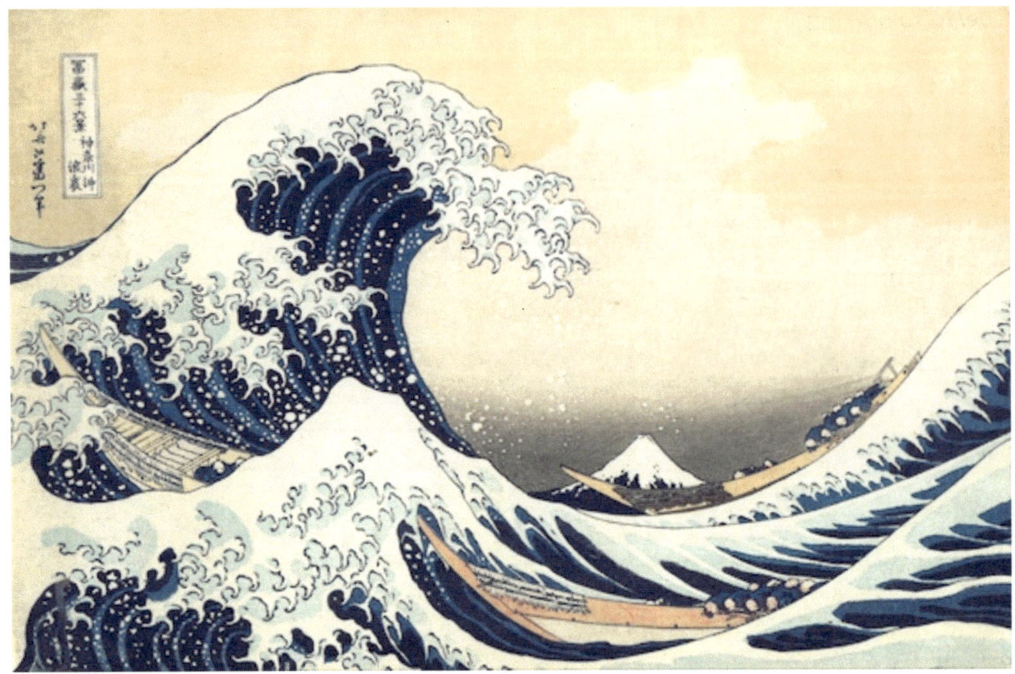

Katsushika Hokusai, Under the Wave off Kanagawa (Kanagawa oki nami ura), also known asThe Great Wave, from the series Thirty-six Views of Mount Fuji (Fugaku sanjūrokkei), c. 1830-32, polychrome woodblock print; ink and color on paper, 10 1/8 x 14 15 /16 inches / 25.7 x 37.9 cm (The Metropolitan Museum of Art)

Katsushika Hokusai's *Under the Wave off Kanagawa*, also called *The Great Wave* has became one of the most famous works of art in the world—and debatably the most iconic work of Japanese art. Initially, thousands of copies of this print were quickly produced and sold cheaply. Despite the fact that it was created at a time when Japanese trade was heavily restricted, Hokusai's print displays the influence of Dutch art, and proved to be inspirational for many artists working in Europe later in the nineteenth century.

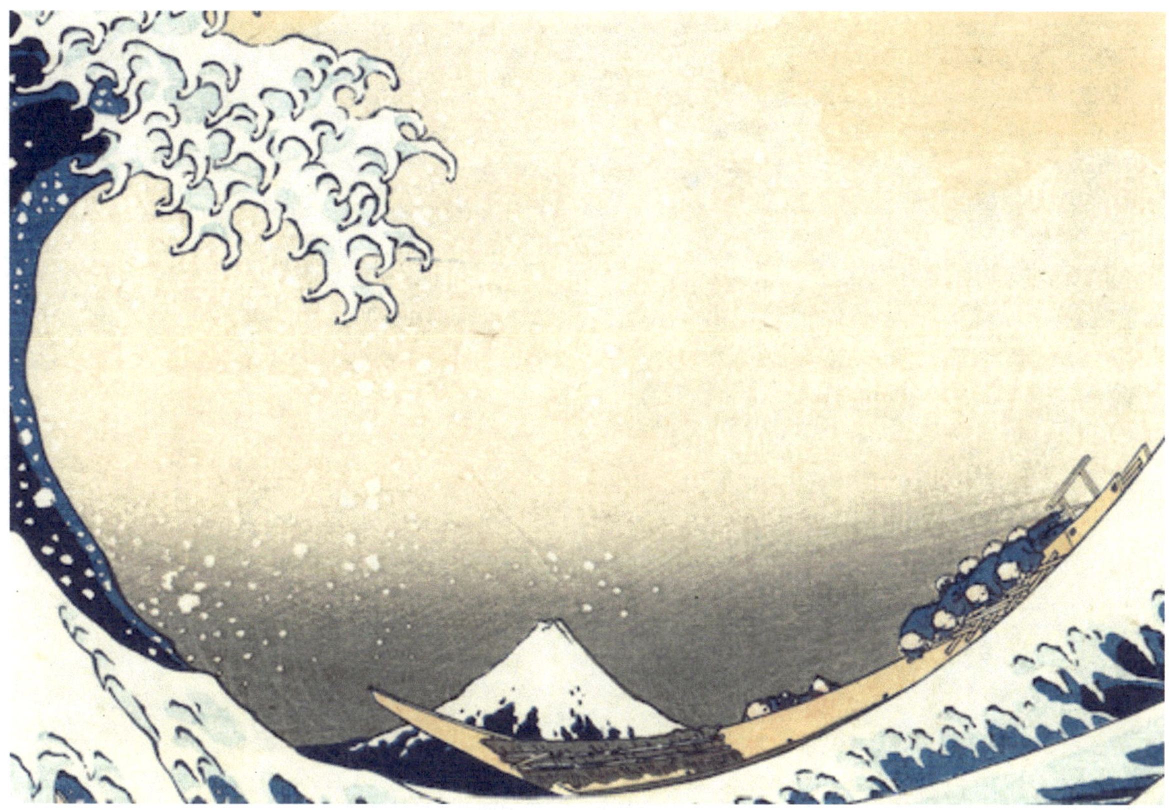

Katsushika Hokusai, Under the Wave off Kanagawa (detail)

Thirty-six Views of Mount Fuji

Under the Wave off Kanagawa is part of a series of prints titled *Thirty-six views of Mount Fuji*, which Hokusai made between 1830 and 1833. It is a polychrome (multi-colored) woodblock print, made of ink and color on paper that is approximately 10 x 14 inches. All of the images in the series feature a glimpse of the mountain, but as you can see from this example, Mount Fuji does not always dominate the frame. Instead, here, the foreground is filled with a massive cresting wave. The threatening wave is pictured just moments before crashing down on to three fishing boats below. *Under the Wave off Kanagawa* is full of visual play. The mountain, made tiny by the use of perspective, appears as if it too will be swallowed up by the wave. Hokusai's optical play can also be lighthearted, and the spray from top of the crashing wave looks like snow falling on the mountain.

Hokusai has arranged the composition to frame Mount Fuji. The curves of the wave and hull of one boat dip down just low enough to allow the base of Mount Fuji to be visible, and the white top of the great wave creates a diagonal line that leads the viewers eye directly to the peak of the mountain top. Across the thirty-six prints that constitute this series, Hokusai varies his representation of the mountain. In other prints the mountain fills the composition, or is reduced to a small detail in the background of bustling city life.

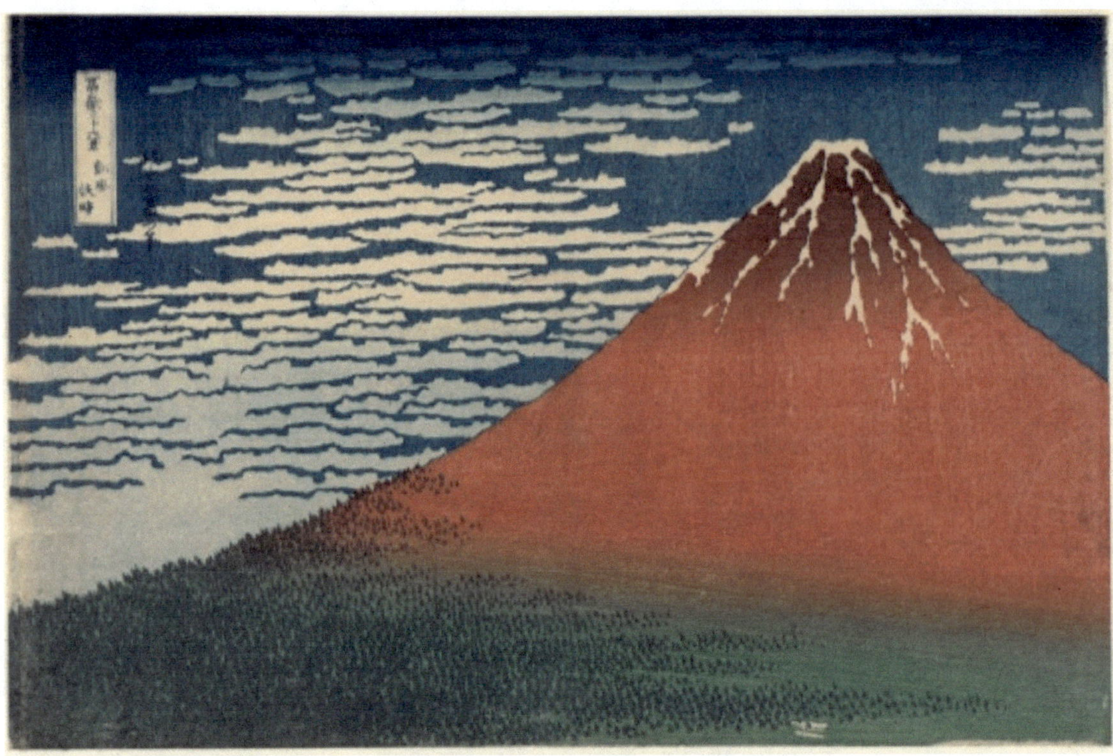

Katsushika Hokusai, Fine Wind, Clear Weather, Also known as Red Fuji, from the series Thirty-six Views of Mount Fuji, c. 1830-31, woodblock print; ink and color on paper, 9 5/8 x 15 inches / 24.4 x 38.1 cm (Museum of Fine Arts, Boston)

Who Was Katsushika Hokusai?

Hokusai was born in 1760 in Edo (now Tokyo), Japan. During the artists' lifetime he went by many different names; he began calling himself Hokusai in 1797. Hokusai discovered Western prints that came to Japan by way of Dutch trade. From the Dutch artwork Hokusai became interested in linear perspective. Subsequently, Hokusai created a Japanese variant of linear perspective. The influence of Dutch art can also be seen in the use of a low horizon line and the distinctive European color, Prussian blue.

Hokusai was interested in oblique angles, contrasts of near and far, and contrasts of manmade and the natural. These can be seen in *Under the Wave off Kanagawa* through the juxtaposition of the large wave in the foreground which dwarfs the small mountain in the distance, as well as the inclusion of the men and boats amidst the powerful waves.

Why Mount Fuji?

Mount Fuji is the highest mountain in Japan and has long been considered sacred. Hokusai is often described as having a personal fascination with the mountain, which sparked his interest in making this series. However, he was also responding to a boom in domestic travel and the corresponding market for images of Mount Fuji. Japanese woodblock prints were often purchased as souvenirs. The original audience for Hokusai's prints was ordinary townspeople who were followers of the "Fuji cult" and made pilgrimages to climb the mountain, or tourists visiting the new capital city. Although the skyscrapers in Tokyo obscure the view of Mount Fuji today, for Hokusai's audience the peak of the mountain would have been visible across the city.

The Making of Ukiyo-e Prints

Ukiyo-e is the name for Japanese woodblock prints made during the Edo Period. Ukiyo-e, which originated as a Buddhist term, means "floating world" and refers to the impermanence of the world. The earliest prints were made in only black and white, but later, as is evident from Hokusai's work, additional colors were added. A separate block of wood was used for each color. Each print is made with a final overlay of black line, which helps to break up the flat colors. Ukiyo-e prints are recognizable for their emphasis on line and pure, bright color, as well as their ability to distill form down to the minimum.

Hokusai moved away from the tradition of making images of courtesans and actors, which was the customary subject of ukiyo-e prints. Instead, his work focused on the daily life of Japanese people from a variety of social levels. Such as the quotidian scene of fishermen battling the sea off the coast of Mount Fuji that we see in *The Great Wave*. This change of subject matter was a breakthrough in both ukiyo-e prints and in Hokusai's career.

Popularity of Ukiyo-e Prints in Europe

Beginning in 1640, Japan was largely closed off to the world and only limited interaction with China and Holland was allowed. This changed in the 1850s, when trade was forced open by American naval commodore, Matthew C. Perry. After this, there was a flood of Japanese visual culture into the West. At the 1867 International Exposition in Paris, Hokusai's work was on view at the Japanese pavilion. This was the first introduction of Japanese culture to mass audiences in the West, and a craze for collecting art called Japonisme ensued. Additionally, Impressionist artists in Paris, such as Claude Monet, were great fans of Japanese prints. The flattening of space, an interest in atmospheric conditions, and the impermanence of modern city life—all visible in Hokusai's prints—both reaffirmed their own artistic interests and inspired many future works of art.

Reading: Becoming Modern

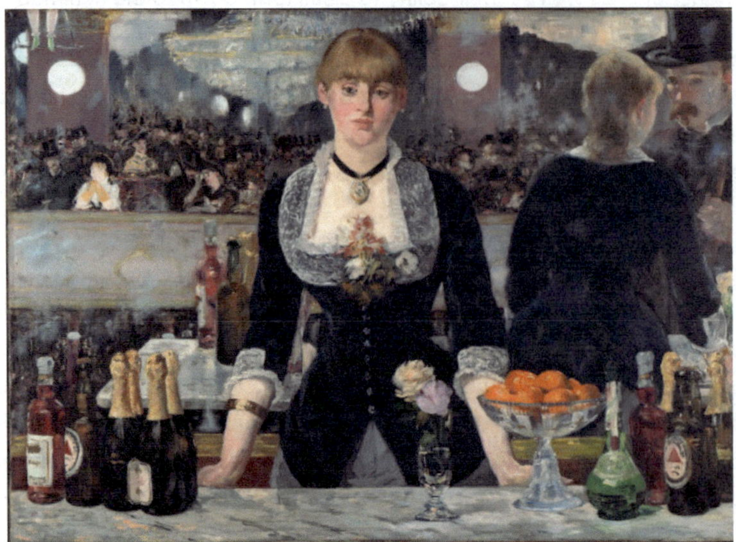

Édouard Manet, A Bar at the Folies-Bergère, oil on canvas, 1882 (Courtauld Gallery, London)

People use the term "modern" in a variety of ways, often very loosely, with a lot of implied associations of new, contemporary, up-to-date, and technological. We know the difference between a modern country and a third world country and it usually has less to do with art and more to do with technology and industrial progress, things like indoor plumbing, easy access to consumer goods, freedom of expression, and voting rights. In the nineteenth century, however, modernity and its connection with art had certain specific associations that people began recognizing and using as barometers to distinguish themselves and their culture from earlier nineteenth century ways and attitudes.

Chronologically, Modernism refers to the period from 1850 to 1960. It begins with the Realist Movement and ends with Abstract Expressionism. That's just a little over one hundred years. During that period the western world experienced some significant changes that transformed Europe and the United States from traditional societies that were agriculturally based into modern ones with cities and factories and mass transportation. Here are some important features that all modern societies share.

1. **Capitalism** replaced landed fortunes and became the economic system of modernity in which people exchanged labor for a fixed wage and used their wages to buy ever more consumer items rather than produce such items themselves. This economic change dramatically affected class relations because it offered opportunities for great wealth through individual initiative, industrialization and technology—somewhat like the technological and dot.com explosion of the late 20th and early 21st century. The industrial revolution which began in England in the late 18th century and rapidly swept across Europe (hit the U.S. immediately following the Civil War) transformed economic and social relationships, offered an ever increasing number of cheaper consumer goods, and changed notions of education. Who needed the classics when a commercial/technically oriented education was the key to financial success? The industrial revolution also fostered a sense of competition and progress that continues to influence us today.

2. **Urban culture** replaced agrarian culture as industrialization and cities grew. Cities were the sites of new wealth and opportunity with their factories and manufacturing potential. People moving from small farms, towns to large cities helped to breakdown traditional culture and values. There were also new complications such as growing urban crime, prostitution, alienation, and depersonalization. In a small town you probably knew the cobbler who made your shoes and such a personal relationship often expanded into everyday economics—you might be able to barter food or labor for a new pair of shoes or delay payments. These kinds of accommodations that formed a substructure to agrarian life were swept away with urbanization. City dwellers bought shoes that were manufactured, transported by railroads, displayed in shop windows, and purchased only for cash. Assembly lines, anonymous labor, and advertising created more consumer

items but also a growing sense of depersonalization. The gap between the "haves" and the "have nots" increased and were more visible in the city.

3. **Technological advances** such as industrialization, railroads, gas lighting, streetcars, factory systems, indoor plumbing, appliances, and scientific advances were rapidly made and these changes dramatically affected the way people lived and thought about themselves. One consequence was that people in industrialized areas thought of themselves as progressive and modern and considered undeveloped cultures in undeveloped countries as primitive and backward.

4. Modernity is characterized by increasing **secularism** and diminished religious authority. People did not abandon religion but they paid less attention to it. Organized religions were increasingly less able to dictate standards, values, and subject matter. Fine art moved from representing human experience and its relationship to God's creation, to a focus on personal emotions and individual spiritual experiences that were not based in any organized and institutionalized religion.

5. The modern world was extremely **optimistic**—people saw these changes as positive. They welcomed innovation and championed progress. Change became a signifier of modernity. Anything that was traditional and static signaled outmoded, old-fashioned, conservative and was to be avoided by the new modern public. Modern Europe and the U.S. internalized these positions and used modernity as a way of determining and validating their superiority. The nineteenth century was also a period of tremendous colonial growth and expansion, in the name of progress and social benefit and all of these activities were spearheaded by newly industrialized western countries.

Many artists closely identified with modernity and embraced the new techniques and innovations, the spirit of progress, invention, discovery, creativity and change. They wanted to participate in creating the modern world and they were anxious to try out new ideas rather than following the more conservative guidelines of Academic art. This is not to say that these mid-nineteenth century artists were the first to challenge an older generation or set of ideas. Many academic artists had argued over formal issues, styles and subject matter but this was much like a good natured agreement within a club; everyone in the group agreed to disagree.

By the mid-1850s polite academic disagreements were being taken out of the Academy and onto the street. Artists were looking increasingly to the private sector for patronage, tapping into that growing group of bourgeois or middle class collectors with money to spend and houses to fill with paintings. This new middle class audience that made its money through industrialization and manufacturing had lots of "disposable income", and they wanted pictures that they could understand, that were easy to look at, fit into their homes, addressed subjects they liked. Not for them the historical cycles of gods, saints and heroes with their complex intellectual associations and references; instead, they wanted landscapes, genre scenes, and still life. They were not less educated than earlier buyers, but educated with a different focus and set of priorities. Reality was here and now, progress was inevitable, and the new hero of modern life was the modern man.

Modernity is then a composite of contexts: a time, a space, and an attitude. What makes a place or an object "modern" depends on these conditions.

The Avant-Garde

Throughout the 19th century there were artists who produced pictures that we do not label "modern art" generally because the techniques or subjects were associated with the conservative academic styles, techniques and approaches. On the other hand, modern artists were often called the "avant-garde." This was originally a military term that described the point man (the first soldier out)—the one to take the most risk. The French socialist Henri de Saint-Simon first used the term in the early 1820s to describe an artist whose work would serve the needs of the people, of a socialist society rather than the ruling classes. The avant-garde is also used to identify artists whose painting subjects and techniques were radical, marking them off from the more traditional or academic styles, but not with any particular political ideology in mind. Avant-garde became a kind of generic term for a number of art movements centered on the idea of artistic autonomy and independence. In some cases the avant-garde was closely associated with political activism, especially socialist or communist movements; in other cases, the avant-garde was pointedly removed from politics and focused primarily on aesthetics. The avant-garde was never a cohesive group of artists and what was avant-garde in one nation was not necessarily the same in others.

Finally, although modern artists were working throughout many countries in Europe and the United States, most 19th art and much twentieth-century modern art is centered in France and produced by French artists. Unlike England which was politically stable in the nineteenth century, France went through a variety of governments and insurrections all of which provided a unique political and cultural environment that fostered what we know as modern art.

Reading: Early Photography

By modern standards, nineteenth-century photography can appear rather primitive. While the stark black and white landscapes and unsmiling people have their own austere beauty, these images also challenge our notions of what defines a work of art.

Photography is a controversial fine art medium, simply because it is difficult to classify—is it an art or a science? Nineteenth-century photographers struggled with this distinction, trying to reconcile aesthetics with improvements in technology.

The Birth of Photography

Although the principle of the camera was known in antiquity, the actual chemistry needed to register an image was not available until the nineteenth century.

Artists from the Renaissance onwards used a camera obscura (Latin for dark chamber), or a small hole in the wall of a darkened box that would pass light through the hole and project an upside down image of whatever was outside the box. However, it was not until the invention of a light sensitive surface by Frenchman Joseph Nicéphore Niépce that the basic principle of photography was born.

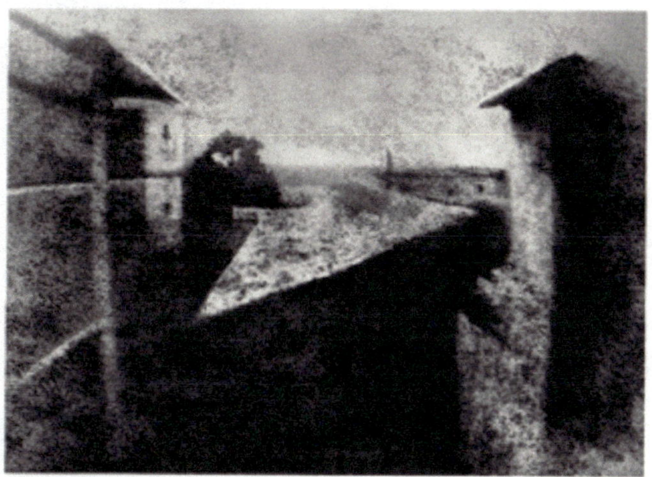

Joseph Nicéphore Niépce, View from the Window at Gras, 1826

From this point the development of photography largely related to technological improvements in three areas, speed, resolution and permanence. The first photographs, such as Niepce's famous *View from the Window at Gras* (1826) required a very slow speed (a long exposure period), in this case about eight hours, obviously making many subjects difficult, if not impossible, to photograph. Taken using a camera obscura to expose a copper plate coated in silver and pewter, Niepce's image looks out of an upstairs window, and part of the blurry quality is due to changing conditions during the long exposure time, causing the resolution, or clarity of the image, to be grainy and hard to read. An additional challenge was the issue of permanence, or how to successfully stop any further reaction of the light sensitive surface once the desired exposure had been achieved. Many of Niepce's early images simply turned black over time due to continued exposure to light. This problem was largely solved in 1839 by the invention of hypo, a chemical that reversed the light sensitivity of paper.

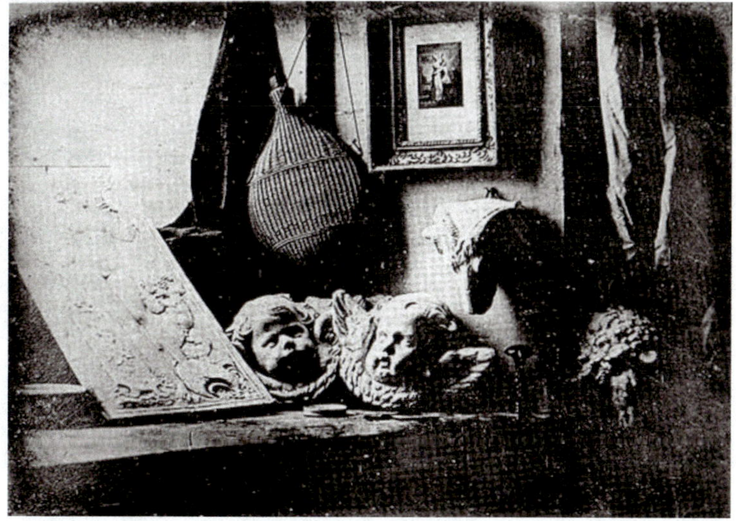

Louis Daguerre, The Artist's Studio, 1837, daguerreotype

Technological Improvements

Photographers after Niepce experimented with a variety of techniques. Louis Daguerre invented a new process he dubbed a daguerrotype in 1839, which significantly reduced exposure time and created a lasting result, but only produced a single image.

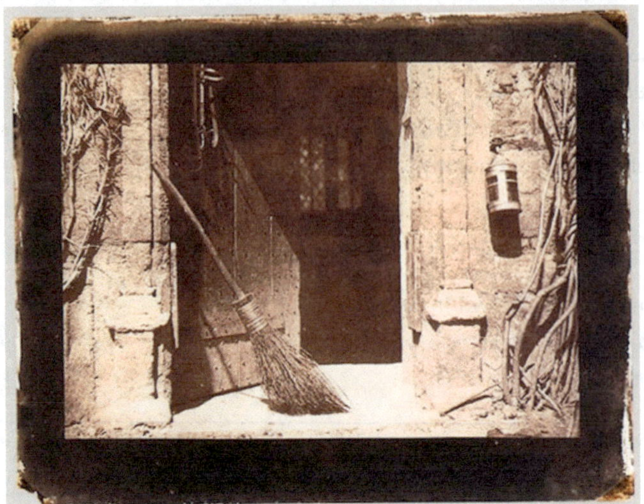

William Henry Fox Talbot, The Open Door, 1844, Salted paper print from paper negative

At the same time, Englishman William Henry Fox Talbot was experimenting with his what would eventually become his calotype method, patented in February 1841. Talbot's innovations included the creation of a paper negative, and new technology that involved the transformation of the negative to a positive image, allowing for more that one copy of the picture. The remarkable detail of Talbot's method can be see in his famous photograph, *The Open Door*(1844) which captures the view through a medieval-looking entrance. The texture of the rough stones surrounding the door, the vines growing up the walls and the rustic broom that leans in the doorway demonstrate the minute details captured by Talbot's photographic improvements.

The collodion method was introduced in 1851. This process involved fixing a substance known as gun cotton onto a glass plate, allowing for an even shorter exposure time (3–5 minutes), as well as a clearer image.

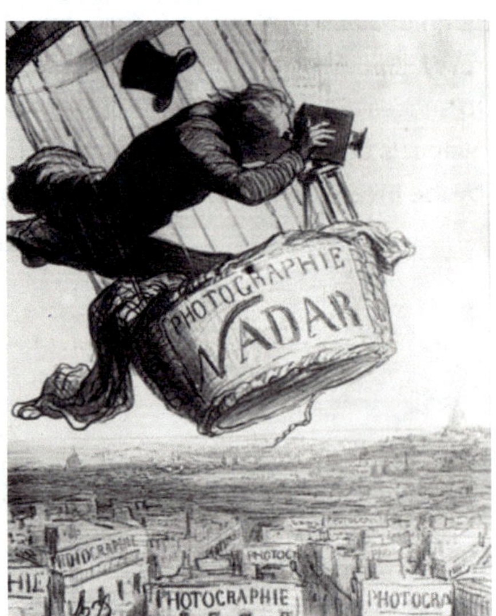

Honoré Daumier, Nadar élevant la Photographie à la hauteur de l'Art (Nadar elevating Photography to Art), lithograph from Le Boulevard, May 25, 1863

The big disadvantage of the collodion process was that it needed to be exposed and developed while the chemical coating was still wet, meaning that photographers had to carry portable darkrooms to develop images immediately after exposure. Both the difficulties of the method and uncertain but growing status of photography were lampooned by Honore Daumier in his *Nadar Elevating Photography to the Height of Art* (1862). Nadar, one of the most prominent photographers in Paris at the time, was known for capturing the first aerial photographs from the basket of a hot air balloon. Obviously, the difficulties in developing a glass negative under these circumstances must have been considerable.

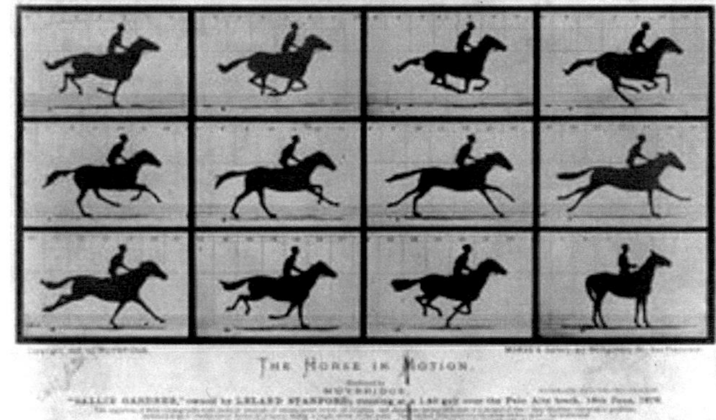

Eadweard Muybridge, The Horse in Motion ("Sallie Gardner," owned by Leland Stanford; running at a 1:40 gait over the Palo Alto track, 19 June 1878)

Further advances in technology continued to make photography less labor intensive. By 1867 a dry glass plate was invented, reducing the inconvenience of the wet collodion method.

Prepared glass plates could be purchased, eliminating the need to fool with chemicals. In 1878, new advances decreased the exposure time to 1/25th of a second, allowing moving objects to be photographed and lessening the need for a tripod. This new development is celebrated in Eadweard Maybridge's sequence of photographs called Galloping Horse (1878). Designed to settle the question of whether or not a horse ever takes all four legs completely off the ground during a gallop, the series of photographs also demonstrated the new photographic methods that were capable of nearly instantaneous exposure.

Finally in 1888 George Eastman developed the dry gelatin roll film, making it easier for film to be carried. Eastman also produced the first small inexpensive cameras, allowing more people access to the technology.

Photographers in the nineteenth century were pioneers in a new artistic endeavor, blurring the lines between art and technology. Frequently using traditional methods of composition and marrying these with innovative techniques, photographers created a new vision of the material world. Despite the struggles early photographers must have had with the limitations of their technology, their artistry is also obvious.

Reading: Impressionism

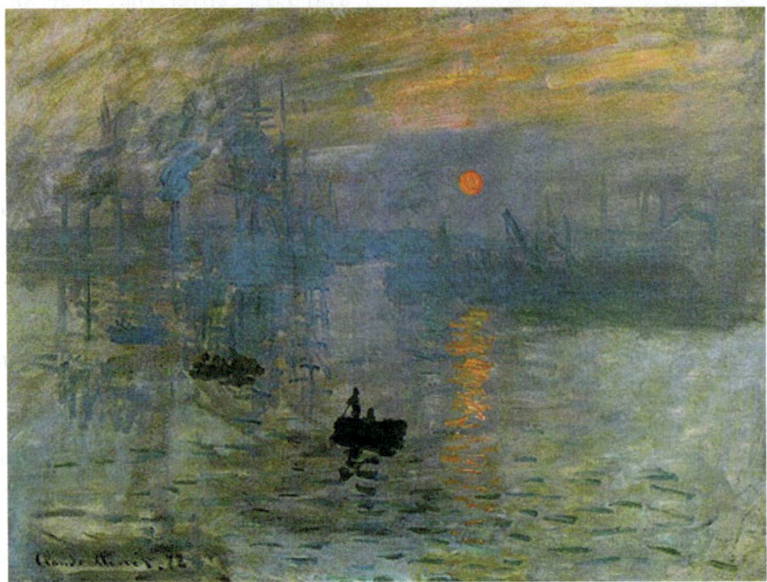

Claude Monet, Impression Sunrise, 1872 (exhibited at the first Impressionist exhibition in 1874)

Establishing Their Own Exhibitions—Apart from the Salon

The group of artists who became known as the Impressionists did something ground-breaking, in addition to their sketchy, light-filled paintings. They established their own exhibition – apart from the annual salon. At that time, the salon was really the only way to exhibit your work (the work was chosen by a jury). Claude Monet, August Renoir, Edgar Degas, Berthe Morisot, Alfred Sisley, and several other artists could not afford to wait for France to accept their work. They all had experienced rejection by the Salon jury in recent years and knew waiting a whole year in between each exhibition was no longer tenable. They needed to show their work and they wanted to sell it.

So, in an attempt to get recognized outside of the official channel of the salon, these artists banded together and held their own exhibition. They pooled their money, rented a studio that belonged to the famous photographer Nadar and set a date for their first exhibition together. They called themselves the Anonymous Society of Painters, Sculptors, and Printmakers. The show opened at about the same time as the annual Salon, May 1874. The Impressionists held eight exhibitions from 1874 through 1886.

The decision was based on their frustration and their ambition to show the world their new, light-filled images.

The impressionists regarded Manet as their inspiration and leader in their spirit of revolution, but Manet had no desire to join their cooperative venture into independent exhibitions. Manet had set up his own pavilion during the 1867 World's Fair, but he was not interested in giving up on the Salon jury. He wanted Paris to come to him and accept him—even if he had to endure their ridicule in the process.

Monet, Renoir, Degas, and Sisley had met through classes. Berthe Morisot was a friend of both Degas and Manet (she would marry Édouard Manet's brother Eugène by the end of 1874). She had been accepted to the Salon, but her work had become more experimental since then. Degas invited Berthe to join their risky effort. The first exhibition did not repay them monetarily but it drew the critics who decided their art was abominable. It wasn't finished. They called it "just impressions." (And not in a complimentary way.)

The Lack of "Finish"

Remember that the look of a J.A.D. Ingres or even a surly Delacroix had a "finished" surface. These younger artists' completed works looked like sketches. And not even detailed sketches but the fast, preliminary "impressions" that artists would dash off to preserve an idea of what to paint later. Normally, an artist's "impressions" were not meant to be sold, but were meant to be aids for the memory—to take these ideas back to the studio for the masterpiece on canvas. The critics thought it was insane to sell paintings that looked like slap-dash impressions and consider these paintings works "finished."

Landscape and Contemporary Life (Not History Painting!)

Also—Courbet, Manet and the Impressionists challenged the Academy's category codes. The Academy deemed that only "history painting" was great painting. These young Realists and Impressionists opened the door to dismantling this hierarchy of subject matter. They believed that landscapes and genres scenes were worthy and important.

Color

In their landscapes and genre scenes of contemporary life, the Impressionist artists tried to arrest a moment in their fast-paced lives by pinpointing specific atmospheric conditions—light flickering on water, moving clouds, a burst of rain. Their technique tried to capture what they saw. They painted small commas of pure color one next to another. The viewer would stand at a reasonable distance so that the eye would mix the individual marks, thus blending the colors together optically. This method created more vibrant colors than those colors mixed on a palette. Becoming a team dedicated to this new, non-Academic painting gave them the courage to pursue the independent exhibition format—a revolutionary idea of its own.

Light

An important aspect of the Impressionist painting was the appearance of quickly shifting light on the surface. This sense of moving rapidly or quickly changing atmospheric conditions or living in a world that moves faster was also part of the Impressionist's criteria. They wanted to create an art that seemed modern: about contemporary life, about the fast pace of contemporary life, and about the sensation of seeing light change incessantly in the landscape. They painted outdoors (en plein air) to capture the appearance of the light as it really flickered and faded while they worked.

Mary Cassatt was an American who met Edgar Degas and was invited to join the group as they continued to mount independent exhibitions. By the 1880s, the Impressionist accepted the name the critics gave them. The American Mary Cassatt began to exhibition with the Impressionists in 1877.

For a very long time, the French refused to find the work worthy of praise. The Americans and other non-French collectors did. For this reason, the U.S. and other foreign collections own most of the Impressionist art. (The Metropolitan Museum of Art owns a good portion of the Havermayer Collection. Louisine Havermayer knew Mary Cassatt, who advised Louisine when she visited Paris.)

Reading: Nkisi Nkondi

Divine Protection

Sacred medicines and divine protection are central to the belief of the BaKongo peoples (Democratic Republic of Congo). The BaKongo believe that the great god, Ne Kongo, brought the first sacred medicine (or nkisi) down from heaven in an earthenware vessel set upon three stones or termite mounds.

A nkisi (plural: minkisi) is loosely translated a 'spirit' yet it is represented as a container of sacred substances which are activated by supernatural forces that can be summoned into the physical world. Visually, these minkisi can be as simple as pottery or vessels containing medicinal herbs and other elements determined to be beneficial in curing physical illness or alleviating social ills. In other instances minkisi can be represented as small bundles, shells, and carved wooden figures. Minkisi represent the ability to both 'contain' and 'release' spiritual forces which can have both positive and negative consequences on the community.

Nkisi Nkondi

A fascinating example of a nkisi can be found in a power figure called nkisi nkondi (a power figure is a magical charm seemingly carved in the likeness of human being, meant to highlight its function in human affairs.). A nkisi nkondi can act as an oath taking image which is used to resolve verbal disputes or lawsuits (mambu) as well as an avenger (the term nkondi means 'hunter') or guardian if sorcery or any form of evil has been committed. These minkisi are wooden figures representing a human or animal such as a dog (nkisi kozo) carved under the divine authority and in consultation with an nganga or spiritual specialist who activates these figures though chants, prayers and the preparation of sacred substances which are aimed at 'curing' physical, social or spiritual ailments.

Insertions

Nkisi nkondi figures are highly recognizable through an accumulation pegs, blades, nails or other sharp objects inserted into its surface. Medicinal combinations called bilongo are sometimes stored in the head of the figure but frequently in the belly of the figure which is shielded by a piece of glass, mirror or other reflective surface. The glass represents the 'other world' inhabited by the spirits of the dead who can peer through and see potential enemies. Elements with a variety of purposes are contained within the bilongo. Seeds may be inserted to tell a spirit to replicate itself; mpemba or white soil deposits found near cemeteries represent and enlist support from the spiritual realm. Claws may incite the spirits to grasp something while stones may activate the spirits to pelt enemies or protect one from being pelted.

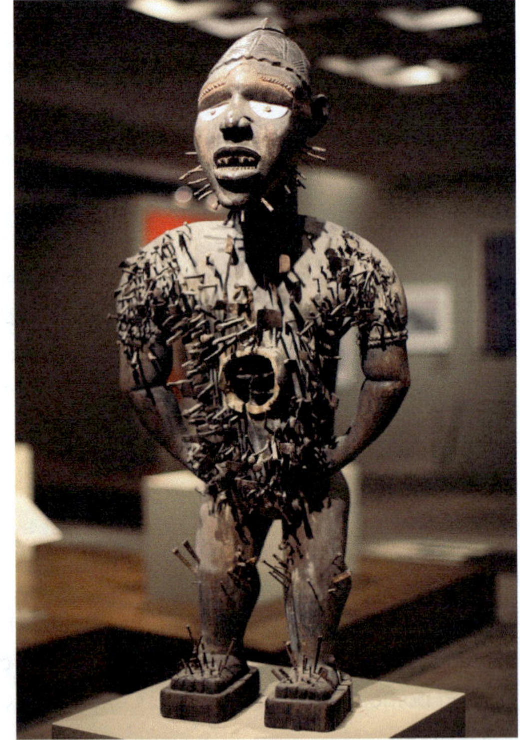

Power Figure (Nkisi N'Kondi: Mangaaka), mid to late nineteenth century, wood, paint, metal, resin, ceramic, 46 7/16" / 118 cm high, Democratic Republic of Congo (The Metropolitan Museum of Art)

The insertions are driven into the figure by the nganga and represent the mambu and the type or degree of severity of an issue can be suggested through the material itself. A peg may refer to a matter being 'settled' whereas a nail, deeply inserted may represent a more serious offense such as murder. Prior to insertion, opposing parties or clients, often lick the blades or nails, to seal the function or purpose of the nkisi through their saliva. If an oath is broken by one of the parties or evil befalls one of them, the nkisi nkondi will become activated to carry out its mission of destruction or divine protection.

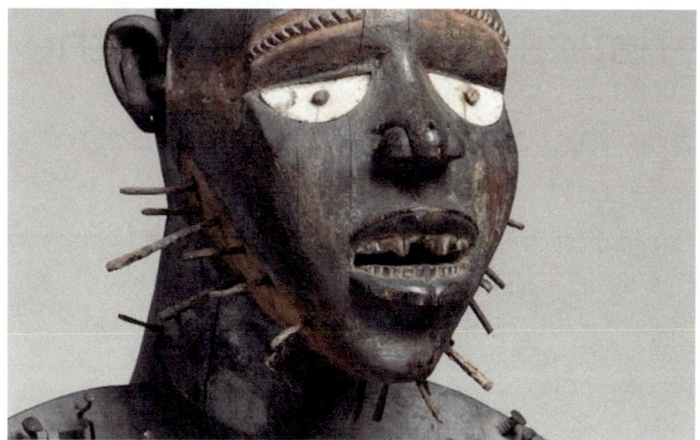

Detail: Power Figure (Nkisi N'Kondi: Mangaaka), mid to late nineteenth century (The Metropolitan Museum of Art)

Migrations

Europeans may have encountered these objects during expeditions to the Congo as early as the 15th century. However, several of these "fetish" objects, as they were often termed, were confiscated by missionaries in the late 19th century and were destroyed as evidence of sorcery or heathenism. Nevertheless, several were collected as objects of fascination and even as an object of study of BaKongo culture. BaKongo traditions such as those of the nkisi nkondi have survived over the centuries and migrated to the Americas and the Caribbean via Afro-Atlantic religious practices such as vodun, Palo Monte, and macumba. In Hollywood these figures have morphed into objects of superstition such as New Orleans voodoo dolls covered with stick pins. Nonetheless, minkisi have left an indelible imprint as visually provocative figures of spiritual importance and protection.

Suggested Readings

Driskell, David C., Michael D. Harris, Wyatt Macgaffey, and Sylvia H. Williams. 1993. *Astonishment and Power*. Washington: Published for the National Museum of African Art by the Smithsonian Institution Press.

Thompson, Robert Farris. 1983. *Flash of the Spirit: African and Afro-American Art and Philosophy.* New York: Random House.

Key Characteristics of Art: 1900 to the Present

Identify and describe key characteristics and defining events of art from 1900 to the present

LEARNING ACTIVITIES

The learning activities for this section include:

- Reading: Cubism and Picasso's Still Life with Chair Caning
- Video: Wassily Kandinsky, Composition VII, 1913, Abstract Expressionism
- Reading: British Art and Literature During WWI
- Reading: Italian Futurism: An Introduction
- Reading: Dada and Surrealism
- Reading: Art in Nazi Germany
- Reading: The Origins of Abstract Expressionism
- Reading: Photography
- Reading: Contemporary Art
- Reading: Warhol's Gold Marilyn Monroe
- Reading: Conceptual Art
- Reading: Mary Kelly's Post-Partum Document
- Reading: Appropriation (The "Pictures Generation")

Take time to review and reflect on each of these activities in order to improve your performance on the assessment for this section.

Reading: Cubism and Picasso's Still Life with Chair Caning

The Evolution of Cubism

Beginning in 1908, and continuing through the first few months of 1912, Braque and Picasso co-invent the first phase of Cubism. Since it is dominated by the analysis of form, this first stage is usually referred to as Analytic Cubism. But then during the summer of 1912, Braque leaves Paris to take a holiday in Provence. During his time there, he wanders into a hardware store, and there he finds a roll of oil cloth. Oil cloth is an early version of contact paper, the vinyl adhesive used to line the shelves or drawers in a cupboard. Then, as now, these materials come in a variety of pre-printed patterns.

Braque purchased some oil cloth printed with a fake wood grain. That particular pattern drew his attention because he was at work on a Cubist drawing of a guitar, and he was about to render the grain of the wood in pencil. Instead, he cut the oil cloth and pasted a piece of the factory-printed grain pattern right into his drawing. With this collage, Braque changed the direction of art for the next ninety years.

Collage

As you might expect, Picasso was not far behind Braque. Picasso immediately begins to create collage with oil cloth as well—and adds other elements to the mix (but remember, it was really Braque who introduced collage—he never gets enough credit). So what is the big deal? Oil cloth, collage, wood grain patterns—what does this have to do with art and Cubism? One of the keys to understanding the importance of Cubism, of Picasso and Braque, is to consider their actions and how unusual they were for the time. When Braque, and then Picasso placed industrially-produced objects ("low" commercial culture) into the realm of fine art ("high" culture) they acted as artistic iconoclasts (icon=image/clast=destroyer).

Moreover, they questioned the elitism of the art world, which had always dictated the separation of common, everyday experience from the rarefied, contemplative realm of artistic creation. Of equal importance, their work highlighted—and separated—the role of technical skill from art-making. Braque and Picasso introduced a "fake" element on purpose, not to mislead or fool their audience, but rather to force a discussion of art and craft, of high and low, of unique and mass-produced objects. They ask: "Can this object still be art if I don't actually render its forms myself, if the quality of the art is no longer directly tied to my technical skills or level of craftsmanship?"

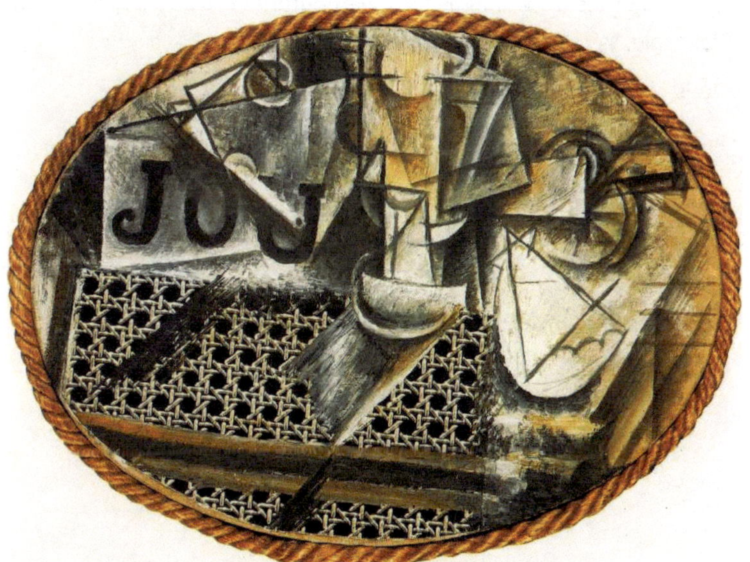

Pablo Picasso, Still Life with Chair Caning, 1912 (Musee Picasso)

Still-Life with Chair Caning

Virtually all avant-garde art of the second half of the twentieth century is indebted to this brave renunciation. But that doesn't make this kind of Cubism, often called Synthetic Cubism (piecing together, or synthesis of form), any easier to interpret. At first glance, Picasso's *Still-Life with Chair Caning* of 1912 might seem a mishmash of forms instead of clear picture. But we can understand the image—and other like it—by breaking down Cubist pictorial language into parts. Let's start at the upper right: almost at the edge of the canvas (at two o'clock) there is the handle of a knife. Follow it to the left to find the blade. The knife cuts a piece of citrus fruit. You can make out the rind and the segments of the slice at the bottom right corner of the blade.

Below the fruit, which is probably a lemon, is the white, scalloped edge of a napkin. To the left of these things and standing vertically in the top center of the canvas (twelve o'clock) is a wine glass. It's hard to see at first, so look carefully. Just at the top edge of the chair caning is the glass's base, above it is the stem (thicker than you might expect), and then the bowl of the glass. It is difficult to find the forms you would expect because Picasso depicts the glass from more than one angle. At eleven o'clock is the famous "JOU," which means "game" in French, but also the first three letters of the French word for newspaper (or more literally, "daily"; journal=daily). In fact, you can make out the bulk of the folded paper quite clearly. Don't be confused by the pipe that lays across the newspaper. Do you see its stem and bowl?

Looking Down and Looking Through

But there are still big questions: why the chair caning, what is the gray diagonal at the bottom of the glass, and why the rope frame? (Think of a ship's port hole. The port hole reference is an important clue.) Also, why don't the letters sit better on the newspaper? Finally, why is the canvas oval? It has already been determined that this still life is composed of a sliced lemon, a glass, newspaper, and a pipe. Perhaps this is a breakfast setting, with a citron pressé (French lemonade). In any case, these items are arranged upon a glass tabletop. You can see the reflection of the glass. In fact, the glass allows us to see below the table's surface, which is how we see the chair caning—which represents the seat tucked in below the table.

Okay, so far so good. But why is the table elliptical in shape? This appears to be a café table, which are round or square but never oval. Yet, when we look at a circular table, we never see it from directly above. Instead, we see it at an angle, and it appears elliptical in shape as we approach the table to sit down. But what about the rope, which was not mass-produced, nor made by Picasso, but rather something made especially for this painting? We can view it as the bumper of a table, as it was used in some cafés, or as the frame of a ship's port hole, which we can look "through," to see the objects represented. The rope's simultaneous horizontal and vertical orientation creates a way for the viewer (us) to read the image in two ways—looking down and looking through/across. Put simply, Picasso wants us to remember that the painting is something different from that which it represents. Or as Gertrude Stein said, "A rose is a rose is a rose."

- https://youtu.be/286FiUvOeFs

Video: Wassily Kandinsky, Composition VII, 1913, Abstract Expressionism

Cubism is an important development in freeing painting from traditional representational depiction. The coming decades of painting will be a wealth of exploration of levels of abstraction and focus on how painting uniquely articulates formal aspects like color, line, and the flatness of the two-dimensional pictorial surface.

- https://youtu.be/i16sGRY7SZ4

Reading: British Art and Literature During WWI

A Brief Introduction to WWI and Its Representation

When shots rang out in Sarajevo on June 28, 1914, Europe began hurtling towards one of the deadliest conflicts the world has ever seen. Gavrilo Princip's assassination of Austro-Hungarian Archduke Franz Ferdinand and his wife, Sophie, brought long-brewing political tension to a head. By August 4, 1914, the Central Powers (Germany, Bulgaria, Austro-Hungary, and the Ottoman Empire) and the Entente or Allied Powers (France, Britain, Russia, Italy, and later the United States), were officially engaged in the First World War.

The crisis would last until November 11, 1918 and claim millions of lives, with battlefronts in Europe, European waters, and in the Middle and Near East. World War I, also known as the Great War, was a distinctly modern conflict in many ways. However, like wars throughout history, it inspired a tremendous amount of creative output from artists and writers, civilians and combatants, men and women.

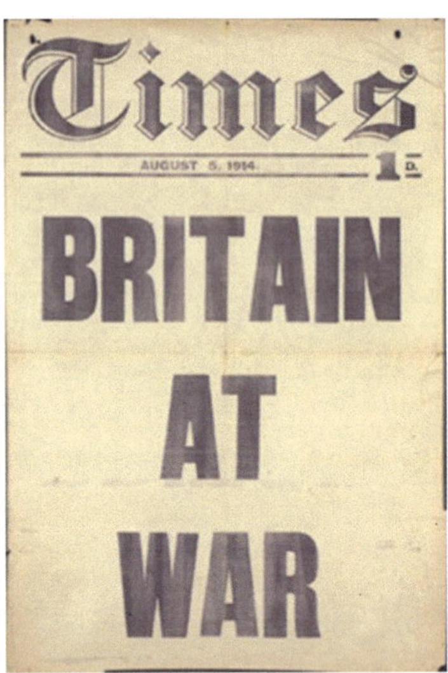

Placard for The Times, "Britain At War" 5 August 1914

Though we may read about dates and numbers when we study historic conflicts, the lived reality of a war becomes much more vivid when we look at the diverse creative expressions it inspires. The varied perspectives represented in the First World War art show us that there was not one single uniform war experience for Britons, whether on the battlefield or at home. In fact, we could say that British artists and writers witnessed and experienced different wars even though only one conflict is recorded in history. War-related art also had many purposes, whether to document, commemorate, appeal, revise, expose, obscure, or protest.

The Conflict between Real and Ideal

Propaganda posters often urged men to enlist in the British Army by appealing to ideals of masculinity, heroism, pride, and loyalty. These widely circulated posters relied on a viewer's positive response to imagery of healthy, stalwart soldiers or emblems of the British nation. A propaganda poster asks its viewer to identify with what is depicted, which usually concerns political, gender, and/or social identity. As part of making such an appeal, propagandists often obscure more realistic aspects of combat or service.

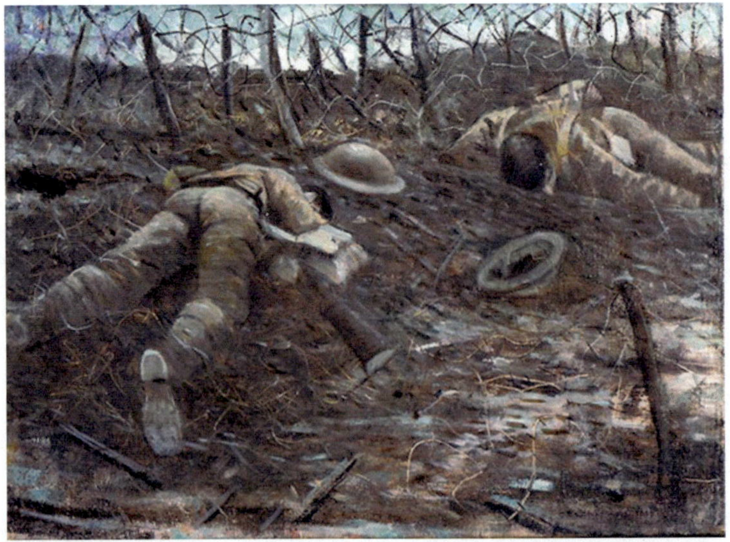

C.R.W. Nevinson, Paths of Glory, 1917, oil on canvas, 467 x 609 mm (Imperial War Museum, London)

In contrast, many war artists offered harsh but realistic visual depictions of the death and destruction that resulted from combat. For example, when we look at C.R.W. Nevinson's stark painting, *Paths of Glory*, irony comes to the forefront. Though the piece has an idealistic-sounding title, we shudder at the sight of two dead soldiers lying in the battlefield mud. We cannot identify with, or even identify these soldiers at all. Their faces are obscured and their bodies merge with the murky earth, suggesting the loss of identity and the waste of young lives. The brownish grey mud almost threatens to rise up and swallow the entire scene.

Paul Nash's 1917 work, *The Menin Road*, depicts a ruined Belgian landscape. Before us, dead tree trunks rise in a wasteland of mud and standing water. This spooky, alienating, place includes strange clouds of smoke penetrated here and there by searchlights. Despite these beams of light, we cannot see anything past the immediate scene. Here is chaos, irrevocable change, and devastation.

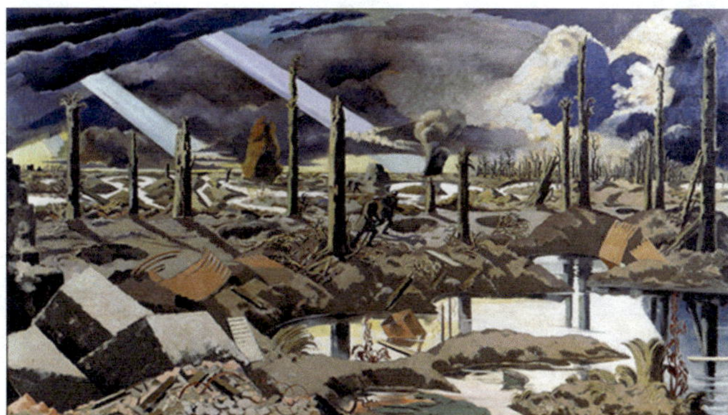

Paul Nash, The Menin Road, 1919, oil on canvas, 1828 x 3175 mm (Imperial War Museum, London)

Carrying Poetry to War

First World War literature also presents a range of perspectives. Rupert Brooke's patriotic '1914' sonnet sequence became hugely popular in the early years of the war. At the outset of the war, many Britons were touched by the heroic sentiments of the poems, in particular, "The Soldier." This poem's combatant speaker assures the reader that his death in battle will mean that "there's some corner of a foreign field/That is for ever England." Brooke's poems pictured military service and death as purifying and noble. At the start of the war, when such nationalistic feeling was strong, many British soldiers departed for training with a copy of Brooke's poems tucked into their kits.

However, after years of devastating losses and with no clear resolution to the seemingly endless fighting, poets depicting the hard reality of the soldier's experience gained more recognition. Wilfred Owen's gloomy 1917 "Anthem for Doomed Youth" pictures the war's fallen "d[ying] as cattle," for example. Siegfried Sassoon's 1918 piece, "Counter-Attack," offers us the gruesome vision of a battlefield "place rotten with dead" where corpses "face downward, in the sucking mud,/Wallow..." Sassoon's shocking verbal image recalls the horrible tableau of Nevinson's dead soldiers lying facedown in the mud.

A Note on WWI and Modernism

During the years leading up to the war, many modernists began to turn their attention to their media; writers and authors broke free of traditional parameters of form and imagery and brought the very materials of their crafts to the forefront. They questioned the solidity of the bond between representation and meaning. Works like T.S. Eliot's poem, "The Waste Land," Mark Gertler's *Merry-Go-Round* (Tate Britain), or Virginia Woolf's *Mrs. Dalloway* sought to shock, alienate, or provoke audiences and to thereby explore new sensory and intellectual effects in art and literature.

While the modernist movement had begun prior to the war, the conflict's vast scale, brutality, and costs fascinated many artists and writers. The war definitively ended many social and cultural traditions that survived the nineteenth century and made clear the modern, mechanized world we were entering, a world where the older expressive forms and techniques no longer seemed adequate, appropriate, or compelling.

Women Writers and Artists

Women artists and writers played a significant role in documenting civilian and service experiences. Vera Brittain, who volunteered as a nurse, recorded her impressions of work and loss in her memoir, *Testament of Youth*, one of the war's most recognized autobiographical works. Women artists documented other civilian realities such as female workers in factories—doing jobs vacated by men in the military— who had become crucial for war-related production.

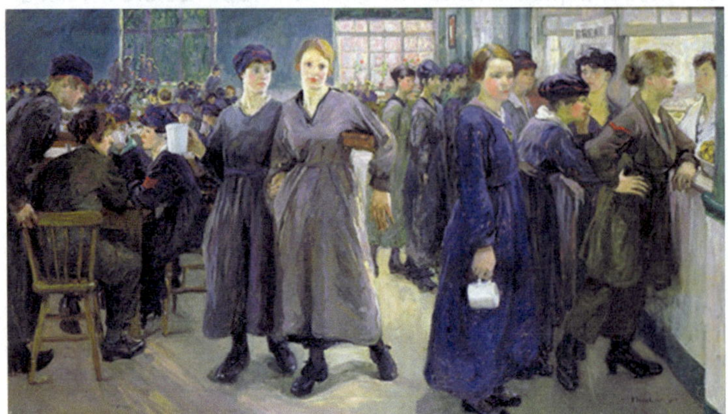

Flora Lion, Women's Canteen at Phoenix Works, Bradford, 1918, oil on canvas, 1066 x 1828 mm (Imperial War Museum)

Flora Lion for example, shows us a canteen for women munitions (weapons) workers in her painting, *Women's Canteen at Phoenix Works, Bradford*. We can see the exhaustion that the workers are feeling. The women here look somewhat relieved for their tea break. Their resigned expressions and slouching posture underscore the mental and physical fatigue of this critical but dangerous line of work, but they also make us recognize the more emotional weariness of the civilian war experience.

WWI's Aftermath: Public and Private Commemoration

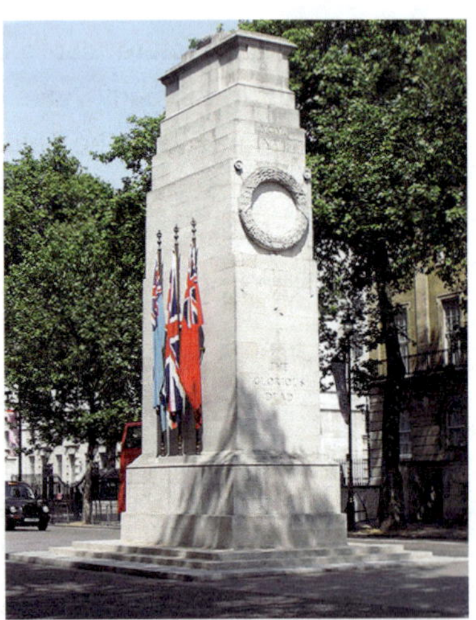

When the war concluded in November 1918, nearly a million Britons were dead. British soldiers killed in action were buried overseas, so that public officials and grieving families were challenged to represent both personal and national losses. To recognize individual sacrifices, the British government issued memorial bronze plaques and paper scrolls to the family of each serviceperson who died as a result of the war. And, on November 11, 1920, a solemn ceremony dedicated two of Britain's most famous public war monuments, Edward Luytens's *Whitehall Cenotaph* and the *Unknown Soldier*, buried in Westminster Abbey.

Edward Luytens, Whitehall Cenotaph, unveiled 1920, portland stone, London

The creative work of giving textual, visual, or plastic form to First World War experiences would go on into the 1930s and after. Even as Britain neared the fearful prospect of a second major international conflict, the Great War continued to haunt those who had lived through it.

Reading: Italian Futurism: An Introduction

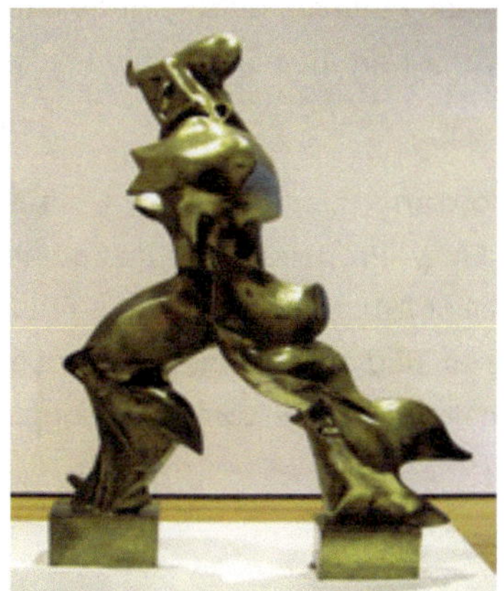

Umberto Boccioni, Unique Forms of Continuity in Space, 1913 (cast 1931), bronze, 43 7/8 x 34 7/8 x 15 3/4" (MoMA)

Can you imagine being so enthusiastic about technology that you name your daughter Propeller? Today we take most technological advances for granted, but at the turn of the last century, innovations like electricity, x-rays, radio waves, automobiles and airplanes were novel and extremely exciting. Italy lagged Britain, France, Germany, and the United States in the pace of its industrial development. Culturally speaking, the country's artistic reputation was grounded in Ancient, Renaissance and Baroque art and culture. Simply put, Italy represented the past.

In the early 1900s, a group of young and rebellious Italian writers and artists emerged determined to celebrate industrialization. They were frustrated by Italy's declining status and believed that the "Machine Age" would result in an entirely new world order and even a renewed consciousness. Filippo Tommaso Marinetti, the ringleader of this group, called the movement Futurism. Its members sought to capture the idea of modernity, the sensations and aesthetics of speed, movement, and industrial development.

A Manifesto

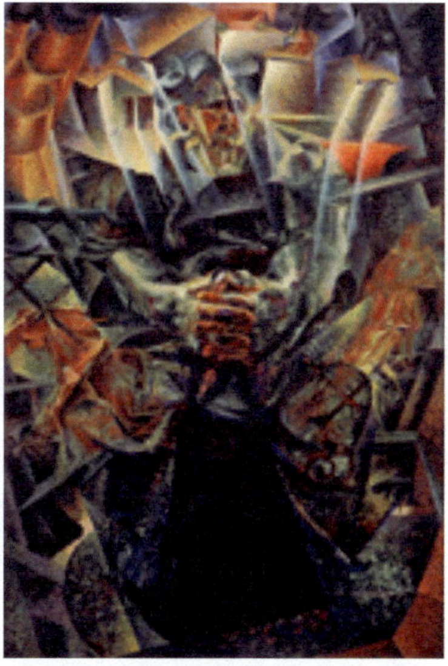

Umberto Boccioni, Materia, 1912 (reworked 1913), oil on canvas, 226 x 150 cm (Mattioli Collection loaned to Peggy Guggenheim Collection, Venice)

Marinetti launched Futurism in 1909 with the publication his "Futurist manifesto" on the front page of the French newspaper *Le Figaro*. The manifesto set a fiery tone. In it Marinetti lashed out against cultural tradition (*passatismo*, in Italian) and called for the destruction of museums, libraries, and feminism. Futurism quickly grew into an international movement and its participants issued additional manifestos for nearly every type of art: painting, sculpture, architecture, music, photography, cinema—even clothing.

The Futurist painters—Umberto Boccioni, Carlo Carrà, Luigi Russolo, Gino Severini, and Giacomo Balla—signed their first manifesto in 1910 (the last named his daughter Elica—Propeller!). Futurist painting had first looked to the color and the optical experiments of the late 19th century, but in the fall of 1911, Marinetti and the Futurist painters visited the Salon d'Automne in Paris and saw Cubism in person for the first time. Cubism had an immediate impact that can be seen in Boccioni's *Materia* of 1912 for example. Nevertheless, the Futurists declared their work to be completely original.

Dynamism of Bodies in Motion

The Futurists were particularly excited by the works of late 19th-century scientist and photographer Étienne-Jules Marey, whose chronophotographic (time-based) studies depicted the mechanics of animal and human movement.

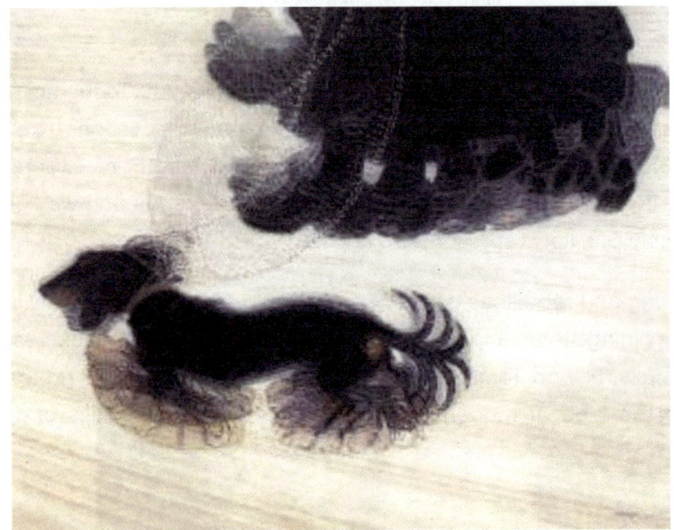

Giacomo Balla, Dynamism of a Dog on a Leash, 1912, oil on canvas, 35 1/2 x 43 1/4 " (Albright-Knox Art Gallery, Buffalo)

A precursor to cinema, Marey's innovative experiments with time-lapse photography were especially influential for Balla. In his painting *Dynamism of a Dog on a Leash*, the artist playfully renders the dog's (and dog walker's) feet as continuous movements through space over time.

Entranced by the idea of the "dynamic," the Futurists sought to represent an object's sensations, rhythms and movements in their images, poems and manifestos. Such characteristics are beautifully expressed in Boccioni's most iconic masterpiece, *Unique Forms of Continuity in Space* (see above).

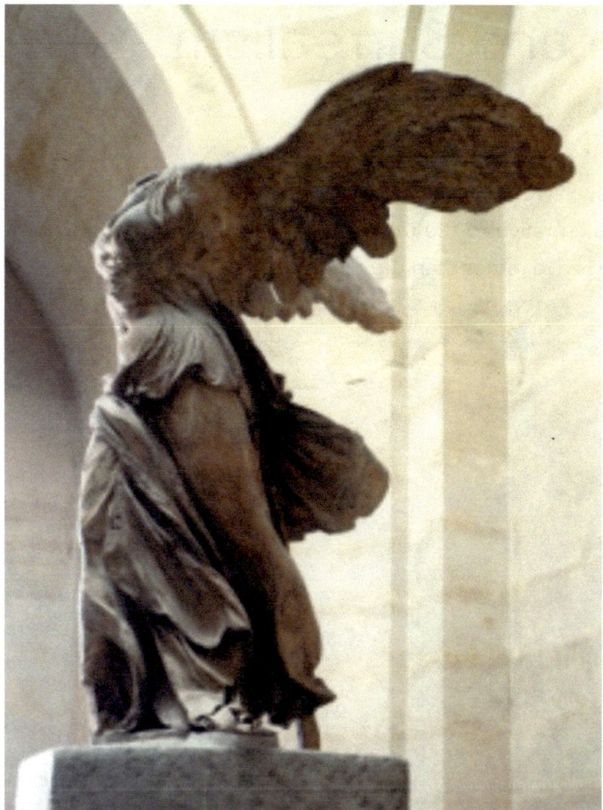

Nike of Samothrace, marble, c. 190 B.C.E. (Louvre, Paris)

The choice of shiny bronze lends a mechanized quality to Boccioni's sculpture, so here is the Futurists' ideal combination of human and machine. The figure's pose is at once graceful and forceful, and despite their adamant rejection of classical arts, it is also very similar to the *Nike of Samothrace*.

Politics and War

Futurism was one of the most politicized art movements of the twentieth century. It merged artistic and political agendas in order to propel change in Italy and across Europe. The Futurists would hold what they called *serate futuriste*, or Futurist evenings, where they would recite poems and display art, while also shouting politically charged rhetoric at the audience in the hope of inciting riot. They believed that agitation and destruction would end the status quo and allow for the regeneration of a stronger, energized Italy.

These positions led the Futurists to support the coming war, and like most of the group's members, leading painter Boccioni enlisted in the army during World War I. He was trampled to death after falling from a horse during training. After the war, the members' intense nationalism led to an alliance with Benito Mussolini and his National Fascist Party. Although Futurism continued to develop new areas of focus (*aeropittura*, for example) and attracted new members—the so-called "second generation" of Futurist artists—the movement's strong ties to Fascism has complicated the study of this historically significant art.

Reading: Dada and Surrealism

- https://youtu.be/9E1cA3j_xY8

One of the most important and subversive movements of the twentieth century, Surrealism flourished particularly in the 1920s and 1930s and provided a radical alternative to the rational and formal qualities of Cubism. Unlike Dada, from which in many ways it sprang, it emphasized the positive rather than the nihilistic.

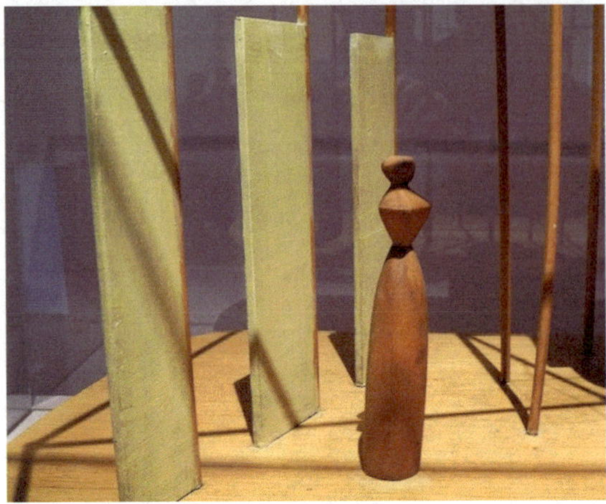

Alberto Giacometti, The Palace at 4 a.m., 1932. Wood, glass, wire, and string, 25 x 28-1/4 x 15-3/4 inches (The Museum of Modern Art)

Surrealism sought access to the subconscious and to translate this flow of thought into terms of art. Originally a literary movement, it was famously defined by the poet André Breton in the First Manifesto of Surrealism (1924):

> SURREALISM, noun, masc. Pure psychic automatism by which it is intended to express either verbally or in writing the true function of thought. Thought dictated in the absence of all control exerted by reason, and outside all aesthetic or moral preoccupations.

A number of distinct strands can be discerned in the visual manifestation of Surrealism. Artists such as Max Ernst and André Masson favoured automatism in which conscious control is suppressed and the subconscious is allowed to take over. Conversely, Salvador Dali and René Magritte pursued an hallucinatory sense of super-reality in which the scenes depicted make no real sense. A third variation was the juxtaposition of unrelated items, setting up a startling unreality outside the bounds of normal reality.

Common to all Surrealistic enterprises was a post-Freudian desire to set free and explore the imaginative and creative powers of the mind. Surrealism was originally Paris based. Its influence spread through a number of journals and international exhibitions, the most important examples of the latter being the International Surrealist Exhibition at the New Burlington Galleries, London and the Fantastic Art Dada, Surrealism at the Museum of Modern Art, New York, both held in 1936.

With the outbreak of the Second World War, the centre of Surrealist activity transferred to New York and by the end of the War the movement had lost its coherence. It has retained a potent influence, however, clearly evident in aspects of Abstract Expressionism and various other artistic manifestations of the second half of the twentieth century.

Reading: Art in Nazi Germany

Nazi Art Policy

How do you destroy an artwork? You can hide it, scratch it, tear it, put a slogan over it, burn it, or, as the Nazis did in 1937, simply show it to millions of people.

If you visited Munich in the summer of that year, you could see two spectacular exhibitions that were held only a few hundred meters apart. One was the Great German Art Exhibition, showcasing recent leading examples of 'Aryan' art. The other was the Degenerate Art Exhibition, which offered a tour through the art that the National Socialist Party had rejected on ideological grounds. It was made up of art that was not considered 'Aryan' and offered a last glimpse before these works of art disappeared.

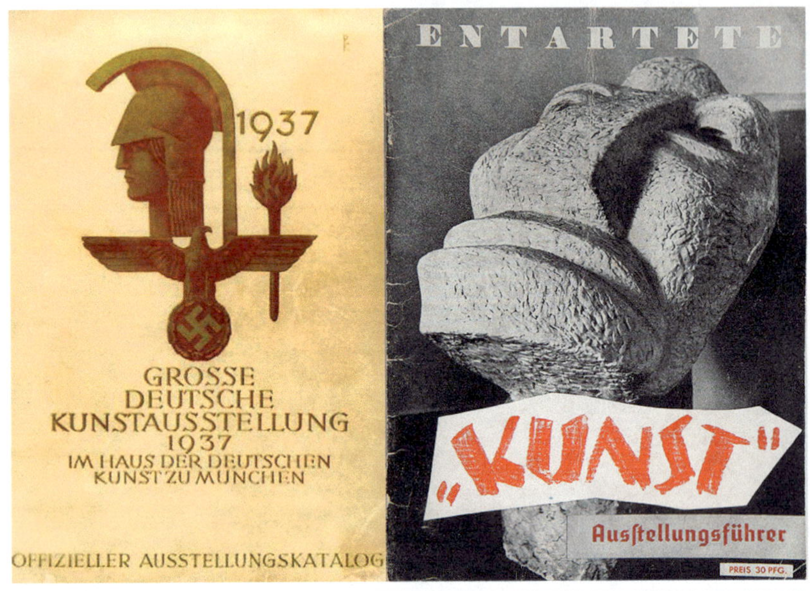

1937 Great German Art Exhibition and Degenerate Art Exhibition catalogue covers

The Degenerate Art Exhibition cleverly manipulated visitors to loathe and ridicule the art on exhibit, in part by erasing their original meaning. Until shortly before the exhibition, these paintings and sculptures had been displayed at the nation's greatest museums, but now they were the principal performers in a freak show. The shock-value was enhanced by only allowing over-18s into the exhibition. The lines for the Degenerate Art Exhibition went around the block. Inside, many pictures had been taken out of their frames, and were attached to walls that were emblazoned with outraged slogans. Rather than whispering respectfully, people pointed and snickered. The paintings and sculptures had lost their status as artworks, and were now reduced to dangerous and outrageous rubbish.

Visual symbolism was important to the Nazis, and Hitler himself had been a painter, so it is not surprising that they dedicated significant resources promoting their ideals through art. So how was the decision made? How were 'degenerate' and 'Aryan' artworks selected? If you look at the works of art that were glorified and compare them to those that were attacked by the Nazis, the differences usually seem clear enough; experimental, personal, non-representational art was rejected, whilst conventionally 'beautiful,' stereotypically heroic art was revered. This seems like an obvious line to be taken by a totalitarian regime: everyone will find these artworks beautiful, and everyone will feel and think the same thing about them, without the risk of unwanted, random, personal, or unclear interpretations.

A Very Simple Decision

And the Nazis presented it as a very simple decision, any true German would immediately be able to tell the difference. But in reality, a four-year battle was fought all the way to the top echelons of the Nazi hierarchy over what 'Aryan' art was supposed to be, exactly. The opinions on this could not have been more contradictory, and top Nazi officials such as Heinrich Himmler, Joseph Goebbels and Alfred Rosenberg championed the art they each preferred.

Surprisingly, before 1937, Goebbels—and many other Nazis—collected modern art. Goebbels had works of modern art in his study, his living room and was a fan of many artists that eventually ended up in the Degenerate Art Exhibition. Heinrich Himmler was interested in mystical, Germanic art that harked back to a tribal past. Another influential Nazi, Alfred Rosenberg, liked the pastoral, romantic style that depicted humble farmers, rural landscapes and blond maidens.

Hitler would have none of it. He loathed Expressionism and modern art whilst pastoral idylls were not serious enough. Goebbels reversed himself and became one of the driving forces behind the Degenerate Art Exhibition, prosecuting the same artworks he had once enjoyed. Rosenberg also let go, albeit reluctantly, whilst Himmler changed tack and stole artworks by the wagonload behind Hitler's back throughout the war.

So How Was "Aryan" Art Defined?

In a sense, the concept of "Aryan" art was defined by what it was not: anything that was ideologically problematic (that did not fit with the extremist beliefs of the regime) was removed until there little left but an academic style that celebrated youth, optimism, power and eternal triumph. Nevertheless, it remained difficult for even the most influential Nazis to understand the selection criteria for art sanctioned by the state.

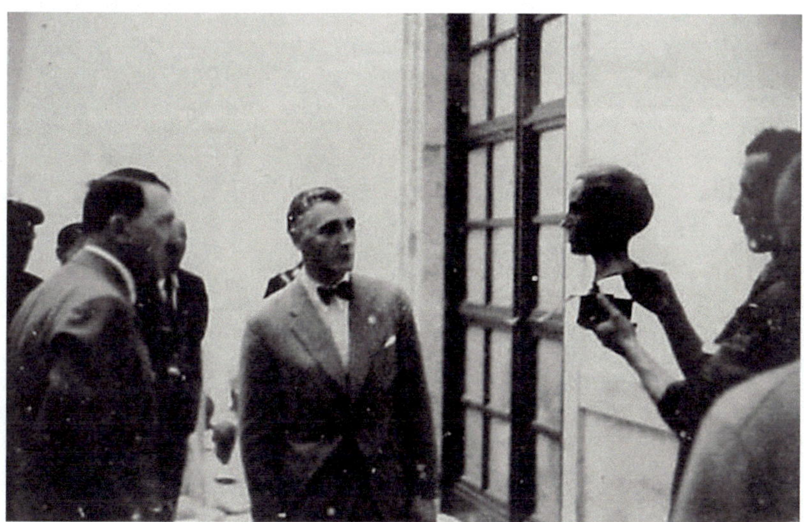
Hitler and Ziegler judging the Great German Art Exhibition, 1937

Take for example Adolf Ziegler, who had been in charge of selecting the artwork to be exhibited in the Great German Art Exhibition. Just before the show opened, Hitler visited in order to inspect the artwork chosen to represent the eternal future of Nazi Germany. He was not pleased with the selection his most loyal followers had made. On the 5th of June, 1937, Goebbels wrote in his diary that the Führer was "wild with rage" and subsequently issued a statement declaring "I will not tolerate unfinished paintings," meaning that the exhibition had to be reconceived at the last minute.

Even opportunistic "hard-liners" like Adolf Ziegler, an artist favored by Hitler, were not quite able to fulfill their patron's vision. However, it would not be right to conclude that the criteria for art that represented the 'Aryan' state appears to have been based principally on the eye of Adolf Hitler rather than a set of delineated characteristics. Even Hitler's taste was not the ultimate indicator of 'Aryan' art: whilst planning what great artworks he would take from the conquered museums of Europe for his never-realized Führer-Museum, he was convinced by his newly appointed museum director that his taste was not up to standard for the world-class museum he envisaged. Rather than firing the man, Hitler deferred to this Dr. Hans Posse, despite the fact that he had recently been fired from his post as museum director in Dresden for endorsing "degenerate art."

What Was Actually on Display in the Two Exhibitions?

The Degenerate Art Exhibition mostly exhibited Expressionism, New Objectivism and some abstract art. Strangely, very few works came from Jewish artists, and a lot of artworks had until recently been favorites of many Nazis. Renowned works by artists such as Ernst Ludwig Kirchner, Karl Schmidt-Rotluff and Ernst Barlach now hung on walls marked with graffiti. The works ranged from quiet and traditional looking, such as Ernst Barlach's *The Reunion (Das Wiedersehen)*, 1926 which showed two poised, realistically carved wooden figures holding each other, to more grotesquely painted works, such as Otto Dix' *War Cripples (Kriegskrüppel)*, 1920. This work shows a procession of cartoonesque yet morbid war veterans, painfully moving forward with the aid of pushchairs, prosthetic legs and crutches, smoking cheerfully, though one soldier's face is half eaten away, revealing a rictus grin of clenched teeth.

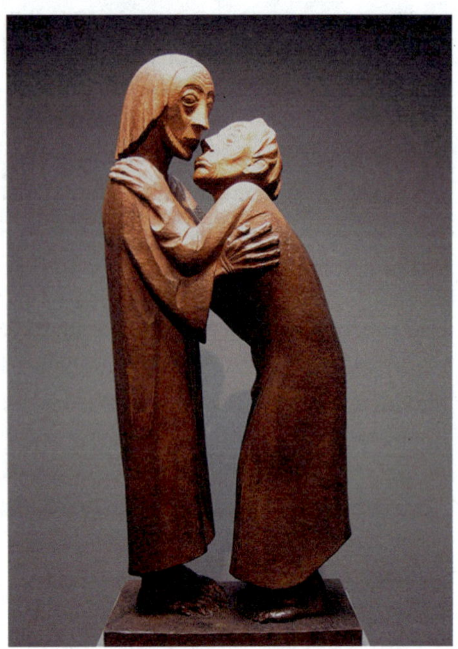

Ernst Barlach, The Reunion (Das Wiedersehen), 1926 mahogany, 90 x 38 x 25 cm, Ernst Barlach Haus, Hamburg (photo: Rufus46, CC: BY-SA)

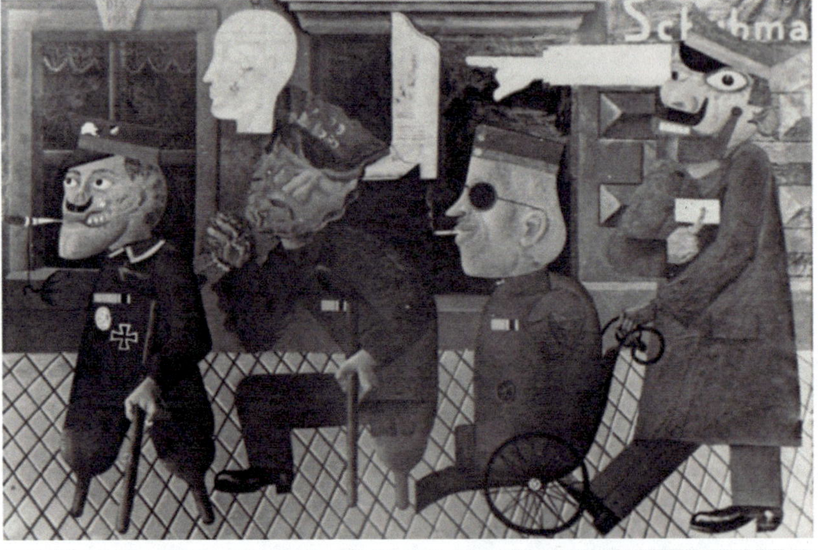

Otto Dix, War Cripples (45% Fit for Service), 1920, oil on canvas, lost work

In contrast, the Great German Art Exhibition showed art with the hallmarks of classical tradition, large sculptures of tall and muscular bodies and paintings of heroic soldiers by artists such as Josef Thorak and Arno Breker. Prominent position was given to Breker's *Decathlete ('Zehnkämpfer')* and *Victory ('Siegerin')*, both made in 1936, showing two bronze figures over three metres high, their impersonal facial expressions and perfectly proportioned bodies almost archetypical examples of the classical style.

However, in later editions of the Great German Art Exhibition, works that did not fit the ideals of beauty, youth and optimism crept back in. Realistically painted works depicting soldiers despairing in the trenches by Albert Heinrich and sad, emaciated figures like the bust *Der Walzmeister* by Fritz Koelle began to share the space with oversized muscular bronze men and paintings of serene nude women.

The random nature of Nazi art policy continued after these exhibitions closed. Breker and Thorak, superstars of the Nazi regime, actually had some works branded as degenerate (though this was quickly covered up), whereas the artist Emil Nolde, who joined the Nazi party and was an early and enthusiastic supporter, had been issued a so-called *Malverbot* forbidding him to paint even in the privacy of his own home. He received regular visits from the Gestapo, the secret police, who came to touch his brushes to ensure that they had not been used. Nolde became a water-color painter. The brushes dried a lot faster than with oil paint.

Reading: The Origins of Abstract Expressionism

What's in a Name?

The group of artists known as Abstract Expressionists emerged in the United States in the years following World War II. As the term suggests, their work was characterized by non-objective imagery that appeared emotionally charged with personal meaning. The artists, however, rejected these implications of the name.

They insisted their subjects were not "abstract," but rather primal images, deeply rooted in society's collective unconscious. Their paintings did not express mere emotion. They communicated universal truths about the human condition. For these reasons, another term—the New York School—offers a more accurate descriptor of the group, for although some eventually relocated, their distinctive aesthetic first found form in New York City.

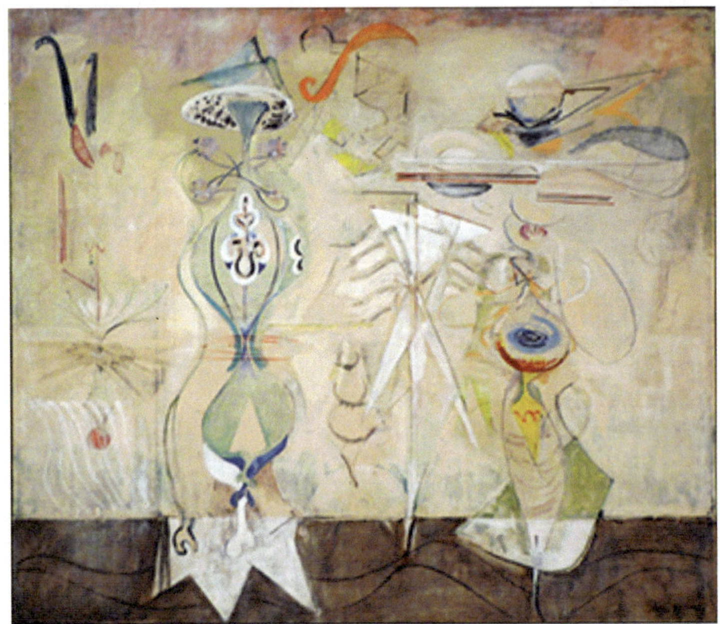

Mark Rothko, Slow Swirl at the Edge of the Sea, 1944, oil on canvas, 191.4 x 215.2 cm (MoMA)

The rise of the New York School reflects the broader cultural context of the mid-twentieth century, especially the shift away from Europe as the center of intellectual and artistic innovation in the West. Much of Abstraction Expressionism's significance stems from its status as the first American visual art movement to gain international acclaim.

Art for a World in Shambles

Barnett Newman wrote:

Although distinguished by individual styles, the Abstract Expressionists shared common artistic and intellectual interests. While not expressly political, most of the artists held strong convictions based on Marxist ideas of social and economic equality. Many had benefited directly from employment in the Works Progress Administration's Federal Art Project. There, they found influences in Regionalist styles of American artists such as Thomas Hart Benton, as well as the Socialist Realism of Mexican muralists including Diego Rivera and José Orozco.

The growth of Fascism in Europe had brought a wave of immigrant artists to the United States in the 1930s, which gave Americans greater access to ideas and practices of European Modernism. They sought training at the school founded by German painter Hans Hoffmann, and from Josef Albers, who left the Bauhaus in 1933 to teach at the experimental Black Mountain College in North Carolina, and later at Yale University. This European presence made clear the formal innovations of Cubism, as well as the psychological undertones and automatic painting techniques of Surrealism.

Whereas Surrealism had found inspiration in the theories of Sigmund Freud, the Abstract Expressionists looked more to the Swiss psychologist Carl Jung and his explanations of primitive archetypes that were a part of our collective human experience. They also gravitated toward Existentialist philosophy, made popular by European intellectuals such as Martin Heidegger and Jean-Paul Sartre.

Given the atrocities of World War II, Existentialism appealed to the Abstract Expressionists. Sartre's position that an individual's actions might give life meaning suggested the importance of the artist's creative process. Through the artist's physical struggle with his materials, a painting itself might ultimately come to serve as a lasting mark of one's existence. Each of the artists involved with Abstract Expressionism eventually developed an individual style that can be easily recognized as evidence of his artistic practice and contribution.

What Does It Look Like?

Although Abstract Expressionism informed the sculpture of David Smith and Aaron Siskind's photography, the movement is most closely linked to painting. Most Abstract Expressionist paintings are large scale, include non-objective imagery, lack a clear focal point, and show visible signs of the artist's working process, but these characteristics are not consistent in every example.

1. Barnett Newman, "Response to the Reverend Thomas F. Mathews," in Revelation, Place and Symbol (Journal of the First Congress on Religion, Architecture and the Visual Arts), 1969.

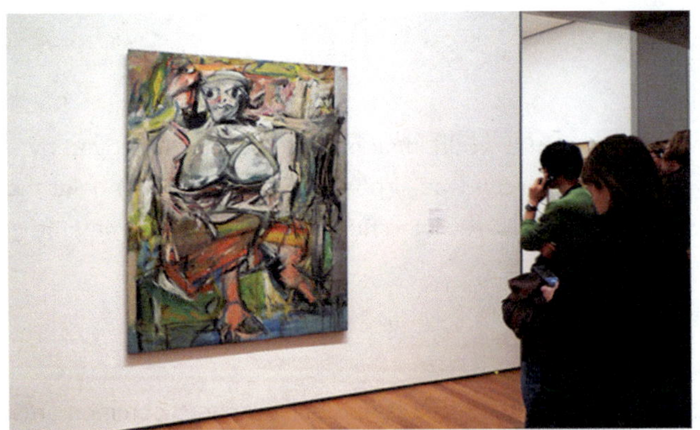

Willem de Kooning, Woman, I, 1950–52, oil on canvas, 192.7 x 147.3 cm (MoMA)

In the case of Willem de Kooning's *Woman I*, the visible brush strokes and thickly applied pigment are typical of the "Action Painting" style of Abstract Expressionism also associated with Jackson Pollock and Franz Kline. Looking at *Woman I*, we can easily imagine de Kooning at work, using strong slashing gestures, adding gobs of paint to create heavily built-up surfaces that could be physically worked and reworked with his brush and palette knife. De Kooning's central image is clearly recognizable, reflecting the tradition of the female nude throughout art history. Born in the Netherlands, de Kooning was trained in the European academic tradition unlike his American colleagues. Although he produced many non-objective works throughout his career, his early background might be one factor in his frequent return to the figure.

In contrast to the dynamic appearance of de Kooning's art, Mark Rothko and Barnett Newman exemplify what is sometimes called the "Color Imagist" or "Color Field" style of Abstract Expressionism. These artists produced large scale, non-objective imagery as well, but their work lacks the energetic intensity and gestural quality of Action Painting.

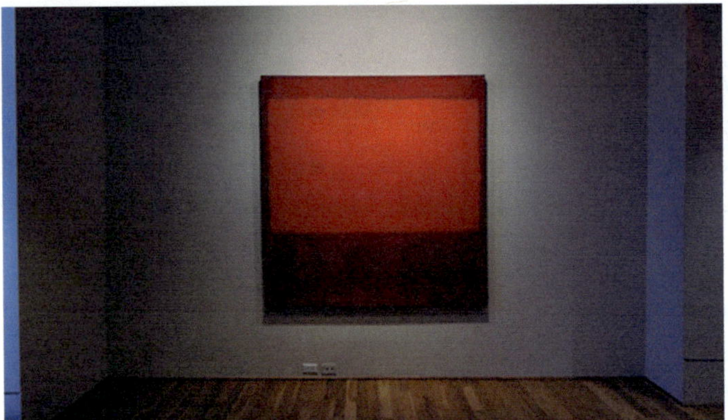

Mark Rothko, Orange and Red on Red, 1957, oil on canvas, 174.9 x 168.5 cm (Phillips Collection, Washington)

Rothko's mature paintings exemplify this tendency. His subtly rendered rectangles appear to float against their background. For artists like Rothko, these images were meant to encourage meditation and personal reflection. Adolph Gottlieb, writing with Rothko and Newman in 1943, explained, "We favor the simple expression of the complex thought."[2]

Barnett Newman's *Vir Heroicus Sublimis* illustrates this lofty goal. In this painting, Newman relied on "zips," vertical lines that punctuate the painted field of the background to serve a dual function. While they visually highlight the expanse of

2. Letter from Mark Rothko and Adolph Gottlieb to Edward Alden Jewell Art Editor, New York Times, June 7, 1943.

contrasting color around them, they metaphorically reflect our own presence as individuals within our potentially overwhelming surroundings. Newman's painting evokes the eighteenth-century notion of the Sublime, a philosophical concept related to spiritual understanding of humanity's place among the greater forces of the universe.

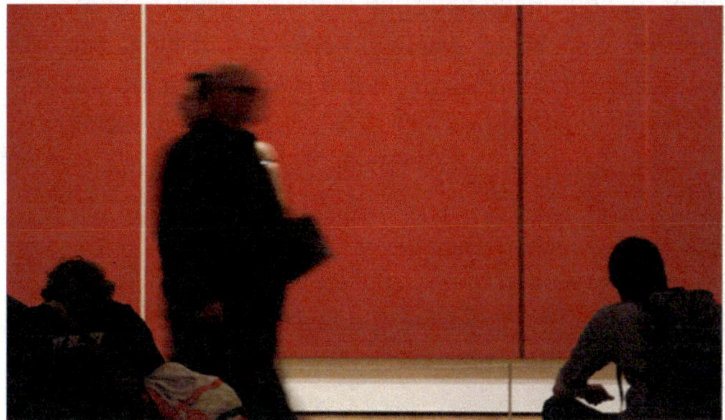

Detail of Barnett Newman, Vir Heroicus Sublimis, 1950 with visitors at MoMA

Abstract Expressionism's Legacy

Throughout the 1950s, Abstract Expressionism became the dominant influence on artists both in the United States and abroad. The U.S. government embraced its distinctive style as a reflection of American democracy, individualism, and cultural achievement, and actively promoted international exhibitions of Abstract Expressionism as a form of political propaganda during the years of the Cold War. However, many artists found it difficult to replicate the emotional authenticity implicit in the stylistic innovations of de Kooning and Pollock. Their work appeared studied and lacked the same vitality of the first generation pioneers. Others saw the metaphysical undertones of Abstract Expressionism at odds with a society increasingly concerned with a consumer mentality, fueled by economic success and proliferation of the mass media. Such reactions would inevitably lead to the emergence of Pop, Minimalism, and the rise of a range of new artistic developments in the mid-twentieth century.

Reading: Photography

Photography undergoes extraordinary changes in the early part of the twentieth century. This can be said of every other type of visual representation, however, but unique to photography is the transformed perception of the medium. In order to understand this change in perception and use—why photography appealed to artists by the early 1900s, and how it was incorporated into artistic practices by the 1920s—we need to start by looking back.

In the later nineteenth century, photography spread in its popularity, and inventions like the Kodak #1 camera (1888) made it accessible to the upper-middle class consumer; the Kodak Brownie camera, which cost far less, reached the middle class by 1900.

In the sciences (and pseudo-sciences), photographs gained credibility as objective evidence because they could document people, places, and events. Photographers like Eadweard Muybridge created portfolios of photographs to measure human and animal locomotion. His celebrated images recorded incremental stages of movement too rapid for the human eye to observe, and his work fulfilled the camera's promise to enhance, or even create new forms of scientific study.

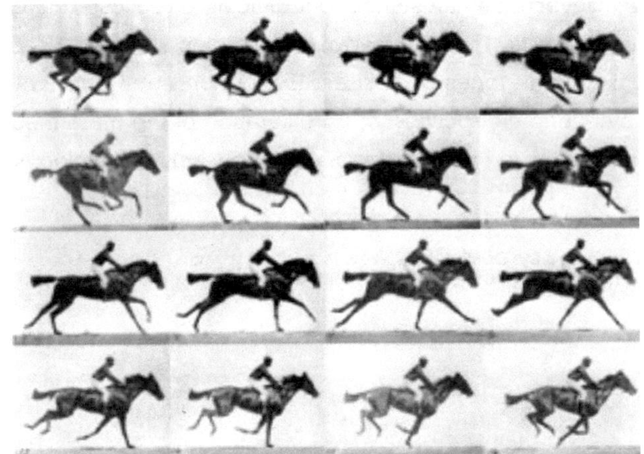

Eastman Kodak Advertisement for the Brownie Camera, c. 1900

Eadweard Muybridge, Thoroughbred bay mare "Annie G." galloping, Human and Animal Locomotion, plate 626, 1887

In the arts, the medium was valued for its replication of exact details, and for its reproduction of artworks for publication. But photographers struggled for artistic recognition throughout the century. It was not until in Paris's Universal Exposition of 1859, twenty years after the invention of the medium, that photography and "art" (painting, engraving, and sculpture) were displayed next to one another for the first time; separate entrances to each exhibition space, however, preserved a physical and symbolic distinction between the two groups. After all, photographs are mechanically reproduced images: Kodak's marketing strategy ("You press the button, we do the rest,") points directly to the "effortlessness" of the medium.

Since art was deemed the product of imagination, skill, and craft, how could a photograph (made with an instrument and light-sensitive chemicals instead of brush and paint) ever be considered its equivalent? And if its purpose was to reproduce details precisely, and from nature, how could photographs be acceptable if negatives were "manipulated," or if photographs were retouched? Because of these questions, amateur photographers formed casual groups and official societies to challenge such conceptions of the medium. They—along with elite art world figures like Alfred Stieglitz—promoted the late nineteenth-century style of "art photography," and produced low-contrast, warm-toned images like *The Terminal* that highlighted the medium's potential for originality.

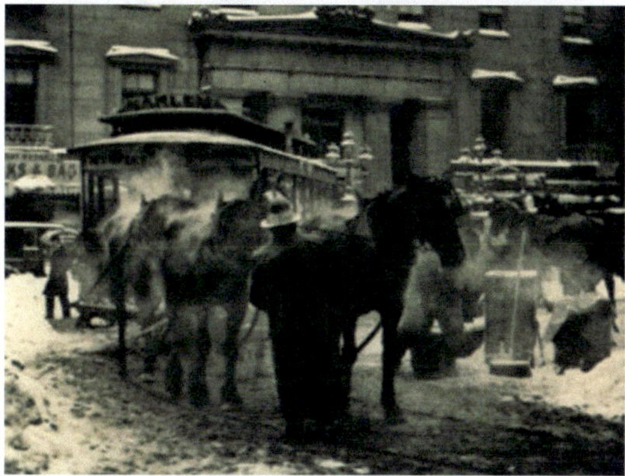

Alfred Stieglitz, The Terminal, photogravure, 1892

So what transforms the perception of photography in the early twentieth century? Social and cultural change—on a massive, unprecedented scale. Like everyone else, artists were radically affected by industrialization, political revolution, trench warfare, airplanes, talking motion pictures, radios, automobiles, and much more—and they wanted to create art that was as radical and "new" as modern life itself. If we consider the work of the Cubists and Futurists, we often think of their works in terms of simultaneity and speed, destruction and reconstruction. Dadaists, too, challenged the boundaries of traditional art with performances, poetry, installations, and photomontage that use the materials of everyday culture instead of paint, ink, canvas, or bronze.

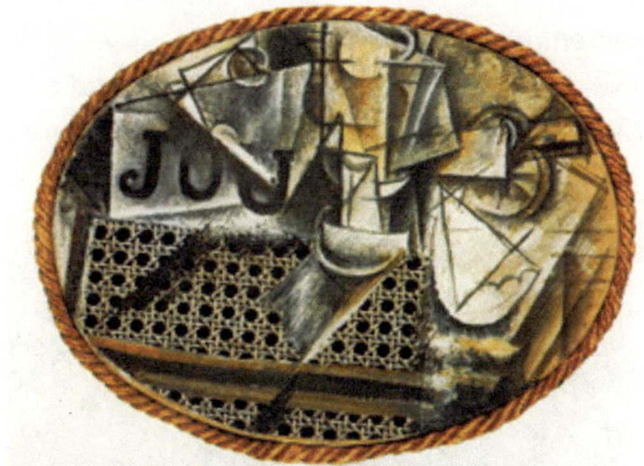

Picasso, Still Life with Chair Caning, 1912, oil, oilcloth and pasted paper on canvas with rope frame

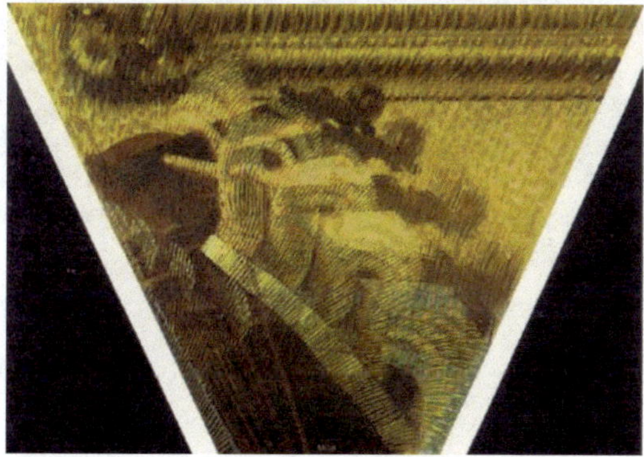

Giacomo Balla, Hand of the Violinist, 1912 (Hand of the Violinist, 1912, oil on canvas (London, priv. col.)

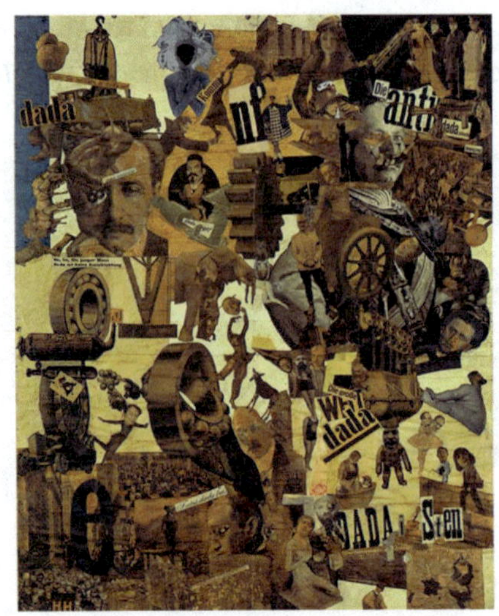

Hannah Höch, Cut with the Kitchen Knife Dada Through the Last Weimar Beer-Belly Cultural Epoch of Germany, 1919-20, photomontage

By the early 1920s, technology becomes a vehicle of progress and change, and instills hope in many after the devastations of World War I. For avant-garde ("ahead of the crowd") artists, photography becomes incredibly appealing for its associations with technology, the everyday, and science—precisely the reasons it was denigrated a half-century earlier. The camera's technology of mechanical reproduction made it the fastest, most modern, and arguably, the most relevant form of visual representation in the post-WWI era. Photography, then, seemed to offer more than a new method of image-making—it offered the chance to change paradigms of vision and representation.

With August Sander's portraits, such as *Secretary at a Radio Station*, *Pastry Cook* or *Disabled Man*, we see an artist attempting to document—systematically—modern types of people, as a means to understand changing notions of class, race, profession, ethnicity, and other constructs of identity. Sander transforms the practice of portraiture with these sensational, arresting images. These figures reveal as much about the German professions as they do about self-image.

Cartier-Bresson's leaping figure in *Behind the Gare St. Lazare* reflects the potential for photography to capture individual moments in time—to freeze them, hold them, and recreate them. Because of his approach, Cartier-Bresson is often considered a pioneer of photojournalism. This sense of spontaneity, of accuracy, and of the ephemeral corresponded to the racing tempo of modern culture (think of factories, cars, trains, and the rapid pace of people in growing urban centers).

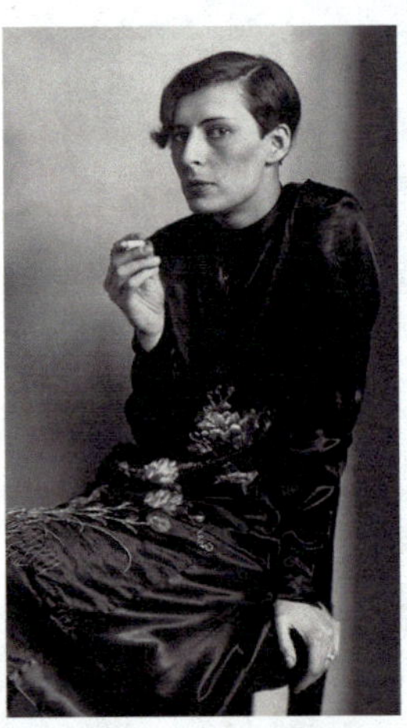

August Sander, Secretary at a Radio Station, Cologne, 1931

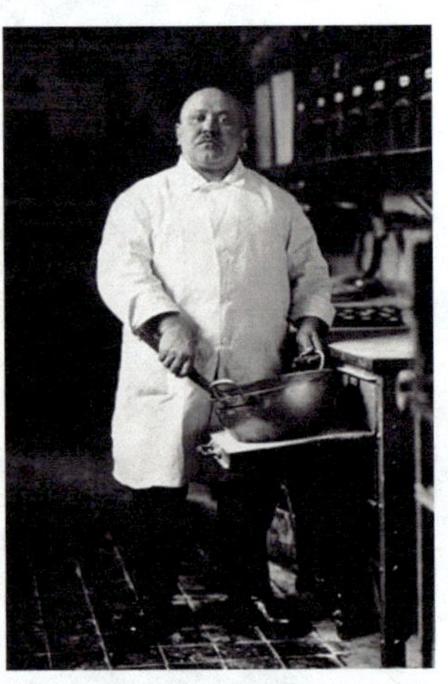

August Sander, Pastry Chef, 1928

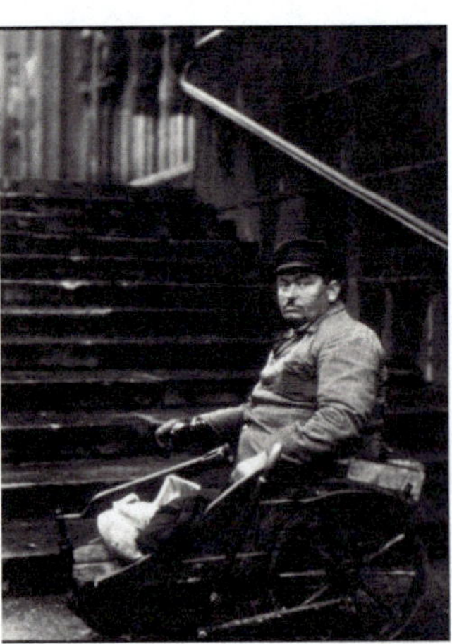

August Sander, Disabled Man, 1926

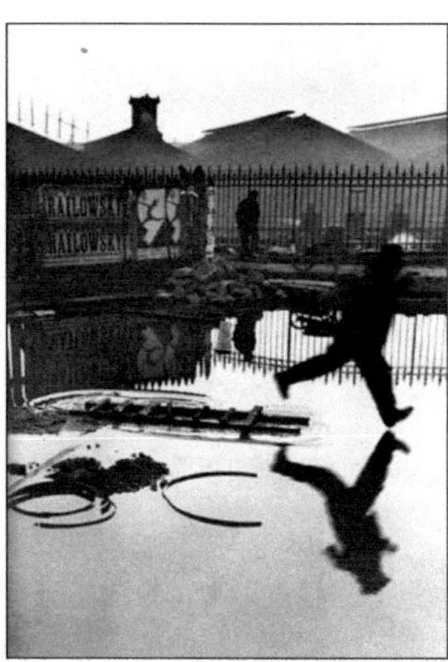

Henri Cartier-Bresson, Behind the Gare St. Lazare, 1932

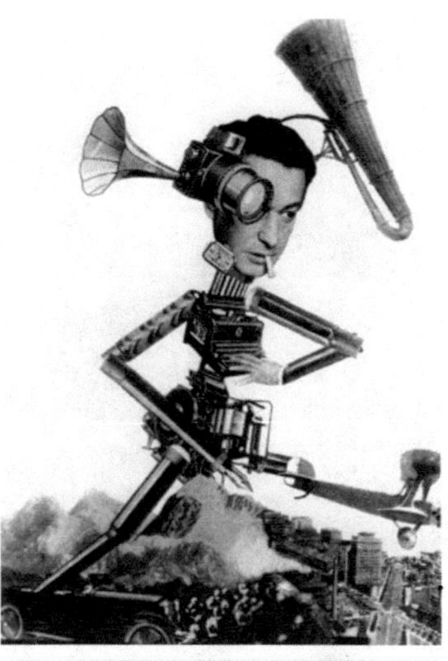

Umbo (Otto Umbehr), The Roving Reporter, photomontage, 1926

Umbo's photomontage *The Roving Reporter* shows how modern technologies transform our perception of the world—and our ability to communicate within it. His camera-eyed, colossal observer (a real-life journalist named Egon Erwin Kisch) demonstrates photography's ability to alter and enhance the senses. In the early twentieth-century, this medium offered a potentially transformative vision for artists, who sought new ways to see, represent, and understand the rapidly changing world around them.

Reading: Contemporary Art

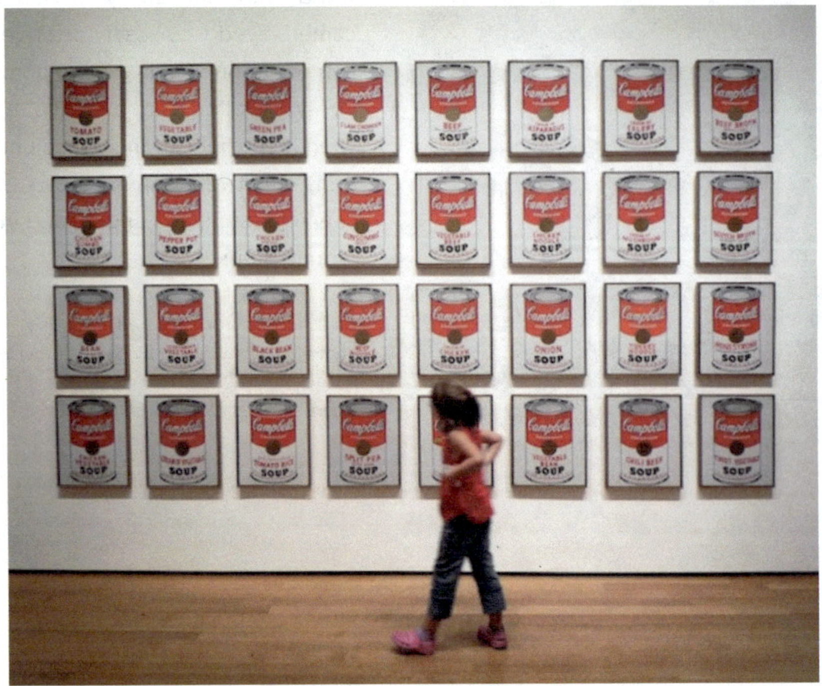

Andy Warhol, Campbell's Soup Cans, 1962, synthetic polymer paint on 32 canvases, each 20 x 16" (The Museum of Modern Art) (photo: Steven Zucker)

"Getting" Contemporary Art

It's ironic that many people say they don't "get" contemporary art because, unlike Egyptian tomb painting or Greek sculpture, art made since 1960 reflects our own recent past. It speaks to the dramatic social, political and technological changes of the last fifty years, and it questions many of society's values and assumptions—a tendency of postmodernism, a concept sometimes used to describe contemporary art. What makes today's art especially challenging is that, like the world around us, it has become more diverse and cannot be easily defined through a list of visual characteristics, artistic themes or cultural concerns.

Minimalism and Pop Art, two major art movements of the early 1960s, offer clues to the different directions of art in the late 20th and 21st century. Both rejected established expectations about art's aesthetic qualities and need for originality. Minimalist objects are spare geometric forms, often made from industrial processes and materials, which lack surface details, expressive markings, and any discernible meaning. Pop Art took its subject matter from low-brow sources like comic books and advertising. Like Minimalism, its use of commercial techniques eliminated emotional content implied by the artist's individual approach, something that had been important to the previous generation of modern painters. The result was that both movements effectively blurred the line distinguishing fine art from more ordinary aspects of life, and forced us to reconsider art's place and purpose in the world.

Shifting Strategies

Minimalism and Pop Art paved the way for later artists to explore questions about the conceptual nature of art, its form, its production, and its ability to communicate in different ways. In the late 1960s and 1970s, these ideas led to a "dematerialization of art," when artists turned away from painting and sculpture to experiment with new formats including photography, film and video, performance art, large-scale installations and earth works. Although some critics of the time foretold "the death of painting," art today encompasses a broad range of traditional and experimental media, including works that rely on Internet technology and other scientific innovations.

Contemporary artists continue to use a varied vocabulary of abstract and representational forms to convey their ideas. It is important to remember that the art of our time did not develop in a vacuum; rather, it reflects the social and political concerns of its cultural context. For example, artists like Judy Chicago, who were inspired by the feminist movement of the early 1970s, embraced imagery and art forms that had historical connections to women.

In the 1980s, artists appropriated the style and methods of mass media advertising to investigate issues of cultural authority and identity politics. More recently, artists like Maya Lin, who designed the Vietnam Veterans' Memorial Wall in Washington D.C., and Richard Serra, who was loosely associated with Minimalism in the 1960s, have adapted characteristics of Minimalist art to create new abstract sculptures that encourage more personal interaction and emotional response among viewers.

These shifting strategies to engage the viewer show how contemporary art's significance exists beyond the object itself. Its meaning develops from cultural discourse, interpretation and a range of individual understandings, in addition to the formal and conceptual problems that first motivated the artist. In this way, the art of our times may serve as a catalyst for an on-going process of open discussion and intellectual inquiry about the world today.

Reading: Warhol's Gold Marilyn Monroe

Popular Culture, "Popular" Art

At first glance, Pop Art might seem to glorify popular culture by elevating soup cans, comic strips and hamburgers to the status of fine art on the walls of museums. But, then again, a second look may also suggest a critique of the mass marketing practices and consumer culture that emerged in the United States after World War II.

Andy Warhol's *Gold Marilyn Monroe* (1962) clearly reflects this inherent irony of Pop. The central image on a gold background evokes a religious tradition of painted icons, transforming the Hollywood starlet into a Byzantine Madonna that reflects our obsession with celebrity. Notably, Warhol's spiritual reference was especially poignant given Monroe's suicide a few months earlier.

Like religious fanatics, the actress's fans worshipped their idol; yet, Warhol's sloppy silk-screening calls attention to the artifice of Marilyn's glamorous façade and places her alongside other mass-marketed commodities like a can of soup or a box of Brillo pads.

Genesis of Pop

In this light, it's not surprising that the term "Pop Art" first emerged in Great Britain, which suffered great economic hardship after the war. In the late 1940s, artists of the "Independent Group," first began to appropriate idealized images of the American lifestyle they found in popular magazines as part of their critique of British society.[1]

Pop Art's origins, however, can be traced back even further. In 1917, Marcel Duchamp asserted that any object—including his notorious example of a urinal—could be art, as long as the artist intended it as such. Artists of the 1950s built on this notion to challenge boundaries distinguishing art from real life, in disciplines of music and dance, as well as visual art.

Robert Rauschenberg's desire to "work in the gap between art and life," for example, led him to incorporate such objects as bed pillows, tires and even a stuffed goat in his "combine paintings" that merged features of painting and sculpture. Likewise, Claes Oldenberg created *The Store*, an installation in a vacant storefront where he sold crudely fashioned sculptures of brand-name consumer goods.

These "Proto-pop" artists were, in part, reacting against the rigid critical structure and lofty philosophies surrounding Abstract Expressionism, the dominant art movement of the time; but their work also reflected the numerous social changes taking place around them.

Post-War Consumer Culture Grab Hold (and Never Lets Go)

The years following World War II saw enormous growth in the American economy, which, combined with innovations in technology and the media, spawned a consumer culture with more leisure time and expendable income than ever before. The manufacturing industry that had expanded during the war now began to mass-produce everything from hairspray and washing machines to shiny new convertibles, which advertisers claimed all would bring ultimate joy to their owners.

---

1. Critic Lawrence Alloway and artist Richard Hamilton are usually credited with coining the term, possibly in the context of Hamilton's famous collage from 1956, Just what is it that makes today's home so different, so appealing? Made to announce the Independent Group's 1956 exhibition "This Is Tomorrow," in London, the image prominently features a muscular semi-nude man, holding a phallically positioned Tootsie Pop.

Significantly, the development of television, as well as changes in print advertising, placed new emphasis on graphic images and recognizable brand logos—something that we now take for granted in our visually saturated world.

It was in this artistic and cultural context that Pop artists developed their distinctive style of the early 1960s. Characterized by clearly rendered images of popular subject matter, it seemed to assault the standards of modern painting, which had embraced abstraction as a reflection of universal truths and individual expression.

Irony and Iron-ons

In contrast to the dripping paint and slashing brushstrokes of Abstract Expressionism—and even of Proto-Pop art—Pop artists applied their paint to imitate the look of industrial printing techniques. This ironic approach is exemplified by Lichtenstein's methodically painted Benday dots, a mechanical process used to print pulp comics.

As the decade progressed, artists shifted away from painting towards the use of industrial techniques. Warhol began making silkscreens, before removing himself further from the process by having others do the actual printing in his studio, aptly named "The Factory." Similarly, Oldenburg abandoned his early installations and performances, to produce the large-scale sculptures of cake slices, lipsticks, and clothespins that he is best known for today.

- https://youtu.be/lXfzq27fGvU

Reading: Conceptual Art

A widespread movement from the mid-1960s through the 1970s, conceptual art emphasized the artist's thinking, making any activity or thought a work of art without the necessity of translating it into physical form. The term gained currency after the publication in the summer 1967 issue of *Artforum* of the Minimal artist Sol Lewitt's article "Paragraphs on Conceptual Art." This dealt with the "primary structures" of Robert Morris, simple polyhedrons which could be "visualized" from any point of view.

In its broadest sense, conceptual art can be traced back to the primitive artist who included the backbone in his drawing of a fish because he 'knew' it was there, even though it was outwardly invisible. The Renaissance, with its concern for accurate depiction, could be said to have firmly placed the emphasis on the perceptual rather than the conceptual.

See works by conceptual artist John Baldessari: http://www.moma.org/collection/artist.php?artist_id=304

Reading: Mary Kelly's Post-Partum Document

Anyone who has been in the unpleasant position of changing a dirty nappy will know that normally your first instinct is to get it as far away from it as possible. So it might seem strange that American artist Mary Kelly (born 1941) took the liners of her son's used cloth nappies, printed them with details of his diet, and displayed them as artworks. Causing some controversy at their debut exhibition, the nappy liners formed the first part of the epic and fascinating *Post-Partum Document* (1973-79)

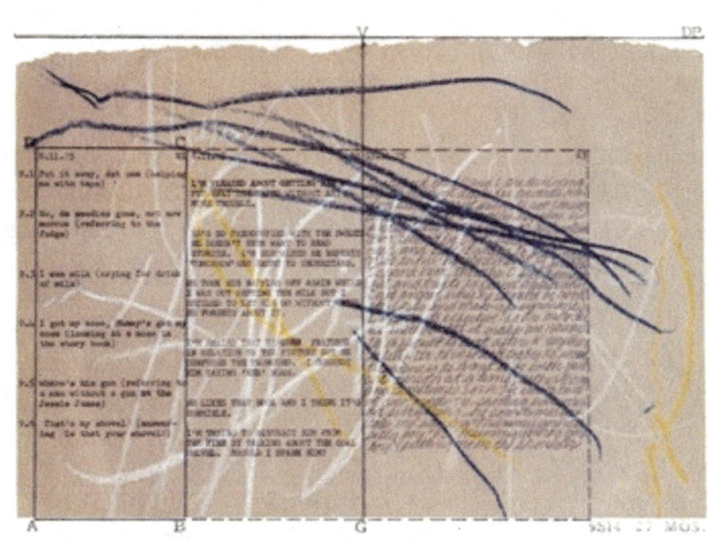

Mary Kelly, Post-Partum Document, 1973–79

Kelly has made works that examine complicated social issues such as the ramifications of war, and the politics of how our identities are constructed. In *Post-Partum Document*, she was engaging in a discussion that was happening at the emergence of second-wave feminism about the way in which women worked in the home. At a time where many feminist artists were looking at reclaiming the body through performance – such as Marina Abramovic and Carole Schneeman – or revising history in order to incorporate our foremothers – such as Judy Chicago – Kelly looked more directly at the invisible daily experience of women engaged in domestic labour.

Post-Partum Document consists of six sections of documentation that follow the development of Kelly's son, Kelly Barrie, from birth until the age of five. Kelly intricately charts her relationship with her son, and her changing role as a mother by writing on artefacts associated with child care: baby clothes, his drawings, items he collects, and his first efforts at writing. In addition, there are detailed analytical texts that exist in parallel to the objects.

In "Documentation III: Analysed Markings and Diary Perspective Schema," Kelly includes three types of text. She describes them in the documentation that accompanies their exhibition as:

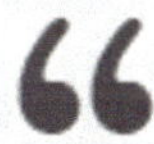

R1 A condensed transcription of the child's conversation, playing it back immediately following the recording session

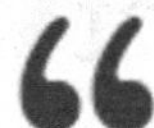

> R2 A transcription of the mother's inner speech in relation to R1, recalling it during a playback later the same day
> R3 A secondary revision of R2, one week later, locating the conversation (as object) within a specific time interval (as spatial metaphor) and rendering it "in perspective" (as a mnemic system)

Kelly's documentations that accompany the work are heavily indebted to Lacanian psychoanalysis, which conceives of the unconscious as being structured like a language. This is interesting in relation to *Post-Partum Document* because it is so layered with text. The quote above strongly contrasts with extracts taken from column R1 (the transcripts) from the piece dated 27.9.75, which is written in lowercase on a typewriter. They state:

> Come'n do it (wants to fly the kite)
> Down dis, its falling. (I'm pretending to fly the kite)]
> Ask Daddy flying the kite, go ask him (I say Daddy will fly it tomorrow)

We can see how much range there is in the text that she uses. Adding to this, there are the sections in R2 that provide a picture of an adult's day to day interaction with a small child. This column is typed in capital letters, using the aesthetic of the text in order to separate the voices. From the same piece R2 reads:

> I say it would be nice to take it outside as it's very windy but it's also very late so I try to change the subject.
> As I started this game of pretending to fly the kite standing on a chair holding it and making sounds like wind, now I'm stuck with it.
> He remembers promises very well.

Finally, in section R3, Kelly describes her anxiety following an accident in which her son drank liquid aspirin and had to be rushed to hospital. This section is handwritten and is much longer, with candid text that explores the difficulties of childrearing. A part of this section states:

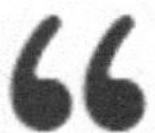

Sometimes I forget to give him his medicine which makes me feel totally irresponsible or I just feel I wish it was all over i.e. he was "grown up" but my mother says it never ends the worry just goes on and on

Over the top of all this worry and analysis are Kelly Barrie's drawings. They are typical of the drawings made by a young child, not much more than scribbles on rice paper. However, his lines cut over his mother's careful work; their carelessness seems all the more free when contrasted with her deliberations.

What makes this piece important is the way in which motherhood – so often seen in art history as a sentimental connection between mother and child – is shown as a difficult and complex relationship. Kelly's voice does not overbear her son's, instead it exists in tandem; we see Kelly developing and adapting as much as her child.

This is an extensive project (comprising in total of 139 individual parts) and Kelly's attention to the material qualities of these mundane objects is outstanding. This piece is a central work within feminist art that is still a relevant and a fascinating picture of what motherhood means for women.

Reading: Appropriation (The "Pictures Generation")

Appropriation—the strategy of selective borrowing—is a common theme in the history of modern art. Since the late nineteenth century artists have both copied and imitated the work of other artists. Consider, for example, the work of Vincent Van Gogh, who copied the format and the compositions of Japanese color woodcuts (ukiyo-e). In the twentieth century, Pablo Picasso imitated the form of African masks for the faces of several female figures in his well-known painting, *Les Demoiselles d'Avignon* of 1907. The appropriation of Leonardo da Vinci's *Mona Lisa* by Marcel Duchamp in 1919 was a radical gesture, where Duchamp drew a handlebar mustache and goatee onto a postcard-size reproduction of Leonardo's famous painting.

The Pictures Generation

In the late 1970s appropriation took on new significance. Artists later identified as belonging to the "Pictures Generation" moved beyond the use of appropriation as a formal strategy, and instead made appropriation the content of the works as well. Repositioning the forms and ideas from previous works of art, these artists were invested in creating new meanings in new contexts. Through the manipulation of media like film and photography in particular, these artists questioned both the possibility and the significance of "originality."

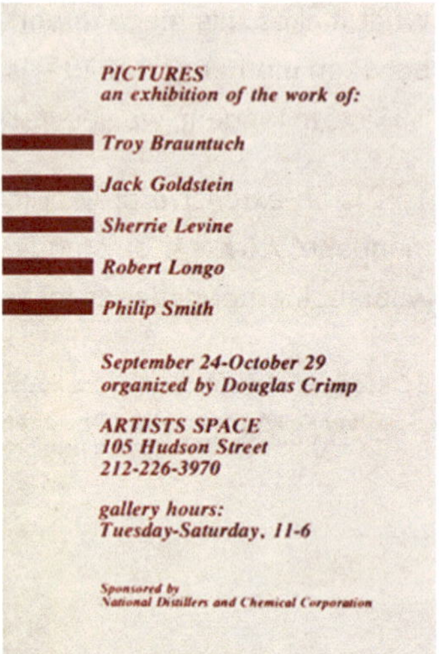

Invitation to the 1977 Artists Space exhibition, "Pictures"

Many of the artists now known as the "Pictures Generation" were so named mainly because of their inclusion in the 1977 exhibition "Pictures" at Artists Space in New York City. The five artists included in this exhibition—Troy Brauntuch, Jack Goldstein, Sherrie Levine, Robert Longo, and Philip Smith—explored the boundaries between reality and images, originals and reproductions. This concern with "pictures" expanded beyond those five original artists to include many others working in this period as well. In a retrospective exhibition at the Metropolitan Museum of Art in 2009 the work of artists Barbara Kruger, Louise Lawler, Richard Prince, David Salle, Cindy Sherman, and Michael Zwack was included under the broad category of Pictures Generation art. Despite the diversity in the subjects and approaches of these artists, most did work in photography and film—two media particularly suited to the blurring of boundaries between originals and reproductions, and between the real world and the world of images. From the moment of its invention, photography inspired debates around the question of originality; with one negative image capable of producing an unknown number of positive prints, can we consider any of those as original?

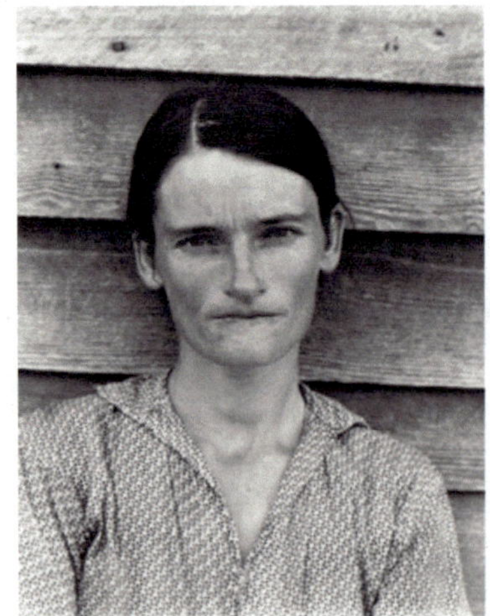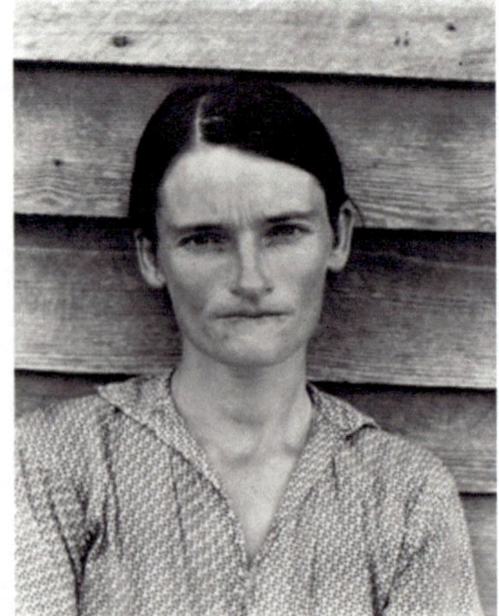

Left: Walker Evans, Alabama Tenant Farmer Wife, 1936, gelatin silver print, 20.9 x 14.4 cm, Metropolitan Museum of Art. Right: After Walker Evans, 1981, gelatin silver print 12.8 x 9.8 cm, Metropolitan Museum of Art

The work of Sherrie Levine, one of the artists included in the 1977 "Pictures" exhibition engages with these questions of originality via her use of photography. For Levine's *After Walker Evans*, 1981, for example, the artist rephotographed a 1936 black-and-white portrait by Walker Evans of the wife of an Alabama sharecropper. Although it may be difficult to distinguish the 1936 and 1981 photographs, it is important to note that Levine did not produce her image from Evans's negative or even his gelatin silver print; rather, Levine's *After Walker Evans* was taken from of a catalog reproduction of Evans's 1936 image. Levine's specific appropriation of Evans's reproduced image confronts the contradiction between photography (an infinitely reproducible medium) and fine art (which favors the unique object). In other words, Levine's reproductions of photographic reproductions intervene directly in the debates surrounding the medium of photography—as a document or a work of art, as a unique image or an endlessly reproducible copy. When we look at Levine's *After Walker Evans* we are reminded of the words of the historian and critic Douglas Crimp, who curated the 1977 "Pictures" exhibition. "Underneath each picture," Crimp wrote, "there is always another picture."

Postmodernism

Artists directly engaged with appropriation in the 1970s were doing so under the influence of postmodernism. In previous generations, artists were praised for their ability to create new ideas and objects. Originality was the hallmark of modernism, and artists were presumed to be independent creators of objects and their meaning. However, by the late 1960s such ideas were beginning to break down. New theories about the impossibility of originality developed in the field of literary theory began to permeate the art world. A key text of this period was a 1968 essay by French philosopher Roland Barthes entitled "Death of the Author." Barthes realigned the focus of literary theory from the creation of language to its enunciation. This meant that the act of interpretation was more important than the act of creation. Artists were suddenly freed from the burden and the expectations of complete originality; what mattered now was how artists could interpret, reconfigure, and reposition already extant works and ideas to create other meanings. Levine's *After Walker Evans* expresses these postmodern ideas. It can be difficult to locate the "original" in Levine's image. Instead, the focus here is on how the artist uses the medium of photography to disrupt modernist lineages, which frequently put white, heterosexual males at the "origin" of these trajectories. The "After" in her title refers to the existence of a prior model but underscores Levine's break with it.

Artists have continued to explore strategies of appropriation. For example, in the early 1990s the photographer Carrie Mae Weems appropriated daguerreotype photographs of slaves taken in 1850 by J.T. Zealy in her *Sea Island Series*.

See Carrie Mae Weems, *A Negroid Type / You Became a Scientific Profile / An Anthropological Debate/ & A Photographic Subject:* http://carriemaeweems.net/galleries/from-here.html

As in the work of Levine, Weems's use of these photographs was more than an appropriation of the image itself; the focus here is on reworking the meaning of these original photographs. The nineteenth-century daguerreotypes objectify the bodies of South Carolina slaves, reducing them to specimens in order to prove a theory about the innate inferiority of people of African descent. In her re-presentation of these nineteenth-century images, however, Weems transforms the sitters of the photographs from objects to people. Her tinting of the photographs and their installation alongside a narrative gives the subjects of these images a new voice of their own, acknowledging the history of oppression from which they came.

Compare Artworks—Similar Period

Compare and contrast two works of art from a similar period

LEARNING ACTIVITIES

The learning activities for this section include:

- Reading: Modern Storytellers: Romare Bearden, Jacob Lawrence, Faith Ringgold

Take time to review and reflect on this activity in order to improve your performance on the assessment for this section.

Reading: Modern Storytellers: Romare Bearden, Jacob Lawrence, Faith Ringgold

Read "Modern Storytellers: Romare Bearden, Jacob Lawrence, Faith Ringgold," which is part of the Heilbrunn Timeline of Art History series (Metropolitan Museum of Art).

- http://www.metmuseum.org/toah/hd/most/hd_most.htm

Compare Artworks—Different Periods and Cultures

Compare and contrast two works of art from different cultures and periods in terms of formal qualities, context, and meaning

Take time to review and reflect on this activity in order to improve your performance on the assessment for this section.

Reading: African Influences in Modern Art

Read "African Influences in Modern Art," which is part of the Heilbrunn Timeline of Art History series (Metropolitan Museum of Art).

- http://www.metmuseum.org/toah/hd/aima/hd_aima.htm

Historical Influence of Art

Analyze a modern work of art and describe how it borrows from or is influenced by an earlier work of art

LEARNING ACTIVITIES

The learning activities for this section include:

- Reading: Classical Art and Modern Dress

Take time to review and reflect on this activity in order to improve your performance on the assessment for this section.

Reading: Classical Art and Modern Dress

Read "Classical Art and Modern Dress," which is part of the Heilbrunn Timeline of Art History series (Metropolitan Museum of Art).

- http://www.metmuseum.org/toah/hd/god2/hd_god2.htm

Putting It Together

While it may not seem like it, the prior content was only a brief survey that places the visual record within the trajectory of the historical context. The history of humanity can be seen through art history, from early prehistoric cave paintings to the artwork we will return to now by Felix Gonzalez-Torres.

- How do artworks build on what came before them?
- How was Marcel Duchamp's 'readymades' a kind of seismic shift in the world of art, that impacted what kinds of things are considered art today?
- How is this installation by Gonzalez-Torres a product of the time it was created in?

    - https://youtu.be/37bSb-aQ4BM

Artwork from one era to the next is rarely an outright rejection of what came before, rather the breaks between periods and stylistic movements is more a fuzzy transition than a hard one. Without doubt every artwork is impacted by what came before it. Consider the invention of photography. Until photography, drawing and painting were the primary mediums for realistic representational imagery. Photography quickly assumes this role, and after its invention in late 19th century, painting enters a dramatic period of experimentation from impressionism, to cubism, to abstraction expressionism.

Marcel Duchamp's readymades destabilized what could be considered legitimate art objects, boldly paving the way for conceptual installations like Felix Gonzalez-Torres Candies. Gonzalez-Torres was a gay man making art in America during the AIDS epidemic of the 1980's and 90's. At the time there was an erroneous stigma that the disease was a gay epidemic. This encouraged already bigoted attitudes towards gay men, in particular, and further discrimination. Candies is a product of this time, not only a memorial to the love of his life, Ross, dying of AIDS, but a product of people's attitudes towards those suffering with AIDS.

CHAPTER 5: FINE ART MEDIA AND TECHNIQUE

Why It Matters

Examine the materials, processes, and techniques used in the making of art (course level learning objective)

Introduction

In this module will will discuss some of the major materials, processes, and techniques used in making art.

Creating a work of art is a process. When an artist chooses to work with a certain medium, or use specific techniques, those choices are some of the most defining parameters of the entire creative process.

Let's return to the caves at Chauvet-Pont-d'Arc, where, roughly 35,000 years ago, humans transformed the space into a kind of canvas. Those prehistoric artists were using the technologies available to them—charred bones or charcoal from the fire. It's surprising how the nature of the work surface figures into the end result, too. In the same way that a painter might select a particular type of brush for the kind of brushstroke it will produce, the prehistoric artists made thoughtful choices about where to place specific renderings of animals so they could use the natural contours and fissures in the cave rocks to create bas-relief giving a horn, a hump, or a haunch realistic depth (Thurman).

If art is a process of seeing, imagining, and making, as Henry Sayre explains, then media and techniques give voice to the imagination (3). All media bring specific visual effects that affect how we interpret them as viewers. As you work through the content in this section, consider how the visual effects of a figure drawn by hand with charcoal are different from a figure drawn with a digital vector-based drawing program. How would an artist's drawn rendering of a scene in a courtroom be different from a photograph of the same thing?

MODULE LEARNING OUTCOMES

- Describe the basic techniques of drawing, painting, photography, and printmaking
- Distinguish between additive and subtractive sculpture techniques
- Describe traditional methods and materials of building design
- Explain the techniques of film and video art
- Discuss and describe the growing impact of computers and digital tools on art making of the 21st century

---

How to Study for the Performance Assessment (PA)

The PA for this module involves answering short answer and short essay questions that are designed to test your understanding of the Learning Outcomes for this module. The questions deal with specific aspects of the different art mediums discussed in the module content. Read through the performance assessment for this module BEFORE you begin the module content. I suggest printing it out, or making notes on the keywords/concepts in each PA question. Use what you noted on the PA as a study guide. As you read through the module content, take notes on the subjects or anything that you find relevant to the PA questions. Be sure to document the page or place in the content where you found each note, in case you need to return to that content, or need to ask me a specific question citing module content. Once you are ready to complete the PA, you will have these notes to help you answer the questions thoughtfully.

OK, let's get started!

Works Cited

Sayre, Henry. *A World of Art*, Sixth edition. Boston: Prentice Hall, 2010. Print.

Thurman, Judith. *First Impressions, What Does the World's Oldest Art Say About Us*. New Yorker Magazine. 2008. Web. 31 May 2015.

CC licensed content, Original
- Why It Matters: Fine Art Media and Technique. **Authored by**: Wendy Riley and Lumen Learning. **License**: *CC BY: Attribution*

Two-Dimensional Arts

Describe the basic techniques of drawing, painting, photography, and printmaking

<table>
<tr><td align="center">LEARNING ACTIVITIES</td></tr>
<tr><td>

The learning activities for this section include:

- Reading: Drawing
- Reading: Painting
- Reading: Printmaking
- Reading: Modern Developments in Photography

</td></tr>
</table>

Take time to review and reflect on each of these activities in order to improve your performance on the assessment for this section.

Reading: Drawing

Introduction

Drawing is the simplest and most efficient way to communicate visual ideas, and for centuries charcoal, chalk, graphite and paper have been adequate enough tools to launch some of the most profound images in art. Leonardo da Vinci's *The Virgin and Child with Saint Anne and Saint John the Baptist* wraps all four figures together in what is essentially an extended family portrait. Da Vinci draws the figures in a spectacularly realistic style, one that emphasizes individual identities and surrounds the figures in a grand, unfinished landscape. He animates the scene with the Christ child pulling himself forward, trying to release himself from Mary's grasp to get closer to a young John the Baptist on the right, who himself is turning toward the Christ child with a look of curious interest in his younger cousin.

The traditional role of drawing was to make sketches for larger compositions to be manifest as paintings, sculpture or even architecture. Because of its relative immediacy, this function for drawing continues today. A preliminary sketch by the contemporary architect Frank Gehry captures the complex organic forms of the buildings he designs.

Types of Drawing Media

Dry Media includes charcoal, graphite, chalks and pastels. Each of these mediums gives the artist a wide range of mark making capabilities and effects, from thin lines to large areas of color and tone. The artist can manipulate a drawing to achieve desired effects in many ways, including exerting different pressures on the medium against the drawing's surface, or by erasure, blotting or rubbing.

This process of drawing can instantly transfer the sense of character to an image. From energetic to subtle, these qualities are apparent in the simplest works: the immediate and unalloyed spirit of the artist's idea. You can see this in the self-portraits of two German artists; Kathe Kollwitz and Ernst Ludwig Kirchner. Wounded during the first world war, his *Self-Portrait Under the Influence of Morphine* from about 1916 presents us with a nightmarish vision of himself wrapped in the fog of opiate drugs. His hollow eyes and the graphic dysfunction of his marks attest to the power of his drawing.

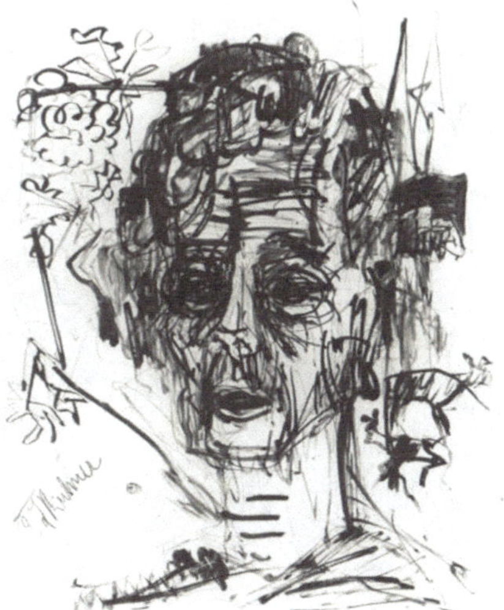

Ernst Ludwig Kirchner, Self Portrait Under the Influence of Morphine, around 1916. Ink on paper. Licensed under Creative Commons.

Graphite media includes pencils, powder or compressed sticks. Each one creates a range of values depending on the hardness or softness inherent in the material. Hard graphite tones range from light to dark gray, while softer graphite allows a range from light gray to nearly black. French sculptor Gaston Lachaise's *Standing Nude with Drapery* is a pencil drawing that fixes the energy and sense of movement of the figure to the paper in just a few strokes. And Steven Talasnik's contemporary large-scale drawings in graphite, with their swirling, organic forms and architectural structures are testament to the power of pencil (and eraser) on paper.

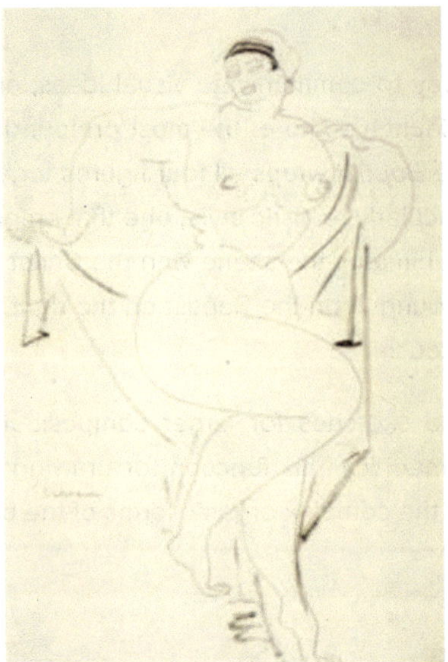

Gaston Lachiase, Standing Nude with Drapery, 1891. Graphite and ink on paper. Honolulu Academy of Arts. Licensed under Creative Commons.

Charcoal, perhaps the oldest form of drawing media, is made by simply charring wooden sticks or small branches, called **vine** charcoal, but is also available in a mechanically **compressed** form. Vine charcoal comes in three densities: soft, medium and hard, each one handling a little different than the other. Soft charcoals give a more velvety feel to a drawing. The artist doesn't have to apply as much pressure to the stick in order to get a solid mark. Hard vine charcoal offers more control but generally doesn't give the darkest tones. Compressed charcoals give deeper blacks than vine charcoal, but are more difficult to manipulate once they are applied to paper.

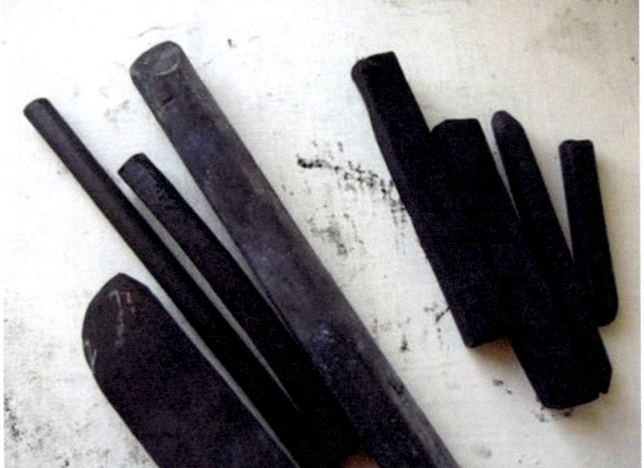

Left: vine charcoal sticks. Right: compressed charcoal squares. Vine Charcoal examples, via Wikipedia Commons. Licensed under Creative Commons.

Charcoal drawings can range in value from light grays to rich, velvety blacks. A charcoal drawing by American artist Georgia O'Keeffe is a good example.

Pastels are essentially colored chalks usually compressed into stick form for better handling. They are characterized by soft, subtle changes in tone or color. Pastel pigments allow for a resonant quality that is more difficult to obtain with graphite or charcoal. Picasso's Portrait of the Artist's Mother from 1896 emphasizes these qualities.

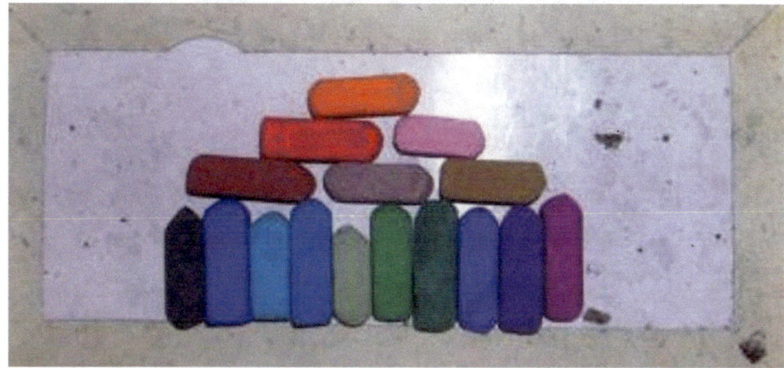

Pastels, digital image licensed through Creative Commons.

More recent developments in dry media are **oil pastels**, pigment mixed with an organic oil binder that deliver a heavier mark and lend themselves to more graphic and vibrant results. The drawings of Beverly Buchanan reflect this. Her work celebrates rural life of the south centered in the forms of old houses and shacks. The buildings stir memories and provide a sense of place, and are usually surrounded by people, flowers and bright landscapes. She also creates sculptures of the shacks, giving them an identity beyond their physical presence.

Wet Media

Ink: Wet drawing media traditionally refers to ink but really includes any substance that can be put into solution and applied to a drawing's surface. Because wet media is manipulated much like paint – through thinning and the use of a brush – it blurs the line between drawing and painting. Ink can be applied with a stick for linear effects and by brush to cover large areas with tone. It can also be diluted with water to create values of gray. The Return of the Prodigal Son by Rembrandt shows an expressive use of brown ink in both the line qualities and the larger brushed areas that create the illusion of light and shade.

Felt tip pens are considered a form of wet media. The ink is saturated into felt strips inside the pen then released onto the paper or other support through the tip. The ink quickly dries, leaving a permanent mark. The colored marker drawings of Donnabelle Casis have a flowing, organic character to them. The abstract quality of the subject matter infers body parts and viscera.

Other liquids can be added to drawing media to enhance effects – or create new ones. Artist Jim Dine has splashed soda onto charcoal drawings to make the surface bubble with effervescence. The result is a visual texture unlike anything he could create with charcoal alone, although his work is known for its strong manipulation. Dine's drawings often use both dry and liquid media. His subject matter includes animals, plants, figures and tools, many times crowded together in dense, darkly romantic images.

Traditional Chinese painting uses water-based inks and pigments. In fact, it is one of the oldest continuous artistic traditions in the world. Painted on supports of paper or silk, the subject matter includes landscapes, animals, figures and **calligraphy**, an art form that uses letters and script in fluid, lyrical gestures.

Two examples of traditional Chinese painting are seen below. The first, a wall scroll painted by Ma Lin in 1246, demonstrates how adept the artist is in using ink in an expressive form to denote figures, robes and landscape elements, especially the strong, gnarled forms of the pine trees. There is sensitivity and boldness in the work. The second example is the opening detail of a copy of "Preface to the Poems Composed at the Orchid Pavilion" made before the thirteenth century. Using ink and brush, the artist makes language into art through the sure, gestural strokes and marks of the characters.

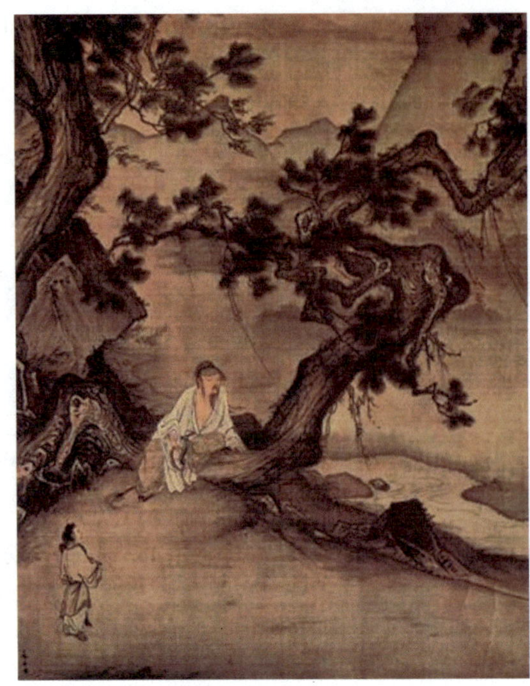

Ma Lin, Wall Scroll, ink on silk. 1246 Used under GNU Free
Documentation License

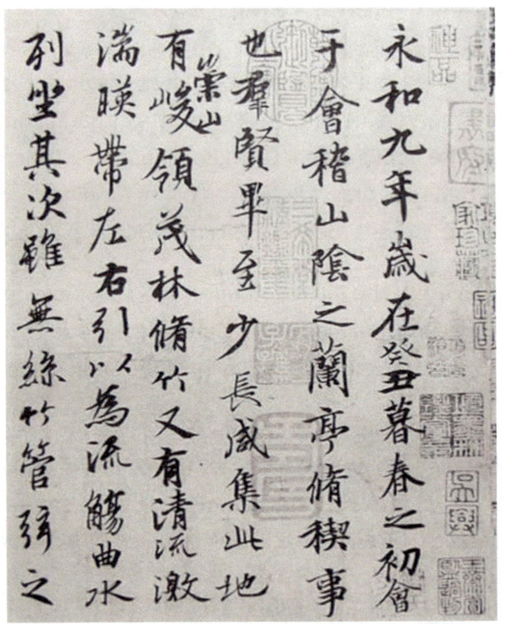

Opening detail of a copy of Preface to the Poems
Composed at the Orchid Pavilion. Before the
thirteenth century. Hand scroll, ink on paper. The Palace
Museum, Beijing. Licensed through Creative Commons.

Drawing is a foundation for other two and three-dimensional works of art, even being incorporated with digital media that expands the idea of its formal expression. The art of Matthew Ritchie starts with small abstract drawings. He digitally scans and projects them to large scales, taking up entire walls. Ritchie also uses the scans to produce large, thin three-dimensional templates to create sculptures out of the original drawings.

Reading: Painting

Painting is the application of pigments to a support surface that establishes an image, design or decoration. In art the term "painting" describes both the act and the result. Most painting is created with pigment in liquid form and applied with a brush. Exceptions to this are found in Navajo sand painting and Tibetan mandala painting, where powdered pigments are used. Painting as a medium has survived for thousands of years and is, along with drawing and sculpture, one of the oldest creative media. It's used in some form by cultures around the world.

Three of the most recognizable images in Western art history are paintings: Leonardo da Vinci's *Mona Lisa*, Edvard Munch's *The Scream* and Vincent van Gogh's *The Starry Night*. These three art works are examples of how painting can go beyond a simple mimetic function, that is, to only imitate what is seen. The power in great painting is that it transcends perceptions to reflect emotional, psychological, even spiritual levels of the human condition.

Painting media are extremely versatile because they can be applied to many different surfaces (called **supports**) including paper, wood, canvas, plaster, clay, lacquer and concrete. Because paint is usually applied in a liquid or semi-liquid state it has the ability to soak into porous support material, which can, over time, weaken and damage the it. To prevent this a support is usually first covered with a ***ground***, a mixture of binder and chalk that, when dry, creates a non-porous layer between the support and the painted surface. A typical ground is gesso.

There are six major painting media, each with specific individual characteristics:

- Encaustic
- Tempera
- Fresco
- Oil
- Acrylic
- Watercolor

All of them use the following three basic ingredients:

- Pigment
- Binder
- Solvent

Pigments are granular solids incorporated into the paint to contribute color. The **binder**, commonly referred to as the *vehicle*, is the actual film-forming component of paint. The binder holds the pigment in solution until it's ready to be dispersed onto the surface. The **solvent** controls the flow and application of the paint. It's mixed into the paint, usually with a brush, to dilute it to the proper *viscosity*, or thickness, before it's applied to the surface. Once the solvent has evaporated from the surface the remaining paint is fixed there. Solvents range from water to oil-based products like linseed oil and mineral spirits.

Let's look at each of the six main painting media:

1. Encaustic paint mixes dry pigment with a heated beeswax binder. The mixture is then brushed or spread across a support surface. Reheating allows for longer manipulation of the paint. Encaustic dates back to the first century C.E. and was used extensively in funerary mummy portraits from Fayum in Egypt. The characteristics of encaustic painting include strong, resonant colors and extremely durable paintings. Because of the beeswax binder, when encaustic cools it forms a tough skin on the surface of the painting. Modern electric and gas tools allow for extended periods of heating and paint manipulation.

Below is an example of encaustic painting by José María Cano.

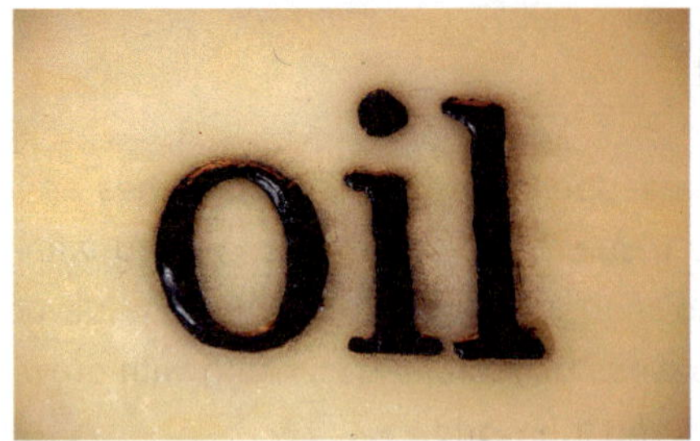

José María Cano, detail of painting made in encaustic, 2010

2. Tempera paint combines pigment with an egg yolk binder, then thinned and released with water. Like encaustic, tempera has been used for thousands of years. It dries quickly to a durable matte finish. Tempera paintings are traditionally applied in successive thin layers, called glazes, painstakingly built up using networks of cross hatched lines. Because of this technique tempera paintings are known for their detail.

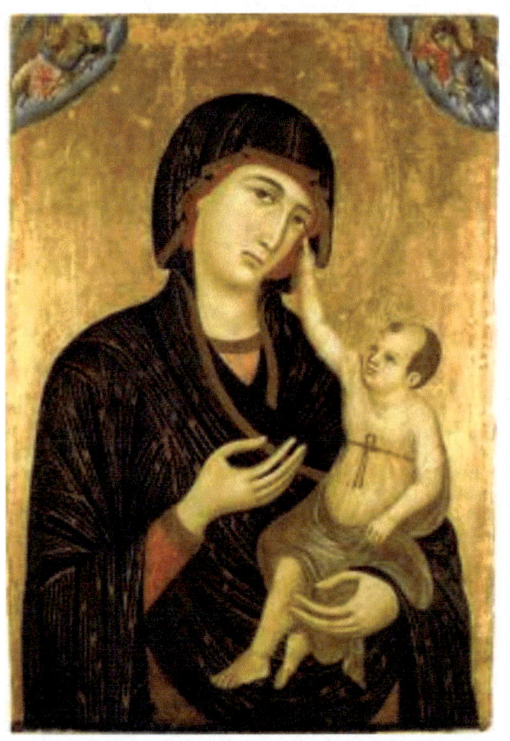

Duccio, The Crevole Madonna, c. 1280. Tempera on board Museo dell'Opera del Duomo, Siena, Italy. Image is in the public domain

In early Christianity, tempera was used extensively to paint images of religious icons. The pre-Renaissance Italian artist Duccio (c. 1255 – 1318), one of the most influential artists of the time, used tempera paint in the creation of *The Crevole Madonna* (above). You can see the sharpness of line and shape in this well-preserved work, and the detail he renders in the face and skin tones of the Madonna (see the detail below).

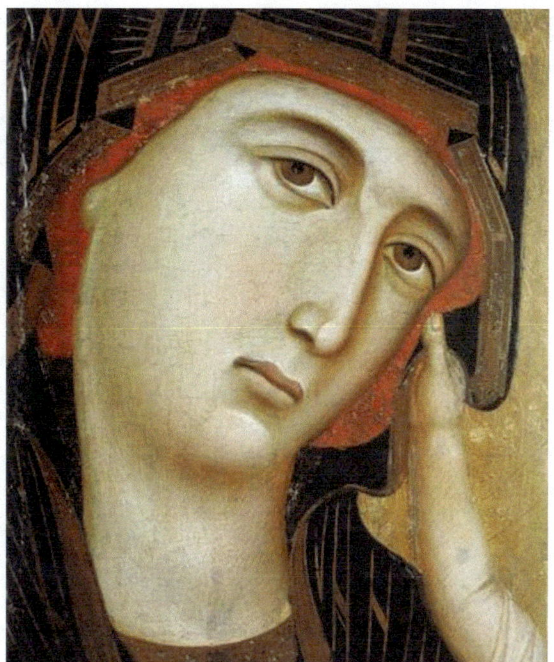

Duccio, The Crevole Madonna (detail), c. 1280. Tempera on board. Museo dell'Opera del Duomo, Siena, Italy. Image is in the public domain

Contemporary painters still use tempera as a medium. American painter Andrew Wyeth (1917-2009) used tempera to create *Christina's World*, a masterpiece of detail, composition and mystery.

3. Fresco painting is used exclusively on plaster walls and ceilings. The medium of fresco has been used for thousands of years, but is most associated with its use in Christian images during the Renaissance period in Europe.

There are two forms of fresco: **Buon** or "wet," and **secco**, meaning "dry."

Buon fresco technique consists of painting in pigment mixed with water on a thin layer of wet, fresh lime mortar or plaster. The pigment is applied to and absorbed by the wet plaster; after a number of hours, the plaster dries and reacts with the air: it is this chemical reaction that fixes the pigment particles in the plaster. Because of the chemical makeup of the plaster, a binder is not required. Buon fresco is more stable because the pigment becomes part of the wall itself.

Domenico di Michelino's *Dante and the Divine Comedy* from 1465 (below) is a superb example of buon fresco. The colors and details are preserved in the dried plaster wall. Michelino shows the Italian author and poet Dante Aleghieri standing with a copy of the *Divine Comedy* open in his left hand, gesturing to the illustration of the story depicted around him. The artist shows us four different realms associated with the narrative: the mortal realm on the right depicting Florence, Italy; the heavenly realm indicated by the stepped mountain at the left center – you can see an angel greeting the saved souls as they enter from the base of the mountain; the realm of the damned to the left – with Satan surrounded by flames greeting them at the bottom of the painting; and the realm of the cosmos arching over the entire scene.

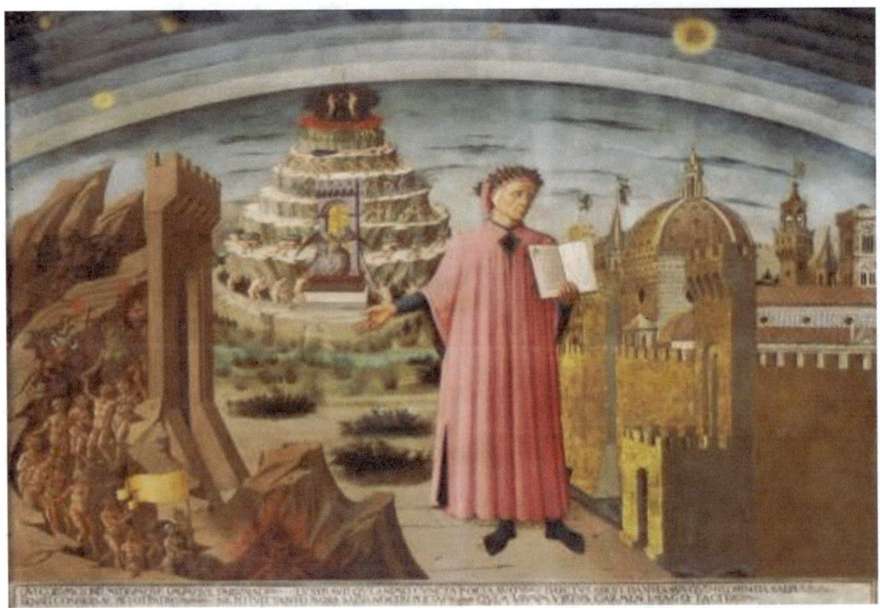

Domenico di Michelino, Dante's Divine Comedy, 1465, buon fresco, the Duomo, Florence, Italy. This image is in the public domain

Secco fresco refers to painting an image on the surface of a dry plaster wall. This medium requires a binder since the pigment is not mixed into the wet plaster. Egg tempera is the most common binder used for this purpose. It was common to use secco fresco over buon fresco murals in order to repair damage or make changes to the original.

Leonardo Da Vinci's painting of *The Last Supper* (below) was done using secco fresco.

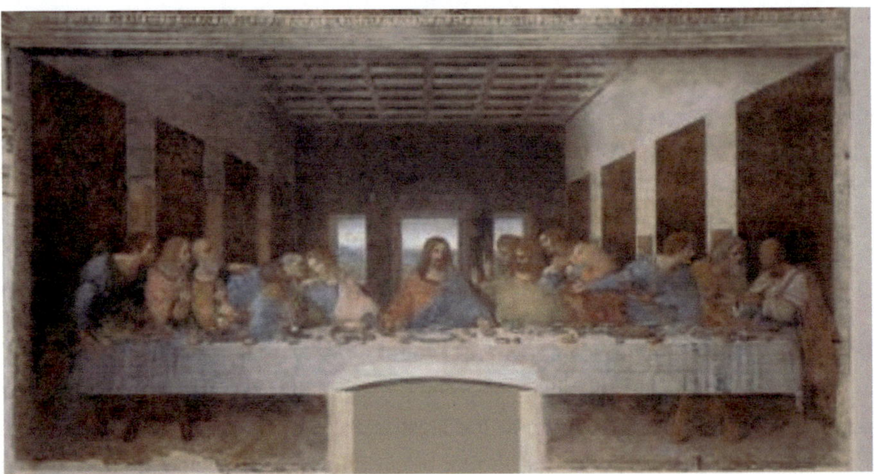

Leonardo Da Vinci, The Last Supper, 1495–98, dry fresco on plaster. Church of Santa Maria delle Grazie, Milan. This image is in the public domain

4. Oil paint is the most versatile of all the painting media. It uses pigment mixed with a binder of linseed oil. Linseed oil can also be used as the vehicle, along with mineral spirits or turpentine. Oil painting was thought to have developed in Europe during the fifteenth century, but recent research on murals found in Afghanistan caves show oil based paints were used there as early as the seventh century.

Some of the qualities of oil paint include a wide range of pigment choices, its ability to be thinned down and applied in almost transparent glazes as well as used straight from the tube (without the use of a vehicle), built up in thick layers called **impasto** (you can see this in many works by Vincent van Gogh). One drawback to the use of impasto is that over time the body of the paint can split, leaving networks of cracks along the thickest parts of the painting. Because oil paint dries slower than other media, it can be blended on the support surface with meticulous detail. This extended working time also allows for adjustments and changes to be made without having to scrape off sections of dried paint.

In Jan Brueghel the Elder's still life oil painting you can see many of the qualities mentioned above. The richness of the paint itself is evident in both the resonant lights and inky dark colors of the work. The working of the paint allows for many different effects to be created, from the softness of the flower petals to the reflection on the vase and the many visual textures in between.

Richard Diebenkorn's *Cityscape #1* from 1963 shows how the artist uses oil paint in a more fluid, expressive manner. He thins down the medium to obtain a quality and gesture that reflects the sunny, breezy atmosphere of a California morning. Diebenkorn used layers of oil paint, one over the other, to let the under painting show through and a flat, more geometric space that blurs the line between realism and abstraction.

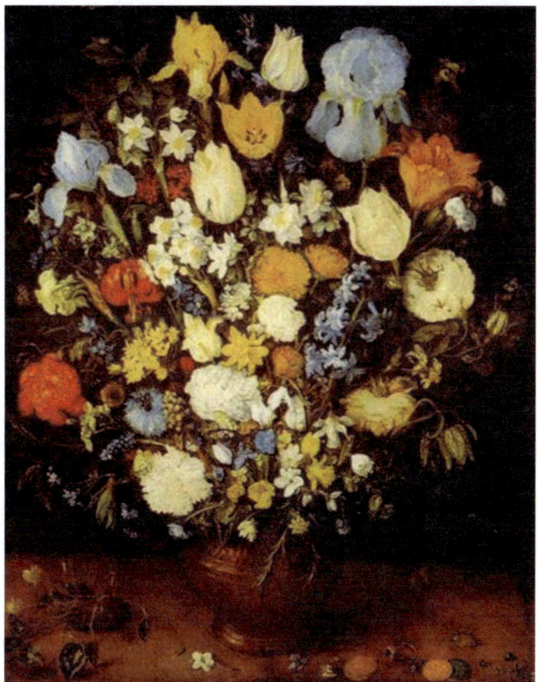

Jan Brueghel the Elder, Flowers in a Vase, 1599. Oil on wood. Kunsthistorisches Museum, Wien, Germany. Used under GNU Documentation Licensing .

Georgia O'Keeffe's oil paintings show a range of handling between soft and austere to very detailed and evocative. You rarely see her brushstrokes, but she has a summary command of the medium of oil paint.

The abstract expressionist painters pushed the limits of what oil paint could do. Their focus was in the *act* of painting as much as it was about the subject matter. Indeed, for many of them there was no distinction between the two. The work of Willem de Kooning leaves a record of oil paint being brushed, dripped, scraped and wiped away all in a frenzy of creative activity. This idea stays contemporary in the paintings of Celia Brown.

5. Acrylic paint was developed in the 1950's and became an alternative to oils. Pigment is suspended in an acrylic polymer emulsion binder and uses water as the vehicle. The acrylic polymer has characteristics like rubber or plastic. Acrylic paints offer the body, color resonance and durability of oils without the expense, mess and toxicity issues of using heavy solvents to mix them. One major difference is the relatively fast drying time of acrylics. They are water soluble, but once dry become impervious to water or other solvents. Moreover, acrylic paints adhere to many different surfaces and are extremely durable. Acrylic impastos will not crack or yellow over time.

The American artist Robert Colescott (1925-2009) used acrylics on large-scale paintings. He uses thin layers of underpainting, scumbling, high-contrast colors, and luscious surfaces to bring out the full range of effects that acrylics offer.

6. Watercolor is the most sensitive of the painting media. It reacts to the lightest touch of the artist and can become an over worked mess in a moment. There are two kinds of watercolor media: **transparent** and **opaque**. Transparent watercolor operates in a reverse relationship to the other painting media. It is traditionally applied to a paper support, and relies on the whiteness of the paper to reflect light back through the applied color (see below), whereas opaque paints (including opaque watercolors) reflect light off the skin of the paint itself. Watercolor consists of pigment and a binder of gum arabic, a water-soluble compound made from the sap of the acacia tree. It dissolves easily in water.

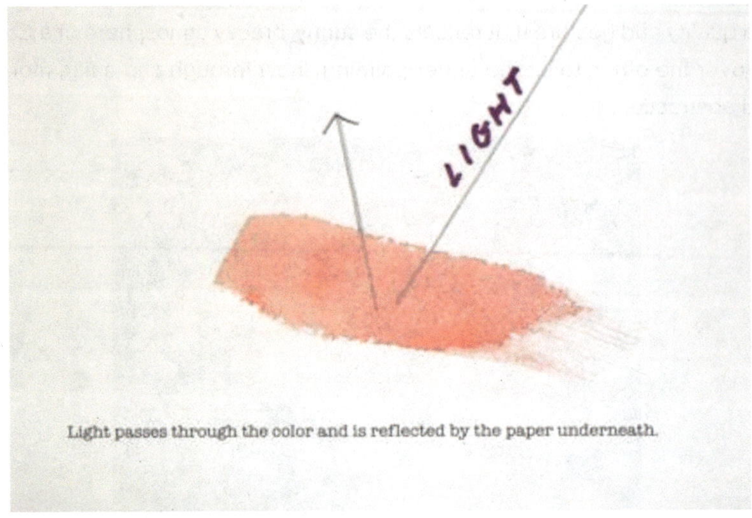

Light passes through the color and is reflected by the paper underneath.

Image by Christopher Gildow. Used here with permission.

Watercolor paintings hold a sense of immediacy. The medium is extremely portable and excellent for small format paintings. The paper used for watercolor is generally of two types: hot pressed, which gives a smoother texture, and cold pressed, which results in a rougher texture. Transparent watercolor techniques include the use of **wash**; an area of color applied with a brush and diluted with water to let it flow across the paper. **Wet-in-wet** painting allows colors to flow and drift into each other, creating soft transitions between them. **Dry brush** painting uses little water and lets the brush run across the top ridges of the paper, resulting in a broken line of color and lots of visual texture.

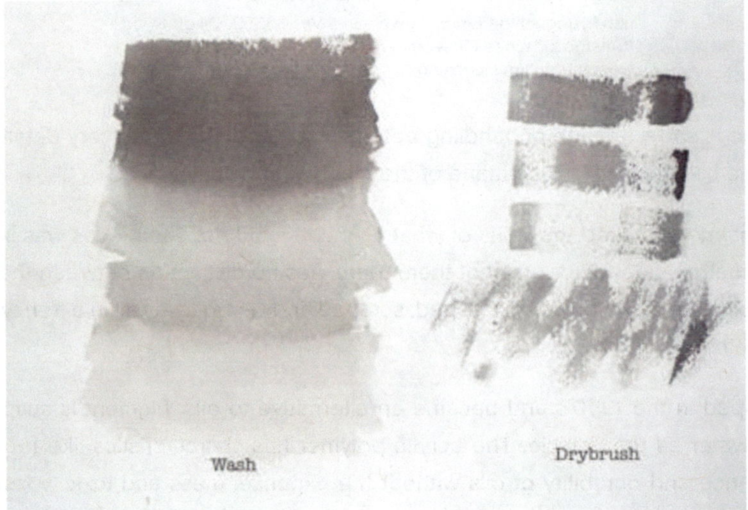

Examples of watercolor painting techniques: on the left, a wash. On the right, dry brush effects. Image by Christopher Gildow. Used here with permission.

John Marin's Brooklyn Bridge (1912) shows extensive use of wash. He renders the massive bridge almost invisible except for the support towers at both sides of the painting. Even the Manhattan skyline becomes enveloped in the misty, abstract shapes created by washes of color.

Boy in a Red Vest by French painter Paul Cezanne builds form through nuanced colors and tones. The way the watercolor is laid onto the paper reflects a sensitivity and deliberation common in Cezanne's paintings.

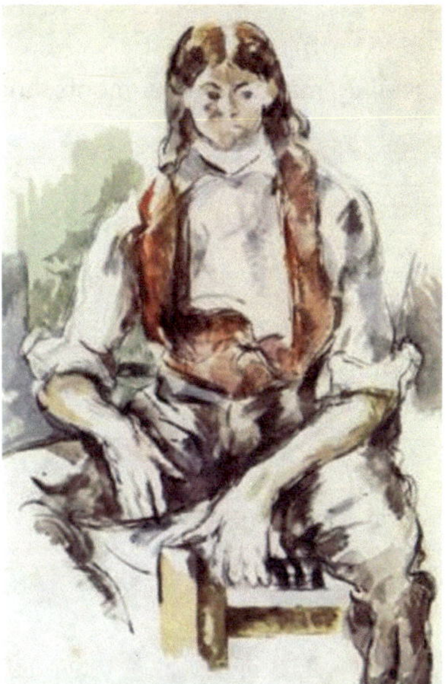

Paul Cezanne, Boy in a Red Vest, c. 1890. Watercolor on paper. This image is licensed under the GNU Free Documentation License

The watercolors of Andrew Wyeth indicate the landscape with earth tones and localized color, often with dramatic areas of white paper left untouched. Brandywine Valley is a good example.

Opaque watercolor, also called **gouache**, differs from transparent watercolor in that the particles are larger, the ratio of pigment to water is much higher, and an additional, inert, white pigment such as chalk is also present. Because of this, gouache paint gives stronger color than transparent watercolor, although it tends to dry to a slightly lighter tone than when it is applied. Gouache paint doesn't hold up well as impasto, tending to crack and fall away from the surface. It holds up well in thinner applications and often is used to cover large areas with color. Like transparent watercolor, dried gouache paint will become soluble again in water.

Jacob Lawrence's paintings use gouache to set the design of the composition. Large areas of color – including the complements blue and orange, dominate the figurative shapes in the foreground, while olive greens and neutral tones animate the background with smaller shapes depicting tools, benches and tables. The characteristics of gouache make it difficult to be used in areas of detail.

Gouache is a medium in traditional painting from other cultures, too. Zal Consults the Magi, part of an illuminated manuscript form sixteenth-century Iran, uses bright colors of gouache along with ink, silver and gold to construct a vibrant composition full of intricate patterns and contrasts. Ink is used to create lyrical calligraphic passages at the top and bottom of the work.

Other painting media used by artists include the following:

Enamel paints form hard skins typically with a high-gloss finish. They use heavy solvents and are extremely durable.

Powder coat paints differ from conventional paints in that they do not require a solvent to keep the pigment and binder parts in suspension. They are applied to a surface as a powder then cured with heat to form a tough skin that is stronger than most other paints. Powder coats are applied mostly to metal surfaces.

Epoxy paints are polymers, created mixing pigment with two different chemicals: a resin and a hardener. The chemical reaction between the two creates heat that bonds them together. Epoxy paints, like powder coats and enamel, are extremely durable in both indoor and outdoor conditions.

These industrial grade paints are used in sign painting, marine environments, and aircraft painting.

Reading: Printmaking

Printmaking uses a transfer process to make multiples from an original image or template. The multiple images are printed in an **edition**, with each print signed and numbered by the artist. All printmaking media result in images reversed from the original. Print results depend on how the template (or **matrix**) is prepared. There are three basic techniques of printmaking: **relief, intaglio and planar**. You can get an idea of how they differ from the cross-section images below, and view how each technique works from this site at the Museum of Modern Art in New York.

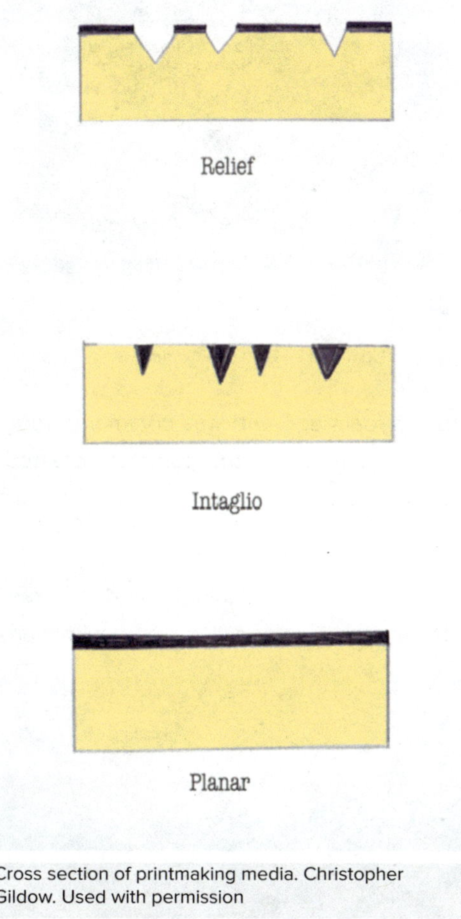

Cross section of printmaking media. Christopher Gildow. Used with permission

The black areas indicate the inked surface.

A **relief print**, such as a woodcut or linoleum cut, is created when the areas of the matrix (plate or block) that are to show the printed image are on the original **surface**; the parts of the matrix that are to be ink-free having been cut away, or otherwise removed. The printed surface is in relief from the cut away sections of the plate. Once the area around the image is cut away, the surface of the plate is rolled up with ink. Paper is laid over the matrix, and both are run through a press, transferring the ink from the surface of the matrix to the paper. The nature of the relief process doesn't allow for lots of detail, but does result in graphic images with strong contrasts. Carl Eugene Keel's *Bar* shows the effects of a woodcut printed in black ink.

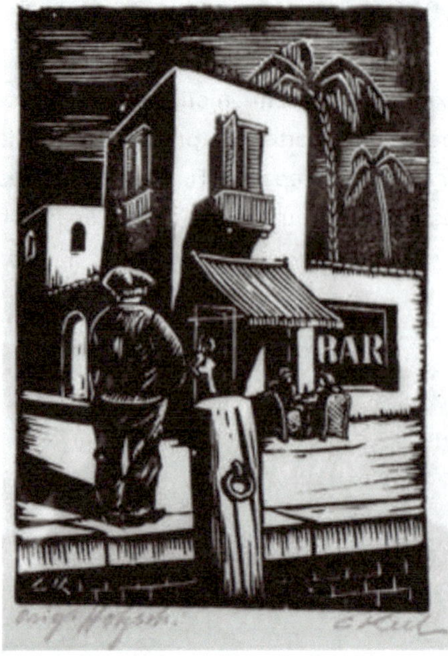

Carl Eugene Keel, Bar, 2006. Woodcut print on
paper. Licensed by Creative Commons

Block printing developed in China hundreds of years ago and was common throughout East Asia. The Japanese woodblock print below shows dynamic effects of implied motion and the contrasts created using only one color and black. Ukiyo-e or "floating world" prints became popular in the nineteenth century, even influencing European artists during the Industrial Revolution.

Relief printmakers can use a separate block or matrix for each color printed or, in **reduction** *prints* a single block is used, cutting away areas of color as the print develops. This method can result in a print with many colors.

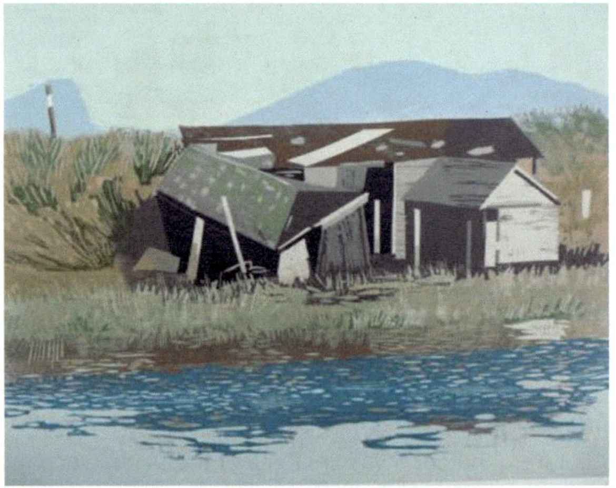

Christopher Gildow, Boathouse, 2007, from the Stillaguamish
Series. Reduction woodcut print. Used with permission

Intaglio prints such as etchings, are made by incising channels into a copper or metal plate with a sharp instrument called a **burin** to create the image, inking the entire plate, then wiping the ink from the surface of the plate, leaving ink only in the incised channels **below** the surface. Paper is laid over the plate and put through a press under high pressure, forcing the ink to be transferred to the paper.

Examples of the intaglio process include etching and **dry point**: In dry point, the artist creates an image by scratching the burin directly into a metal plate (usually copper) before inking and printing. Today artists also use plexiglass, a hard clear plastic, as plates. Characteristically these prints have strong line quality and exhibit a slightly blurred edge to the line as the result of burrs created in the process of incising the plate, similar to clumps of soil laid to the edge of a furrowed trench. A fine example of dry point is seen in Rembrandt's Clump of Trees with a Vista. The velvety darks are created by the effect of the burred-edged lines.

Etching begins by first applying a protective wax-based coating to a thin metal plate. The artist then scratches an image with a burin through the protective coating into the surface of the metal. The plate is then submersed in a strong acid bath, etching the exposed lines. The plate is removed from the acid and the protective coating is removed from the plate. Now the bare plate is inked, wiped and printed. The image is created from the ink in the etched channels. The amount of time a plate is kept in the acid bath determines the quality of tones in the resulting print: the longer it is etched the darker the tones will be. *Correccion* by the Spanish master Francisco Goya shows the clear linear quality etching can produce. The acid bath removes any burrs created by the initial dry point work, leaving details and value contrasts consistent with the amount of lines and the distance between them. Goya presents a fantastic image of people, animals and strange winged creatures. His work often involved biting social commentary. *Correccion* is a contrast between the pious and the absurd.

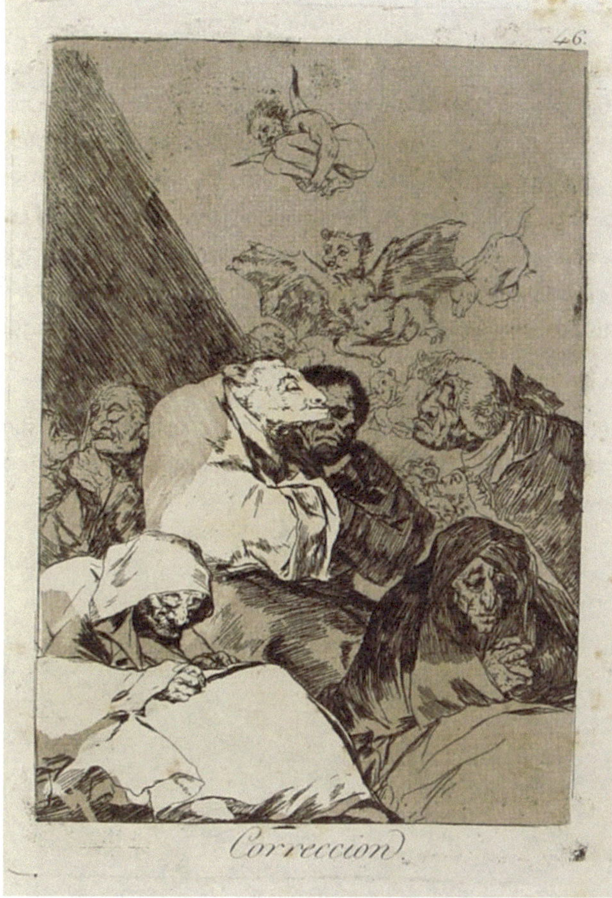

Francisco Goya, Correccion, 1799. Etching on paper. Work is in the public domain

There are many different techniques associated with intaglio, including aquatint, scraping and burnishing.

Planar prints like monoprints are created on the *surface* of the matrix without any cutting or incising. In this technique the surface of the matrix (usually a thin metal plate or Plexiglass) is completely covered with ink, then areas are partially removed by wiping, scratching away or otherwise removed to form the image. Paper is laid over the matrix, then run through a press to transfer the image to the paper. Monoprints (also monotypes) are the simplest and painterly of the printing media. By definition monotypes and monoprints cannot be reproduced in editions. Kathryn Trigg's monotypes show how close this print medium is related to painting and drawing.

Lithography is another example of planar printmaking, developed in Germany in the late eighteenth century. "Litho" means "stone" and "graph" means "to draw." The traditional matrix for lithography is the smooth surface of a limestone block.

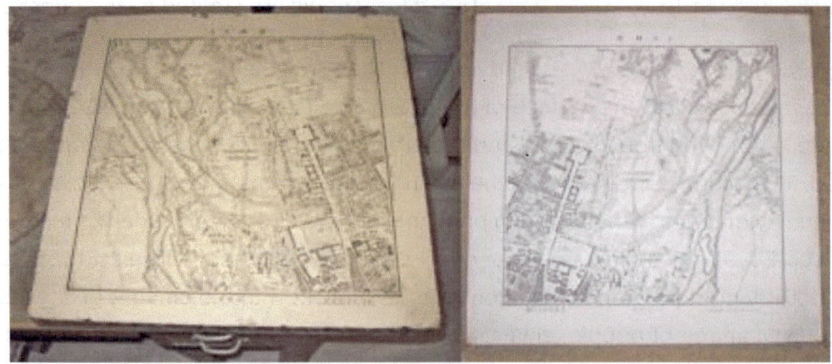

Lithographic stone is on the left with the negative image. Printed positive image is on the right.
Image by Chris73. Licensed under Creative Commons.

While this matrix is still used extensively, thin zinc plates have also been introduced to the medium. They eliminate the bulk and weight of the limestone block but provide the same surface texture and characteristics. The lithographic process is based on the fact that grease repels water. In traditional lithography, an image is created on the surface of the stone or plate using grease pencils or wax crayons or a grease-based liquid medium called tusche. The finished image is covered in a thin layer of gum arabic that includes a weak solution of nitric acid as an etching agent. The resulting chemical reaction divides the surface into two areas: the positive areas containing the image and that will repel water, and the negative areas surrounding the image that will be water receptive. In printing a lithograph, the gum arabic film is removed and the stone or metal surface is kept moist with water so when it's rolled up with an oil based ink the ink adheres to the positive (image) areas but not to the negative (wet) areas.

Because of the media used to create the imagery, lithographic images show characteristics much like drawings or paintings. In *A Brush for the Lead* by Currier and Ives (below), a full range of shading and more linear details of description combine to illustrate a winter's race down the town's main road.

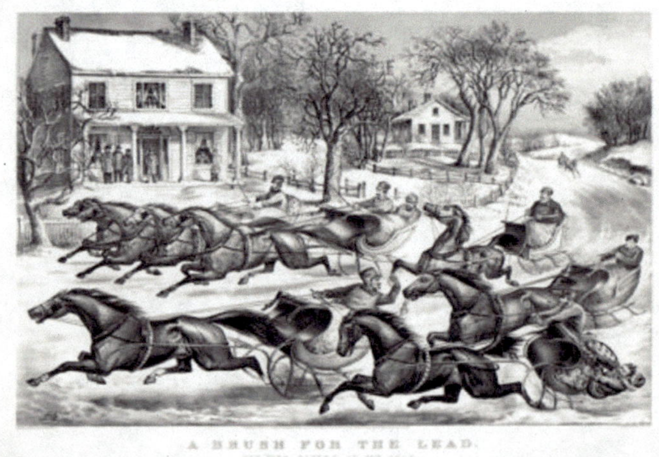

Currier and Ives, A Brush for the Lead; New York Flyers on the Snow, 1867.
Lithograph Library of Congress. Image is in the public domain.

Serigraphy, also known as **screen printing**, is a third type of planar printing medium. Screen printing is a printing technique that uses a woven mesh to support an ink-blocking stencil. The attached stencil forms open areas of mesh that transfer ink or other printable materials that can be pressed through the mesh as a sharp-edged image onto a substrate such as paper or fabric. A roller or squeegee is moved across the screen stencil, forcing or pumping ink past the threads of the woven mesh in the open areas. The image below shows how a stencil's positive (image) areas are isolated from the negative (non-image) areas.

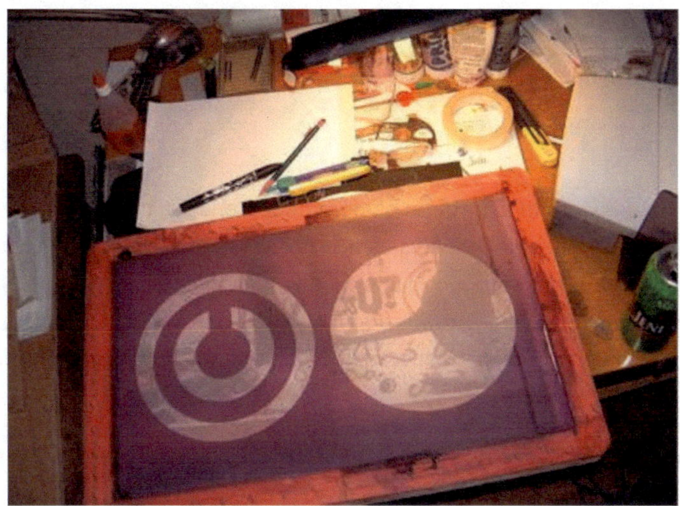

Silkscreen box and stencil, image by Meul. Licensed through Creative Commons.

In serigraphy, each color needs a separate stencil. You can watch how this process develops in the accompanying video. Screen printing is an efficient way to print posters, announcements, and other kinds of popular culture images. Andy Warhol's silk screens use images and iconography from popular culture.

Reading: Photography

EARLY DEVELOPMENT

The first attempts to capture an image were made from a camera obscura, used since the 16th century. The device consists of a box or small room with a small hole in one side that acts as a lens. Light from an external scene passes through the hole and strikes the opposite surface inside where it is reproduced upside-down, but with color and perspective preserved. The image is usually projected onto paper adhered to the opposite wall, and can then be traced to produce a highly accurate representation. Experiments in capturing images on film had been conducted in Europe since the late 18th century.

Using the camera obscura as a guide, early photographers found ways to chemically fix the projected images onto plates coated with light sensitive materials. Moreover, they installed glass lenses in their early cameras and experimented with different exposure times for their images. View from the Window at Le Gras is one of the oldest existing photographs, taken in 1826 by French inventor Joseph Niepce using a process he called heliograpy ("helio" meaning sun and "graph" meaning write). The exposure for the image took eight hours, resulting in the sun casting its light on both sides of the houses in the picture. Further developments resulted in apertures– thin circular devices that are calibrated to allow a certain amount of light onto the exposed film. Apertures allowed photographers better control over their exposure times.

During the 1830's Louis Daguerre, having worked with Niepce earlier, developed a more reliable process to capture images on film by using a polished copper plate treated with silver. He termed the images made by this process "Daguerreotypes". They were sharper in focus and the exposure times were shorter. His photograph Boulevard du Temp from 1838 is taken from his studio window overlooking a busy Paris street. Still, with an exposure of ten minutes, none of the moving traffic or pedestrians (One exception. See if you can find it!) stayed still long enough to be recorded.

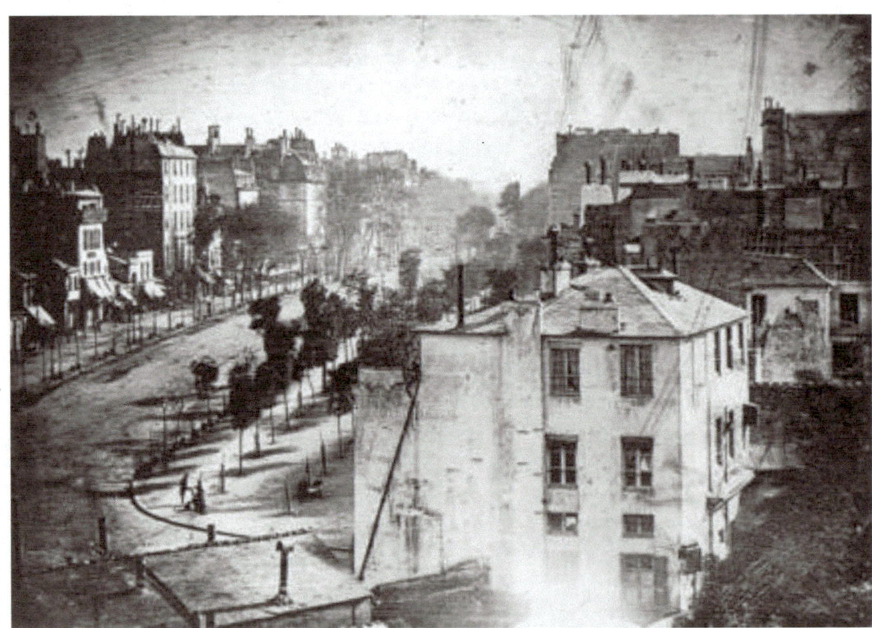

Louis Daguerre, Boulevard du Temps, 1838. Image in the public domain

At the same time in England, William Henry Fox Talbot was experimenting with other photographic processes. He was creating photogenic drawings by simply placing objects (mostly botanical specimens) over light sensitive paper or plates, then exposing them to the sun. By 1844 he had invented the calotype; a photographic print made from a negative image. In contrast, Daguerreotypes were single, positive images that could not be reproduced. Talbot's calotypes allowed for multiple prints from one negative, setting the standard for the new medium. Though Daguerre won the race to be first in releasing his photographic process, Talbot's negative to positive process would eventually become the dominant process.

IMPACT ON OTHER MEDIA

The advent of photography caused a realignment in the use of other two-dimensional media. The photograph was now in direct competition with drawing, painting and printmaking. The camera turns its gaze on the human narrative that stands before it. The photograph gave (for the most part), a realistic and unedited view of our world. In its early beginning, photography was considered to offer a more "true" image of nature because it was created mechanically, not by the subjective hand of an artist. Its use as a tool for documentation was immediate, which gave the photo a scientific role to play. The sequential, instantaneous exposures by Eadweard Muybridge helped to understand human and animal movement, but also highlighted that photography could be used to expand human vision, imaging something that could not be seen with the naked eye. The relative immediacy and improved clarity of the photographic image quickly pitted the camera against painting in the genre of portraiture. Before photography, painted portraits were afforded only to the wealthy and most prominent members of society. They became symbols of social class distinctions. Now portraits became available to individuals and families from all social levels.

Photography as an Art

It wasn't long before photographers recognized the aesthetic value of a photograph. As a new medium, photography began the march towards being considered a high form of art. Alfred Stieglitz understood this potential, and as a photographer, editor and gallery owner, was a major force in promoting photography as an art form. He led in forming the Photo Secession in 1902, a group of photographers who were interested in defining the photograph as an art form in itself, not just by the subject matter in front of the lens. Subject matter became a vehicle for an emphasis on composition, lighting and textural effects. His own photographs reflect a range of themes. The Terminal (1892) is an example of "straight photography": images from the everyday taken with smaller cameras and little manipulation. In The Terminal Stieglitz captures a moment of bustling city street life on a cold winter day. The whole cold, gritty scene is softened by steam rising off the horses and the snow provides highlights. But the photo holds more than formal aesthetic value. The jumble of buildings, machines, humans, animals and weather conditions provides a glimpse into American urban culture straddling two centuries. Within ten years from the time this photo was taken horses will be replaced by automobiles and subway stations will transform a large city's movement into the twentieth century.

Photojournalism and photography's many subject placements

Photography is a medium that has multiple subject placements. It is used as an art medium, in journalism, in advertising, the fashion industry, and we use it to personally document our lives. It is one, if not the most, pervasive form of documentation in the world. These multiple subject placements make it a complex phenomena to analyze.

The news industry was fundamentally changed with the invention of the photograph. Although pictures were taken of newsworthy stories as early as the 1850's, the photograph needed to be translated into an engraving before being printed in a newspaper. It wasn't until the turn of the nineteenth century that newspaper presses could copy original photographs. Photos from around the world showed up on front pages of newspapers defining and illustrating stories, and the world became smaller as this early mass medium gave people access to up to date information...with pictures!

Photojournalism is a particular form of journalism that creates images in order to tell a news story and is defined by these three elements:

Timeliness — the images have meaning in the context of a recently published record of events.

Objectivity — the situation implied by the images is a fair and accurate representation of the events they depict in both content and tone.

Narrative — the images combine with other news elements to make facts relatable to the viewer or reader on a cultural level.

As visual information, news images help in shaping our perception of reality and the context surrounding them.

Photographs taken by Mathew Brady and Timothy O'Sullivan during the American Civil War (below) gave sobering witness to the carnage it produced. Images of soldiers killed in the field help people realize the human toll of war and desensitize their ideas of battle as being particularly heroic.

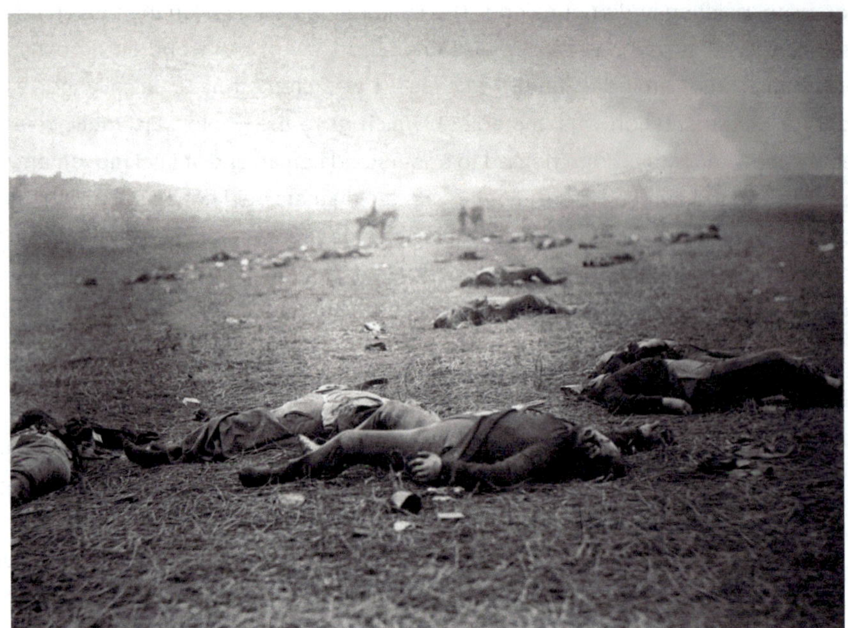

"The Harvest of Death" Union dead on the battlefield at Gettysburg, Pennsylvania, photographed July 5–6, 1863. Image in Public Domain. Available through US Library of Congress

Photojournalism's "Golden Age" took place between 1930 and 1950, coinciding with advances in the mediums of radio and television.

Dorothea Lange was employed by the federal government's Farm Security Administration to document the plight of migrant workers and families dislocated by the Dust Bowl and the Great Depression in America during the 1930's. Migrant Mother, Florence Owens Thompson, Nipomo Valley, California is an iconic image of its hardships and the human resolve to survive. Like O'Sullivan's civil war photos, Lange's picture puts a face on human tragedy. Photographs like this helped win continued support for president Franklin Roosevelt's social aid programs.

Modern Developments

Edwin Land invented the instant camera, capable of taking *and* developing a photograph, in 1947, followed by the popular SX-70 instant camera in 1972. The SX-70 produced a 3-inch-square-format positive image that developed in front of your eyes. The beauty of instant development for the artist was that during the two or three minutes it took for the image to appear, the film emulsion stayed malleable and able to manipulate. The artist *Lucas Samaras* used this technique of manipulation to produce some of the most imaginative and visually perplexing images in a series he termed photo-transformations. Using himself as subject, Samaras explores ideas of self-identity, emotional states and the altered reality he creates on film.

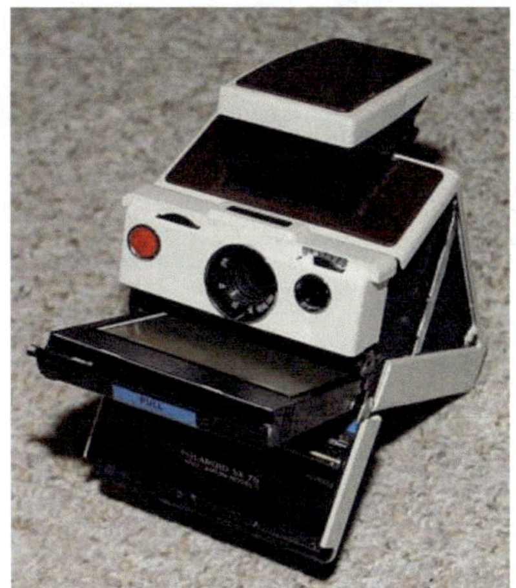

Polaroid SX-70 Instant Camera. Licensed through Creative Commons

Digital cameras appeared on the market in the mid 1980s. They allow the capture and storage of images through electronic means (the charge-coupled device) instead of photographic film. This new medium created big advantages over the film camera: the digital camera produces an image instantly, stores many images on a memory card in the camera, and the images can be downloaded to a computer, where they can be further manipulated by editing software and sent anywhere through cyberspace. This eliminated the time and cost involved in film development and created another revolution in the way we access visual information.

Digital images start to replace those made with film while still adhering to traditional ideas of design and composition. *Bingo Time* by photographer Jere DeWaters (below) uses a digital camera to capture a visually arresting scene within ordinary surroundings. He uses a rational approach to create a geometric order within the format, with contrasting diagonals set up between sloping pickets and ramps, with an implied angle leading from the tire on the lower left to the white window frame in the center and culminating at the clock on the upper right. And even though the sign yells out to us for attention, the black rectangle in the center is what gets it.

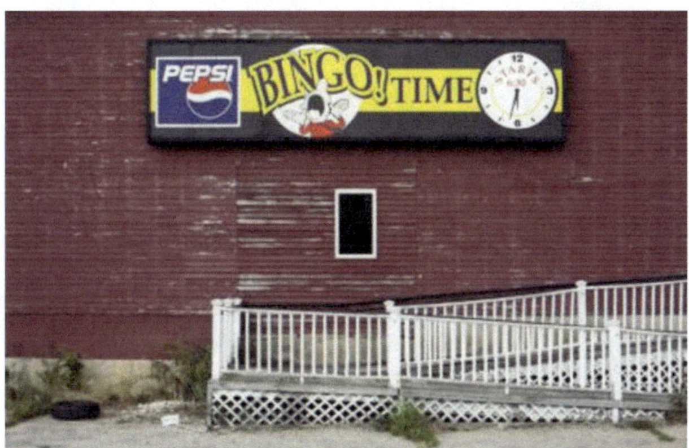

Jere DeWaters, Bingo Time, 2006, digital color print. Used by permission.

In addition, digital cameras and editing software let artists explore the notion of *staged reality*: not just recording what they see but creating a *new* visual reality for the viewer. Sandy Skogland creates and photographs elaborate tableaus inhabited by animals and humans, many times in cornered, theatrical spaces. In a series of images titled True Fiction Two she uses the digital process — and the irony in the title to build fantastically colored, dream like images of decidedly mundane places. By straddling both installation and digital imaging, Skoglund blurs the line between the real and the imagined in art.

The photographs of Jeff Wall are similar in content—a blend of the staged and the real, but presented in a straightforward style the artist terms "near documentary."

Three-Dimensional Techniques

Distinguish between additive and subtractive sculpture techniques

LEARNING ACTIVITIES

The learning activities for this section include:

- Reading: Types of Sculpture and Other Three-Dimensional Media
- Reading: Methods
- Reading: Installation Art

Take time to review and reflect on this activity in order to improve your performance on the assessment for this section.

Reading: Types of Sculpture and Other Three-Dimensional Media

Sculpture is any artwork made by the manipulation of materials resulting in a three-dimensional object. The sculpted figure of the Venus of Berekhat Ram, discovered in the Middle East in 1981, dates to 230,000 years BCE. It is the oldest example of artwork known. The crudely carved stone figure will fit in the palm of your hand. Its name derives from the similarity in form with so-called female fertility figures found throughout Europe, some of which date to 25,000 years ago. For example, the form of the *Venus of Willendorf* below shows remarkable skill in its carving, including arms draped over exaggerated breasts, an extended abdomen and elaborate patterning on the head, indicating either a braided hairstyle or type of woven cap. Just as remarkable, the figure has no facial detail to indicate identity. The meaning behind these figures is difficult to put into context because of the lack of any written record about them or other supporting materials.

These earliest images are indicative of most of the cultural record in sculpture for thousands of years; singular figurative objects made within an iconographic context of myth, ritual or ceremony. It's not until the Old Kingdom period of Egyptian sculpture, between 3100 and 2180 BCE, that we start to see sculpture that reflects a resemblance of specific figures.

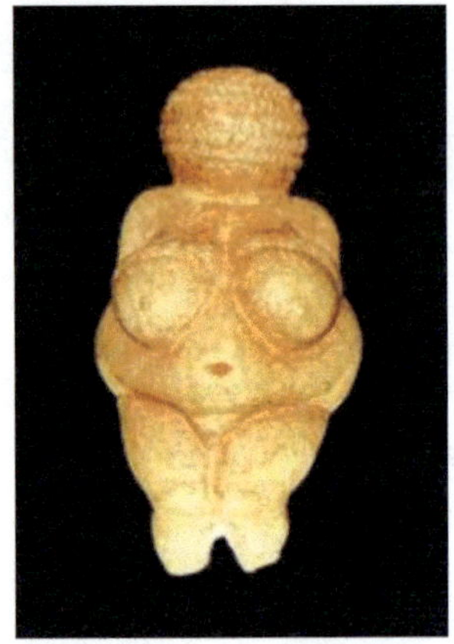

Sculpture can be **freestanding**, or self-supported, where the viewer can walk completely around the work to see it from all sides, or created in **relief,** where the primary form's surface is raised above the surrounding material, such as the image on a coin. **Bas-relief** refers to a shallow extension of the image from its surroundings, **high relief** is where the most prominent elements of the composition are undercut and rendered at more than half in the round against the background. Rich, animated bas-relief sculpture exists at the Banteay Srei temple near Angor Wat, Cambodia. Here humans and mythic figures combine in depictions from ancient Hindu stories.

Venus of Willendorf, c.25,000 BCE. Natural History Museum, Vienna. Image in the public domain

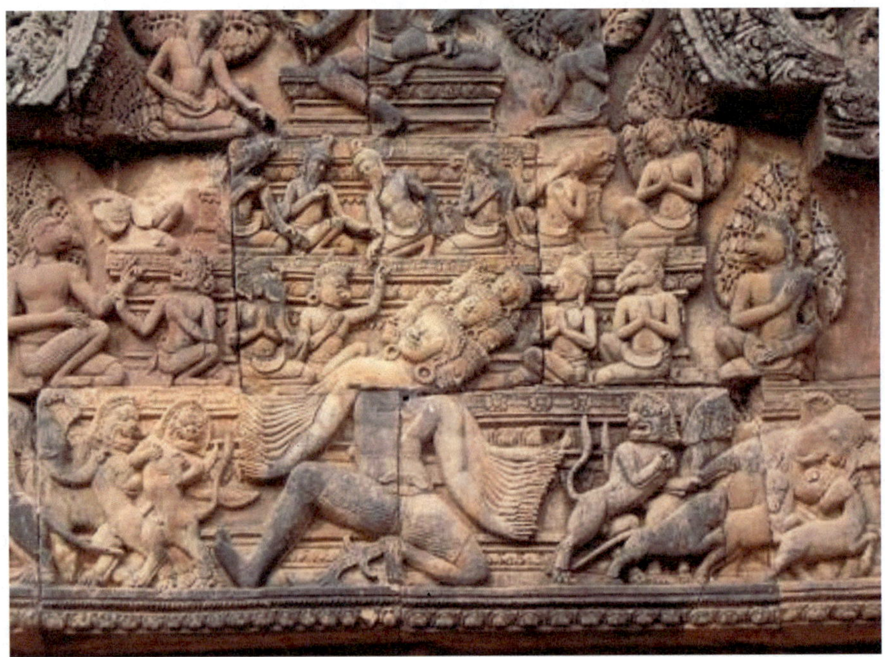

Bas-relief sculpture at the temple Banteay Srei, Angor, Cambodia. Tenth century. Sandstone. Image in the public domain.

The Shaw Memorial combines freestanding, bas-, and high-relief elements in one masterful sculpture. The work memorializes Colonel Robert Gould Shaw and the Massachusetts Fifty-fourth regiment, the first African American infantry unit to fight for the north in the Civil War.

Reading: Methods

1. Carving uses the subtractive process to cut away areas from a larger mass, and is the oldest method used for three-dimensional work. Traditionally stone and wood were the most common materials because they were readily available and extremely durable. Contemporary materials include foam, plastics and glass. Using chisels and other sharp tools, artists carve away material until the ultimate form of the work is achieved.

A beautiful example of the carving process is seen in the *Water and Moon* Bodhisattva from tenth-century China. The Bodhisattva, a Buddhist figure who has attained enlightenment but decides to stay on earth to teach others, is exquisitely carved and painted. The figure is almost eight feet high, seated in an elegant pose on a lotus bloom, relaxed, staring straight ahead with a calm, benevolent look. The extended right arm and raised knee create a stable triangular composition. The sculptor carves the left arm to simulate muscle tension inherent when it supports the weight of the body.

In another example, you can see the high degree of relief carved from an original cedar wood block in the *Earthquake Mask* from the Pacific Northwest Coast Kwakwaka' wakw culture. It's extraordinary for masks to personify a natural event. This and other mythic figure masks are used in ritual and ceremony dances. The broad areas of paint give a heightened sense of character to this mask.

Wood sculptures by contemporary artist Ursula von Rydingsvard are carved, glued and even burned. Many are massive, rough vessel forms that carry the visual evidence of their creation.

Michelangelo's masterpiece statue of *David* from 1501 is carved and sanded to an idealized form that the artist releases from the massive block, a testament to human aesthetic brilliance.

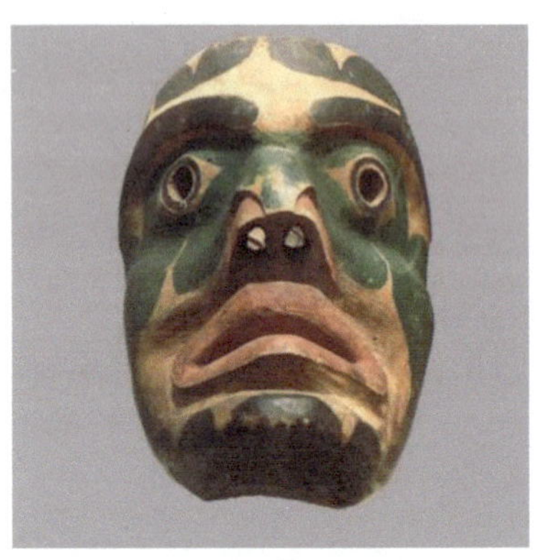

Earthquake Mask, 9" x 7", early twentieth century. Kwakwaka' wakw culture, North American Pacific Coast. Burke Museum, University of Washington, Seattle. Used by permission.

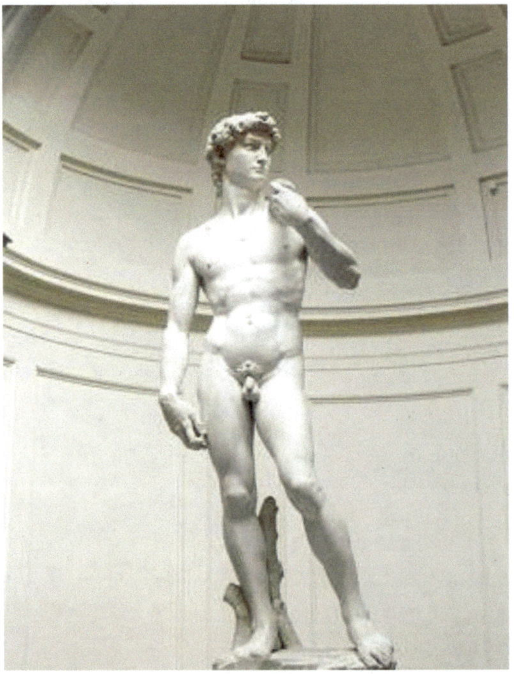

Michelangelo, David, 1501, marble, 17 feet high. Galleria dell'Accademia, Florence. Image in the public domain

2. Casting: The additive method of casting has been in use for more than five thousand years. It's a manufacturing process by which a liquid material is usually poured into a mold, which contains a hollow cavity of the desired shape, and then allowed to solidify. One traditional method of bronze casting frequently used today is the lost wax process. Casting materials are usually metals but can be various cold-setting materials that cure after mixing two or more components together; examples are epoxy, concrete, plaster, and clay. Casting is most often used for making complex shapes that would be otherwise difficult or uneconomical to make by other methods. It's a labor-intensive process that allows for the creation of multiples from an original object (similar to the medium of printmaking), each of which is extremely durable and exactly like its predecessor. A mold is usually destroyed after the desired number of castings has been made. Traditionally, bronze statues were placed atop pedestals to signify the importance of the figure depicted. A statue of William Seward (below), the U. S. Secretary of State under Abraham Lincoln and who negotiated the purchase of the Alaska territories, is set nearly eight feet high so viewers must look up at him. Standing next to the globe, he holds a roll of plans in his left hand.

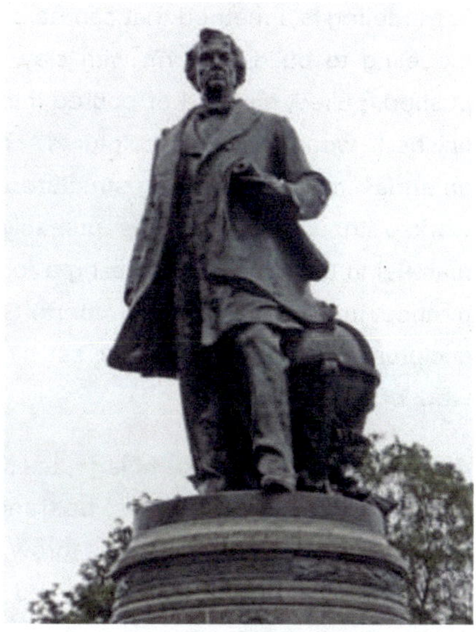

Richard Brooks, William Seward, bronze on stone pedestal, c. 1909. Image by Christopher Gildow. Used with permission.

More contemporary bronze cast sculptures reflect their subjects through different cultural perspectives. The statue of rock guitarist Jimi Hendrix is set on the ground, his figure cast as if performing on stage. He's on both of his knees, head thrown back, eyes shut and mouth open in mid wail. His bell-bottom pants, frilly shirt unbuttoned halfway, necklace and headband give us a snapshot of 1960s rock culture but also engage us with the subject at our level.

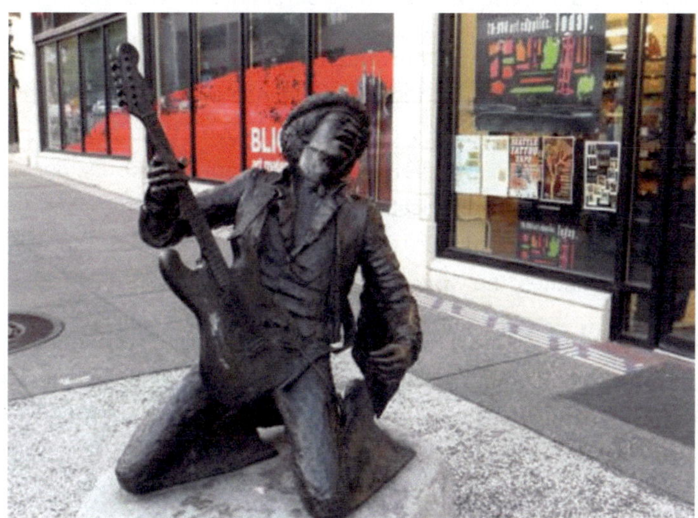

Daryl Smith, Jimi Hendrix, 1996, bronze. Broadway and Pine, Seattle. Image by Christopher Gildow. Used with permission.

Doris Chase was also a strong sculptor. Her large-scale abstract work *Changing Form* from 1971 is cast in bronze and dominates the area around it. The title refers to the visual experience you get walking around the work, seeing the positive and negative shapes dissolve and recombine with each other.

3. Modeling is a method that can be both additive and subtractive. The artist uses modeling to build up form with clay, plaster or other soft material that can be pushed, pulled, pinched or poured into place. The material then hardens into the finished work. Larger sculptures created with this method make use of an **armature**, an underlying structure of wire that sets the physical shape of the work. Although modeling is primarily an additive process, artists do remove material in the process. Modeling a form is often a preliminary step in the casting method. In 2010, Swiss artist Alberto Giacometti's Walking Man (c. 1955), a bronze sculpture first modeled in clay, set a record for the highest price ever paid for a work of art at auction.

4. Construction, or Assemblage, uses found, manufactured or altered objects to build form. Artists weld, glue, bolt and wire individual pieces together. Sculptor Debra Butterfield transforms throw away objects into abstract sculptures of horses with scrap metal, wood and other found objects. She often casts these constructions in bronze.

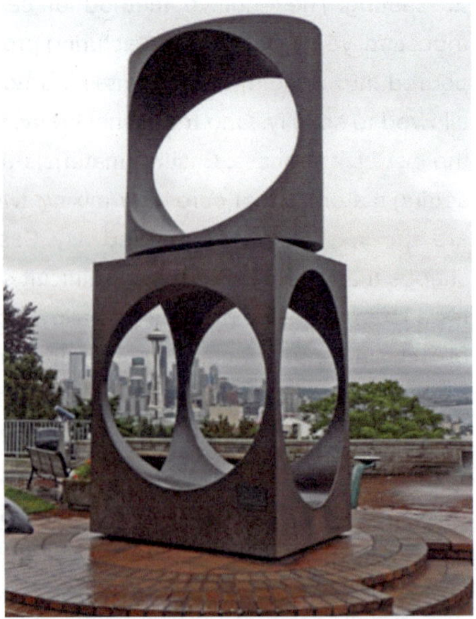

Doris Chase, Changing Form, 1971. Bronze. Image by Christopher Gildow. Used with permission.

Louise Nevelson used cut and shaped pieces of wood, gluing and nailing them together to form fantastic, complex compositions. Painted in a single tone, (usually black or white), her sculptures are graphic, textural façades of shapes, patterns, and shadow.

Traditional African masks often combine different materials. The elaborate Kanaga Mask from Mali uses wood, fibers, animal hide and pigment to construct an other worldly visage that changes from human to animal and back again.

Some modern and contemporary sculptures incorporate movement, light and sound. **Kinetic** sculptures use ambient air currents or motors allowing them to move, changing in form as the viewer stands in place. The artist Alexander Calder is famous for his mobiles, whimsical, abstract works that are intricately balanced to move at the slightest wisp of air, while the sculptures of Jean Tinguely are contraption-like and, similar to Nevelson's and Butterfield's works, constructed of scraps often found in garbage dumps. His motorized works exhibit a mechanical aesthetic as they whir, rock and generate noises. Tinguely's most famous work, Homage to New York, ran in the sculpture garden at New York's Museum of Modern Art in 1960 as part of a performance by the artist. After several minutes, the work exploded and caught fire.

The idea of generating sound as part of three-dimensional works has been utilized for hundreds of years, traditionally in musical instruments that carry a spiritual reference. Contemporary artists use sound to heighten the effect of sculpture or to direct recorded narratives. The cast bronze fountain by George Tsutakawa (below) uses water flow to produce a soft rushing sound. In this instance the sculpture also attracts the viewer by the motion of the water: a clear, fluid addition to an otherwise hard abstract surface.

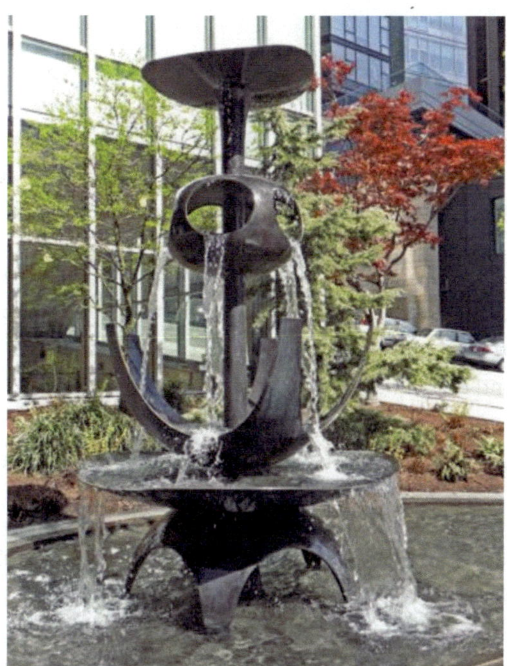

George Tsutakawa, Fountain. Bronze, running water. City of Seattle. Image by Christopher Gildow. Used with permission.

Doug Hollis's A Sound Garden from 1982 creates sounds from hollow metal tubes atop gridlike structures rising above the ground. In weathervane fashion, the tubes swing into the wind and resonate to specific pitch. The sound extends the aesthetic value of the work to include the sense of hearing and, together with the metal construction, creates a mechanical and psychological basis for the work.

Reading: Installation Art

Dan Flavin is one of the first artists to explore the possibilities of light as a sculptural medium. Since the 1960s his work has incorporated fluorescent bulbs of different colors and in various arrangements. Moreover, he takes advantage of the wall space the light is projected onto, literally blurring the line between traditional sculpture and the more complex medium of installation.

Installation art utilizes multiple objects, often from various mediums, and takes up entire spaces. It can be generic or site specific. Because of their relative complexity, installations can address aesthetic and narrative ideas on a larger scale than traditional sculpture. Its genesis can be traced to the Dada movement, ascendant after World War I and which predicated a new aesthetic by its unconventional nature and ridicule of established tastes and styles. Sculpture came off the pedestal and began to transform entire rooms into works or art. Kurt Schwitters' Merzbau, begun in 1923, transforms his apartment into an abstract, claustrophobic space that is at once part sculpture and architecture. With installation art the viewer is surrounded by and can become part of the work itself.

British artist Rachel Whiteread's installation Embankment from 2005 fills an entire exhibition hall with casts made from various sized boxes. At first appearance a snowy mountain landscape navigated by the viewer is actually a gigantic nod to the idea of boxes as receptacles of memory towering above and stacked around them, squeezing them towards the center of the room.

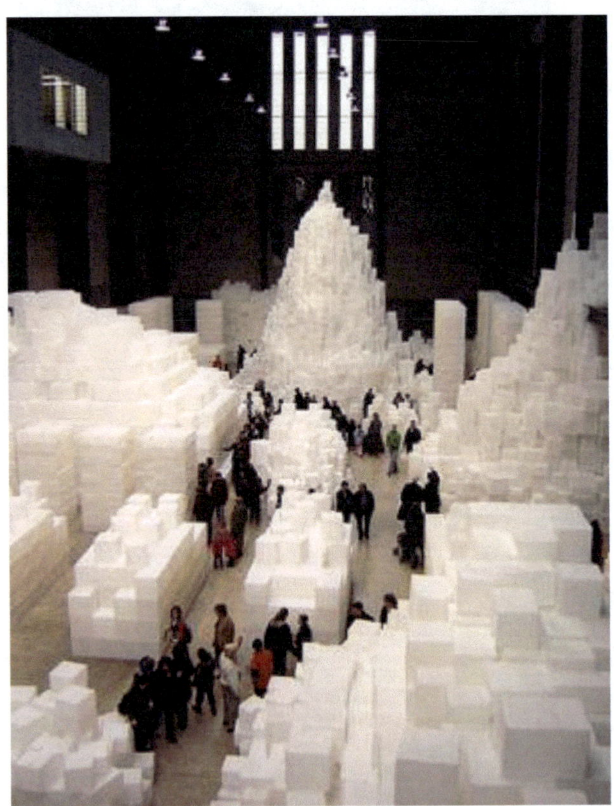
Rachel Whiteread, Embankment, 2005. Source: Wikipedia, licensed through Creative Commons

Ilya Kabakov mixes together a narrative of political propaganda, humor and mundane existence in his installation *The Man Who Flew into Space from His Apartment* from 1984. What we see is the remains of a small apartment plastered with Soviet era posters, a small bed and the makeshift slingshot a man uses to escape the drudgery of his life within the system. A gaping hole in the roof and his shoes on the floor are evidence enough that he made it into space.

Architecture

Describe traditional methods and materials of building design

Take time to review and reflect on this activity in order to improve your performance on the assessment for this section.

Reading: Design, Methods, and Materials

Architecture is an art form that reflects how we present ourselves across the earth's landscape, and, like other expressive mediums, it changes with styles, technologies and cultural adaptations. Architecture not only provides worldly needs of shelter, workspace and storage but also represents human ideals in buildings like courthouses and government buildings and manifestations of the spirit in churches and cathedrals. Traditional architecture has survived over thousands of years in one form or another, while contemporary design offers new approaches in how we use materials and technology to shape the look of our environment.

Early Developments in Building Design and Techniques Methods

The basic methods of building design and construction have been used for thousands of years. Stacking stones, laying brick, or lashing wood together in one form or another are still used today in all parts of the world. But over the centuries, innovations in methods and materials have given new expression to architecture and the human footprint on the landscape. We can look to historical examples for clues that give context to different style periods.

In western culture, one of the earliest settlements with permanent structures was discovered at Catalhoyuk in Turkey (pictured below). The rich soil that surrounds the settlement indicates the inhabitants relied in part on farming. Dated to about 7500 BCE, the dwellings are constructed from dried mud and brick and show wooden support beams spanning the ceilings. The design of the settlement incorporates a cell-like structure of small buildings either sharing common walls or separated by a few feet. The roofs are flat and were used as pathways between buildings.

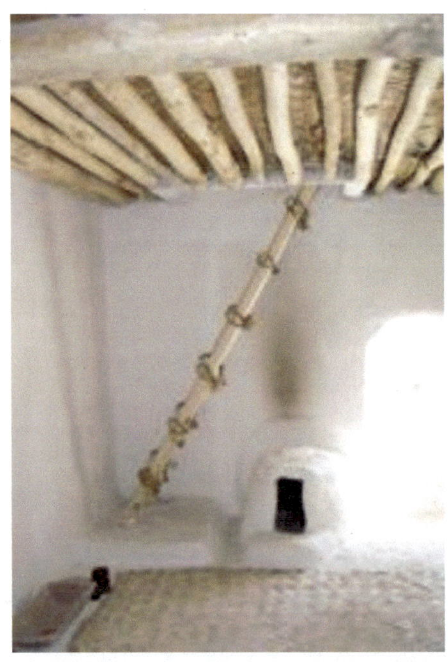

Restoration of interior, Catalhoyuk, Turkey. Image licensed under Creative Commons.

A significant advance came with the development of the **post and lintel** system. With this, a system of posts —either stone or wood — are placed at intervals and spanned by beams at the tops. The load is distributed down the posts to allow for areas of open space between them. Its earliest use is seen at *Stonehenge* (below), a prehistoric monument in southern England dating to about 3000 BCE.

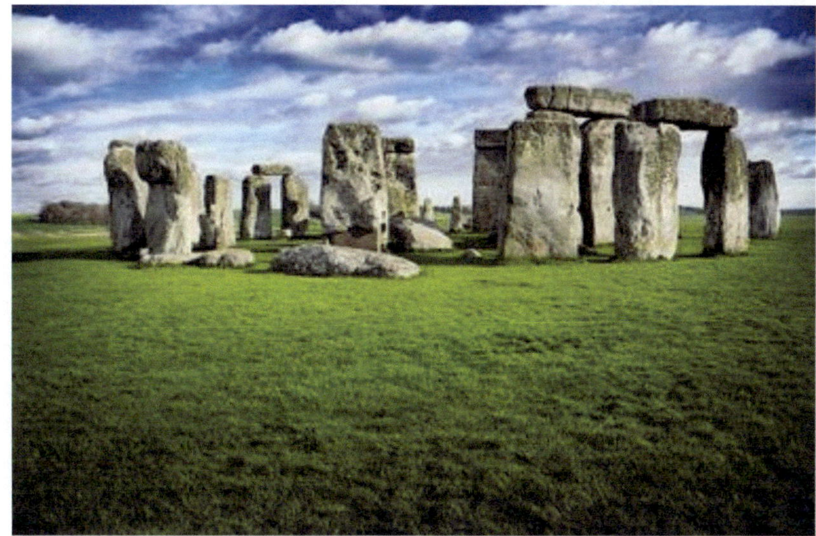

Stonehenge, Wiltshire County, England. Image: David Ball. Image licensed under Creative Commons.

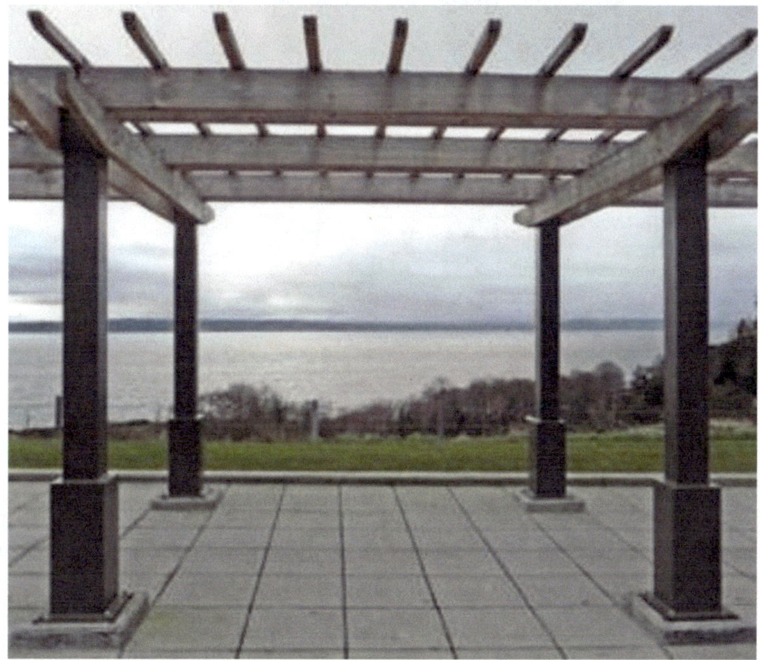

Post and Lintel support in contemporary use. Image by Christopher Gildow. Used with permission.

A **colonnade** continues the post and lintel method as a series of columns and beams enveloping larger areas of space. Colonnades can be free standing or part of a larger structure. Common in Egyptian, Greek and Roman architectural design, their use creates visual rhythm and implies a sense of grandeur. Over time columns became categorized by the capital style at their tops. The smooth and unadorned **Tuscan** and fluted **Doric** columns give way to more elaborate styles: the scrolled **Ionian** and the high relief **Corinthian**.

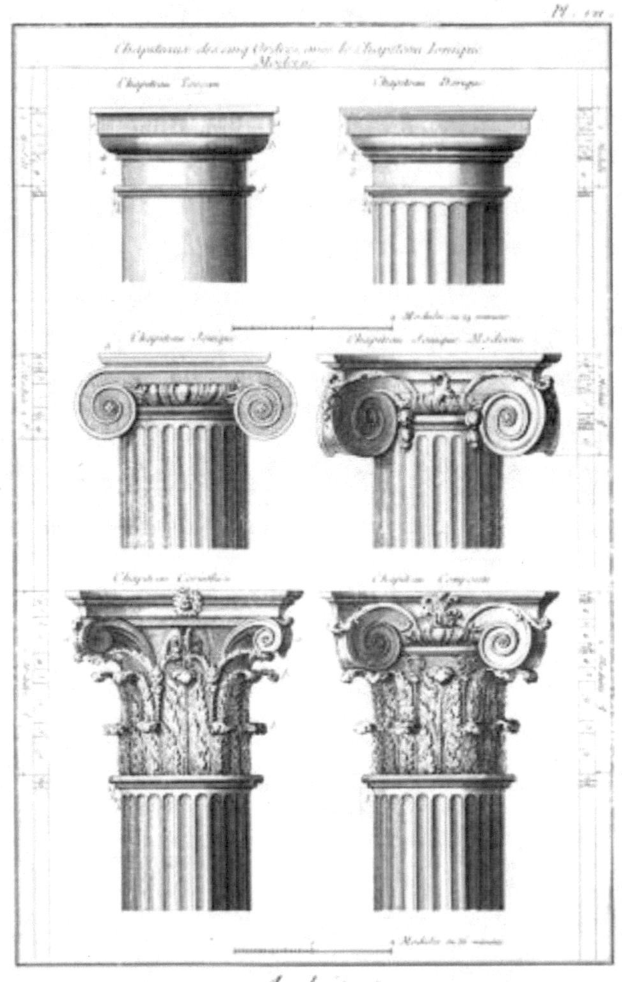

Greek and Roman capitals: Top row: Tuscan, Doric. Middle Row: Ionic. Bottom Row: Corinthian and a composite Ionic Corinthian. Classical Orders, engraving from the Encyclopédie vol. 18. Public domain.

The Parthenon, a Greek temple to the mythic goddess Athena, was built in the fifth century BCE in Athens and is part of a larger community of structures in the Acropolis. All are considered pinnacles of classic Greek architecture. Ionic colonnades march across all sides of the Parthenon, the outer boundary of a very ordered interior floor plan.

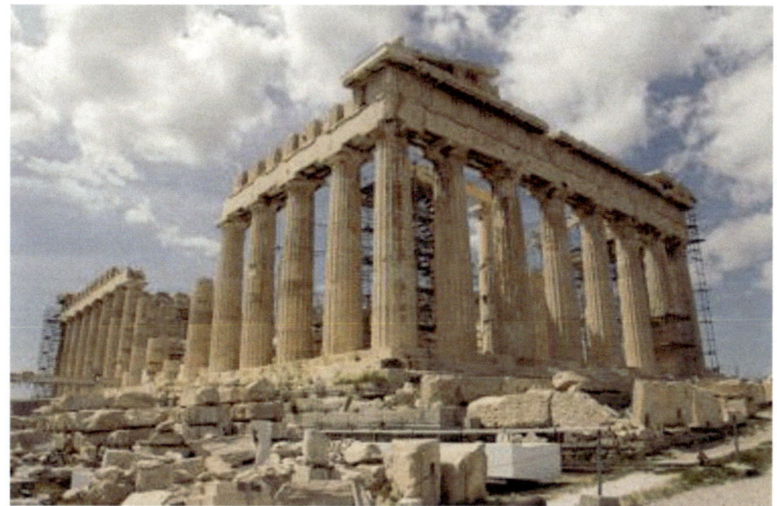

The Parthenon, Athens, Greece. 447 BCE. Digital image by Kallistos and licensed under Creative Commons

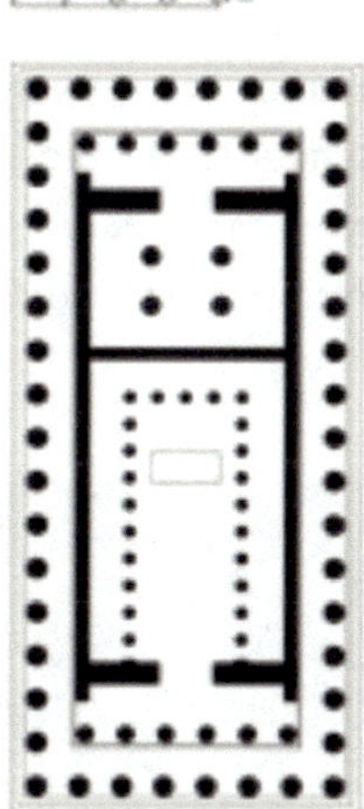

Floor plan of the Parthenon. Licensed through Creative Commons.

Another example is the colonnade surrounding St. Peter's Square in the Vatican, Rome.

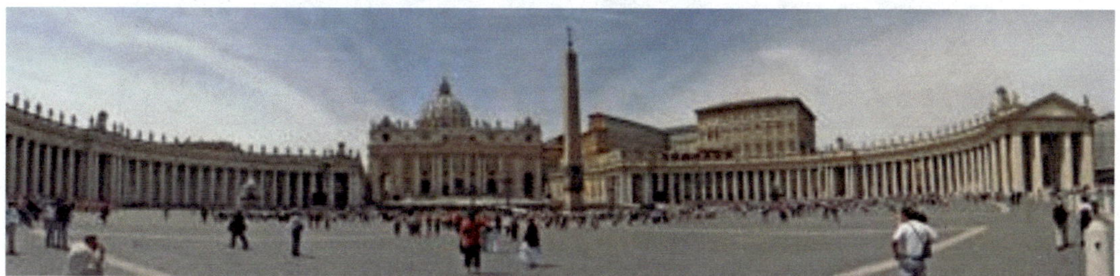

Gian Lorenzo Bernini, Colonnade at St. Peter's Square, the Vatican. 1656–67. Photo by D.F. Malan. Licensed through Creative Commons.

The colonnade is part of our contemporary surroundings too. Parks and other public spaces use them to the same effect: providing visual and material stability in spanning areas of open space.

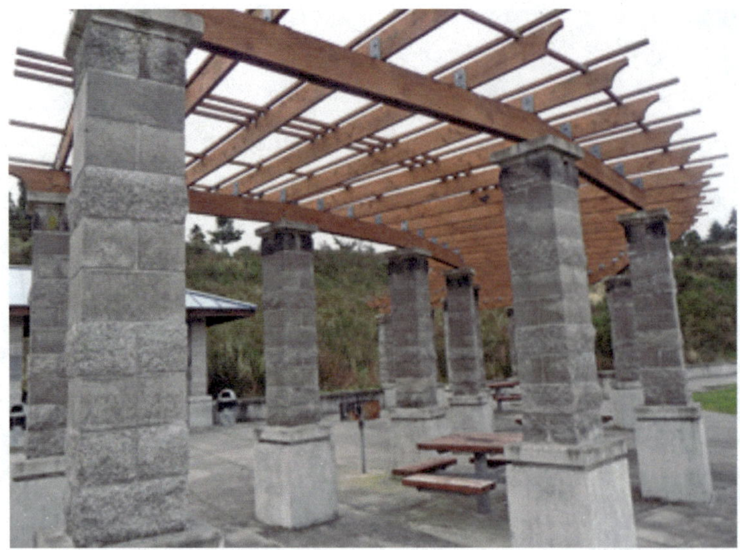

Contemporary colonnade. Image: Christopher Gildow. Used with permission.

The development of the **arch** gave architecture new alternatives to post and lintel construction. Arches appeared as early as the 2nd millennium BC in Mesopotamian brick architecture. They supply strength and stability to walls without massive posts and beams because their construction minimizes the shear load imposed on them. This meant walls could go higher without compromising their stability and at the same time create larger areas of open space between arches. In addition, the arch gave buildings a more organic, expressive visual element. The Colosseum in Rome (below), built in the first century CE, uses repeated arches to define an imposing but decidedly airy structure. The fact that it's still standing today is testament to the inherent strength of the arch.

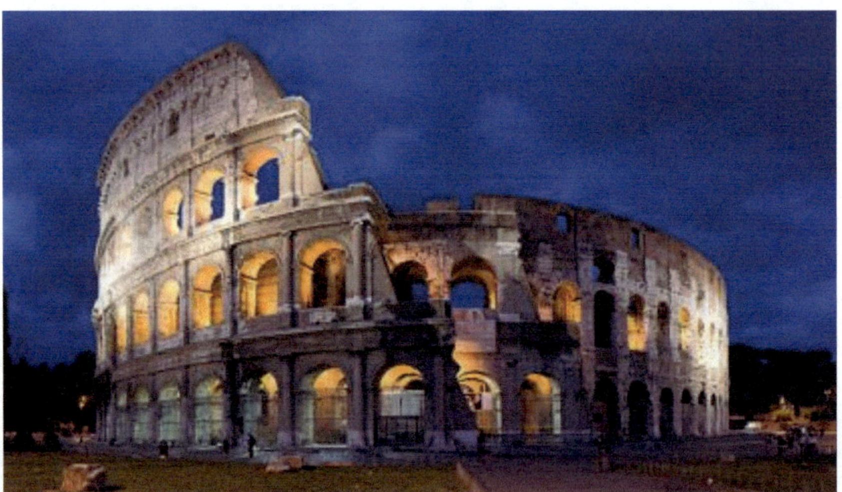

The Colosseum, Rome, Italy. First century CE. Photo by David Iliff. Image licensed through Creative Commons.

Roman aqueducts are another example of how effectively the arch was used. Tall and graceful, the arches support themselves in a colonnade and were used to transport a network of water channels throughout ancient Rome.

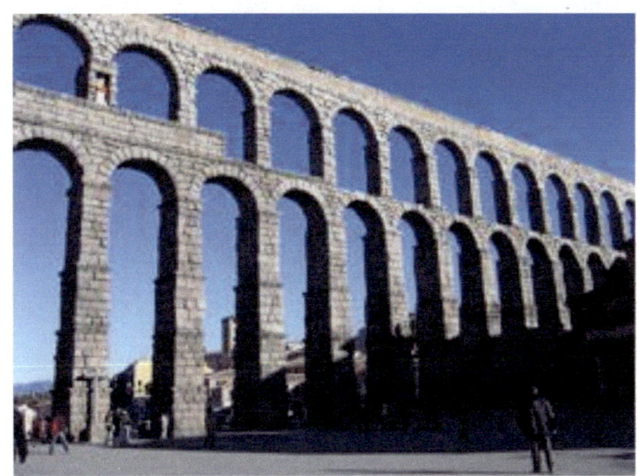

Roman aqueduct, c. First century CE. Image in the public domain.

From the arch came two more important developments: extending an arch in a linear direction formed a **vault**, encapsulating tall, narrow spaces with inverted "U" shaped ceilings. The compressive force of the vault required thick walls on each side to keep it from collapsing. Because of this many vaults were situated underground – essentially tunnels – connecting areas of a larger building or providing covered transport of people, goods and materials throughout the city.

An arch rotated on its vertical axis creates a **dome**, with its curving organic scoop of space reserved for the tops of the most important buildings. The Pantheon in Rome sports a dome with an oculus – a round or elliptical opening at the top, that is the massive building's only light source.

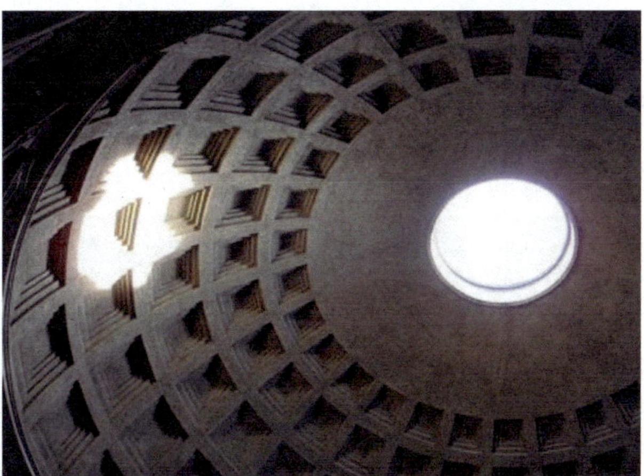

Dome of the Pantheon with oculus, Rome. 126 CE. Image in the public domain.

These elements combined to revolutionize architectural design throughout Europe and the Middle East in the form of bigger and stronger churches, mosques and even sectarian government buildings. Styles changed with technology. **Romanesque** architecture was popular for nearly three hundred years (800 – 1100 CE). The style is characterized by barrel or groin vault ceilings, thick walls with low exterior buttresses and squared off towers. Buildings reached a point where they struggled to support their own weight. The architectural solution to the problem was a **flying buttress**, an exterior load-bearing column connected to the main structure by a segmented arch or "flyer."

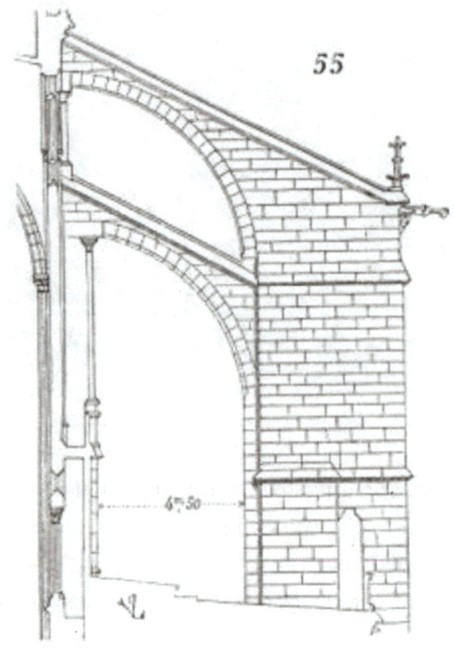

Diagram of a flying buttress from St. Denis basilica, Paris. From the Dictionary of French Architecture from 11th to 16th Century (1856), licensed through Creative Commons.

Flying buttresses became a kind of exoskeleton that transferred the heavy weight of Romanesque stone roofs through their arches and into the ground, away from the building. They became catalysts for the **Gothic** style based on higher, thinner walls, pointed arches, ribbed vaults, and spired towers. Also, the thinner walls of the Gothic style allowed for more stained glass windows and interior illumination.

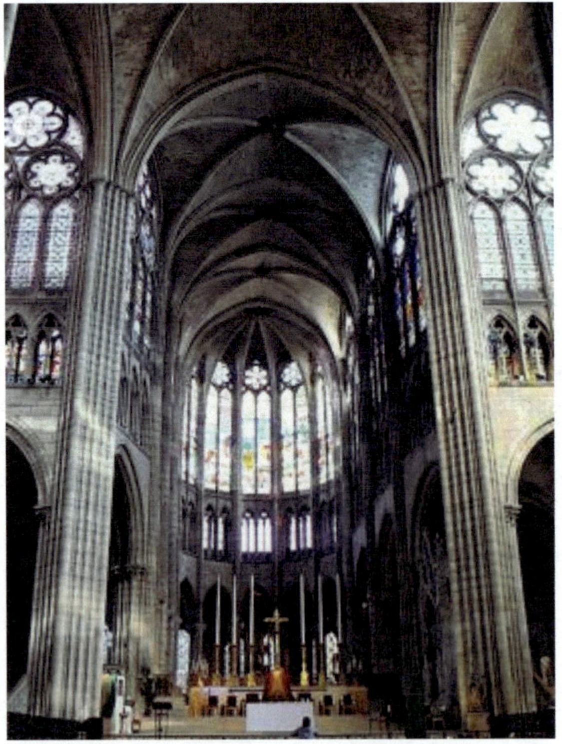

Church of St. Denis, France. Seventh–twelfth centuries CE. Image in the public domain

St. Denis basilica in France (above) is one of the first Gothic-style churches, known for its high vaulted ceilings and extensive use of stained glass windows. The architecture of the church became a symbol of spirituality itself: soaring heights, magnificently embellished interiors and exteriors, elaborate lighting and sheer grandeur on a massive scale.

The Doges Palace in Venice, Italy (pictured below) housed the political aristocracy of the Republic of Venice for a thousand years. Built in 1309 CE, its rhythmic levels of columns and pointed arches, divided by fractals as they rise, give way to elaborate geometric patterns in the pink brick façade. The ornamental additions at the top edge reinforce the patterns below.

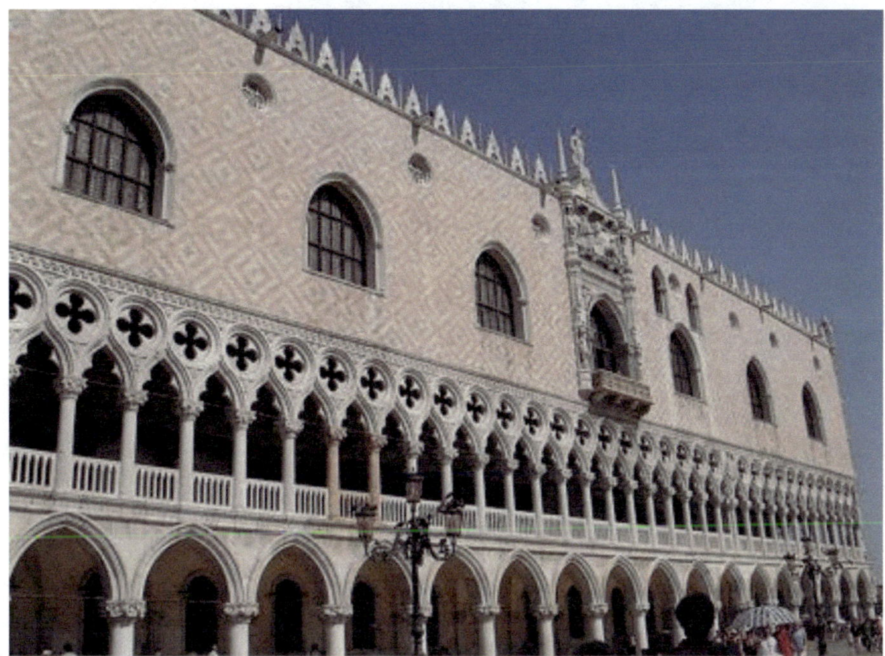

The Doges Palace, 1309 CE, viewed from St. Mark's Square, Venice, Italy. Image by Martti Mustonen and licensed through Creative Commons.

ARCHITECTURE IN CHINA & THE FAR EAST

Chinese architecture refers to a style of architecture that has taken shape in East Asia over many centuries. The structural principles of traditional Chinese architecture have remained largely unchanged. Chinese architectural (and aesthetic) design is based on symmetry, a general emphasis on the horizontal and site layouts that reflect a hierarchy of importance. These considerations result in formal and stylistic differences in comparison to the West, and display alternatives in design.

The Chinese have used stone, brick and wood for centuries. The Great Wall, begun in the 5th century BCE, was intended to keep nomadic invaders out of Northern China. The stone wall covers 5500 miles in its entirety. The rigid material takes on a more flexible appearance as it conforms to the contours of the landscape surrounding it.

CROSS-CULTURAL INFLUENCES

As overland and marine trade routes expanded between Eastern and Western civilizations so did the influence of cultural styles in architecture, religion and commerce. The most important of these passages was the Silk Road, a system of routes that developed over hundreds of years across the European and Asian continents. Along this route are buildings that show cross-cultural influences in their design.

The Dome of the Rock in Jerusalem offers different cultural influences manifest in one building: a classic Greek colonnade at the main entrance, the gold dome and central turret supporting it, western style arches and colorful Islamic surface embellishment.

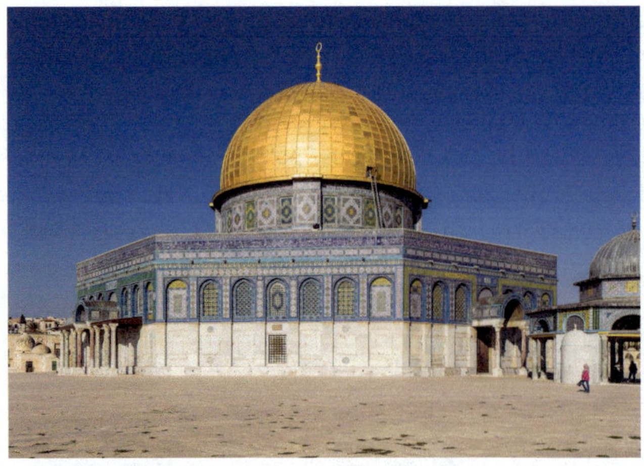

The Dome of the Rock, on the Temple Mount, in the Old City of Jerusalem, Photo Credit Andrew Shiva, Image licensed through Creative Commons

The Louvre Palace in Paris, once the official royal residence and now one of the world's biggest museums, had its beginnings in the 12th century but didn't achieve its present form until recently. The building's style is French Renaissance – marked by a formal symmetry, horizontal stability and restrained ornamentation. The Louvre executive board chose architect I. M. Pei's glass pyramid design as the defining element for the new main entry in 1989. The choice was a great success: the pyramid further defines the public space above ground and gives natural light and a sense of openness to the underground lobby beneath it.

THE INDUSTRIAL REVOLUTION

Beginning in the 18th century the Industrial Revolution made fundamental changes in agriculture, manufacturing, transportation and housing. Architecture changed in response to the new industrial landscape. Prior to the late 19th century, the weight of a multistory building had to be supported principally by the strength of its walls. The taller the building, the more strain this placed on the lower sections. Since there were clear engineering limits to the weight such load-bearing walls could sustain, large designs meant massively thick walls on the ground floors, and definite limits on the building's height.

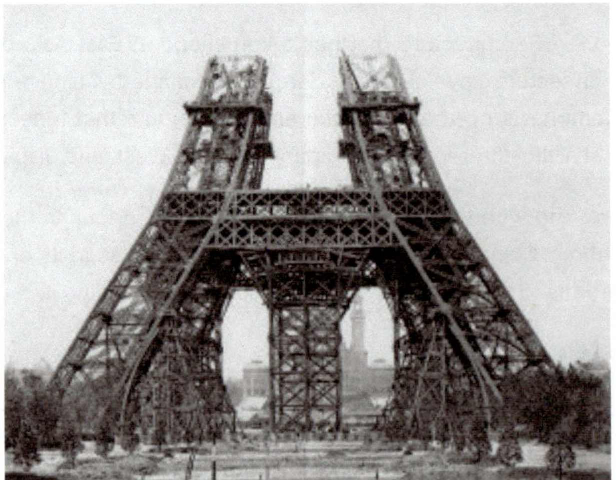

Eiffel Tower, Start of construction of second stage, May 1888. Image in the public domain

Forged iron and milled steel began to replace wood, brick and stone as primary materials for large buildings. This change is encapsulated in the Eiffel Tower, built in 1889. Standing on four huge arched legs, the iron lattice tower rises narrowly to just over 1000 feet high. The Eiffel Tower not only became an icon for France but for industry itself – heralding a new age in materials, design and construction methods.

In America, the development of cheap, versatile steel in the second half of the 19th century helped change the urban landscape. The country was in the midst of rapid social and economic growth that made for great opportunities in architectural design. A much more urbanized society was forming and the society called out for new, larger buildings. By the middle of the 19th century downtown areas in big cities began to transform themselves with new roads and buildings to accommodate the growth. The mass production of steel was the main driving force behind the ability to build skyscrapers during the mid 1880s.

Steel framing was set into foundations of reinforced concrete, concrete poured around a grid of steel rods (re-bar) or other matrices to increase tensile strength in foundations, columns and vertical slabs.

MODERNIST ARCHITECTURE

The move to modernism was introduced with the opening of the Bauhaus school in Weimar Germany. Founded in 1919 by the German architect Walter Gropius, Bauhaus (literal translation "house of construction") was a teaching and learning center for modern industrial and architectural design. Though not a movement or style in itself, Bauhaus instructors and staff reflected different artistic perspectives, all of them born from the modern aesthetic. It was partly the product of a post- World War I search for new artistic definitions in Europe. Gropius's commitment to the principle of bringing all the arts together with a focus on practical, utilitarian applications. This view rejected the notion of "art for art's sake", putting a premium on the knowledge of materials and their effective design. This idea shows the influence of Constructivism, a similar philosophy developed concurrently in Russia that used the arts for social purposes. Bauhaus existed for fourteen years, relocating three times, and influencing a whole generation of architects, artists, graphic and industrial designers and typographers.

In 1924 Gropius designed the Bauhaus main building in Dessau. Its modern form includes bold lines, an asymmetric balance and curtain walls of glass. It's painted in neutral tones of white and gray accented by strong primary colors on selected doors.

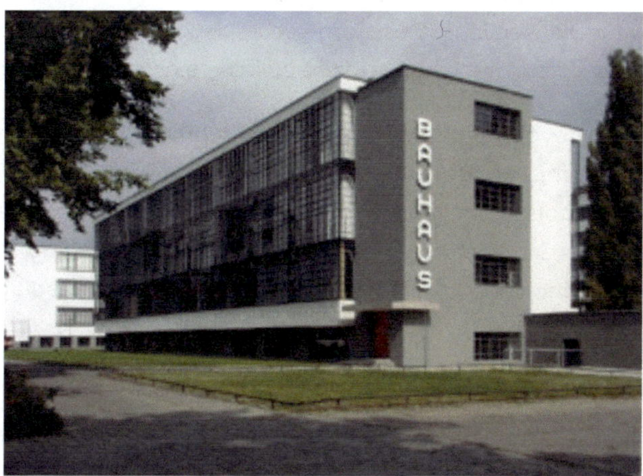

Bauhaus in Dessau, Germany, 1925-26, Image in public domain

Frank Lloyd Wright is considered one of the 20th century's greatest architects. Wright designed buildings, churches, homes and schools, but is best known for his design of Falling Water, a home in the Pennsylvania countryside for Chicago department store owner Edgar Kaufman. His design innovations include unified open floor plans, a balance of traditional and modern materials and the use of cantilevered forms that extends horizontal balance.

The Guggenheim Museum in New York City is an example of Wright's concern with organic forms and utilization of space. The main element in the design is a spiral form rising from the middle of the cantilevered main structure. Paintings are exhibited on its curved walls. Visitors take the elevator to the top floor and view the works as they travel down the gently sloped hallway. This spiral surrounds a large atrium in the middle of the building and a domed skylight at the top.

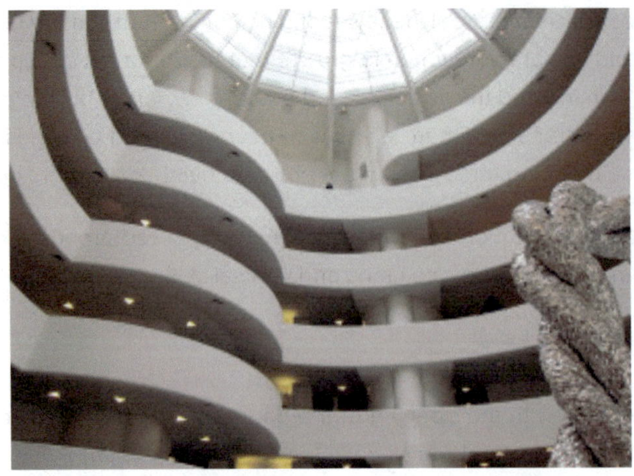
Atrium, Solomon R. Guggenheim Museum, Manhattan, New York, 1959,
Image in the public domain

POST MODERN & CONTEMPORARY ARCHITECTURE

Postmodern architecture began as an international style whose first examples are generally cited as being from the 1950s, but did not become a movement until the late 1970s and continues to influence present-day architecture. Postmodernity in architecture is generally thought to be heralded by the return of "wit, ornament and reference" to architecture in response to the formalism of the International Style.

Michael Graves's Portland Building from 1982 personifies the idea behind postmodernist thought. A reference to more traditional style is evident in the patterned column-like sections. Overt large-scale decorative elements are built into and onto the exterior walls, and contrasts between materials, colors and forms give the building a graphic sense of visual wit.

We can see how architecture is actively evolving in the contemporary work of Frank Gehry and Zaha Hadid. Gehry's work is famous for its rolling and bent organic forms. His gestural, erratic sketches are transformed into buildings through a computer aided design process (CAD). They have roots in postmodernism but lean towards a completely new modern style. They have as much to do with sculpture as they do with architecture. Seattle's Experience Music Project is an example of the complexity that goes into his designs. Its curves, ripples and folds roll across space and the multi-colored titanium panels adorning the exterior accentuate the effect.

GREEN ARCHITECTURE

In the last decade there has emerged a strong interest in developing "green" architecture – designs that incorporate ecologically and environmentally sustainable practices in site preparation, materials, energy use and waste systems. Some are simple: buildings oriented to the south or west helps with passive solar heating. Others are more complex: Solar voltaic cells on the roof to generate power to the building. Green roofs are made of sod and other organic material and act as a cooling agent and recycle rainwater too. In addition, technological innovations in lighting, heating and cooling systems have made them more efficient.

A branch of the Seattle Public Library uses green design. A glass curtain wall on the north side makes use of natural lighting. Overhanging wooden roof beams shades harsh light. The whole structure is nestled under a green roof of sod and over 18,000 low water use plants. Seven skylights on the roof provide more natural lighting.

- Architecture and the Industrial Revolution. **Authored by**: Christopher Gildow. **Located at**: https://learn.canvas.net/courses/24/pages/m9-architecture-and-the-industrial-revolution?module_item_id=44477. **Project**: Open Course Library. **License**: *CC BY-NC-SA: Attribution-NonCommercial-ShareAlike*
- Modern Architecture: A New Language. **Authored by**: Christopher Gildow. **Located at**: https://learn.canvas.net/courses/24/pages/m9-modern-architecture-a-new-language?module_item_id=44478. **Project**: Open Course Library. **License**: *CC BY-NC-SA: Attribution-NonCommercial-ShareAlike*
- Green Architecture. **Authored by**: Christopher Gildow. **Located at**: https://learn.canvas.net/courses/24/pages/m9-green-architecture?module_item_id=44480. **Project**: Open Course Library. **License**: *CC BY-NC-SA: Attribution-NonCommercial-ShareAlike*
- Post-Modern and Contemporary Architecture. **Authored by**: Christopher Gildow. **Located at**: https://learn.canvas.net/courses/24/pages/m9-post-modern-and-contemporary-architecture?module_item_id=44479. **Project**: Open Course Library. **License**: *CC BY-NC-SA: Attribution-NonCommercial-ShareAlike*

Time-Based Art

Explain the techniques of film and video art

LEARNING ACTIVITIES

The learning activities for this section include:

- Reading: Time-Based Media: Film and Video

Take time to review and reflect on this activity in order to improve your performance on the assessment for this section.

Reading: Time-Based Media: Film and Video

With traditional film, what we see as a continuous moving image is actually a linear progression of still photos on a single reel that pass through a lens at a certain rate of speed and are projected onto a screen. We saw a simple form of this process earlier in the pioneering work of Eadweard Muybridge.

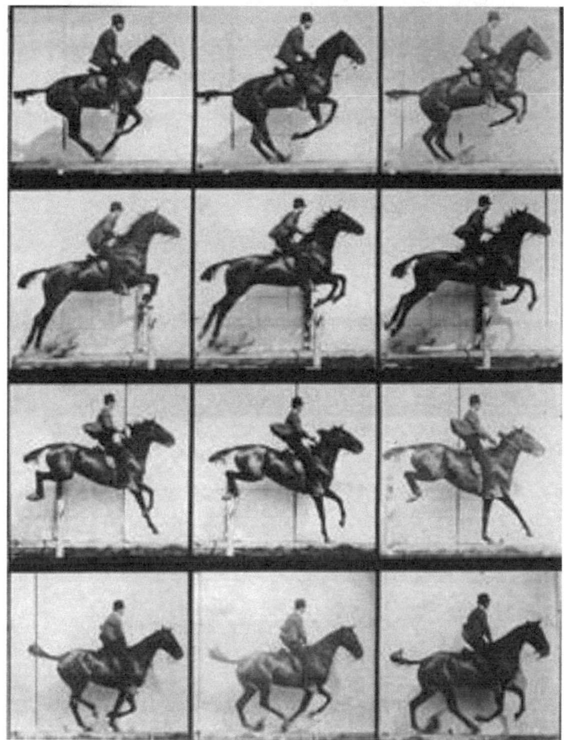

Eadweard Muybridge, Sequence of a Horse Jumping, 1904.
Image is in the public domain

The first motion picture cameras were invented in Europe during the late nineteenth century. These early "movies" lacked a soundtrack and were normally shown along with a live pianist, organ player or orchestra in the theatre to provide the musical accompaniment. In the United States, film went from being a novelty to an art form with D. W. Griffith's *Birth of a Nation* in 1915. In it Griffith presents a narrative of the Civil War and its aftermath but with a decidedly racist view of American blacks and the Ku Klux Klan.

Film scholars agree it contains many new cinematic innovations and refinements, technical effects and artistic advancements, including a color sequence at the end. It had a formative influence on future films and has had a recognized impact on film history and the development of film as art. In addition, at almost three hours in length, it was the longest film to date (from *Filmsite Movie Review: The Birth of a Nation*).

Unique to the moving image is its ability to unfold an idea or narrative over time, using the same elements and principles inherent in any artistic medium. Film stills show how dramatic use of lighting, staging and set compositions are embedded throughout an entire film.

Video art, first appearing in the 1960s and 70s, uses magnetic tape to record image and sound together. The advantage of video over film is its instant playback and editing capability. One of the pioneers in using video as an art form was Doris Chase. She began by integrating her sculptures with interactive dancers, using special effects to create dreamlike work, and spoke of her ideas in terms of painting with light. Unlike filmmakers, video artists frequently combine their medium with installation, an art form that uses entire rooms or other specific spaces, to achieve effects beyond mere projection. South Korean video artist Nam June Paik made breakthrough works that comment on culture, technology and politics. Contemporary video artist

Bill Viola creates work that is more painterly and physically dramatic, often training the camera on figures within a staged set or spotlighted figures in dark surroundings as they act out emotional gestures and expressions in slow motion. Indeed, his work The Greeting reenacts the emotional embrace seen in the Italian Renaissance painter Jocopo Pontormo's work The Visitation below.

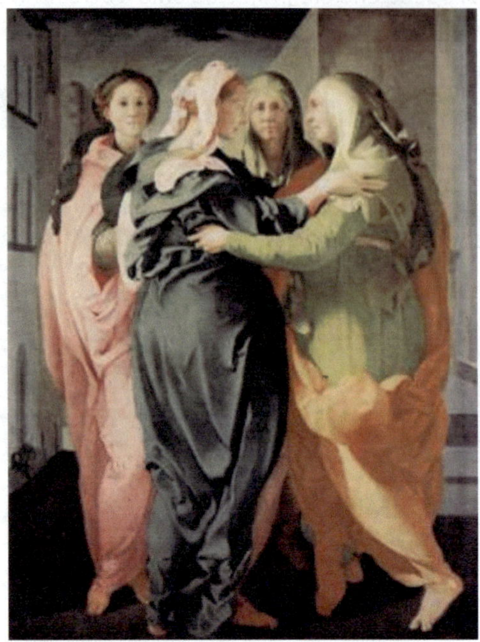

Jacopo Pontormo, The Visitation, 1528, oil on canvas. The Church of San Francesco e Michele, Carmignano, Italy. Image is in the public domain.

- https://youtu.be/Dg0lyGUVXaQ

Digital Technology

Discuss and describe the growing impact of computers and digital tools on art making in the 21st century

Take time to review and reflect on this activity in order to improve your performance on the assessment for this section.

Reading: Digital Technology and Art of the 21st Century

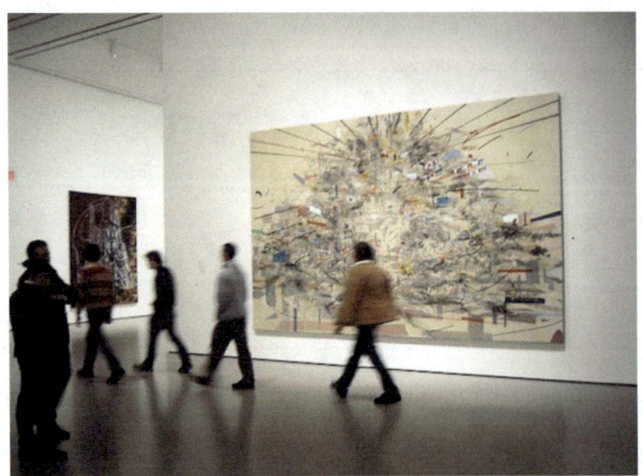

Visitors at The Museum of Modern Art in front of Julie Mehretu, Empirical Construction, Istanbul, 2003. Ink and synthetic polymer paint on canvas, 10′ x 15′ (304.8 x 457.2 cm). Photo: thatgirl

Introduction

Twenty-first-century art is a burgeoning field of practice, research, and publication, making it an incredibly dynamic field of study. Many important topics have been resonating in the new century and inspiring new thinking and scholarly debate, such as the surge of bio art in response to scientific research in the life sciences, and the critical theory known as relational aesthetics that developed in response to an increase in art that invites viewers' participation and interaction. Other topics that were much-discussed in the late twentieth century remain vital for the analysis of twenty-first-century art and visual culture, including semiotics, post-modernism, and feminism.

Art of the twenty-first century emerges from a vast variety of materials and means. These include the latest electronic technologies, such as digital imaging and the Internet; familiar genres with a long history that continue to be practiced with great vigor, such as painting (see, for example, the work of Julie Mehretu and Shahzia Sikander); and materials and processes once associated primarily with handicrafts, re-envisioned to express new concepts. Many artists regularly and freely mix media and forms, making the choices that best serve their concepts and purposes. Activities vary from spectacular projects accomplished with huge budgets and extraordinary production values to modest endeavors that emphasize process, ephemeral experiences, and a do-it-yourself approach. The notion of influences has also shifted with changes in communications and technology; every location around the world has artists who respond to local geographies and histories as well as the sway of global visual culture.

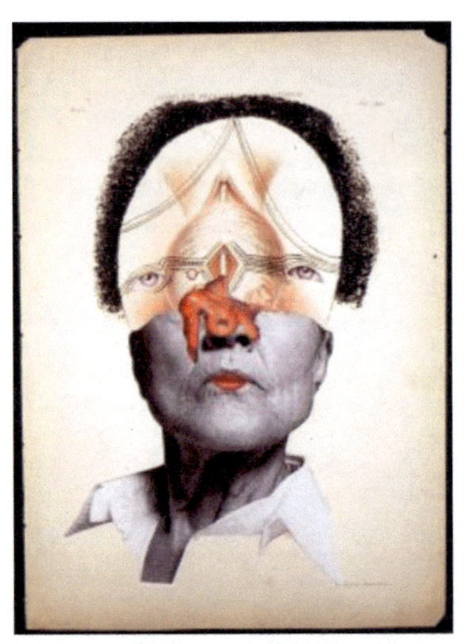

Wangechi Mutu, Complete Prolapsus of the Uterus, 2004, Glitter, ink, collage on found medical illustration paper, 46 x 31cm

Computers and digital technology

Like the camera did more than one hundred and fifty years ago, computers and digital technology have revolutionized the visual art landscape. Some artists now use digital technology to extend the reach of creative possibilities. Sophisticated software allows any computer user the opportunity to create and manipulate images and information. From still images and animation to streaming digital content and digital installations, computers have become high tech creative tools.

In a blending of traditional and new media, artist Chris Finley uses digital templates—software-based composition formats—to create his paintings.

The work of German artist Jochem Hendricks combines digital technology and human sight. His eye drawings rely on a computer interface to translate the process of looking into physical drawings.

Digital technology is a big part of the video and motion picture industries with the capability for high definition images, better editing resources and more areas for exploration to the artist.

The camera arts are relatively new mediums to the world of art but their contributions are perhaps the most significant of all. They are certainly the most complex. Like traditional mediums of drawing, painting and sculpture they allow creative exploration of ideas and the making of objects and images. The difference is in their avenue of expression: by recording images and experiences through light and electronics they, on the one hand, narrow the gap between the worlds of the "real" and the "imagined" and on the other offers us an art form that can invent its own reality with the inclusion of the dimension of time. We watch as a narrative unfolds in front of our eyes. Digital technology has created a whole new kind of spatial dimension: cyberspace.

Globalization

A key feature of the art scene in the twenty-first century (and of many sectors of twenty-first-century life) is the impact of globalization – the accelerating interconnectivity of human activity and information across time and space. Aided by the internet and mass media, awareness of the vitality of contemporary art in localities around the globe has grown exponentially. Anyone with access to the internet can follow developments in Shanghai, Sydney, São Paulo, or Nairobi. Simultaneously the increased movement of artists across borders and oceans has added to the intermixing of influences and artistic vocabularies. For example, Wangechi Mutu, originally from Kenya, pursued further education in South Wales and then in the United States. Her collaged images of women are informed by African tribal arts, 20th-century European and American collage artists, and the latest illustrations from fashion, pornography, and medical sources.

The meaning and consequences of globalization are much debated by scholars. Economically and politically, is globalization a force for growth and freedom in societies everywhere, or does it contribute to further exploitation of developing regions by the wealthy? Does globalization work in different ways in different localities?

Regarding globalization and art, do practices in Asia, Africa, the Middle East, and elsewhere challenge the traditional assumptions and value judgments that are the basis of the Western canon? Are Western institutions rethinking that canon or simply adding art from other places to their rosters in a token and uncritical gesture of inclusivity? How do curated exhibitions that address themes of globalization represent artists from various parts of the world? The expanding art market and the proliferation of biennials and art fairs helped a select group of artists from every continent to gain an international presence; but have the underlying structure and values of the art market changed otherwise?

Visual Culture

In the twenty-first century visual culture has grown as a recognized interdisciplinary field of study, taking a multifaceted approach to understanding how images of all types communicate and participate in the construction of identity, gender, class, power relationships, and other social and political meanings and values. Medicine, science, politics, consumer culture, and religion and spirituality are some of the arenas that visual culture studies examine along with art. Visual culture scholars analyze film, television, graphic novels, fashion design, and other forms of popular culture in addition to established fine art media such as painting, and they draw upon many methodologies and theories, including semiotics, sociology, psychoanalysis, reception theory, feminism, and the concept of the gaze, to name a few.

Just as visual culture scholars are examining images and media of all types so, too, are twenty-first-century artists drawing inspiration, imagery, materials, and concepts from diverse areas of culture, moving well beyond influences from the history of fine art and design. The world of professional sports and fanatic fans has been a topic for Paul Pfeiffer, while the commercial television industry has informed various video installations by Christian Jankowski.

Most contemporary artists do not draw rigid distinctions between high art and popular culture. For instance, a number of contemporary artists embrace traditional techniques of fiber art but use them to create unorthodox forms or address current social and political issues. Along these lines, Ghada Amer has used thread to embroider on canvas repeated motifs of nude women engaged in sexual acts, then partially obscured the embroidered images with gestural painted brushstrokes. Her themes include the expression and repression of female sexuality and eroticism in both Western and Islamic societies. Another example of intermixing visual cultures is the complex array of interactions between science and contemporary art, with many artists engaging with scientific imagery and ideas in their practice. For example, Wim Delvoye's ongoing series called Cloaca imagines humans as cyborgs, representing the human digestive system as a kind of biomechanical contraption. Finally, many twenty-first-century artists are deeply affected by their immersion in global visual culture, which is now made vividly present through online networks. Many artists maintain a personal website, and some create art expressly for dissemination through social media. As always, new technologies provide new opportunities and challenges.

Public and Participatory Art

Public art was a well-established genre by the late twentieth century, attracting both traditional and experimental practitioners. Public art in the twenty-first century has expanded even more as a field of activity in which creative investigation can take place. In addition to continuing familiar forms such as site-specific monuments, murals, graffiti, and collaborations between artists, engineers, and architects, public art encompasses new purposes, forms, and locations, including pop-up art shops, street parades, and online projects. Public artists in the twenty-first century might use established approaches such as installation and performance but introduce new variations. For instance, it is now common for artists to hire other people, sometimes with special skills, to undertake performances on their behalf. In this vein, Vanessa Beecroft hired fashion models for performances, and the collaborative artists Allora & Caldazilla directed professional athletes as performers in some of their installations.

A pronounced tendency in the twenty-first century has been art that is participatory, in which the social interactions prompted by a work become its content. Often called relational art, the work literally engages the public in some way. For instance, Carsten Höller has installed giant slides in museums for visitors to slide down, and Rirkrit Tiravanija has prepared Thai food and served it to gallery goers. Artists attracted by the immediacy and connectivity of globally networked media often create online projects that invite social interaction. Relational aesthetics has developed (and been contested) as a critical theory for analyzing and evaluating such undertakings. Key questions in these debates include: Does it matter if the social interactions prompted by such works promote a better world or are conviviality and entertainment sufficient goals? To what extent should the physical products of relational art (such as Höller's slides) be evaluated aesthetically as well as for their social effects?

The twenty-first century is just beginning – issues and ideas are evolving rapidly and new artists are constantly gaining attention and influence.

*The content was first developed for Oxford Art Online and appears courtesy of Oxford University Press. Visit to learn more about contemporary art and see a list of significant twenty-first-century artists.

Putting It Together

In this module we discussed the following:

- the basic techniques of drawing, painting, photography, and printmaking;
- additive and subtractive sculpture techniques;
- methods and materials in building design;
- techniques and challenges of film and video;
- and the growing impact of computers and digital tools on art making.

The creative process is a kind of critical thinking (Sayre, 3). It involves visual research, trial and error, being open to new information, evaluating results, and being self-critical. The medium or mixed-media are the raw materials that an artist uses to make their idea come to life.

Each medium has its own unique visual effects or characteristics. In the viewer context we read these unique visual effects and draw specific meanings from them. Photography, for example, has the ability to render a selection of life in such realistic detail that it is used in non-artistic practices for evidence collection. Even though Photoshop has become part of our vernacular in the Western world, and we know photographs can be manipulated, if we were to see a photograph of a courtroom scene our first inclination would be that it is a factual record of that moment, as opposed to an artist's drawn rendering, which has a very different set of visual effects.

Works Cited

Sayre, Henry. *A World of Art*, Sixth edition. Boston: Prentice Hall, 2010. Print.

CHAPTER 6: RESEARCH, COMMUNICATE, AND EVALUATE ARTS INFORMATION

Why It Matters

Evaluate and utilize resources to research information about the arts (course level learning objective)

Introduction

Has someone ever related some fact or story you were immediately skeptical of? Of course, we've all had that happen. Information is only as reliable as its source. Often in our information-saturated lives, the value of good-quality information gets lost amid the vast quantity of fairly shallow information available for quick consumption.

It's important to cite your sources for several reasons:

- to demonstrate that your information is trustworthy because it comes from well-researched sources;
- to avoid plagiarism and responsibly credit other people's ideas and work;
- and to allow others to validate your ideas and research by tracking down the sources you used.

As you work through the last module, consider why it's important to follow a specific system for citing works—in the case of the humanities, the MLA format.

Also, consider how newly discovered works of art become authenticated. For example, what does provenance have to do with this recent movie, *The Woman in Gold*? Check out the following trailer, and see if you have some ideas.

- https://www.youtube.com/watch?v=9bx3KTGBEal

MODULE LEARNING OUTCOMES

- Identify and evaluate relevant source materials for arts
- Document research sources appropriately using MLA format

Completing the Final Performance Assessment!

This last PA is the Compare and Contrast paper. This PA is designed for you to demonstrate what you have learned from multiple modules. You will be analyzing form (module 2), researching aspects of period styles of paintings (module 4), researching iconography (module 3), and researching historical context (module 2 & 4). Make sure that you understand how cite sources in MLA style before you begin this assessment. As you do your research make sure you document all your sources as you go! Use the questions listed in the PA as a guide to complete your research before you begin writing the final paper. If at any point, you feel lost or unsure how to proceed, contact me for help.

You're almost finished! OK, here we go!

Work Cited

Anonymous. "Why Citing is Important." MIT Library Guides. Web. 7 June 2015.

Evaluate Source Materials

Identify and evaluate relevant source materials for arts

LEARNING ACTIVITIES

The learning activities for this section include:

- Reading: Research, Supplements, Definitions, Work Hints, and More
- Reading: Writing About Art
- Reading: Writing Processes
- Audio/Reading: Nazi-Era Arts Cache Brings Provenance Issues to Swiss Museum

Take time to review and reflect on these activities in order to improve your performance on the assessment for this section.

Reading: Research, Supplements, Definitions, Work Hints, and More

Here are some things to take into consideration when doing research (discussed in terms of "levels"):

Third Level of Research:

- You might speak to an instructor and they make recommendations for you to follow up on
- You might meet/know someone in the field you need to learn about and they get you started
- Or these days, you might do a general search using your favorite search engine. I would call this a "shotgun search" to get started (by "shotgun" I mean that it's a wide-open, general search that will include a wide range of sources from Encyclopedias to Wikipedia). This kind of search can give you a lot of directions to go further, but can be confusing and may include unreliable, inaccurate, or just plain wrong information.

Second Level of Research:

- Looking at/taking information found in the third level research and going into it deeper. This means finding the sources: like the author, and checking their "works cited" or bibliography and then corroborating, checking the provenance, and credentials of source(s).We need to check and confirm that our research is accurate and correct. This is a place where your instructor should be able to help. REMINDER: Your instructor is one of your resources.
- Corroboration means finding 2 or more sources that say the same thing and have good credentials for reliability that the information is from someone who has training/expertise/experience and/or is knowledgeable in the subject. Corroborating also means checking these credentials – "Why should I listen to this person or source?" 2nd level sources are also when someone is writing or discussing a subject; an artwork; a book or subject, etc. but they are not the person who wrote the text or painted the painting or whatever. In the art world, many of these sources are art historians, historians or theorists or art critics (knowledgeable people who write about art).
- Provenance is the history of something, for example who made the artwork, who owned it after that and where has it been all these years. Provenance is important to confirming that a given artwork is not a fake or a copy or stolen. These days the Provenance of an artwork may be checked by chemical and/or scientific analysis.
- NOTE: corroboration and provenance are important aspects and issues in the art world.

First Level of Research:

- Information is referred to as original sources and sometimes called primary sources. This might be the actual painting, sculpture or artwork being considered. It might be the book, the poem, the drama written; music; dance – it might be an artist's own writings about their work. In the Arts – it is frequently hard to get to the source materials, as those are the original artworks (or the artist's writings). Original artworks like you might find in a museum. If one is looking at a reproduction of an artwork (photos, videos, recordings)–that is a second-level source because it is not the actual original and there can be all kinds of color/quality/image degradations in the process of reproduction (these aspects are inherent in the process of reproduction, in fact)

An example:

1. Let's say we find a video on YouTube fromBob47 about medical illustration, which talks about Leonardo DaVinci's drawings (this is a third-level source). I watch that and then look for his bibliography or cited sources (probably none).
2. So I do a search for DaVinci and medical illustration. Among other things, I find an article in the Washington Academy of Science journal by Joanne Snow-Smith. This is a good article and I can use it for my project, but it is still only a second-level source because she is talking/writing about DaVinci. She will probably have a bibliography and works cited (her research). I can follow up on that.

3. My first-level source for this example would be to go to DaVinci's diaries and sketchbooks related to medical illustration. There, I could look at his writings about medical illustration and his drawings – that would be 1st level source material. Now the problem here is that I would only be able to look at reproductions of his sketchbooks, unless I travel to Italy or wherever his original notebooks are preserved. So, in this case, if I studied those reproductions, we might call that advanced 2nd level sourcing.

Audio/Reading: Nazi-Era Art Cache Brings Provenance Issues To Swiss Museum

Audie Cornish talks to Jonathan Petropolous, professor of European History at Claremont McKenna College, about the acceptance of Nazi-era art by the Museum of Fine Arts Bern in Switzerland. Listen to the audio version or read the transcript: http://www.npr.org/2014/11/24/366379292/nazi-era-art-cache-brings-provenance-issues-to-swiss-museum

Reading: Writing About Art

Take a look at Writing About Art by Marjorie Munsterberg. It's a great resource to help you get started on an art-related writing project. Particularly, read Historical Analysis and Appendix I: Writing the paper.

Reading: Writing Processes

If you need help with basic writing tips and techniques, Writing Commons is a great online resource for doing academic writing of all kinds. This section on Writing Processes to a good place to start.

Document Sources

Document sources appropriately using MLA format

Take time to review and reflect on this activity in order to improve your performance on the assessment for this section.

Reading: Bibliography

When you write, you will need to cite your source in-text and create a bibliography that lists works cited using MLA standards. It is important to give an accurate citation so that the instructor can track down your sources and look at them when necessary.

Use the Perdue OWL MLA Formatting and Style Guide as your model for citations and how to create a bibliography.

Purdue OWL MLA Formatting style guide: https://owl.english.purdue.edu/owl/resource/747/1/

Putting It Together

This course is particularly focused on helping you develop visual literacy skills, but all the college courses you take are to some degree about information literacy. Visual literacy is really just a specialized type of information literacy. The skills you acquire in this course will help you become an effective researcher in other fields, as well.

MLA style is important because it gives you—and all those engaged in scholarly activities on topics within the humanities—a conventional way to cite resources so that they can be corroborated. It takes the guesswork out of demonstrating you did thorough research, and it lends integrity to your work.

Provenance is also about a kind of integrity. It refers to the history of an object—in particular, the object's origin and chain of ownership—and, in art, it can be used to identify and authenticate real (as opposed to fake) works of art. Knowing a work's provenance can also help in the recovery of stolen works of art. Today, there are many new methods of establishing provenance that use chemical analysis. As you heard in the podcast, matters of provenance still haunt Nazi-era artworks suspected of being looted during World War Two. The recent movie *Woman in Gold* is a story about the return of artwork stolen by the Nazis from Jewish families during the war. The case was a shocking victory for Adele Bloch-Bauer's family, who sued the Austrian government and won. As Steve Schlackman of *Art Law Journal* explained, "At the very least, it will make foreign states think twice when receiving works without the proper provenance." You can read more about the court case here: http://artlawjournal.com/the-legal-story-behind-the-woman-in-gold/

Work Cited

Schlackman, Steve. The Story Behind the "Women in Gold". Art Law Journal. 2015. Web. 7 June 2015.

Online Writing Tutor

Class,

The Angel Learning Doc. is about Online Tutoring available through HCCC.

Mr. S.

ANGEL_Learning.docx

Windows Users:

To download the file to your own computer, right-click the location link and select "Save Target As" or "Save Link As" from the pop-up menu. To attempt to view the file from its current location, just left-click the location link.

Mac Users:

To download the file to your own computer, hold the "control" key down and click the mouse button on the location link, or right-click if you are using a two-button mouse. Then select "Download Linked File" from the pop-up menu. To attempt to view the file from its current location, simply click the location link.